MEDITERRANEAN MODERNISMS

Engaging with the work of Nobel Prize-winning poet Odysseus Elytis within the framework of international modernism, Marinos Pourgouris places the poet's work in the context of other modernist and surrealist writers in Europe. At the same time, Pourgouris puts forward a redefinition of European Modernism that makes the Mediterranean, and Greece in particular, the discursive contact zone and incorporates neglected elements such as national identity and geography. Beginning with an examination of Greek Modernism, Pourgouris's study places Elytis in conversation with Albert Camus; analyzes the influence of Charles Baudelaire, Gaston Bachelard, and Sigmund Freud on Elytis's theory of analogies; traces the symbol of the sun in Elytis's poetry by way of the philosophies of Heraclitus and Plotinus; examines the influence of Le Corbusier on Elytis's theory of architectural poetics; and takes up the subject of Elytis's application of his theory of Solar Metaphysics to poetic form in the context of works by Freud, C.G. Jung, and Michel Foucault. Informed by extensive research in the United States and Europe, Pourgouris's study makes a compelling contribution to the comparative study of Greek modernism, the Mediterranean, and the work of Odysseus Elytis.

New Brunswick
New York
Providence
Χαιρέτωσαν!

And I find I keep asking the same question, because of the history:
where do I stand in relation to these writers:
in another country or in this valuing city?

Raymond Williams, *The Country and the City*

Mediterranean Modernisms
The Poetic Metaphysics
of Odysseus Elytis

MARINOS POURGOURIS
University of Cyprus, Cyprus

LONDON AND NEW YORK

First published 2011 by Ashgate Publishing

Published 2016 by Routledge
2 Park Square, Milton Park, Abingdon, Oxfordshire OX14 4RN
711 Third Avenue, New York, NY 10017, USA

First issued in paperback 2016

Routledge is an imprint of the Taylor & Francis Group, an informa business

Copyright © Marinos Pourgouris 2011

Marinos Pourgouris has asserted his right under the Copyright, Designs and Patents Act, 1988, to be identified as the author of this work.

All rights reserved. No part of this book may be reprinted or reproduced or utilised in any form or by any electronic, mechanical, or other means, now known or hereafter invented, including photocopying and recording, or in any information storage or retrieval system, without permission in writing from the publishers.

Notice:
Product or corporate names may be trademarks or registered trademarks, and are used only for identification and explanation without intent to infringe.

British Library Cataloguing in Publication Data
Pourgouris, Marinos.
Mediterranean modernisms: the poetic metaphysics of Odysseus Elytis.
  1. Elytes, Odysseas, 1911–1996 – Criticism and interpretation. 2. Modernism (Literature) – Greece. 3. Modernism (Literature) – Mediterranean Region.
  I. Title
  889.1'32–dc22

Library of Congress Cataloging-in-Publication Data
Pourgouris, Marinos.
  Mediterranean modernisms: the poetic metaphysics of Odysseus Elytis / by Marinos Pourgouris.
    p. cm.
  Includes bibliographical references and index.
  1. Elytes, Odysseas, 1911–1996—Criticism and interpretation. 2. Modernism (Literature)—Greece. 3. Modernism (Literature)—Mediterranean Region. 4. Modernism (Literature)—Europe. I. Title.

PA5610.E43Z84 2011
889'.132—dc22

2010035125

ISBN 13: 978-1-138-25373-5 (pbk)
ISBN 13: 978-1-4094-1000-3 (hbk)

Contents

Acknowledgments		*vii*
Note to Readers		*ix*
Introduction: Odysseus Elytis and the Specter of Nationalism		1
1	Modernism: From Paris to Athens	15
2	Towards a New Mediterranean Culture	37
3	The Theory of Analogies	65
4	Solar Metaphysics	111
5	Architectural Poetics	145
Appendix: Odysseus Elytis: Life and Works		*201*
Works Cited		*213*
Index		*223*

Acknowledgments

This book combines my interest in three themes: modernism, nationalism, and the Mediterranean. I have been preoccupied with these for a number of years now and my explorations would not have been as enjoyable, as enlightening, or as intriguing, without the help of a number of friends and colleagues with whom I spent countless hours discussing some of the ideas that found their way in this book. A number of people at Rutgers University read the early draft of the manuscript and provided me with constructive feedback on many of the book's themes. To Steven Walker—the best Jungian I know—I owe the discussion on the anima and a long-lasting friendship. Together we discussed Jung, Elytis, and the Mediterranean in New Brunswick restaurants, his house in Highland Park, in cars, on trains to New York, and on the shores of the Mediterranean in southern France. To Richard Serrano I owe much of the discussion on Camus's Algeria. I am indebted to Janet Walker for her close reading of the early drafts of the manuscript and particularly for her input on modernism; she understands well the many misconceptions associated with the reading of modernism from a Western lens. Many thanks to Chad Lowen-Schmidt, Sanja Bahun-Radunović, and Tatjana Aleksic for their encouragement and their contributions. Several colleagues in the Department of Comparative Literature at Brown University have been encouraging me all along and have helped me develop many of the themes in this book. I am eternally indebted to Rey Chow—a dear friend and an astonishing theorist—for the countless conversations on poststructuralism, the ethnic, Foucault, postcolonialism, cinema, Greece, China, life, and so many other things. I owe a heartfelt *shokran* to Elliott Colla at Georgetown University: our joint explorations of the Levant, our common interest in poetry, Egypt, and Greece have been invaluable to me. Some of the material on the Mediterranean was first "tested" in a class we taught together on the Levant. My thanks to Nauman Naqvi—a walking encyclopedia of postcolonial theory and philosophy—for always keeping my mind sharp. I salute Ken Haynes for keeping his door always open in Marston Hall and for never getting tired with my questions. I wish to express my appreciation to David Konstan, Elsa Amanatidou, and Kostis Kornetis, my colleagues in the Modern Greek Studies Program at Brown, for their support. Charlie Auger and Carol Wilson, also at Brown, have made writing this book much easier by taking care of so many trivial things for me. Suzanne Steward-Steinberg's interest in the Mediterranean has been inspiring—the course we taught together on "Mediterranean Identities" at Brown gave me plenty of material to work with. My students at Brown and Rutgers have been a priceless source of inspiration; this book would not have been the same without them. They will recognize here many of my lectures on modernism, the Mediterranean, and nationalism (my special thanks to Georgianna Dalaras, Erik Resly, Maggie Taft, Sheila Pakir, Anjana Joshi, Lindsey Meyers, Will Fysh, Qussay Al-Attabi, and Stefanie Sevcik). I owe my gratitude to Vassilis Lambropoulos at the

University of Michigan—the early draft of the second chapter was part of a lecture I gave there after his invitation. To Gregory Jusdanis at Ohio State—for without his books, the study of nationalism and modernity would have been much poorer. My warm regards to Edmund Keeley at Princeton University for providing me with a number of contacts during my research in Athens. I thank him for his encouragement and support. I am indebted to Ioulita Iliopoulou for answering so many questions about Elytis's books, for responding to my letters of inquiry, and for sharing her deep knowledge of Elytis's work with me. Kostas Myrsiades was one of the first people to read the early draft of the manuscript and I thank him for his comments. Robert Fagles was one of the kindest people I met—a natural comparatist, an exceptional teacher, and a true gentleman. I thank him for the many conversations on Yiannis Ritsos, George Seferis, Odysseus Elytis (and Odysseus in general). I also owe my gratitude to my new colleagues in the Department of Byzantine and Modern Greek Studies at the University of Cyprus. During my research in Athens, I had several conversations with one of the most remarkable contemporary Greek poets: Michalis Ganas. I thank him for his kindness and support. The photograph that adorns this book is by the New York based photographer, Dimitri Mellos, whose work I admire very much. I thank him for his generosity. The cover design is Vasillis Ioannou's work; this is the second cover he has designed for me and I am always humbled by his enthusiasm and his assistance. I also wish to express my gratitude to Ashgate Publishing, my editor Kathy Bond Borie for her meticulous work, and Senior Editor Ann Donahue for her guidance.

Some of the support came from people that have always been present in my life. My parents, Costas and Galateia, have unknowingly cultivated my love for literature even when they (or I for that matter) had no idea where on earth it would lead me. Unconditional love might be a burden sometimes; it's been a blessing to me. When I told my two brothers, Christoforos and Rodos, I was working on Elytis they asked me if I meant *Alytis* (vagabond). How right they were! I would gladly yet painfully claim that title myself in my comings and goings between so many homes in Greece, Cyprus, and the United States. And there were so many people I always found waiting for me in these arrivals and departures: Giorgos, Suzanna, Nikos, Vassilis, Nikoletta, Chrystalla, Constantinos, Andri, Andis, Skevi, Savvas, Edel, Olga, Dimitri, Alex, Martha, Penelope, Eva, Mary, Nandia, Giorgos, Nephele; this book is an answer to the question you all asked me, one way or another, over the past few years (what are you working on?). I hope it's a good enough response.

It's curious that the final acknowledgement in many books concerns the person most intricately connected with the project. Perhaps it's because we postpone, we give ourselves time, until we find the appropriate words. Yianna Ioannou has witnessed this book from its inception to its conclusion. She patiently suffered my many moods and whims. She has always been my first and most demanding reader. And for that, and for so many other reasons, I thank her:

Φιλιά που δόθηκαν και άλλα που δεν. Χαιρέτωσαν.
Ανθ' ημών η αγάπη.

Note to Readers

Unless otherwise noted, all translations from the original Greek are mine. I use Jeffrey Carson and Nikos Sarris's translations of Elytis's poetry except for the two collections that are not included in the *Collected Poems* or have not been translated into English: *Εκ του Πλησίον* and *Τα Ρω του Έρωτα*. Transcribing some of Elytis's poems has been a challenge as their formatting is very precise. I tried to maintain the original formatting, in most cases, but I would caution the reader to look to the original poems for an accurate visual and typographical representation. In the bibliographical references the reader will note that I kept the original titles of the Greek texts but chose to Latinize all proper names and places for uniformity.

Introduction: Odysseus Elytis and the Specter of Nationalism

> I became thousands of years old, and already use Minoan script with such ease that the world wonders and believes in the miracle.
> Fortunately they haven't managed to read me.
> —Elytis, *Diary of an Invisible April*

When I first met Elytis's companion, the poet Ioulita Iliopoulou, a few years ago, she explained to me that the late Odysseus Elytis was more or less an ascetic man. He lived in the same apartment in Athens for many years, he did not own a television set, he wrote on the same desk since childhood, and when he would leave his apartment he would usually visit the same café in Kolonaki. He interacted with a small circle of acquaintances and he guarded his private life from the media even after he was awarded the Nobel Prize in 1979. He had donated most of his books to libraries and he kept a very small personal collection for his own use. This "closed up" view of the poet, stereotypical as it may be, might also suggest, metaphorically speaking, the position in which ethnic literatures find themselves today in the postmodern or poststructuralist world. Elytis wrote in Greek and was preoccupied, especially early in his poetic career, along with other poets of the so-called generation of the thirties, with Greek identity (Greekness). In Greece he became known as the poet of the Aegean, of the islands, of the sun, and the sea. Much like Walt Whitman, who celebrated the American landscape, Elytis's poetry is overwhelmingly concerned with a personal redefinition of Greekness and it almost always unfolds in the foreground of the Greek landscape. He was, in other words, a distinctively *Greek* poet living and writing in modernist times. In today's poststructural setting, where, as Rey Chow tells us, *difference* is valorized as the most fundamental discursive principle, where multiculturalism and diversity are celebrated as paradigms of a desirable humanity, what can a Greek poet—a poet so intimately focused on the Greek experience—tell us that we might find worth listening to?

My own approach to Elytis's work in this book is first and foremost an intervention to the deplorable conditions ethnic literatures have found themselves in during the last few decades. In the poststructuralist celebration of what is different, diverse, multicultural, international, or planetary—of what generally challenges the centrality of meaning or the claim to authenticity—ethnic literatures are often perceived as too monocultural, too monolithic, and unable to tell us anything about the urgent theoretical problems of our times. To put it simply, poststructuralism has indeed challenged the foundations of Western Logos but, in doing so, it has also relegated ethnicity to the margins. I find Rey Chow's theoretical contribution to the critique of poststructuralism as an important intervention here—an intervention that outlines, as lucidly as possible, the problems underlining this celebration of difference that describes the theoretical tendencies inherent both in Deconstruction and Cultural Studies. In *The Protestant Ethnic and the Spirit of Capitalism* Chow writes:

> First, poststructuralist theory has made a crucial contribution towards undoing the deadlock in signification by loosening the presumed fixed correspondences between signifier and signified. In terms of signification, difference rather than sameness now becomes the key to a radicalized way of thinking about identity. Second, one of the consequences of theory defined this way is the replication of the dislocated sign in the sociocultural frame of identity formation, so that (the experience of) dislocation per se, as it were, often becomes valorised or even idealized—as what is different, mobile, contingent, indeterminable, and so on. Third, as Pheng Cheah points out, these poststructuralist arguments about identity are, philosophically speaking, traceable to the same tradition in which culture itself is considered definitively as a form of emancipation from the tyranny of the given. Culture, in other words, occupies something of the status of difference, which is associated with fluidity and movement and thus with freedom. Obviously this is not an entirely accurate view of culture, since, far from being essentially emancipatory, culture often also partakes of the constraints, oppressions, and inequalities of the given. Fourth, from this we may understand why culture in the plural—as multiple forms of differences, as cultural diversity, as multiculturalism—is fraught with unresolved questions such as those of racism (inequality between different racial and/or ethnic groups) and class discrimination (inequality between groups of the same racial/ethnic background as well as between groups of different racial ethnic backgrounds). In other words, once transposed into sociocultural and/or geographical terrains, the poststructuralist specialization in difference, a revolution on its own terms, appears inadequate in accounting for how the purportedly liberating movements of difference and hybridity can and do become hierarchically organized as signs of minoritization and inferiority in various contemporary world situations.[1]

For whom, then, does poststructuralism speak? And in what language? What is the position of the ethnic (and ethnic literatures) in the contemporary theoretical focus on the multicultural and the diverse? I believe that the case of Elytis can be instructive in understanding the misconceptions that plague ethnic literatures today.

Like many of the poets and writers of his generation, Elytis is first and foremost a modernist poet. As Peter Bürger argues in his *Theory of the Avant-Garde*, the principal development of art in bourgeois society, was made possible by "the progressive detachment of art from real life contexts, and the correlative crystallization of a distinctive sphere of experience, i.e., the aesthetic." Consequently, the aim of the avantgardist protest is to "reintegrate art into

---

[1] Rey Chow, *The Protestant Ethnic and the Spirit of Capitalism* (New York: Columbia University Press, 2002), p. 134.

the praxis of life."² This bridging of the gap between the aesthetic and the "praxis of life" is exemplified, in the case of Western European modernism, in the attempts of such leading modernist movements as futurism, dadaism, and surrealism, to find a frame within which art would interrelate with reality: futurists integrated technology and the urban space in their work, surrealists went as far as establishing a bureau for the investigation of dreams, dadaists called for the destruction of what hindered aesthetic development (which was pretty much everything from museums to all art), etc. In Greece, the bridging of the aesthetic with the "praxis of life" took a very different expression but was still as emphatic. As many Greek writers of the 1930s saw it, including Elytis, modern Greek identity remained largely unexplored, hindered by the ever-present comparison with the Greek antiquity. In the nineteenth century such comparison was indeed warranted since it also meant that the Greek nation could cater to the imaginings of the many Westerners who always filtered modern Greece through the lens of antiquity—in short, the narrative of a Greek continuity benefitted the nascent Greek nation by providing it with a much needed visibility. But by the 1930s, as I discuss in the first chapter of this book, Greek modernists responded to this representation of Greekness by exploring what they perceived as the suppressed and uncharted dimensions of Greek identity. The aesthetic, then, was a distinctively *Greek* aesthetic and the "Praxis of life" became manifest in the topographical orientations of the text (turning towards the seascape of the Aegean for example) and in promoting the hitherto unexplored facets of Greek identity: folk art, tradition, Cycladic architecture, etc.

An assessment of Elytis's modernist theories allows us, then, to re-examine modernism not simply in the limited confines of what constitutes a "global" modernity but to understand the different meaning that modernist thought acquired once it spread from the cosmopolitan centers of Western Europe to territories where both the local aesthetic and the local cultural idiosyncrasies propelled it into a new dynamic. Such re-examination is especially urgent today when entering the much celebrated category of "World Literature," or as Pascale Casanova puts it "The World Republic of Letters,"³ presupposes the existence of a "universal aesthetic"—this is a cosmopolitan republic that, much like colonial spaces, renders literary space as postnational, benign, a conglomeration of writers writing in the Universal Colors of Benetton.

Goethe's call for a reconsideration of literature in a global context (*Weltliteratur*) perhaps found its most significant paradigm in the advent of modernism. From the great theorists of modernism—from Bradbury and McFarlane to Calinescu, Poggioli, and many others—we learn that it emerged in cosmopolitan and multilingual cities, that it demolished barriers, and, most importantly, that it

---

[2] Peter Bürger, *Theory of the Avant-Garde*, trans. M. Shaw (Minneapolis: University of Minnesota Press, 1984), p. 22–3.

[3] Pascale Casanova, *The World Republic of Letters*, trans. M.B. DeBevoise (Cambridge, MA: Harvard University Press, 2007).

was highly antinational. Much like the concept of "World Literature," European modernism was inclusive and universal: it looked to the East (to Asia) and to the South (Africa) for inspiration traversing and transforming national boundaries into hybrid creative expressions. But even if one stays within European borders, such definition of modernism is both problematic and selectively constructed. Bradbury and McFarlane's volume *Modernism: A Guide to European Literature 1890–1930*[4]—considered one of the most seminal texts in the study of European modernism—traces modernism in North-Western Europe and never seems to go beyond Prague (with the fleeting and notable exception of Moscow). Everything in between (i.e., South-Eastern Europe) is completely bypassed. What do we do, then, with the modernist activity in Belgrade, Krakow, Athens, or Bucharest? In fact, modernism in these cities developed in very different terms and conditions: in cities that were far from the cosmopolitanism of Paris and, often, at a different time (i.e., as late as the 1930s); most importantly, modernism in these settings often had a national or traditional flare. Consequently, these local movements may be seen as mimetic, belated expressions of modernism and as negligible to an essential definition of the modernist phenomenon. Such selective view—selective both in spatial and temporal terms—ignores the fact that these movements were also highly hybrid expressions and potent rebellions against convention.

As Rey Chow argues in *The Age of the World Target*, "From Nietzsche and Heidegger to Derrida and Foucault, Western philosophy and theory's pronouncements of the West's demise and loss of meaning have continued with relative indifference to and ignorance of the histories and languages elsewhere."[5] There is a kind of an orientalist flare in what Chow describes as the "self-referentiality" of poststructuralism, which insists in viewing the "peripheral" through a transnational and distinctly Western lens. In the same way that nineteenth- and early twentieth-century oriental and exotic fantasies restored meaning to what was thought to be an anemic Western life, poststructuralism declares the demise of the World alongside the demise of the West; to rephrase Nietzsche's famous statement: the West is dead, thus, the Rest must now die with it. It should not be a surprise then that national literatures' adaptation of modernism and their response to postmodernism and poststructuralism has often materialized as a clear anti-Western polemic. Chow writes:

> The apparently monolingual, monocultural, and mononational investigations of India, Nigeria, Spanish America, modern Greece, or Japan, in other words, should be understood as full-fledged comparative projects, their precarious and enigmatic enunciations bearing testimony to an interlingual, intercultural, and international historicity that exposes the positivistic limits of the (Western) human sciences—that exposes, indeed, the finitude of (Western) man as a domain of the known and knowable that Foucault so memorably elucidates.[6]

---

[4] Malcolm Bradbury and James McFarlane, *Modernism: A Guide to European Literature 1890–1930*, ed. Malcolm Bradbury and James McFarlane (London: Penguin, 1991).

[5] Rey Chow, *The Age of the Wold Target* (Durham: Duke University Press, 2006), p. 13.

[6] Chow, *The Age*, pp. 85–6.

In this light, the redefinition of Greek identity that Greek modernists of the 1930s undertook, for example, can similarly be perceived as a deconstruction of existing Western preconceptions (and misconceptions) of Greek culture. In other words, Western modernism can be understood as a rebellion of the West against its own logos, whereas Greek modernism was a rebellion of the "margin" against the same Western logos that persistently misread Greekness. In fact, for poets like Elytis, George Seferis, Andreas Empeirikos, and others, the modernist rebellion in Europe was a welcomed reaction that they could use in order to respond both to local and global misperceptions of Greek identity. Yet, there is an important distinction to be made between modernism and poststructuralism in their respective positions vis-à-vis national literatures. Whereas modernism, in its (re)constructive tendencies, often found a sense of revitalization in the margin (albeit with all its exoticism, primitivism, etc.), poststructuralism is less kind and, in a sense, more "democratic" in its deconstructive methodology. In other words, modernism might have been willing to consider the value of the margin (in a spirit akin to T.S. Eliot's emphasis on tradition) but poststructuralism today is deeply committed to equally exposing the national and the imperial, the marginal and the central. As a result, since the early 1980s, many Greek scholars heralded a crisis in Greek literature and literary studies: the achievements of the modernist generation of the thirties seemed over-studied, the theme of literature under the Greek junta (1967–1974) seemed passé, and literature's exploration of political divisions between the Right and the Left since the civil war (1944–1949) seemed outdated. The symptom of this crisis expressed itself in the polarization of the field of modern Greek studies between scholars—mostly in US academic institutions—who supposedly conspire with the enemy (which is none other than Western poststructural theory) and scholars—mostly in Greek academic institutions—who are accused of being too esoteric and indifferent to current theoretical trends. I do not believe that such divisions are helpful but they do exemplify the urgency of defining the position of national literatures within or against the poststructuralist frame. This book, in fact, is an attempt to define this position in reconsidering a poet who has long been described as overtly "national." Inasmuch as my investigation centers on a *Greek* poet it is, perhaps, "monolingual, monocultural, and mononational" but it is also "interlingual, intercultural, and international" in its concern with the unavoidably multidirectional exchange between the so-called centers and margins. His poetry and his theories are a prime paradigm of how ideas circulate, how they are constantly redefined to produce conceptualizations that acquire an entirely new, vibrant, and distinctive dynamic once they are placed in a new cultural context.

What I have outlined so far in introducing this book, are the dangers intrinsic in the mimetic adaptation of the poststructural trope that often neglects the very sociocultural conditions it had set out to defend by deconstructing Eurocentrism. It is perhaps a testimony to our times that to return to the exploration of an "ethnic" poet like Elytis, requires some sort of explanation. Unlike such Greek authors as Nikos Kazantzakis or Constantine Cavafy who have achieved a certain ecumenical status, Elytis, like many other modern Greek authors, remains largely unknown to Western audiences. As Gregory Jusdanis has argued, "what is bought, what is hailed as universal, what is read outside its borders, has to do with rules and issues beyond the specific work."[7] And the criteria, according to Jusdanis, "for determining whether or not a text is world literature have to do with its place of origins, which increasingly is located in Europe's former colonies."[8] Jusdanis further warns of the dangers intrinsic in such a binary conceptualization (i.e., Europe and its former colonies) suggesting that "traditions—say, Armenian, Bulgarian, modern Greek, Hebrew, and Icelandic—that do not fit into either the cosmopolitan or the postcolonial template will not be part of the draft."[9] It is precisely with these dangers in mind that Rey Chow suggests a different sort of conceptualization that offers a more dynamic potential in examining ethnic traditions; she labels this paradigm as "Post European Culture and the West."[10] In this paradigm, "even in the seemingly narcissistic or obsessive preoccupation with itself, a culture such as postcolonial India, postcolonial Africa, Spanish America, modern Greece, or modern Japan already contains, in its many forms of self-writing, imprints of a fraught and prevalent relation of comparison and judgment in which Europe haunts it as the referent of supremacy."[11]

In his *Dream Nation*, Stathis Gourgouris has indeed presented us with a reading of Greek culture through the frame of postcoloniality. "If the story of India," he writes, "is the paradigmatic condition of the colonialist imaginary, then the story of Greece is the paradigmatic colonialist condition *in* the imaginary."[12] Maria Todorova further expanded and reformulated Edward Said's orientalism to read the Balkans as an imaginary space where the region is haunted by the phantasmagoric projections of Europe.[13] Working specifically with the case of Greece, Vangelis Calotychos has adopted a similar model to understand Greece's relationship to the West in a Balkan context.[14] What is stressed in such comparative studies is not

---

[7] Gregory Jusdanis, "World Literature: The Unbearable Lightness of Thinking Globally," *Diaspora* 12, no. 1 (2003): 103–30, p. 122.

[8] Jusdanis, "World Literature," p. 123.

[9] Jusdanis, "World Literature," p. 123.

[10] Chow, *The Age*, pp. 88–91.

[11] Chow, *The Age*, p. 89.

[12] Stathis Gourgouris, *Dream Nation: Enlightenment, Colonization, and the Institution of Modern Greece* (Stanford: Stanford University Press, 1996), p. 6.

[13] Maria Todorova, *Imagining the Balkans* (New York: Oxford University Press, 2009).

[14] I do share Katherine Fleming's reservations concerning the uncritical application of Said's orientalism to the Balkans and the case of Greece. What I am suggesting here is not that we should read Elytis, or modern Greek literature in general, through a postcolonial lens. The designation of Europeaness is undeniably a category that *haunts* modern Greek literature in the sense that local cultural expressions were always measured against developments in Europe. It is not coincidental that Giorgos Theotokas's "Free Spirit," for example, a text that constitutes the closest thing to a manifesto in Greek modernism of the late 1920s, laments the position of Greek literature by comparing it with developments in Europe. Elytis would engage in a similar critique in the 1930s. What I am suggesting,

the hegemonic position of Europe and its influence on national literatures. What is stressed is the potentiality that the redefinition of cultural identity has made possible in this *hauntological* relationship with the West.[15] My interest in Elytis, then, largely focuses on those aspects that constitute a reformulation of identity, and modes of writing, that challenge, redefine, or compliment modernist and postmodernist thought: his interest in the Mediterranean as an alternate modernist space, his crafting new ways to approach a poetic form that corresponds with the content of the poem, his insistence on analogies that are linked to geography, etc. The influence of many towering European thinkers (particularly French) on his thought is indisputable and such names as Picasso, Matisse, Baudelaire, Freud, Jung, Bachelard, or Le Corbusier, are present throughout the book. The intent is not simply to present an accurate comparative account of Odysseus Elytis's influence by these thinkers—it is also, as I have already stressed, to follow how this influence adapts itself to the particular idiosyncrasies of a contemporary Greek poet, how it is challenged, reworked, and re-presented in Greece, away from the cosmopolitan centers of Europe but simultaneously haunted by the modernist rebellion that was unfolding there.

My intention in this book is to map a space through which one can approach Elytis's poetry. Apart from a total of 17 poetry collections, Elytis published two massive volumes of essays, *Open Papers* and *Carte Blanche*. These essays cover the period from 1938 to 1995 and constitute an important resource for anyone who wishes to understand modernist activity in Greece. At the same time, one must keep in mind that Elytis might have been a prolific writer, but he was not a theorist in the traditional sense of the term. As he confesses in the introduction to the *Open Papers*, he does not consider himself to be "a critic or a writer of prose."[16] Yet, one perceives in Elytis's thought a clear theoretical framework. On the one hand, what I have attempted here is a *systematization* of Elytis's thought, which always leads to what I have labeled as his "poetic metaphysics." At the same time, I situate Elytis in the greater context of European and Greek modernism and discuss the influences that have shaped his theories.

Part of the challenge of writing this book has been finding the right balance between theory and literature as well as between an introduction to a relatively unknown poet (to English speaking audiences at least) and a more insightful

---

then, is that an investigation of the relationship between the "developed" West and Greek modernism would reveal, in Chow's words, the "imprints of a fraught and prevalent relation of comparison and judgment in which Europe haunts it as the referent of supremacy." For a more elaborate discussion on the relationship between Orientalism, Balkanism, and Greece, see K.E. Fleming, "Orientalism, the Balkans, and Balkan Historiography," *The American Historical Review* (American Historical Association) 105, no. 4 (Oct 2000): 1218–33.

[15] I am using Derrida's term "hauntology" from *Spectres of Marx*, to describe the neither present nor absent relationship of Greek culture with the West; it's a fitting term, I believe, to describe what Chow calls the "imprints of a fraught and prevalent relation of comparison and judgment in which Europe haunts it as the referent of supremacy."

[16] Odysseus Elytis, *Ανοιχτά Χαρτιά* (Athens: Ikaros, 1995), p. 3.

commentary on his work. For the readers who are unfamiliar with Elytis and his work, I have included an appendix that might introduce them to some important biographical and bibliographical details. As far as the wider theoretical framework of the book is concerned, each chapter attempts, on the one hand, an explication of Elytis's theories and, on the other, it attempts to place these theories in relation to a pertinent theoretical framework. To put it simply, each chapter is concerned with a subtheme that offers potential ways in which Elytis's theories can inform scholars who are working on modernism, the Mediterranean, the relationship between national identity and culture, or the position of ethnic literatures in the current theoretical environment.

I should clarify, at this point, my persistent use of the term "metaphysics" throughout the book. Generally speaking, when I use the term I am referring to the tendency, that begins with Aristotle, to understand ontology, the relationship between man and nature, or between science and empiricism, as a transcendent phenomenon that reveals a certain (subjective) truth. Many of the thinkers that I am considering here have either fallen out of favor today or are approached, understandably so, with a degree of skepticism. What can one make of Heidegger's insistence that man inhabits the world poetically? Where exactly does Jung's metapsychological conception of the anima archetype, Freud's celebrated unconscious, or Lacan's "gaze" reside in objective/scientific terms? Do Camus's Mediterranean aesthetics constitute anything more than a sensual (or, worst, a *colonial*) fantasy? What of Sapir and Whorf's outdated and sharply criticized linguistic determinism? Aren't all these merely creative attempts to fill the void of meaninglessness that culminated in the final epiphany of poststructuralism to reject the stability of any meaning? I began this project as an attempt to understand Elytis's theoretical positions—many of these theories are central in the formulation of his metaphysical poetics and, therefore, they are important in my effort to outline a comprehensive presentation of his thought in the modernist context. It is admittedly difficult to speak of postcoloniality and metaphysics in the same breath. Yet, it is precisely in this metaphysical space—a space that we can go as far as calling *spiritual*—that national autonomy and ethnic literature evolve. Elytis persistently incorporates metaphysical theories in order to situate his own understanding of poetry and his own view of Greekness. To reject such a metaphysical approach seems as absurd to me as the simplistic understanding of the "imaginary nation" as an unreal (i.e., false) construction; however *imaginary* nations might be, the consequences in the process of imagining them are fundamentally and undeniably real.

In the first chapter of the book I concentrate on Elytis's formative years, his involvement with surrealism and the influence of Éluard's poetry on his early work. My aim is twofold: first, to place Elytis in the historical and literary context of his time and, second, to follow the evolution of his own aesthetics. I discuss, for example, the influence of Paul Éluard's poetry on Elytis as well as his introduction to French surrealism. At the same time, I am interested in redefining the general description of European modernism by emphasizing the centrality of ethnicity in the case of Greek modernism (but also, as I discuss, in the examples of the Bulgarian,

Polish, and Romanian avant-garde). This reassessment of European modernism is a project that I have been preoccupied with for a number of years now; in a sense, this chapter is an extension of a volume I co-edited with Sanja Bahun-Radunović on the Avant-Garde in 2006.[17] What I hope a discussion on Elytis's work can add to this topic is a reconfiguration and a challenge of modernism's supposed cosmopolitanism, its multiculturalism, and its antinational position.

The second chapter focuses on the Mediterranean and begins by exploring the fantasy that situates the region in the imaginary of European travelers and writers. This discussion will form the background for the subsequent examination of Albert Camus and Odysseus Elytis's construction of a Mediterranean aesthetic. The two writers knew each other personally and, as I explain in this chapter, many of Elytis's ideas are in fact extensions of Camus's theories on the Mediterranean. As Camus found a justification of his philosophy in the Algerian landscape and seascape, we might say, Elytis discovered a similar *ethos* in the islands of the Aegean. In essence, what a comparative study of their Mediterranean philosophy reveals is, first, the effort to create a modernist framework that is distinctly Mediterranean (as opposed to Northern European) and, second, the political reverberations of such positioning when measured against their respective positions on Algeria and Greece. Naturally, as I hope my early examination of the Mediterranean fantasy indicates, I am interested in theories that approach the Mediterranean as a singular cultural entity and the problems inherent in such representation. As I will argue, I find that Elytis and Camus offer us two entirely different Mediterranean models—for Camus the Mediterranean region *in its totality* has the potential to challenge European rationalism, whereas for Elytis the Mediterranean can only be expressed in the local or in a culturally specific topos.

This orientation of the poet's thought, and more specifically his reading of the Greek (Mediterranean) landscape, will lead us to a discussion of his two central metaphysical constructs: the theory of Analogies and the theory of Solar Metaphysics. The third chapter concentrates on an examination of analogies in relation to three main influences: Charles Baudelaire, Gaston Bachelard, and Sigmund Freud. Elytis admits the influence of these three on his thought and especially on the formation of his theory of Analogies. Generally, we can say that the term "analogies" is grounded in Baudelairean "correspondences," Freudian "dream symbolism," and what Bachelard calls "material imagination." My intention here is to elucidate the way in which Elytis transposes and merges these concepts in his poetic creations. Even though he was influenced by many European thinkers, it is important to stress that his ideas were always adapted to the Greek experience. When Elytis speaks of a synaesthetic evaluation of the world as Baudelaire conceives it, for example, he is referring to the interaction of the senses in a *specifically Greek* geographical context. For him, the way in which a Greek

---

[17] Sanja Bahun-Radunović and Marinos Pourgouris, *The Avant-Garde and the Margin: New Territories of Modernism*, ed. Sanja Bahun Radunović and Marinos Pourgouris (Newcastle: Cambridge Scholars Press, 2006).

understands the words "olive tree," or "sea," or "mountain" differs significantly from that of, let us say, an Englishman. The same can be said of dream symbols and Bachelard's four elements of the imagination (air-wind-earth-fire). To further explicate this point I discuss Elytis's conception of Greece and "Greekness" in relation to the (now controversial) theories of the American linguists Edward Sapir and Benjamin Whorf. In this chapter I also discuss the theory of Analogies alongside Lacan's concept of "the Gaze." The exchange between the subject and the object, as Bachelard and Baudelaire perceive it, is described here in psychoanalytic terms and is linked to Elytis's poem "The Garden Gazes" and his collage of the same title. Finally, in this chapter's conclusion, I return to Fredric Jameson's contentious reading of third world literatures as *national allegories*. What specifically interests me, in the context of my discussion on Elytis and his theory of Analogies, is the relationship between analogy and allegory. To the extent that Elytis's analogies are necessarily national—to the extent that they present us with a poetic space within which Greekness is expressed—I find that Jameson's essay might offer, despite the fierce opposition of many critics to its essentialisms, a useful framework through which the relationship between literature and ethnicity can be approached.

The theory of Solar Metaphysics, which is the focus of the fourth chapter, approaches the poem as a conflation of components that move around a central nucleus in the same way, as Elytis argues, that the planets revolve around the sun. After defining the theory, I continue to trace the symbol of the sun in Elytis's poetry and through the philosophies of Heraclitus and Plotinus. In the case of Heraclitus, I distinguish three major concepts that Elytis appropriates in his own thought: the discovery of an alternative reality, the synthesis of opposites, and the view of the sun as an ethical symbol. In my discussion on Plotinus, I explore Elytis's interest in the concept of the "divine light" as a source of ethos. The ethos that we encounter in Heraclitus and Plotinus is here linked to a redefinition of justice and truth in Elytis. The concept of truth is further linked to Heidegger's definition of truth [*alētheia*] as a *process* of revelation and discovery. The greater part of the chapter concentrates on the influence of Le Corbusier on Elytis's theory of Solar Metaphysics. That is because the theory finds its most profound expression in what Elytis calls "architectural [poetic] design." I conclude this chapter with a discussion of the relationship between architecture and poetry and, more specifically, with what I believe is Elytis's most important contribution to the modernist crisis of form: the suggestion of an elaborate and precise poetic structure that corresponds with poetic content. In the same way that Cleanth Brooks attempted, in the 1940s, a structural reading of poetry along the lines of what he called the "structure of meanings," Elytis's theory of Solar Metaphysics is an elaboration on what we could label as *the meaning of structure*.

If Solar Metaphysics is a theory that comments on the relationship between content and form, Architectural Poetics may be described as the application of this theory to the poem's structure. In other words, the poem is structured, for Elytis, as a self-containing universe that revolves around a luminous nucleus. I find this application to be Elytis's most unique and profound technique; he is, perhaps, the first and only modernist poet to appropriate structure in such a complex and elaborate method. For this reason, I devote the entire fifth chapter to an examination of architectural poetics in four collections: *The Monogram, The Axion Esti, The Little Seafarer, and Maria Nephele*. In order to better understand the relationship between structure and meaning, or content and form, I will further discuss these collections in the context of three theories/texts: Sigmund Freud's "Mourning and Melancholia" (in *The Monogram*), Michel Foucault's "Nietzsche, Genealogy, History" (in *The Axion Esti* and The *Little Seafarer*), and C.G. Jung's description of the *anima* archetype (in *Maria Nephele*). The influence of Jung and Freud on Elytis is indisputable; he makes ample references to Freud in his essays and had many of Jung's books in his personal library. Foucault is simply used in correlation to Elytis's perception of the tension between literature and history. In the same way that Foucault turns to a genealogical approach to redefine history more effectively, Elytis uses the body and the creation of a "dream nation" as an alternative and a more accurate meta-historical narrative.

From the first poem of *Orientations* to the last of *From Nearby*, Elytis's entire poetic creation is intentionally structured: it begins with the word έρωτας (Eros) and it concludes with the word αγάπη (love). The publication of his collected poems was delayed for four years until the right printing paper was found: he wanted the book to be small enough to fit in the bag of a schoolgirl. He also disliked such grand titles as "Complete Poems" or "Oeuvres"; when his poems were eventually collected in one very small volume in 2002, it was simply titled Ποίηση (Poetry). This attention to presentation characterizes all of Elytis's collections; he is attentive to typography, the distance between words, and the color of the cover, as he is to the lithographs, photographs, and paintings that accompany each collection.

In contrast to the meticulous structure of his entire poetic work, his theories are presented in a more fragmentary manner. His essays read more like prose poems— when he wants to communicate a complex philosophical or aesthetic idea he struggles hard, phrasing and rephrasing the same concept. "I speak theoretically," he writes at one such moment, "and I hope I am forgiven in my attempt to reach the Absolute. After all, in action, the instinct realizes instantaneously those things that analysis interprets coordinately."[18] Still, Elytis's essays sketch out a lucid metaphysical system that compliments his poetry; beyond their coordinated interpretation they provide a key to the deeper understanding of his poetic metaphysics and trace his evolution as a poet for a period of about 65 years. The poet's most painstaking effort, as it emerges in his essays, was probably the search for a space that would render the poem "public" without compromising its complexity.

As Mario Vitti writes, throughout his poetic career, Elytis longed to merge with the "ideal reader." His desire went unfulfilled as, time after time, he intervened in protest against the misreading of his poetry; "... the ideal reader that he dreamt

---

[18] Elytis, *Ανοιχτά Χαρτιά*, p. 451.

of did not exist either in the East or in the West."[19] His appropriation by modern Greek culture, especially in the decade following his death, has removed him further from his ideal reader. The degree to which Elytis has been misread, in a (mis)placement alongside the "national" or the "Christian-Orthodox" narrative, is indeed astounding. High-school official study-guides emphasize "the historical/national dimension" of his poetry and stress his role as "a national poet."[20] In a speech delivered in Kozani on September 22, 2004, at an event commemorating the Asia Minor disaster, the late Greek Archbishop Christodoulos incorporated Elytis in Orthodoxy's dream of "unforgotten homelands":

> ... the pale angels of refugees will take our icons in hand and set out for the unforgotten homelands, traversing the blue Aegean "on the wings of winds." It will be the day that, as Elytis writes, "the last of men shall speak his first word and the dreams shall take revenge." In the moments of that dream, we will live a different Apocalypse—the Apocalypse of Asia Minor.[21]

This brief segment encompasses all the fallacious, baseless, and pointless associations against which Elytis fought to protect his poetry. The national appropriation of the poet after the Nobel Prize has manifested itself in a continuous inclusion of his name in cultural and national symbolism: more than a dozen streets in Greece and Cyprus are named after him, a full-life statue sculpted by Yiannis Papas was placed in one of Kolonaki's most central squares (Plateia Dexamenis), and a cruise ship,[22] a theatre on the island of Ios, and a hotel in Thessaly have been given his name. Biographical information and scattered lines from his poetry adorn tourist pamphlets, enticing visitors to travel to the Greek islands. Such cultural incorporation comes as a stark contrast, not only in relation to the deeper essence of his poetry, but also to the ascetic life he had led in his small apartment of Skoufa Street. Ironically, one might say that, in this respect, his poetry has reached the public sphere, albeit without penetrating the public consciousness.

It is inevitable and understandable that, after so many international recognitions, Elytis has become a national commodified symbol in a country that sees itself on the periphery of Europe. The scholarly discussions that persistently situate his work in the frame of the "Generation of the Thirties" have also contributed, to a certain extent, to a misreading of Elytis. Undoubtedly, the early scholarship

---

[19] Mario Vitti, "Εισαγωγή: Το Εργο του Ελύτη και η Ελληνική Κριτική," in *Εισαγωγή στο Εργο του Ελύτη*, ed. Mario Vitti (Heraklion: Panepistimiakes Ekdoseis Kritis, 2000), pp. 36–7.

[20] The quotations refer to the most popular high-school study guide in Greece in the 1980s and 1990s: David Antoniou, Than. Kokovinos and Kostas Petropoulos, *Ερμηνευτικές Αναλύσεις Κειμένων Νεοελληνικής Λογοτεχνίας (Μέρος Β')* (Athens: Pataki, 1982).

[21] Ελευθεροτυπία, "Αιχμές για τις Χαμένες Πατρίδες από Χριστόδουλο," August 23, 2004.

[22] The cruise ship belonged to NEL (Maritime Company of Mytilini) and was active in the period 1982–1985. It was then sold to a non-Greek company and was renamed "Scandinavian Sky," sailing out of Florida.

on Elytis necessitated this kind of appropriation. His turn to the Aegean, his exploration of alternative loci of Greekness, were thus placed in the wider search of that generation for an authentic Greek voice—a voice that was neither classical nor exclusively Western. At the same time, it is important to note that Elytis's poetry continued to develop and evolve well beyond the thirties and the forties and that he wrote his most exceptional poems, I would say, from the 1970s to the 1990s. This book aspires, precisely, to challenge such superficial characterizations that portray Elytis as a surrealist, a national poet, an erotic poet, a poet of the Aegean, an optimist, etc. I find no contradiction in simply describing him as a "Modernist Greek poet"—"Modernist," because he constantly experimented with new ways of expression, both structurally and conceptually, and "Greek" because his poetry is rooted in the Greek language, geography, and tradition. This is where Elytis's work becomes important, especially for scholars in Comparative Literature: it simultaneously allows for a study of the personal and the cultural, the traditional and the modernist; it allows for a more comprehensive and inclusive definition of modernism as it evolved beyond the boundaries of Western Europe. But ultimately, if this study should lead the reader somewhere, it should be to a discovery of Elytis's poetry itself. The last collection he saw published before his death, in 1996, ends with the following lines:

> What remains
> Is Poetry alone. Poetry. Just and essential and straight
> The way the first two-created might have imagined it
> Just in the garden's acridness and infallible in the clock.[23]

---

[23] Odysseus Elytis, *The Collected Poems of Odysseus Elytis*, trans. Jeffrey Carson and Nikos Sarris (Baltimore: Johns Hopkins, 1997), p. 554. Ποίηση μόνον είναι / Κείνο που απομένει. Ποίηση. Δίκαιη και ουσιαστική κι ευθεία / Όπως μπορεί και να τη φαντασθήκαν οι πρωτόπλαστοι / Δίκαιη στα στυφά του κήπου και στο ρολόι αλάθητη (Elytis, *Ποίηση*, Athens: Ikaros, 2003, p. 558).

Chapter 1
Modernism: From Paris to Athens

> Grab the ONE MUST by the T and skin it back to O.
> —Elytis, *The Little Seafarer*

During the first two decades of the twentieth century, while much of Western Europe was living in a frenzy of manifestos, proclamations, and the formation of new literary and artistic movements, Greece remained secluded and largely apathetic to the literary happenings in the West. As late as 1925, George Seferis (1900–1971), an emerging poet at the time, was writing in his journal: "The state of the young people who wish to write in Greece is miserable. There is no one to guide them. Not even an essential book for them to learn, somehow, the language. The moral atmosphere is minimal. There are no elders."[1] At the same time, European modernist movements seemed to lose their vitality and power by the time they reached the Balkans. To put it simply, the more radical strain of modernism restricted itself, from the 1890s to the 1920s, to Central and Western Europe with the notable exception of Yugoslavia where the rise of surrealism was concurrent with its French counterpart. As Franz Kuna writes, until the late 1920s, Vienna and Prague stood on the "*easternmost fringe* of the map of European Modernism."[2] Malcolm Bradbury further "maps" modernism as follows:

> When we think of Modernism, we cannot avoid thinking of these urban climates, and the ideas and campaigns, the new philosophies and politics, that ran through them: through Berlin, Vienna, Moscow, and St. Petersburg, around the turn of the century and into the early years of the war; through London in the years immediately before the war; through Zürich, New York and Chicago during it; and through Paris at all times.[3]

Modernism moved westward easily and swiftly: from Zürich to Berlin, Paris and New York, as in the case of dadaism. Its spread eastward was more sluggish: even when it reached Russia, it still bypassed Greece and other Balkan countries,

---

[1] George Seferis, *Μέρες Α'* (Athens: Ikaros, 2003), p. 17. All the excerpts from *Μέρες Α'* have been translated by Marinos Pourgouris.

[2] Franz Kuna, "Vienna and Prague 1890–1928," in *Modernism: A Guide to European Literature 1890–1930*, ed. Malcolm Bradbury and James McFarlane, 120–33 (London: Penguin, 1991), p. 120. My emphasis.

[3] Malcolm Bradbury, "The Cities of Modernism," in *Modernism: A Guide to European Literature 1890–1930*, ed. Malcolm Bradbury and James McFarlane, 96–104 (London: Penguin, 1991), p. 96.

failing to stir the vociferous collective and far-reaching commotions it had caused in the West. The reasons for this resistance are certainly embedded in the cultural idiosyncrasies of each country and their refusal, in many cases, to recognize an "imported" movement as their own. In the case of Greece, further historical and political reasons explain its absence from the modern literary scene in the first years of the twentieth century.

European modernism had reached its peak in the years immediately preceding and the years following the Great War.[4] In his 1944 *The History of Surrealism*— written, interestingly, during the Second World War—Maurice Nadeau comments on the traumatic realizations that followed the most catastrophic war Europe had experienced until then:

> A regime incapable of disciplining its forces except to make them serve the diminution and destruction of man is bankrupt. Bankrupt, too, the elites applauding the generalized massacre in every country, doing their best to find ways to make it last. Bankrupt the science whose noblest efforts produced nothing better than a new explosive, perfected only another extermination weapon. Bankrupt the philosophies seeing nothing in man but his uniform and eagerly fabricating excuses to keep him in ignorance of the shameful trade he was being made to ply. Bankrupt the art good for nothing better than camouflage, bankrupt the literature, merely an appendage to the military communiqué. Universally bankrupt the civilization turning against itself, devouring itself.[5]

After the war, even such pre-war "revolutionary" movements as futurism and cubism seemed futile attempts to understand a chaotic and incomprehensible world, and even worse, to compromise art within a world that had proven itself a failure. The complete distrust of all established institutions was most notably expressed by Tristan Tzara in his 1918 Dada Manifesto: "Thus DADA was born, out of a need for independence, out of mistrust for the community. People who

---

[4] Malcolm Bradbury and James McFarlane point out that this is a view commonly held by the "New York-London-Paris Axis," as opposed to the chronological profile presented from the point of view of "Berlin, or Vienna, or Copenhagen, or Prague, or St. Petersburg" (Malcolm Bradbury and James McFarlane, "The Name and Nature of Modernism," in *Modernism: A Guide to European Literature 1890–1930*, ed. Malcolm Bradbury and James McFarlane [London: Penguin, 1991, p. 36]). Attempting to isolate a specific chronological frame for the evolution of modernism is a difficult task. The most inclusive definition Bradbury and McFarlane provide for modernism is the tendency to "see the universe as contingent, poverty stricken, denuded until it has been reimagined, its local virilities apprehended through the planes and conjunctions available to the fictionalizing mind" ("The Name and Nature of Modernism," p. 51). What constitutes World War I as a pivotal point in the history of modernism, then, is that it brought about and made more emphatic the conception of the universe as contingent, poverty stricken, and in need of reconstruction.

[5] Maurice Nadeau, *The History of Surrealism*, trans. Richard Howard (Cambridge, MA: The Belknap Press of Harvard University, 1989), p. 44–5.

join us keep their freedom. We don't accept any theories. We've had enough of the cubist and futurist academies: laboratories of formal ideas."⁶

In Greece, on the other hand, the historical, social, and political circumstances at the turn of the century were entirely different from those in Western Europe. Two years before the outbreak of World War I, Greece had fought in two Balkan Wars—the first (1912–1913) against the fading Ottoman Empire, and the second (1913) against Bulgaria. A year after the end of World War I, Greece attempted to regain much of the Asia Minor region. After some momentary gains, Greek forces suffered a major defeat, and by 1922 Greece withdrew any claims on Asia Minor. This territorial retreat resulted not only in a widespread feeling of defeatism but also, and more importantly, in the shattering of the national dream of the "Megali Idea" (the Great Idea): the unification of all the regions where Greeks resided under one nation, with Constantinople as its capital.⁷

From the decades preceding the outbreak of the War of Independence (1821) until the early 1920s, Greek intellectual activity concentrated, to a great extent, on the revival of national culture. It became clear to the Greek intellectuals in the formative years of the Greek nation that "literature and language were key components of a national culture" and that "literature was the imaginary mirror in which the nation reflected itself."⁸ During the nineteenth century many Greek poets appropriated the poetic style of the European Romantics and Parnassians, adding, in most cases, an emphatic tone of patriotism. Contrary to the French and English Romantics, for example, Greek Romantics mainly used "a stilted purist diction" and were "painstakingly patriotic."⁹ Even Andreas Kalvos (1792–1869) and Dionysios Solomos (1798–1857), who developed a distinctive style embodying the complex idiomorphic qualities of the Ionian Islands, largely wrote poetry inspired by the 1821 revolution and the heroic achievements of the Greeks.¹⁰

---

⁶ Tristan Tzara, *Seven Dada manifestos and Lampisteries*, trans. Barbara Wright (London: Calder, 1977), p. 5. The "1918 Dada Manifesto" was famously first read in Zurich on March 23, 1918. Later, in the same year, it was published in *Dada 3*.

⁷ The term "Megali Idea" was first declared in parliament in 1844 by the prominent politician Ioannis Kolettis (see Richard Clogg, Συνοπτική Ιστορία της Ελλάδας [Athens: Katoptro, 1995], p. 50). Essentially, the national dream that the Idea implied was the reconstruction of what once was the Byzantine Empire.

⁸ Gregory Jusdanis, *Belated Modernity and Aesthetic Culture: Inventing National Literature* (Minneapolis: University of Minnesota Press, 1991), p. 46.

⁹ Constantine Trypanis, ed., *The Penguin Book of Greek Verse* (New York: Penguin, 1971), p. lx. Greek Romanticism flourished in Athens immediately following the end of the insurrection against the Ottomans (1828). The leading poet of this school was Alexandros Soutsos (1803–1863), who was educated in Paris and was an ardent admirer of Victor Hugo and Lord Byron.

¹⁰ It is important to note that the poetry of both Solomos and Kalvos became particularly important to Odysseus Elytis, who saw them as forefathers of modern Greek poetry. What Elytis discovered in their work, however, was not nineteenth-century Greek patriotism but a vibrant and rejuvenating Greek language.

It was precisely because the nineteenth-century Greek poets did not perceive a unified notion of a national culture that they emphatically attempted to define it in their works. The political turmoil of the early twentieth century, the military failures, and the territorial losses intensified the feeling of disorientation and made the re-assessment of a national identity even more pressing.

On the social level, the striking differences between Greece and the Western European nations made the importation of European modernist movements to Greece a difficult task. Early twentieth-century Athens was certainly not the cultural capital Paris and Zürich were. In fact, there was more cultural exchange in cities like Constantinople, Smyrna, and Alexandria than in Athens. Malcolm Bradbury links modernism to the modern city inasmuch as it "has appropriated most of the functions and communications of society, most of its population, and the furthest extremities of its technological, commercial, industrial and intellectual experience."[11] At the turn of the century, Athens was still in an early formative stage of becoming a modern city. But soon after, the increasing difficulties in the provinces caused a massive movement of the population to Athens. By the 1920s, Athens had one of the largest bureaucratic systems in Europe, and this resulted in the formation of a new middle class.

What Greek writers sought during this period of intensified modernization was not the disjuncture and chaos expressed in literary modernism, particularly in its futurist, vorticist, and dadaist manifestations, but the achievement of national integration. After the 1880s and as late as the 1920s, the reigning current influencing Greek poetry was Symbolism, with its offer of a much more fitting creative space, at a time when order, form, and an objective all-encompassing reality were the primary concerns of the poets. Order was sought in what Baudelaire had described as "the forest of symbols."[12] The leading poet of the period was undoubtedly Kostis Palamas (1859–1943), whose poetry, apart from employing an austere structure, rhyme, and rhythm, uses the Greek tradition (folk and ancient) as its subtext.[13] The adherence to symbolism and, to some extent, the Parnasse, is fundamentally linked to what we can call the three loci of literary orientation: from the late nineteenth century to the 1920s, the contemporary Greek experience was expressed in relation to the folk tradition, the Byzantine inheritance, and ancient Greece. These three loci coexisted, for the most part, without tension: Palamas's *Twelve Words of the Gypsy* [Ο Δωδεκάλογος του Γύφτου] and the *King's Flute* [Η Φλογέρα του Βασιλιά] both draw from all three traditions without conflict. Their congruity was also related to the more general desire to establish a narrative of continuity

---

[11] Malcolm Bradbury, "The Cities of Modernism," 96–104, p. 97.

[12] "des forêts de symboles," see Baudelaire's sonnet "Correspondences."

[13] Roderick Beaton writes: "Of all the writers active around the turn of the century who aspired to achieve a synthesis of indigenous tradition with contemporary artistic developments elsewhere in Europe, far and away the most influential was Kostis Palamas." Roderick Beaton, *An Introduction to Modern Greek Literature* (Oxford: Oxford University Press, 1999), p. 84.

(from ancient Greece to Byzantium to modern Greece) and to the "Megali Idea."[14] In the 1920s, however, there appeared to be a split between the three. For some poets, especially those that supported the ideas of Pericles Yiannopoulos and Ionas Dragoumis, Ancient Greece was more of a burden than an inspiration and more of a Western idea than an expression of Greek authenticity.

In his book *Five Faces of Modernity*, Matei Calinescu distinguishes two kinds of modernities:

> ... at some point during the first half of the nineteenth century an irreversible split occurred between modernity as a stage in the history of Western civilization—a product of scientific and technological progress, of the industrial revolution, of the sweeping economic and social changes brought about by capitalism—and modernity as an aesthetic concept. Since then, the relations between the two modernities have been irreducibly hostile ....[15]

Paradoxically, as the hostility between the two modernities intensified in the early twentieth century, their relationship became one of powerful interdependence. With the exception of futurism, which attempted to reconcile the two in its emphatic glorification of the machine, wartime and postwar movements such as dadaism and surrealism gained adherence precisely through their vicious and uncompromising attack on reason, the concept of objective reality, and capitalism. In these cases, reaction to the process of modernization formed and sustained an important aspect of literary modernism. Literature's function became that of understanding the human condition beyond the order and logic of science but also beyond the fragmentation and chaos caused by modernization.

Malcolm Bradbury's description of modernism as "the distillation of many capitals and nations, and many different intellectual and aesthetic endeavors and moods"[16] implies both its growth in an urban environment and also its cosmopolitan and global tendencies. In this light, it is difficult to define modernism as a national phenomenon; Bradbury and McFarlane for example, resort to such general terms as "Anglo-American Modernism," or "Germanic Modernism," referring to the "combined and conflated literature of Germany, Austria and Scandinavia."[17] In fact, there exists an apparent hostile relationship between nationalism and modernism that permeates the proclamations and manifestoes of movements such as surrealism and dadaism.

---

[14] Consider, for instance, Yiannis Psycharis's famous statement in *My Journey* [Το Ταξίδι μου]: "In order for a nation to become a nation, two things are needed: it must broaden its borders and it must create its own literature." Yiannis Psycharis, *Το Ταξίδι μου* (Athens: Ermis, 1971), p. 37.

[15] Matei Calinescu, *Five Faces of Modernity: Modernism, Avant-Garde, Decadence, Kitsch, Postmodernism* (Durham: Duke University Press, 1987), p. 41.

[16] Malcolm Bradbury, "The Cities of Modernism," 96–104, p. 103.

[17] Malcolm Bradbury and James McFarlane, "The Name and Nature of Modernism," p. 36.

"Modernization," Gregory Jusdanis argues, "eventually pushes peripheral cultures into an aesthetics of autonomy." Consequently, the "confrontation with modernity" allowed for the emergence of "ideological contradictions in Greek culture," and literature in the 1930s "enabled readers to transcend the incongruity between Western constructs and indigenous practices."[18] What is considerably different in the case of Greece, in comparison to Western Europe, is the infusion *of a national discourse* in the tension between the two versions of modernity. The Greek supporters of surrealism could simultaneously turn against the conservatism of the State and the academia, and glorify the Greek landscape, use the purist and elitist katharevousa, and admire such "national" poets as Solomos and Kalvos.

At the same time, it was natural for modern Greek poets to rebel, like many of their European counterparts, against what they also saw as the corrupt values of the West. Western Europe had traced the origins of its civilization to ancient Greece and the Renaissance refueled the ancient Greece–West connection; but by positioning Greece at the "cradle of civilization," they had also, as Greek modernists saw it, left Greece *in* that cradle. In rejection of the Western European misconceptions of Greek values, the 1930s saw a flourishing of a poetry that attempted a disengagement from the ancient Greek locus. Nevertheless, the relationship of modern Greek poets to the classical tradition remained ambivalent: Seferis found an answer to this dilemma in T.S. Eliot's "mythical method," which utilized the diachronic elements of myth; Yiannis Ritsos attempted to negotiate the communist unease with antiquity by an extensive use of the mythical subtext.[19] What will become important over the course of this study is the rise of a debate in Greek modernism on the "orientation" of Greek identity. This debate was simultaneously expressed spatially and temporally. In other words, it centered on the spatial tension between East and West, North and South, as well as on the temporal tension between antiquity and modernity. The rise of surrealism in the early 1930s, and Elytis's support of its potential, is inexorably linked to the attempt to create a poetic tradition that is both modern—detached from conventional forms of expression—and expressive of the Greek experience.

"As a child, I remember, poetry didn't say much to me," Elytis writes in the "Chronicle of a Decade."[20] His first serious contact with poetry came around the age of 16. Suffering from a nervous breakdown and confined to his bed for two

---

[18] Jusdanis, *Belated*, p. 88.

[19] Communism's unease with classical Greece is aptly addressed by Herbert Marcuse: "Marxist aesthetics must explain why Greek tragedy and the medieval epic, for example, can still be experienced today as 'great,' 'authentic' literature, even though they pertain to ancient slave society and feudalism respectively.... One simply cannot explain the attraction of Greek art for us today as our rejoicing in the unfolding of the social 'childhood of humanity.'" Herbert Marcuse, *The Aesthetic Dimension—Toward a Critique of Marxist Aesthetics* (Boston: Beacon Press, 1978), p. 15. In his poetry, Ritsos often returns to these uneasy moments in Greek mythology in order to address the emotional state of his characters in an oppressive society.

[20] Elytis, *Ανοιχτά Χαρτιά*, p. 332.

months, he turned to the study of literature and read, for the first time, the poetry of C.P. Cavafy and Kostas Karyotakis. The extent to which these two poets influenced Elytis's early attempts to write his own poetry is not well documented since, throughout his life, Elytis meticulously destroyed unnecessary or unsatisfactory compositions, including his early poems.[21] Elytis's first contact with surrealism came in 1928 when he discovered, in Kaufmann's Stadiou Street bookstore, Paul Éluard's *Capitale de la douleur* and *Défense de savoir*. It was a unique moment of an apocalyptic epiphany, which the poet would later often recall in his writings. The timing of this unexpected discovery is noteworthy:

> Well, I was eighteen, full of perplexity about my future and my studies, in a house where mourning had not left an open window, and I heard that all the things I was seeing around me had a minimally real existence.[22]

In 1925, Elytis's father died of pneumonia. Earlier, in 1918, his eldest sister Myrsini had also passed away. In a house plunged into mourning, surrealism, with its rejection of reality and its emphasis on the power of dreams, had become for Elytis an escape into a world where "the life we lived might have been the sleep of the real life which continued every night from dream to dream."[23] It was also an important diversion from the pessimism of Karyotakis and what Elytis saw as the wrinkled didacticism of Cavafy. Éluard's poems were youthful, playful, an "outflanking of the grammatical rules," an ecstatic experience that made "the blood circulate more warmly" and "the cheeks shine at last."[24]

Elytis's excitement with Éluard's poetry was such that he wrote a letter to the renowned publisher José Corti, whose small Parisian press published most of the surrealist poets, requesting more information about Éluard and surrealism. Corti responded by sending him a brochure and a catalogue of titles. The echo of the French surrealist activity was so distant that it was not until two years later, in 1931, that Elytis had a synoptic, yet important, introduction to the surrealist proclamations. A rather unknown magazine published an article on surrealism written by a young man by the name of Dimitris Mentzelos. As Elytis explains, Mentzelos happened to spend some time in Lausanne's "Source" Hospital with René Crevel (1900–1935), both suffering from tuberculosis.[25] Crevel, one of the most active surrealist members, initiated Mentzelos into surrealism and the latter's impressions were published in the Greek literary magazine *Logos*. Although

---

[21] Ioulita Iliopoulou (personal communication). Also see Mario Vitti, *Οδυσσέας Ελύτης* (Athens: Ermis, 1991), p. 15.

[22] Elytis, *Ανοιχτά Χαρτιά*, pp. 338–9.

[23] Elytis, *Ανοιχτά Χαρτιά*, p. 339.

[24] Elytis, *Ανοιχτά Χαρτιά*, p. 337.

[25] Crevel and Mentzelos's hospitalization took place sometime between 1927 and 1929. Crevel was diagnosed with tuberculosis in 1927 and after that he was admitted to various sanatoria, hospitals, and clinics in Switzerland. They possibly met in October 1929, when he was admitted to a Lausanne hospital to undergo an operation.

Mentzelos's study on surrealism was brief and general, it had a powerful impact on Elytis. He now discovered that the poetry of Éluard was composed within a particular ideological and theoretical framework. Unlike the Parnassians and other "art for art's sake" movements, the surrealists had a "perspective on life, not just for the art of poetry."[26] The surrealist revolution became for the young Elytis first and foremost an *action* against all the social and political restrictions around him.

This first contact of the poet with surrealism also came at a time when, in Greece, youth had found its voice in the poetry of C.P. Cavafy and Kostas Karyotakis. The latter's suicide in 1928 had made him an instant idol, and by 1934 the Greek youth worshipped him, Elytis remembers, as a newfound god.[27] Caught between a bureaucratic machine, as a civil servant, and an overwhelming personal pessimism, Karyotakis represented for the disillusioned youth the devastating limitations of life and humans' inability to express themselves outside social and historical strictures. In the context of the aftermath of World War I, the defeat in Asia Minor, the final collapse of the "Megali Idea," and the increasing pace of industrialization, his poetry seemed an appropriate representation of the widespread feeling of defeatism and failure. Though Elytis was first intrigued by Karyotakis, he soon realized that there was no correspondence "between the way in which the poet perceived things and the way we saw our fellow students fight all day, or the way we met our girls each evening in the narrow streets of Lycavetos."[28] Karyotakis's rhyming poetry was confined in a defeatism and pessimism that inevitably led to inaction.

Elytis's fascination with C.P. Cavafy was greater but also short-lived. He first read Cavafy's poetry when he was 16, during the time he spent in bed following his nervous breakdown. As he recalls in "The Chronicle of a Decade," it was the first time he felt a "shaking" and a "curiosity."[29] The Alexandrian poet was not as popular as Karyotakis, since the first collected edition of his work did not appear until 1935, two years after his death, but his poems were regularly published in literary magazines. Though intrigued by Cavafy's poetry, Elytis would eventually see it as "wrinkled," at a time when his "instinctual urge" wished to "exorcise with every means possible, the world's old age."[30] Cavafy was lacking precisely that youthful Dionysian outburst that Elytis would discover about a year later, in Éluard's *Capitale de la douleur* and *L'Amour la poésie*.

---

[26] Elytis, *Ανοιχτά Χαρτιά*, p. 338.

[27] Elytis's description of his fellow university students in 1934 is most telling: "Pale, seized by dreams, they all wrote similar poems that confessed their faith to the one and only god: Karyotakis" (Elytis, *Ανοιχτά Χαρτιά*, p. 322).

[28] Elytis, *Ανοιχτά Χαρτιά*, p. 323.

[29] Elytis, *Ανοιχτά Χαρτιά*, p. 334.

[30] Elytis, *Ανοιχτά Χαρτιά*, p. 336.

If "Elytis" and "Éluard" sound alike, it is because Elytis most likely chose his pen name based on its phonetic proximity to the name of the French poet.[31] The 23-year-old Odysseus Alepoudellis was officially "baptized" Elytis in 1934 at Barba Yiannis's Tavern in the presence of his friends and "amidst a pandemonium of glasses smashing on walls, pans rolling underfoot, wild voices, head-blows, and joyous cries."[32] In 1935, his first poems appeared in the November edition (eleventh) of the magazine *Nea Grammata*; this was the first public introduction of his pen name. Elytis never explained the reasons why he chose this particular name, but his choice has frequently been discussed in relation to such words as "Eleni" [Helen], "Eleftheria" [Freedom], "Ellada" [Greece], and "Elpida" [Hope]—concepts and names that appear throughout in his work. This suggestion, mainly promulgated by the critic Mario Vitti, interesting as it may be, supposes that Elytis was concerned with these themes from the onset of his poetic career, when in fact his very first poems circle more around the concepts of Eros and Nature (particularly the sea and nocturnal images). It is more likely that Elytis's choice of pen name is based on the "hellenization" of Éluard's name by the replacement of the common French ending "ard" with the Greek "ytis."[33]

The anecdote concerning Elytis's choice of pen name reveals further interesting information about the idiosyncrasies of the young poet and his first public presentation. Initially, the name "Vranas," his mother's maiden name, was suggested to him as a possible pen name by his friend and editor of *Nea Grammata*, Giorgos Katsimbalis. "He knew," Elytis writes, "that I would be forced to use a pen name."[34] The reasons that "forced" Elytis to use a pen name are also clear. Apart from his "foresight not to publish" until he was certain he possessed "ways of expression that did not resemble anything else,"[35] he was also reluctant to publish because of his family background. The Alepoudellis family was a known aristocratic family of merchants that grew desperate about the poetic and revolutionary aspirations of their son, believing that "he would expose them irreparably."[36] The young Elytis lived in two worlds: in the first, he was surrounded by his family, the comforts of an aristocratic life, and his conservative fellow students at the Law school of the University of Athens; in the second, he lived in the world of poetry, revolution,

---

[31] Mario Vitti notes that Elytis's friends jokingly referred to the proximity of "Elytis" to "Éluard" and to *alytis* [vagabond] (Vitti, *Οδυσσέας Ελύτης*, p. 18). Kimon Friar suggests that the ending "ytis" rhymes with *politis* [citizen], which gives it a common and inclusive tone (qtd in Vitti, *Οδυσσέας Ελύτης*, p. 18).

[32] Elytis, *Ανοιχτά Χαρτιά*, p. 362.

[33] In Greek "u" is a lowercase "Y." Since Elytis was fluent in French he certainly knew that the French letter "y" is described as "i grec." Consequently, the names "Éluard" and "Elytis" share, in fact, the first three letters.

[34] Elytis, *Ανοιχτά Χαρτιά*, p. 362.

[35] Odysseus Elytis, *Αυτοπροσωπογραφία σε Λόγο Προφορικό* (Athens: Ypsilon, 2000), p. 13. All the excerpts are translated by Marinos Pourgouris.

[36] Elytis, *Ανοιχτά Χαρτιά*, p. 355.

and of individuals often accused by the press and the academia for turning their back on Greek traditional values. Surrealism "helped me find my path and fight against the defenses that I naturally had as a twenty-year-old kid," he would later say in an interview on National Greek Television.[37] The choice of the pen name "Elytis" placed the young poet far from a world of his family's capitalist ventures and initiated him, that raucous evening of his baptism at Barba-Yiannis's Tavern, into his newfound poetic identity.

Elytis's first compositions appeared in the eleventh edition of *Nea Grammata* under the general title "First Poems," and were signed with his newfound name "Elytis." These poems were composed about a year before Andreas Empeirikos officially introduced Elytis to surrealism and they testify to the vast influence of Éluard on his early work. The years between Elytis's initial contact with Éluard's poetry, in 1929, and the composition of his first poems in 1934 are clouded in silence. In the chronology used for the English edition of Elytis's *Collected Poems*, Jeffrey Carson suggests that in 1929 Elytis wrote "his first poems imitating Cavafy."[38] According to Carson, in 1935 Elytis destroyed the Cavafian poems and wrote the "First Poems." In Mario Vitti's chronology, it is suggested that in 1929 Elytis sent his first poems for publication to various literary magazines under different pen names. Given Elytis's tendency to destroy unwanted manuscripts, none of these early attempts into poetry has survived, and his official appearance can be traced only as far back as the November 1935 edition of *Nea Grammata*. His biographical essays included in the volume *Open Papers* are of little help, since Elytis describes there his first creative attempts *after* his meeting with Empeirikos in 1935. What is certain is that, between 1929 and 1934, Elytis went through a creative fermentation that resulted in the crystallization of his thought in the seven poems that appeared in *Nea Grammata*.[39] It is important to note here, that even in 1934, he was reluctant to submit his poems for publication. In fact, they wouldn't have been published had not Katsimbalis forcefully convinced him to do so.[40]

The degree to which Éluard's poetry influenced Elytis in his first poetic attempts can be discussed, in a more comprehensive way, against the background of two publications: a short essay on Éluard, published in *Nea Grammata* in 1936 (which also appears in *Open Papers*), and Elytis's translations of about 35 of Éluard's poems, which appear in a collected volume of translations under the title

---

[37] Elytis, *Αυτοπροσωπογραφία*, p. 15.

[38] Elytis, *Collected Poems*, p. 569.

[39] All of Elytis's chronologists present the years from 1929–1934 as a period of crisis for the young poet. Even though he discovered poetry, wrote poems in imitation of Cavafy, and explored surrealism, he was also enrolled, in 1930, in the Law School at Athens University. During this period, Elytis fluctuated between his interest in poetry and his academic obligations, between the Left (he translated Trotsky and read Marx), and political disengagement. The tension was such that, as Dimitris Daskalopoulos writes, in 1932 "he ceases to write and to read literary magazines." Dimitris Daskalopoulos, "Χρονολόγιο Οδυσσέα Ελύτη (1911–1986)," *Χάρτης* 21-3 (1986): 261–80, p. 263.

[40] Elytis, *Ανοιχτά Χαρτιά*, p. 362.

Second Writing.[41] Though the 1936 essay was written about two years after the composition of his first poems, Elytis's analysis can be used to describe his own early attempts at poetry. He gives three general observations to characterize Éluard's poetry:

1. Éluard's poetry employs a number of "originalities": "Fanatic anti-rhetoric, fragmentation, abolishment of punctuation, brave treatment of the adjective, in most cases short but very inclusive verses."[42] The absence of punctuation aims to create a "magical" and "hyperlogical" atmosphere.
2. Each of Éluard's poems is a "kingdom of images," presented not in a photographic manner but in accordance with what Rimbaud described as "dérèglement de tous les sens"; "An outward projection of the unconscious in a cataract of images."[43]
3. In contrast with older poetry, new poetry (which Éluard represents) doesn't have to be understood cerebrally; the modern poem attempts to shake the entire psychical and material being of the reader.

The essay is clearly influenced by Elytis's formal introduction to surrealism in 1936, as indicated by his references to Rolland de Renéville, Jean Cassou, Bernard Fay, and other literary critics he was probably not familiar with until Empeirikos made his library of surrealist publications available to him. His apparent fascination with Éluard, however, persists, and the striking similarities between his "First Poems" and Éluard's *Capitale* and *L'Amour* are evident. Generally, the "First Poems" are also short, fragmentary, and make little use of punctuation. They present images in a succession that resists a logical understanding, and aim to stimulate the senses rather than to challenge the mind:

> Dreams and dreams came
> To the birthday of jasmine
> Nights and nights to the white
> Sleeplessness of swans
> The dew is born in leaves
> As clear feeling
> In the boundless sky[44]

---

[41] Odysseus Elytis, *Δεύτερη Γραφή* (Athens: Ikaros, 1980). This volume includes Elytis's translations of poems by Rimbaud, Lautréamont, Éluard, Jouve, Ungaretti, Lorca, and Mayakovski.
[42] Elytis, *Ανοιχτά Χαρτιά*, p. 617.
[43] Elytis, *Ανοιχτά Χαρτιά*, p. 618.
[44] Elytis, "Seven Nocturnal Heptastichs," in Elytis, *Collected Poems*, p. 9. Όνειρα κι όνειρα ήρθανε / Στα γενέθλια των γιασεμιών / Νύχτες και νύχτες στις λευκές / Αϋπνίες των κύκνων / Η δροσιά γεννιέται μες στα φύλλα / Όπως μες στον απέραντο ουρανό / Το ξάστερο συναίσθημα (Elytis, *Ποίηση*, pp. 14–15).

Nature interacts with the senses so that the distinction between the body and its surroundings is completely obliterated. What remains is a dreamlike interaction of the senses with the things of the world.

"None of Éluard's poems has a specific subject," writes Elytis in the *Nea Grammata* essay on Éluard. "Whether there is a title or not, none of the poems deal with anything in specific a priori."[45] If the 23-year-old Elytis imitated something in Éluard, it is indeed a sense of playfulness that is more concerned with abstract sensual images than specific concepts. What he had found in the French poet was a youthful exploration of Eros in a dreamlike and unconventional language that Greek poetry seemed to lack. In certain instances the influence is more apparent. Some of the titles Elytis uses for his poems also correspond to similar titles in Éluard's early collections: Éluard's "Seconde Nature" in *L'Amour la poésie* to Elytis's "Second Nature" in the "First Poems"; Éluard's "Absences" in "Nouveaux Poèmes" to Elytis's "Climate of Absence" in the "First Poems"; Elytis's song "I told you about the Clouds" of *The Rhos of Eros* is reminiscent of Éluard's poem "Je te l'ai dit pour les nuages" in *L'Amour la poésie*.[46]

Éluard's poetry became a door that literally led the young Elytis from the dark caverns of the existing poetic conventions "to a *meltemi*[47] of feelings."[48] His "First Poems" testify to Éluard's early influence on him but, as has been already noted, they also reveal his commitment not to publish until he "possessed ways of expression that did not resemble anything else."[49] Indeed, Elytis's poems do not resemble Éluard's, or anything else that was published in Greece at the time, in at least two important ways. The most important difference is the placement of natural elements in a uniquely Greek space. Éluard's natural images are almost never distinctively "French." At their best, they are attempts to inject the natural image within the human body:

> Nature was caught in the nets of your life.
> The tree, your shadow, shows its naked flesh: the sky.
> It has the voice of the sand and the gestures of the wind
> And everything you say moves behind you.[50]

---

[45] Elytis, *Ανοιχτά Χαρτιά*, pp. 618–19.

[46] *The Rhos of Eros* was published as late as 1972, which testifies to the long-lasting influence of Éluard on Elytis.

[47] "Meltemi" is a brisk northern wind that blows every summer (approximately from June to August). It is both refreshing and hot.

[48] Elytis, *Ανοιχτά Χαρτιά*, p. 121. In his essay "Luck-Art-Risk" Elytis recalls the moment when, still a high-school student, he stumbled upon the poetry of Éluard. In Kaufmann's bookstore he remembers reading "Si tu t'en vas la porte s'ouvre sur le jour / Si tu t'en vas la porte s'ouvre sur moi-même" (Elytis, *Ανοιχτά Χαρτιά*, p. 121).

[49] Elytis, *Αυτοπροσωπογραφία*, p. 13.

[50] Paul Éluard, *Capital of Pain*, trans. Richard Weisman (New York: Grossman Publishers, 1973), p. 84. La nature s'est prise au filet de ta vie. / L'arbre, ton ombre montre sa chair nue: le ciel. / Il a la voix du sable et les gestes du vent. / Et tout ce que tu dis

Nature serves as a tool with which the poet can recreate the world and, with it, a new mythology of the body. For the *surrealist* Éluard, in nature one finds a projection of the unconscious that is never described in cultural or national terms; consequently, the invisible world the surrealists so vociferously attempted to paint is disinterested in the concept of ethnicity. For the surrealists, "the word 'nature,' which for centuries had been used synonymously with reality, is now used to designate merely the exterior world."[51] Elytis on the other hand, does not feel constricted by the idea of a Greek landscape. His opening poem in *Orientations* is titled "Of the Aegean," and even after his official encounter with surrealism, his references to nature remain grounded in the Greek landscape: "Sporades," "Ode to Santorini," "Age of Glaucous Memory," "Melancholy of the Aegean," "Image of Boeotia," etc.

The second important difference pertains to the structure of the poems. Even though Éluard's poetry is sometimes presented in resembling stanzas (triplets, quatrains, etc.), there is no strict numerological relation between structure and content. Elytis, on the other hand, builds much of his poetry around the number 7, and places the poems in unique structural forms.[52] The use of what Elytis calls architectural poetics will later become, after the publication of *The Axion Esti*, one of the most distinctive characteristics of his poetry.

The Discovery of Surrealism

Elytis's discovery of Éluard was naturally concurrent with his discovery of surrealism. His official contact with surrealism came in February of 1935, when he met the psychoanalyst and poet Andreas Empeirikos, who had recently arrived from France. For the first time, Elytis was introduced to the ideology of the movement beyond its poetical potential, which he had already explored, to some extent, in the poetry of Éluard. His first meeting with Empeirikos is elaborately described in *Open Papers*, and testifies to the deep impact it had on the young poet:

> It wasn't a usual city house. On the walls the great paintings with the absurd themes pacified instead of bewildering me; I recognized, in flesh and bone, that which for such a long time I was seeing published in the pages of foreign magazines. After a while, I was even able to determine the painters by myself: that one over there is Max Ernst, the other is Yves Tanguy, the other Oscar Domínguez—what a miracle![53]

---

bouge derrière toi (Paul Éluard, *Capitale de la douleur suivi de l'amour la poésie* [Paris: Gallimard, 1966]), p. 83.

[51] Anna Balakian, *Literary Origins of Surrealism. A New Mysticism in French Poetry* (New York: New York University Press, 1947), p. 9.

[52] See Chapters 4 and 5 for a more detailed discussion of Elytis's structural, or architectural, poetics.

[53] Elytis, *Ανοιχτά Χαρτιά*, p. 348.

The first warm meeting between the two men signaled the beginning of a strong friendship that would last until the death of Empeirikos in 1975. Elytis discovered in Empeirikos a true proponent of surrealist theory and a mentor who gave him a unique glimpse into the contemporary European literary world. Most importantly, it affirmed in him the existence of a frame within which Greek poetry could be rejuvenated, not in imitation of Western canons and expressions, but in an exploration of its own linguistic, cultural, and natural idiosyncrasies. He perceived surrealism as an aesthetic philosophy that allowed space for the expression of both thought and sensuality within the parameters of the Greek experience.

Nevertheless, his relationship with surrealist techniques of composition remained an ambiguous one. On the one hand, no other young poet in the 1930s supported the movement with such fervor and dedication as Elytis did. On the other, from the very first article he published in defense of surrealism, he clearly excludes himself from any membership in the movement. In outlining the common misperceptions of Greek critics of surrealism he writes:

> There are other and much more serious objections with which a cultivated person could confront surrealism, as there are other objections that did not allow me to enter its order, but which, gradually, compelled me to recognize a great portion of its preaching and to generally undertake its defense.[54]

It was this zealous defense of surrealism that misled many of Elytis's later critics to label him a surrealist and to group him with Empeirikos, Rantos, and Engonopoulos as the first Greek surrealists. "Obviously, I was never an orthodox surrealist" he would tell Ivar Ivask in a 1972 interview, and in the process of the same interview he would repeat: "I was never a disciple of the surrealist school."[55] In "The Chronicle of a Decade" he generally defines his relationship to the movement:

> It was in this way that surrealism touched me. As a protest against our slavery, which instead of becoming, as it had in the past, a lament, it utilizes exaltation and the infinite combinations of the imagination in order to suggest, at a sophisticated level, solutions in accord with the eternal human desires. Here is something that was not in disharmony with the open white shirts the boldest of us had begun to wear in those years.[56]

His most elaborate attempt to clarify his relationship with surrealism in his early youth was given in the context of a documentary on his life and works filmed by the Greek National Television in 1980. Once more, Elytis defines surrealism as a broad attitude rather than an abstract system of literary composition:

---

[54] Elytis, *Ανοιχτά Χαρτιά*, p. 466.
[55] Odysseus Elytis, "Odysseus Elytis on his Poetry. From an Interview with Ivar Ivask," *Books Abroad* 49, no. 4 (1975): 631–43, pp. 631, 642.
[56] Elytis, *Ανοιχτά Χαρτιά*, pp. 324–5.

> As a theoretical school, surrealism may have supported things I disagreed with, but as a wider cultural movement that fought against Western censorship, that preached the omnipotence of imagination and dream, that preached the freedom of love, and supported the idea that material phenomena were also phenomena of the spirit, it naturally overwhelmed me, especially in my twenties.
>
> In retrospect, I think that it helped me find my path and fight against the defenses I naturally had as a twenty-year-old. For me it was magic—unexpected oxygen in a burnt-out and hydrocephalic Europe. And, as I see it today, it helped me tremendously; only I asked surrealism to serve me and not the other way around. That's where the difference is.[57]

Elytis distinguishes here between two currents in surrealism: its theoretical, or methodological formulations and its revolutionary spirit. This split was also the seed of the schism in French surrealism. Its revolutionary attitude was aligned with the concurrent communist revolutionary politics, but its poetical techniques made it too abstract to be understood by the public. Consequently, most French surrealists had to proclaim their faith either in communism or in Breton's more "orthodox" surrealism. In terms of its poetical methodologies, chiefly expressed in the process of "automatic writing," the movement did not simply fail to interest Elytis but also most of the writers of the generation of the thirties in Greece. The only poets who generally applied Breton's suggestions for surrealist composition were Nikitas Rantos, Andreas Empeirikos, and Nikos Engonopoulos.[58] In terms of its revolutionary attitude, however, its influence in Greece was significant, as it commenced an intense and productive dialogue that upset the conservative literary establishment of the time.

Elytis's defense of surrealism as a much-needed and healthy revolutionary attitude was not characterized by the same reactions as the ones that guided French surrealists. Greek surrealism did not produce any manifestoes, and membership in the movement was almost nonexistent. Most importantly, it evolved against a vastly different cultural, historical, and social background. Firstly, French surrealism, as well as dadaism, had primarily developed as an immediate reaction to the conditions that brought about the First World War, whereas Greek surrealism was introduced more than a decade after the Greek defeat in Asia Minor. The collapse of the "Megali Idea" and the national dream of a "Greece of the three continents and the five seas," led to collective disenchantment rather than furious reaction against the State. Secondly, French surrealism came as a natural aftermath of Romanticism

---

[57] Odysseus Elytis, *Αυτοπροσωπογραφία*, p. 15.

[58] Elytis admits his experimentation with the technique of automatic writing in his essay "Luck-Art-Risk," where he provides examples of his playful poetic games with Empeirikos. Elytis would ask, for example, "What is the color red?" and Empeirikos would *automatically* respond with "a slap by poppies" (Elytis, *Ανοιχτά Χαρτιά*, p. 143). For other examples of Elytis's "automatic" attempts at composition see Elytis, *Ανοιχτά Χαρτιά*, pp. 143–4, 146–52.

and Symbolism, and within the existing turmoil brought about by cubism and futurism as well as even less popular movements such as vorticism and imagism. The coming of surrealism in Greece was concomitant only with a more general and largely uneventful discussion on modernist poetry. To comprehend the effect of this belatedness one must simply consider that very few poets used free verse in Greece in the early 1930s. Thirdly, French surrealism was connected, almost from the beginning, with communism, while the relationship between surrealism and communism in Greece was at its best indifferent and at its worst hostile. The question of a merger between communism and surrealism was hardly discussed in Greece. Fourthly, Paris was a diverse city where writers and poets of various national backgrounds could be found at any point in the early twentieth century, whereas Athens, the center of modernist activity in Greece, was an exceedingly homogeneous and monolingual space where the Greek poets were trying to find their place in the swiftly changing modernist landscape.

The position of surrealism in Greek literary history is so ambiguous, particularly when compared to the French group's achievements, that one could go so far as to claim that the movement never quite *officially* existed in Greece. Its defense and promotion was not undertaken by a particular circle but rather by specific individuals. It was never an organized movement that produced manifestoes and periodicals, or that sparked social disorder to the extent that French surrealism did. In this light, Elytis's justification of the movement's spiritual and revolutionary proclamations is not only a unique moment in Greek literary history, but also part of an intense dialogue that completely altered the existing perceptions of poetry in Greece.

When surrealism gradually began to gain some adherents in Greece, it was fervently attacked primarily by two ideological camps: the Marxists and the traditionalists. Elytis's response to these often-vehement attacks was the publication of many long articles in defense of the movement. These articles, composed in the decade 1935–1945, testify not only to the importance of surrealism in the formation of a personal philosophy for Elytis, but also to the captivating tension between tradition and modernity, particularly in the Greek case of belated modernity. In a 1938 letter in defense of surrealism, Elytis provides a clear outline of what he thinks are the common misconceptions of Greek critics on the subject of the surrealist movement. His objections to their arguments are numerous and center on the following assertions: he maintains that the opponents of surrealism tend to generalize, superficially labeling "surreal" all the poetry they cannot comprehend. Also they claim that the movement had arrived in Greece belatedly, when, in fact, Elytis suggests, the movement's arrival in Greece coincided, chronologically, with its most important contemporary activity and the formation of surrealist circles in many countries (such as Sweden, Switzerland, Belgium, England, Yugoslavia, and Japan). Finally, they perceive surrealism as a "fixed" ideology, whereas the movement kept evolving and going into new directions. Part of this erroneous approach was the constant reference to "automatism" as the main technique of composition when, in fact, Elytis claims, "automatism has been surpassed."[59]

Three of the most important misconceptions of the critics of surrealism in Greece concentrated, according to Elytis, on a complete misplacement of the movement in European literary history. Firstly, surrealism was not merely another literary school but "a perception towards life, the world, things that existed and will always exist...." Breton's "school" did nothing more than to "systematize and organize, and give it a characteristic name."[60] Secondly, surrealism was not simply a new Romantic school. According to their personal idiosyncrasies, surrealists were "romantic or classical, Apollonian or Dionysian, etc." and one of the movement's deepest aspirations was precisely to reconcile life's deepest contradiction utilizing "man's body, nature, and dreams."[61] Thirdly, surrealism was not concerned with an abstract utopian world indifferent to human concerns, but aimed to present an alternative view of reality. In this sense, it follows more in the tradition of the German Romantics, "who suggested for the first time the problem of internal reality and supported that thoughts, feelings, and dreams are equally able to stand within life and affect it."[62]

The surrealist attitude lies at the foundation of Elytis's formation of a personal ideology. Its influence on the poet was long-lasting and channeled his interest in other philosophical or aesthetic positions. From surrealism, Elytis easily proceeded to the discovery of Novalis and Hölderlin, and the exploration of Heraclitus, Camus, Le Corbusier, and others. His outline of the major principles that he found useful in the movement, and which he thought could be utilized by other Greek poets, is important in understanding his subsequent philosophical and poetical stances:

1. Deeply exploring and conquering reality.
2. Raising man above the dismembering a disrupted society imposed on him, reintegrating him with nature, and re-projecting him into the concepts of a national and social totality.
3. Reappraisal of the concept of "chance" and reconciliation of Fantastic and Real elements. An endless exploration and revelation of the marvelous (*merveilleux*).
4. Moving beyond skepticism, dexterity, personal introspection and, generally, the return to the springs of the spirit and the combative promotion of ideals.
5. Grasping and expressing the fascinating and dramatic elements in life in the juxtaposition of two or more things, outside their conventional understanding. Search for and establishment of an objective artistic world through the creation of new symbols.

---

[59] Elytis, *Ανοιχτά Χαρτιά*, p. 470.
[60] Elytis, *Ανοιχτά Χαρτιά*, p. 503.
[61] Elytis, *Ανοιχτά Χαρτιά*, p. 504.
[62] Elytis, *Ανοιχτά Χαρτιά*, p. 504.

6. Emotional reevaluation of the world. Abolition of logic's absolutism and reintroduction, in the right measure, of the "illogical" which, having imagination as its foundation, can allow for the broad understanding of people.
7. Utilization of the vibrant elements of Greek tradition and their reinsertion into free, contemporary means of expression.[63]

Most of Elytis's observations on surrealism are indeed "surreal" in the way Breton envisioned them. The surrealist Manifestoes launch an attack against reality and logic, assert complete *nonconformism*, emphasize the importance of chance and the marvelous, and polemically proclaim a revolution for the liberation of the mind. The concepts of the "national" and "traditional," however, had no place in Breton's vision of surrealism: "Everything remains to be done, every means must be worth trying, in order to lay waste to the ideas of *family, country, religion*. No matter how well-known the surrealist position may be with respect to this matter, still it must be stressed that on this point there is no room for compromise."[64] Elytis, on the other hand, speaks of surrealism's ability to reintegrate man within a "national totality" and its possibility of "utilizing the vibrant elements of Greek tradition." The attempt to find a compromise between surrealism, or modern poetry in general, and the national tradition was often the apple of discord in Greek intellectual circles.

Before long, Elytis found himself at the center of controversy, admittedly gaining "many enemies and the disdain of the philological establishment."[65] The most controversial and intense exchanges in this process were his personal responses (in the form of open letters) to some of the colossi of Greek literary life of the time. Elytis did not hesitate to challenge, among others, such well-known figures as Giorgos Theotokas, Evangelos Papanoutsos, Constantinos Tsatsos, Markos Avgeris, Angelos Sikelianos, and Takis Papatsonis. His challenges went unanswered at times, and were caustically and often mockingly answered at other times. At the end of this long and intense period, some of it taking place during the German occupation of Greece, Elytis saw, in retrospect, a significant transformation in the perceptions toward Art in Greece:

> Since 1930, when the first attempts to surpass an academic perception of Art and reform poetry and painting appeared in Greece, until today—that is after thirteen years only—a tremendous transformation has occurred in the perception of most lettered people. Every day, new ideas supported by the vibrant elements of our land, mostly the younger generation, move full of trust toward the future. Life itself gave the best answer to the ironies of journalists, the facile approach of chronographers, and the people of the literary establishment who had contemptibly turned their backs on us.[66]

---

[63] Elytis, *Ανοιχτά Χαρτιά*, pp. 517–18.

[64] André Breton, *Manifestoes of Surrealism*, trans. Richard Seaver and Helen R. Lane (Ann Arbor: The University of Michigan Press, 1972), p. 128.

[65] Elytis, *Ανοιχτά Χαρτιά*, p. 472.

[66] Elytis, *Ανοιχτά Χαρτιά*, p. 491.

As the Second World War came to a destructive conclusion and as the debate on surrealism and modern poetry in general subsided, Elytis felt, in 1945, that it was time to write the epilogue of the decade. In a long article titled "Assessment and a New Beginning" he reaffirms surrealism's importance in altering past conservative perceptions and emphatically concludes his involvement in one of the most intense and productive periods in modern Greek literature with a hopeful look into the future:

> 1935–1945! An important decade in the chronicles of modern poetry permanently completes its circle. *The polemical period is coming to an end ...*
>
> Goodbye then to bohemianism, goodbye to Wildeism,[67] goodbye to petty laments, goodbye to aristocratism, goodbye to the sadomasochistic misfortunes of the tavern with its wine and the 'alas, us miserable folk,' goodbye to pseudo-revolution with its empty words in the air, yes, goodbye, goodbye....[68]

In many respects, the 1935–1945 decade was indeed an "explosive" period, whether one assesses it historically (with Ioannis Metaxas' dictatorship and the German Occupation) or literary. Surrealism, be it French or Greek, Marxist or Bretonian, aimed at overthrowing established conventions and liberating man from social impositions. Change, for Elytis, would not be achieved through a pseudo-revolution of false promises or through a total rejection of tradition.

Furthermore, surrealism's attack on convention implied, as its alternative, an exploration of the "peripheral other." Greece, for Elytis, was situated at the periphery of Europe and carried the burden of its ancient inheritance. Poetry's revolutionary force would have to be launched against the peripherization of the "other" and the post-World War II rising tendency towards globalization, which threatened to obliterate minor literatures and languages. It is in this context that Elytis's meeting with Albert Camus and their subsequent exploration of specific geographical topoi (Algeria, the Aegean) become important. The revolution they both envisioned focused on the relocation of the center away from Western Europe and towards the South and Eastern regions of the Mediterranean. Their joint attempt to define a new Mediterranean cultural space will be the focus of the second chapter.

National Modernisms

What becomes obvious in this brief introduction to Elytis's first contact with surrealism, as I described it above, is that the most fundamental difference that underlies a comparison between Greek and Western European modernist activity is the concept of ethnic identity. In short, the reconsideration of Greek literature

---

[67] Wildeism [ουαϊλδισμός]: Elytis is referring here to Oscar Wilde.
[68] Elytis, *Ανοιχτά Χαρτιά*, p. 531.

in the 1930s was simultaneously a reconsideration of Greek national identity. The reassessment of ethnicity by modernist poets in this period was not, by any means, a Greek prerogative. Consider, for example, Bogdana Carpenter's description of the Polish Avant-Garde in the period 1918–1939:

> Young poets who began to write around 1918 had no models to follow either spiritually or formally. Their rebellion was total, and their need to invent a new poetic language overwhelming. They tried to absorb simultaneously the lessons of European symbolism and the experiments of the most recent poetic movements such as Futurism, Dada and surrealism. Hence they fused, poetically as well as geographically, Mallarmé with F.T. Marinetti, Guillaume Apollinaire with Vladimir Mayakovski, Bely with André Breton. Even more importantly, they wanted to move their own century-long poetic heritage onto new tracks, to map out a new, indigenous and specifically Polish poetic project.[69]

Much like Greek modernists, Polish avantgardists also attempted, in their incorporation of Western European modernism, to "map out a new, indigenous and specifically Polish poetic project." In fact, modernist activity in Egypt, Japan, postcolonial India and Pakistan, Bulgaria, or Romania, follows a similar trajectory where indigenous traditions are reevaluated in the context of the modernist project. In these places, the exclusion of ethnicity did not take the same absolutist form that we see in, say, French dadaism or surrealism. In fact, as Andriana Varga has convincingly argued, even the works of such celebrated Romanian avant-garde writers as Tristan Tzara and Eugene Ionesco "show the development of a literary discourse which questions both Western and Eastern hegemony and coexists with Western influences on Romanian literature, culture, and society."[70]

---

[69] Bogdana Carpenter, "Between DADA and Constructivism: The Polish Avant-Garde Poetic Project," in *The Avant-Garde and the Margin: New Territories of Modernism*, ed. Sanja Bahun-Radunović and Marinos Pourgouris, 113–28 (Newcastle: Cambridge Scholars Press, 2006), p. 115.

[70] Andriana Varga, "Periphery to Center and Back: Exploring Dada and the Absurd in the Context of Romanian Literary Traditions," in *The Avant-Garde and the Margin: New Territories of Modernism*, ed. Sanja Bahun-Radunović and Marinos Pourgouris, 129–53 (Newcastle: Cambridge Scholars Press, 2006), p. 151. In addition to these important mutations and adaptations of modernism in particular cultural contexts, I would add here the intriguing ways in which particular non-native authors become relevant in some countries whereas they remain peripheral in others. It is interesting, for example, to note that Elytis's poetry became quite popular in China since the 1980s. (See Michelle Yea, "Contemporary Chinese Poetry Scenes," *Chicago Review* 39, no. 3/4 [1993]: 279–83). In a 2009 interview with *World Literature Today*, the young Albanian poet Luljeta Lleshanaku noted that contemporary Greek poets (Elytis, Seferis, Ritsos, and Cavafy) "were really a good school for [her]: their philosophy, found out more in light than in darkness, their vital Mediterranean temperament, their strong and essential metaphors that have to do with this life, awareness of their tradition, adapted very carefully within the individual poetic awareness." (Michele Frucht Levy, "A Conversation with Luljeta Lleshanaku," *World Literature Today* 83, no. 1

To reconsider, then, the position of the ethnic in the advent of modernism is as imperative as the reconsideration of its position today within the frame of poststructuralist discourse. What do we make of the fact, for example, that new translations of C.P. Cavafy's poetry keep appearing every three or four years, that monographs on Nikos Kazantzakis's philosophy are still being published, whereas Greece's two Nobel laureates, Odysseus Elytis and George Seferis, are still largely understudied? Who belongs to the "global" literature of the world and who doesn't? Addressing the reemergence of the category of "World Literature" as a response to "Comparative Literature," Gregory Jusdanis writes:

> Critics concerned with the struggle for freedom will more likely read Rigoberta Menchú, Isabel Allende, or J.M. Coetzee than such Greek authors as Alki Zei, Maro Douka, or Aris Alexandrou. The Greek authors are talented, practice postmodern writing, and are widely read in Greece, but they never acquire an international audience, for reasons outside their control. It is perhaps not a coincidence that the Nobel Prizes awarded to Greek authors, George Seferis in 1963 and Odysseus Elytis in 1979, were given at this time of heightened interests in Greek things.[71]

Interestingly, Seferis and Elytis are two of the most explicitly "comparative" poets in Greece, allowing scholars who are interested in their work to explore influences and exchanges that are already present in their writing (i.e., Seferis's interest in T.S. Eliot or symbolism and Elytis's interest in surrealism or the poetry of Paul Éluard are extensively documented in their journals, essays, and poetry). What makes international audiences less interested in their work is precisely the fact that these audiences are *international*: Seferis and Elytis, in other words, are also markedly *Greek* poets—that is to say they are perceived as too "ethnic." In the current climate that valorizes diversity, difference, and cosmopolitanism, these poets represent a monocultural expression that poststructuralism has already deconstructed and that cultural studies have often designated as too narrow.

The paradox in such conceptualization of national poetry is that ethnicity is, on the one hand, part of that which is rejected and stigmatized as nationalistic and, on the other, it bears the signs of the struggle for recognition and visibility. In the same way that postcolonial writers express something of that colonial relationship that still haunts their writing, as Rey Chow would have it, ethnic writing in general can similarly reveal the tensions that underlie the uneven distribution of cultural capital between different nations.

I find Partha Chatterjee's description of nationalism, as it emerged in the colonial context, central in understanding this preoccupation with the category

---

[Jan–Feb 2009]: 16–20, p. 18). Translations of Elytis's poems appear throughout the Balkans. Such influences are testimonies to the multilayered ways in which literature, even when we label it as *ethnic*, can be adapted to new cultural contexts.

[71] Jusdanis, "World Literature: The Unbearable Lightness of Thinking Globally." *Diaspora* 12, no. 1 (2003): 103–30, p. 122.

of the ethnic in the modernist context. Chatterjee suggests that "anti-colonial nationalism creates its own domain of sovereignty within colonial society well before it begins its political battle with the imperial power. It does this by dividing the world of social institutions and practices into two domains: the material and the spiritual."[72] This split enabled colonial societies to imitate Western technological advancements on the one hand and develop an independent national aesthetic on the other. Responding to this argument, Jusdanis claims that this split goes beyond the colonial setting and describes the relationship of nation states to modernization in general—the cases of Greece, Germany, and Egypt show, for Jusdanis, that "nationalism has resisted political and cultural universal systems from the beginning and has sought in national culture the resources for modernization."[73]

Chatterjee's distinction between the material and the spiritual should be understood here as diachronic—the realm of materiality is not simply the condition that describes the technological or scientific superiority of the West but also the cultural products that progress bestowed upon the West. The reaction to the misreading of Greekness by the Renaissance artists, for example, is one of the many manifestations of this split. The glorification of multiculturalism and cosmopolitanism by the already diverse West is another—a valorization that, as I have already stressed, and as Rey Chow writes, neglects the sociocultural position of the ethnic in these societies. From the perspective of many ethnic poets, their nations always seem to be catching up to the consequences of Western progress and its byproducts. Elytis's position can be read in the background of a similar split. It is a testimony to the evasions and the transformations ethnic identity goes through against the background of a perpetually changing world. What one should see in his poems is not the confident assertion of patriotism but, on the contrary, the desperate plea of a poet to reassert the place of ethnicity in a world that continuously deconstructs it (be it in the modernist, postmodernist, or poststructural context). The second chapter of the book will consider the ways in which such reassertions were expressed in Elytis's turn to the Mediterranean (and particularly the Aegean) as an alternative cultural topos. His theories of Solar Metaphysics and Architectural Poetics, that are the subject of the fourth and fifth chapters, are also expressive of the way in which the redefinition of ethnicity can reveal new and intriguing poetic forms: i.e., how poetic *content* can also point to a very precise *form* that the poem can take.

---

[72] Partha Chatterjee, *The Nation and its Fragments: Colonial and Postcolonial Histories* (Princeton: Princeton University Press, 2007), p. 6.

[73] Gregory Jusdanis, *The Necessary Nation* (Princeton: Princeton University Press, 2001), pp. 8–9.

Chapter 2
Towards a New Mediterranean Culture

> I brought my life this far
> To this point that struggles
> Always near the sea
> —Elytis, *Orientations*

Being Mediterranean

In his *Commentary on the Stranger*, Sartre describes Camus as a "Mediterranean," meaning that "the way in which he reasons, the clarity of his ideas, the cut of this essayistic style, and a certain kind of solar, orderly, ceremonious, and desolate melancholy, all reveal a classical temperament, a Mediterranean."[1] Derrida told the participants at a conference on the island of Capri that "almost all of us (i.e., the participants) are Mediterranean by origin and each of us Mediterranean by a sort of magnetism."[2] In a letter to Melchor Fernandez Almagro, Federico Garcia Lorca wrote that in Barcelona "one finds the Mediterranean, the spirit, the adventure, the elevated dream of perfect love."[3] And one of the most remarkable identifications with the Mediterranean identity comes from a very unlikely thinker, Sigmund Freud. In a letter to Carl Jung, Freud compares Ernest Jones with Jung and himself in the following way: "he [Jones] is a Celt and consequently not quite accessible to us, the Teuton [Jung] and the Mediterranean man [Freud]."[4] As strange as this last one may sound, it is indeed true in at least two ways: a) Freud was deeply immersed in the study of ancient Greek civilization and, b) this is, perhaps, one of these rare moments where he implicitly acknowledges his Jewish identity. Be that as it may, the Mediterranean is a concept that one gravitates towards: it is passionate yet melancholic, an elevated dream and a projected identity, it is simultaneously distinctive and general enough that one can assume it as an identity. It is perhaps with this elusive Mediterranean in mind that the Turkish novelist Orhan Pamuk

---

[1] Jean Paul Sartre, *Existentialism is a Humanism: Including, A Commentary on the Stranger*, trans. Carol Macomber (New Haven: Yale University Press, 2007), p. 76.

[2] Jacques Derrida, "Faith and Knowledge: the Two Sources of 'Religion' at the Limits of Reason Alone," in *Religion*, ed. Jacques Derrida and Gianni Vattimo, trans. David Webb (Stanford: Stanford University Press, 1998), p. 7.

[3] Federico García Lorca, *Selected Letters*, trans. David Gershator (New York: New Directions Publishing, 1983), p. 69.

[4] Sigmund Freud, "Letter from Sigmund Freud to C.G. Jung, July 18, 1908," *The Freud/Jung Letters: The Correspondence between Sigmund Freud and C.G. Jung*, ed. William McGuire (Princeton: Princeton University Press, 1974), p. 165.

writes that "the idea of the Mediterranean as a single entity, is artificial, and the single Mediterranean character that derives from it is, likewise, a thing that had to be invented and elaborated before it was discovered." And then he proceeds, playfully and jokingly, to offer his own guide, "some ground rules" as he calls them, "for those wishing to acquire Mediterranean identity":

1. Foster the view of the Mediterranean as a unified entity; it would be a good thing if such it were. This would provide a new doorway to the place of which we are a part for those of us who cannot travel to Spain, France, and Italy without visas.
2. The best definitions of Mediterranean identity are in books written by non-Mediterraneans. Don't complain about this; just try to become like the Mediterraneans they describe, and you will have your identity.
3. If a writer wants to see himself as Mediterranean, he must give up certain other identities. For example, a French writer who wants to be Mediterranean must give up a part of his Frenchness. By the same logic, a Greek writer wishing to be Mediterranean must give up part of his Balkan and European identities.
4. For those who want to become real Mediterranean writers, whenever you write about it don't say "the Mediterranean," just say "the sea." Speak of its culture and its particularities without naming them and without using the word *Mediterranean* at all. Because the best way to become Mediterranean is never to talk about it.[5]

As playful as it may be, Pamuk's essay captures, quite effectively, the stereotypes surrounding the so-called Mediterranean identity or the Mediterranean character, but also the tension that describes the short and turbulent history of Mediterranean Studies as a field. We might generally say, that the problem of Mediterranean identity is also entangled in the problem of anthropology itself as a field. In other words, it is precisely the strive of anthropology to rid itself of its own colonial historical beginnings, or such categories as "primitive" versus "civilized" people, that poses the greatest opposition to an assumed Mediterranean identity. From a conventional anthropological perspective, the Mediterranean is too "balkanized"— to use an adjective that describes yet another contested field—to be considered a singular cultural entity. The Mediterranean Sea is surrounded by 21 countries in three different continents, it is home to three major religions with multiple denominations, and its inhabitants speak multiple languages and dialects. Yet, as Michael Herzfeld writes, the conceptualization of the Mediterranean as a single entity persists particularly in literature and in popular imagination:

> The tendency to conceptualize the Mediterranean as a single, more or less homogeneous entity has certainly remained strong to this day, not only in

---

[5] Orhan Pamuk, *Other Colors: Essays and a Story*, trans. Maureen Freely (New York: Vintage, 2007), p. 196.

anthropological writings but also, notably, in popular prejudice. Stereotypical images of "Mediterranean peoples" abound in the English-language literature and superficially seem borne out by at least some of the findings of anthropologists. Popular writers credit the region with "voluptuousness" and "austerity" in a supposedly unique combination, while others of self-consciously Mediterranean origin have accepted such characterizations and even quoted them with enthusiastic approval.[6]

At the same time, we must wonder, along with Peregrine Horden and Nicholas Purcell, authors of *The Corrupting Sea*, what constitutes a cultural entity: what is "Europe"? What is "the Middle East"?[7] Even if the Mediterranean is more fragmented than such geographical entities, it still offers the historian abundant examples for the potential study of unities: the great ports that connected most of these countries from antiquity to the early twentieth century (these were simultaneously trade *and* cultural routes); the shared colonial history of many of the Mediterranean countries; the great division between North and South (a division that describes many countries on the European side of the Mediterranean); the shared trade and the shared climate that for Ferdinand Braudel constitute the most unifying characteristic of the Mediterranean; or, as Iain Chambers writes, its function as a "contested sea" (with an entire population of immigrants transiting through it from Africa to the shores of Europe).[8] I shall return to this point since I find it is most pertinent when one speaks of *unities* in the age of poststructuralism.

If we look at travel accounts from the seventeenth to the nineteenth century, the fascination with the Mediterranean concentrates on two areas: sex and ruins (in some cases the two are combined in what we can describe, in jest, as sex on ruins). The most profound example of the Mediterranean's sexualization is undoubtedly Sir Richard Francis Burton's designation, in 1885, of what he called a *Sotadic Zone*: an area where pederasty and homosexuality, or *the Vice* as he labeled it, were common. This zone, according to Burton is

> bounded westwards by the northern shores of the Mediterranean (N. Lat. 43°) and by the southern (N. Lat. 30°). Thus the depth would be 780 to 800 miles including meridional France, the Iberian Peninsula, Italy and Greece, with the coast-regions of Africa from Morocco to Egypt.[9]

Even though the Sotadic Zone includes, apart from the Mediterranean, much of India, Southeast Asia, and much of America, Burton's analysis concentrates

---

[6] Michael Herzfeld, "The Horns of the Mediterraneanist Dilemma," *American Ethnologist* 11.3 (1984): 439–54, p. 440.

[7] Peregrine Horden and Nicholas Purcell, *The Corrupting Sea: A Study of Mediterranean History* (Malden, MA: Blackwell Publishing, 2000).

[8] Iain Chambers, *Mediterranean Crossings: The Politics of an Interrupted Modernity* (Durham: Duke University Press, 2008).

[9] Richard Francis Burton, *One Thousand and One Arabian Nights*, Vol. 10 (Forgotten Books, 2008), p. 140.

primarily on the inheritance of ancient Greece. There are two significant points Burton makes that are important to this discussion: a) his claim that *the Vice* is popular in these areas for "geographical and climatic reasons" and b) that there is a clear distinction between those who inhabit the Sotadic Zone, where "the Vice is popular and endemic," and the northern Europeans, who "are physically incapable of performing the operation and look upon it with the liveliest disgust."[10] The British scholar Havelock Ellis would later reprint Burton's findings in his seminal *Sexual Inversions* (1901) where he would similarly write that "in dealing with a northern country, like England, homosexual phenomena do not present themselves in the same way as they do in southern Italy today or in ancient Greece."[11] Both of these (i.e., geography/climate and the distinction between inhabitants of the Sotadic Zone and those outside of it) are central to the modernist context that I will turn to shortly. For now, suffice it to say that this sort of mapping allows the British traveler (including Burton) to enter and exit this phantasmagoric region of hypersexuality and "perversity" safely and at will. Particular sites of the Mediterranean in fact functioned, and still do, as such heterotopic escapes. From the 1940s until the 1980s, Morocco functioned as such a site where European and American travelers looked for an escape through drugs, sex, and Sufist rituals (with visitors including Tennessee Williams, Allen Ginsburg, Jack Kerouac, Truman Capote, Ornette Coleman, Steve Lacy, Jimi Hendrix, The Rolling Stones, Robert Plant, Jimmy Page, and many others).[12] In Italy, at the turn of the century, the island of Capri served a similar function becoming, in the words of Robert Aldrich, "the homosexual mecca in the South."[13] Mykonos and Santorini in Greece, Sharm El Sheikh in Egypt, Agia Napa in Cyprus, and of course Ibiza in Spain, are some contemporary examples of such sites of escape in the Mediterranean.

The Western travelers' fascination with ruins, particularly Greek and Roman, is well documented and needs no further analysis. What is interesting, however, is that we often find in Western European literature a combination of these two fantasies: i.e., the fantasy of sexual disinhibition and the fantasy of the ancient origins of the West in the Mediterranean (Greece and Rome). It is not surprising, for example, that in his famous essay "A Disturbance of Memory on the Acropolis," Freud connects the visit to the ancient site with the working-through of his own Oedipus Complex and the overcoming of the Father.[14] Freud's fascination with ruins is easily discernible in his writings—one might recall here the famous Rome

---

[10] Burton, *One Thousand*, p. 140.

[11] Havelock Ellis, *Sexual Inversion* (Philadelphia: F.A. Davis Company, 1908), p. 28.

[12] I owe these references to Elliott Colla.

[13] Robert Aldrich, *The Seduction of the Mediterranean: Writing, Art and Homosexual Fantasy* (New York: Routledge, 1993), p. 135.

[14] Sigmund Freud, "A Disturbance of Memory on the Acropolis," in *The Standard Edition of the Complete Psychological Works of Sigmund Freud, Volume XXII (1932–1936): New Introductory Lectures on Psychoanalysis and Other Works*, trans. James Strachey (London: Hogarth Press, 1964).

metaphor in *Civilization and its Discontents* where the architecture of the city is likened to the traumatic experiences of hysterics—and in his personal collection of antiquities that included items from ancient Greece, Rome, and Cyprus. With Freud, we are already mapping here the modernist experiment where both ruins and sexuality become central expressions and are situated in the Mediterranean basin. One might even argue that the entire psychoanalytic project is largely founded upon an exploration of sexuality as expressed in the primordial mythical Mediterranean space: from Oedipus to Antigone and from Christ to Moses. Mythology, or more precisely "the fantasizing (*fabulation*) of antiquity," as Lacan argues, "has also come to something in the form of psychoanalysis."[15] The same combination of sexual disinhibition and the rumination on ruins is found, in the modernist tradition, in the works of E.M. Forster, Laurence Durrell, Henry Miller—who sees at the Acropolis the image of the woman whose lust turns to "forbidden objects of desire"[16]—or in the photographs of Wilhelm von Gloeden, Gaetano D' Agata, Rudolf Koppitz, and Herbert List.[17]

What I am proposing here is that the search for the origins of Western civilizations and the claim to the inheritance of classical Greece that had its foundation in the Renaissance was simultaneously, in the nineteenth century and through the modernist period, a search for and an examination of sexual identity. The Mediterranean functioned as a space where such exploration became possible, where perversity was normalized and where Western sexual fantasies could be acted out in a contained space.[18]

If for Northern European writers the Mediterranean functioned as a phantasmagoric space of sexual perversion and passion, and if it was situated at the beginning of the primordial origins of Western civilization—the navel of the earth or the center of the earth as its etymology suggests—for many Mediterranean writers, it played a central role in the redefinition of identity—both national and sexual. One of the most profound and fairly recent examples of such redefinition is the reconsideration of the concept of "Levantinism" by contemporary Israeli writers. The word was used in European travelers' writings to designate an individual, not necessarily a native of the Levant, who has been "infected" by the sluggishness, disorganization, and undisciplined life of the Levant. As Gil Hochberg argues

---

[15] Jacques Lacan, *On Feminine Sexuality the Limits of Love and Knowledge*, ed. Jacques Alain Miller, trans. Bruce Fink (New York: W.W. Norton & Company, 1999), p. 115.

[16] Henry Miller, *The Colossus of Maroussi* (New York: New Directions, 1958), p. 112.

[17] For a discussion on the Mediterranean and photography see Robert Aldrich, *The Seduction of the Mediterranean: Writing, Art and Homosexual Fantasy*.

[18] James Joyce's *Ulysses* provides us with what we could read as a very amusing commentary on the Western claim to ancient Greek heritage—a claim, we might add, that is often misperceived as Joyce's indebtedness to the Homeric tradition when in fact it's a complete subversion of it. One of the most memorable incidents in *Ulysses* is Leopold Bloom's visit to a museum to inquire whether ancient Greek statues have a hole in their behind. Bloom's curiosity captures nicely, in a rather sarcastic manner, the obsessive quest for both ruins and sexual reinvigoration in Mediterranean archaeology.

"the affiliated term, Levantinism, came to mean, in this context, a state of cultural impurity: a failed attempt on the side of the colonized to imitate the ways of the West, resulting in poor performance of (Western) culture."[19] It was the Egyptian Jewish writer Jacqueline Kahanoff who first attempted a rehabilitation of the term in the 1950s arguing that "the time has come for the Levant to reevaluate itself by its own light, rather than see itself through Europe's sight, as something quaintly exotic, tired, sick and almost lifeless."[20]

There is no doubt that Kahanoff's reconstitution of Levantinism was influenced by her reading of Albert Camus, to whom I will now turn to discuss what is probably the clearest and most systematic attempt to reinvigorate a New Mediterranean Identity in opposition to Northern European projections. I will primarily focus on the shared attempt between Camus and Elytis that went as far as the launching of a periodical that would promote this redefined Mediterranean identity. In Camus's case, as I will discuss, such perception is undermined by his own paradoxical position as both French and Algerian—it is impossible, in other words to approach his discussion on the Mediterranean independently of the French colonization of Algeria. At the same time, I am interested in the ways Camus's views on the Mediterranean are shared or have influenced Elytis. Consequently, I will read several passages from both writers in an attempt to situate this exchange that constitutes a very distinctive attempt in the modernist context, to define the ambiguous space that constitutes Mediterranean aesthetics.

Mediterranean Modernisms: From Algeria to the Aegean

In the late 1940s, Albert Camus and René Char decided to launch a new magazine.[21] "It will probably be called 'Empédocle,'" Camus confided in a letter to his mentor Jean Grenier, noting in parenthesis: "remember Nietzsche, 'Empedocles uses all his virulence in describing the ignorance [of man].'"[22] Elytis, who was by then familiar with both Camus and Char, was asked to write an article to be published in the inaugural issue of the magazine. *Empédocle*, as Elytis recalls, would be published "under the austere principle of defending light and the Mediterranean sensation. Already these two elements were being inscribed with rare energy in the poems of the former [Char], and with adamantine lucidity in the essays of the

---

[19] Gil Hochberg, "'Permanent Immigration': Jacqueline Kahanoff, Ronit Matalon, and the Impetus of Levantinism," *boundary 2* (Duke University Press) 31, no. 2 (2004): 219–43, p. 221.

[20] Qtd in Ammiel Alcalay, *After Jews and Arabs: Remaking Levantine Culture* (Minneapolis: University of Minnesota Press, 1993), p. 72.

[21] Apart from Camus and Char, the editorial board of the magazine included Albert Béguin, Guido Meister, and Jean Vagne (Albert Camus and Jean Grenier, *Correspondences 1932–1960*, trans. Jan Rigaud [Lincoln: University of Nebraska Press, 2003], p. 237).

[22] Camus and Grenier, *Correspondences*, p. 127. Letter dated January 15, 1949.

latter [Camus]."²³ This ambitious plan would also provide the literary space for a unique merging of Camus's philosophy and well-known fiction with his less known aesthetic ideas appearing in *Noces* and *L'Eté*. When Camus and Char asked Elytis to more or less write what he had been telling them in their conversations, he drafted an essay under the title "Pour un lyricisme d' inventions architecturales et de métaphysique solaire" ["For a lyricism of architectural inventions and Solar Metaphysics"]. The concept of Solar Metaphysics would later be crystallized in the poetry of Elytis as one of the most important ideas that underlie his own poetic metaphysics.²⁴

Camus's enthrallment with the Mediterranean landscape, and particularly Algeria, reached its peak in the late 1930s, when he wrote most of the essays included in *Noces* (published in 1939) and *L'Eté* (published in 1954). His views were not merely aesthetic expressions that glorified the Mediterranean region but, rather, a determined philosophical construction based on the paradigm of Mediterranean sensation. In a lecture given at the Maison de la Culture on February 8, 1937, he attempted for the first time to unify his ideas on the subject under a comprehensive philosophy of *action*. From the beginning of this lecture he points out that his effort is not to restore empty traditionalism, celebrate the superiority of one culture over the other, adopt an inverted form of fascism, or incite the Latin against the Nordic peoples. Rejecting the notion of "Mediterranean Nationalism" and of "higher and lower cultures," he proceeds to examine what he calls "obvious facts": a) "There is a Mediterranean sea, a basin linking about ten different countries." These countries "belong to the same family," their inhabitants are "casually dressed" and live a "violent, colorful life." They know what joy is, how to relax, and are not "buttoned right up to the neck" like the Central and Northern Europeans.²⁵ Most importantly however, the Mediterranean is a way of feeling: "a certain smell or scent that we do not need to express: we all feel it through our skin."²⁶ b) "Each time a doctrine has reached the Mediterranean basin,

---

²³ Elytis, *Ανοιχτά Χαρτιά*, p. 448.

²⁴ Some biographical facts might be of interest to the reader here. Elytis and Camus share more than their deep love for the Mediterranean. Both were born and grew up near the sea, in places that they perceived as peripheral to mainstream European culture. Camus's childhood was marked by harsh financial difficulties and the death of his father. Elytis's family was more affluent but he also "grew up in a house where mourning hadn't left one window open" (Elytis, *Ανοιχτά Χαρτιά*, p.64); his eldest sister died when he was seven and his father when he was 14. Both were good athletes, Camus a soccer player and Elytis a long distance runner, and both had to end their athletic careers because of illnesses: Camus contracted tuberculosis at 17 and Elytis suffered a severe nervous breakdown at 16. They also shared a wider circle of acquaintances, which included, among others, Pierre Jean Jouve and René Char.

²⁵ Camus associates the Mediterranean region with "joy," which is different from the "laughter" of the Northern Europeans.

²⁶ Albert Camus, *Lyrical and Critical Essays*, trans. Ellen Conroy Kennedy (New York: Vintage, 1970), p. 191.

in the resulting clash of ideas, the Mediterranean has always remained intact, the land has overcome the doctrine."[27]

Camus illustrates this by juxtaposing Mediterranean Catholicism, with Central European Protestantism. He even goes as far as comparing German with Italian fascism: "What you see first of all in a German is a Hitlerite who greets you with a "Heil Hitler!"; in an Italian, the cheerful and gay human being."[28] The argument Camus pursues here, however abstract and problematic it may be, is that the Mediterranean man lives outside the constraints of history and is thus able to "live un-oppressed" even "in a country of inhuman laws."[29] Ironically, this is precisely the attitude that many revisionist Italian historians will adopt in dealing with Italian atrocities during the Fascist era—a revisionism that is exemplified through such films as Gabriele Salvatores' *Mediterraneo* or John Madden's *Captain Corelli's Mandolin* (based on De Bernières's novel) that portray "cheerful and gay" Italians as opposed to rigid, disciplined, and blood-thirsty Germans. This "inherent" ability of the Mediterranean region to transform doctrines based on the power granted to it by its geographic location is, always according to Camus, the only hope for the present and future of the region: "… the very land that transformed so many doctrines must transform the doctrines of the present day."[30] The Left's future is not to be found in the fake and oppressive collectivism of Stalinist Russia, but in the service of life and the inheritance of the sun. Camus concludes his lecture with an emphatic affirmation for change: "Can we achieve a new Mediterranean culture that can be reconciled with our social ideas? Yes. But both we and you must help to bring it about."[31]

The obvious difficulty in defining a form of action that would be in accordance with the liberating principles of the Mediterranean culture, resides in the argument's theoretical limitations. Disenchanted with Russian communism under the fierce Stalinist regime, Camus searched for a collectiveness that "favors man instead of crushing him."[32] In the Mediterranean culture, he found a nature that had carved humans to its likeness and that was able "to give back all its true meaning to the mind by restoring to culture its true visage of health and sunlight."[33] Once more, it is important to remember that the lecture on "The New Mediterranean Culture" was an attempt to create a frame of action in which Camus's views on Mediterranean aesthetics would find an expression. But it is in his lyrical essays that, according to Elytis, Camus's ideology is expressed "with adamantine lucidity."[34]

---

[27] Camus, *Lyrical*, p. 192.
[28] Camus, *Lyrical*, p. 192.
[29] Camus, *Lyrical*, p. 192.
[30] Camus, *Lyrical*, p. 195.
[31] Camus, *Lyrical*, p. 198.
[32] Camus, *Lyrical*, p. 196.
[33] Camus, *Lyrical*, p. 196.
[34] Elytis, *Ανοιχτά Χαρτιά*, p. 448.

Camus's construction of a Mediterranean ethos is most prominently discussed in relation to Algeria. Any approach to his Mediterranean aesthetics is thus bound to confront his ambiguous relationship to Algerian nationalism. On the one hand, he presented himself as an Algerian, writing caustic critiques about the treatment of Algerians as colonial subjects. On the other, his perception of Algeria strikes one as orientalist and Francocentric. His Algeria, as David Caroll notes, is an "imaginary place," in accord with his philosophical, political, and aesthetic ideas but in discord with the "real Algeria":

> Camus's Algeria, the Algeria of his literary texts and essays, is an imaginary place that is related in various and complex ways to the 'real Algeria' where Camus was born and grew up and to which he remained deeply attached throughout his life. It is a place whose physical characteristics and social dynamics owe as much, if not more, to Camus's desires, fears, and his imaginative faculty or his literary-aesthetic sensibilities as to his sense of history or politics or his critical, analytical faculties. Camus's Algeria is rooted as much in his dreams (and nightmares) as in lived experiences....[35]

His zealous Mediterranean aestheticism has also been criticized as a nullification of historical brutality. As Emily Apter observes, "Critical reception of Camus's work has, until relatively recently, tended to downplay how he compromised his moral stance by taking the French side, focusing instead on the deconstructive metaphysics of his landscapes of absence."[36] One of the most apt critics of Camus's Mediterraneanism and his aestheticization of the Algerian landscape is undoubtedly Edward Said. As Said writes, "the Arabs of *La Peste* and *L'Etranger* are nameless beings used as background for the portentous European metaphysics explored by Camus, who, we should recall, in his Chronique algerienne denied the existence of an Algerian nation."[37] I will return to Said and his critique of Camus shortly since I find it central in understanding Camus and Elytis's shared positions on the Mediterranean on the one hand, and the vastly different cultural geographies these positions embrace. Suffice it to say, for now, that the position of Elytis as a Greek in Greece is less complex, at least politically, than that of Camus in Algeria.[38] What Elytis presents us with is a geographical locus that is

---

[35] David Caroll, "Camus's Algeria: Birthrights, Colonial Injustice, and the Fiction of a French-Algerian People," *MLN* 112, no. 4 (1997): 517–49, pp. 517–18.

[36] Emily Apter, "Out of Character: Camus's French Algerian Subjects," *MLN* 112, no. 4 (1997): 499–516, p. 500.

[37] Edward Said, "Representing the Colonized: Anthropology's Interlocutors," *Critical Inquiry* 15, no. 2 (Winter 1989): 205–25, p. 223.

[38] This point is of particular importance in discussing *The Stranger*. Once more, Apter points to the problems scholars may face in approaching Camus's metaphysics: "For critics steeped in postcolonial perspectives, Camus's name triggers not only a deplorable record on the Algerian War that rightly cost him friendships on the left, but also his systematic nullification of Arab characters, particularly evident in *L'étranger*, *La peste*, and the short stories included in *L'exil et le royaume*. Dissolving the contours of Algerian cities and coastal

indisputably, and in his own admission, personal; his "Greece" is in fact situated at the antipode of the "real Greece." It is a poetical/metaphysical construction that *both* Westerners and Greeks ignore alike.

Noces and *L'Eté* are composed of 12 essays linked by their lyrical portrayal of the Mediterranean landscape. Camus is careful to describe the Mediterranean in all its contrasting qualities: the sky is "raw blue," the sun is "black,"[39] drenching the spectator in a "violent bath,"[40] and light turns everything into "black and white."[41] Nature's blessings in Algiers are described as utterly desiccating:

> There is nothing here for people seeking knowledge, education, or self-improvement. The land contains no lessons. It neither promises nor reveals anything. It is content to give, but does so profusely. Everything here can be seen with the naked eye, and is known the very moment it is enjoyed. The pleasures have no remedies and their joys remain without hope. What the land needs are clear-sighted souls, that is to say, those without consolation. It asks that we make an act of lucidity as one makes an act of faith.[42]

For Camus, the human need for order, consolation, meaning, and eternity do not find an answer in this landscape; the Mediterranean is geographically and temporally an expression of a sensual moment. It is not coincidental, he argues, that tragedy was born in this climate:[43] "The Mediterranean has a solar tragedy that has nothing to do with mists.... Such moments make one realize that if the Greeks knew despair, they experienced it always through beauty and its oppressive quality."[44] Greek tragedy "was always based on the idea of limits," and the Mediterranean landscape, with its punishing yet benevolent sun, is based on the same principles of balance.[45] In a lecture delivered in Athens in 1955, Camus reiterates this point: "Tragedy is

---

landscape into sibilant friezes or projection walls of the European mind, erasing the signs of precursory Algerian secessionism by recording not a trace of the protests and massacres at Sétif in the immediate aftermath of Liberation; and converting the site-specificity of a soon-to-be imploding colonial war into a labyrinthine tectonics of European postwar melancholia, Camus presents colonial unease in a metaphysically abstract worldscape" (Apter, "Out of Character," pp. 502–3). My discussion of *The Stranger* and the "absurd" is concerned more with the common metaphysical space that Camus and Elytis shared and less with their distinctly different relationship to the "nation." One should also keep in mind that, whereas Camus was a self-defined (albeit, disenchanted) Leftist, Elytis completely disengaged his work from political affiliations.

[39] Camus, *Lyrical*, p. 65.
[40] Camus, *Lyrical*, p. 75.
[41] Camus, *Lyrical*, p. 144.
[42] Camus, *Lyrical*, p. 81.
[43] Albert Camus, *Notebooks 1935–1951*, trans. Justin O'Brian (New York: Marlow & Company, 1998), p. 23.
[44] Camus, *Lyrical*, p. 148.
[45] Camus, *Lyrical*, p. 148.

born between light and darkness and rises from the struggle between them."[46] As a projection of the Mediterranean landscape, Greek tragedy seeks a balance in its neutral representation of "right and wrong," "justice and injustice," and in this setting "clear-lighted souls" recover "the innocence and truth that gleamed in the eyes of the ancients face to face with destiny."[47] On the contrary, modern man has turned his back on nature, and "the world has been deliberately cut off from what gives it permanence: nature, the sea, hills, evening meditations."[48]

The sun and the sea are at the core of Camus's Mediterranean experience.[49] Both elements, so emphatically present in the region, are linked with the sense of balance in this landscape. In Oran, man is confronted by "the *permanence* of an unchanging sea"[50] and in Algiers "*unity* expresses itself ... in terms of sea and sky."[51] Both elements are closely related to Camus's theory of the Absurd. The sun, the most important of the two in Camus's philosophical system, is an amoral energy, and our relationship to it determines our ability to overcome, as Sisyphus did, the world's absurdity. In *L'Eté*, Camus links this cosmic understanding the sun represents with the deepest essence of Aeschylus' plays:

> Aeschylus is often heartbreaking; yet he radiates light and warmth. At the center of his universe, we find not fleshless nonsense but an enigma, that is to say, a meaning which is difficult to decipher because it dazzles us. Likewise, to the unworthy but nonetheless stubborn sons of Greece who will still survive in this emaciated century, the scorching heat of our history may seem unendurable, but they endure it in the last analysis because they want to understand it. In the center of our world, dark though it may be, shines an inexhaustible sun, the same sun that shouts today across the hills and plains.[52]

Quoting Heraclitus, Camus further links the sun with the natural order: "The sun will not go beyond its bounds, for otherwise the Furies who watch over justice will find out."[53] The unity of nature revolves around the sun, and the human attempts to create a parallel order (religious, legal, national, etc.) are eternally condemned to failure. And this is precisely the dazzling meaning we are called to decipher: nature is foreign to us because we are far removed from its unity.

---

[46] Camus, *Lyrical*, p. 303. Camus briefly summarizes the complexity that rises from the quest for balance in ancient Greek tragedy in the following examples: "Antigone is right, but Creon is not wrong. Similarly, Prometheus is both just and unjust, and Zeus who pitilessly oppresses him also has right on his side" (Camus, *Lyrical*, p. 301).

[47] Camus, *Lyrical*, p. 77.

[48] Camus, *Lyrical*, p. 150.

[49] The original title for the eight essays of *L'Eté* was, in fact, "Solar Essays" (Camus, *Notebooks*, p. 245).

[50] Camus, *Lyrical*, p. 118.

[51] Camus, *Lyrical*, p. 90.

[52] Camus, *Lyrical*, pp. 160–61.

[53] Camus, *Lyrical*, p. 149.

When the illusory meanings with which we have clothed nature collapse, "the world evades us because it becomes itself again."[54] "If I were a tree among trees, a cat among animals, this life would have a meaning, or rather this problem would not arise, for I should belong to this world."[55] Yet, Camus writes in *The Myth of Sisyphus*: "[o]ne must imagine Sisyphus happy."[56] Sisyphus' absurd condition of stubbornly pushing the rock up the hill for all eternity makes him a rebel, "a proletariat of the gods, powerless and rebellious," and the struggle towards the heights "is enough to fill a man's heart."[57]

In this context, the sun has a dual function in Camus's philosophical system. On the one hand, its position at the center of natural life makes it the most profound reminder of the absurdity of the human condition. On the other hand, this harsh awakening is the solution to the enigma of life. Once man becomes conscious of the world's absurdity, he simultaneously becomes conscious of himself for the first time. He becomes a silently joyous rebel who embraces the ephemeral moment and who realizes that "there is no sun without shadow, and it is essential to know the night."[58] The harsh and merciless sun radiates an awakening of consciousness:

> Where is the absurdity of the world? ... With so much sun in my memory, how could I have wagered on nonsense? People around me are amazed; so am I, at times. I could tell them, as I tell myself, that it was in fact the sun that helped me, and that the very thickness of its light coagulates the universe and its forms into a dazzling darkness.[59]

In the Mediterranean, the overwhelming presence of the sun sustains nature with its life-giving energy and forms landscapes to its liking. Most importantly, however, it affects the people and their attitude toward life. "What I love about the cities of Algeria" Camus writes in *L'Eté*, "is not separate from their inhabitants."[60] The Mediterranean people are indifferent to the mind, and worship the body,[61] and in this landscape one keeps in pace with the sun and the seasons.[62] Young people in this region are dazzling in the summer because they are less clothed and because the "sun gives them the somnolent eyes of great beasts."[63] These beings are "charged with violence from the sky in which their desires revolve."[64]

---

[54] Albert Camus, *The Myth of Sisyphus and Other Essays*, trans. Justin O'Brien (New York: Vintage, 1988), p. 14.
[55] Camus, *Sisyphus*, p. 51.
[56] Camus, *Sisyphus*, p. 123.
[57] Camus, *Sisyphus*, p. 123.
[58] Camus, *Sisyphus*, p. 123.
[59] Camus, *Lyrical*, p. 155.
[60] Camus, *Lyrical*, p. 147.
[61] Camus, *Lyrical*, p. 89.
[62] Camus, *Lyrical*, p. 83.
[63] Camus, *Lyrical*, p. 145.
[64] Camus, *Lyrical*, p. 86.

In Algiers, the transforming qualities of the sun are profoundly evident in their impact on the human body:

> Swimming in the harbor in the summertime, you notice that everybody's skin changes at the same time from white to gold, then to brown, and at last to a tobacco hue, the final stage the body can attain in its quest for transformation.[65]

Though in discussing the Absurd Camus sees nature as indifferent to human affairs and even responsible for the feeling of alienation, he also perceives the Mediterranean landscape as the main factor that distinguishes people in that area from Northern Europeans. Affected by the sun's transforming power, "every year, the young girls come into flower on the beaches. They have only one season."[66] Elsewhere in his *Notebooks* Camus writes: "Heat ripens people like fruit. They are ripe before having lived. They know everything before having learned anything."[67] The Philosophy of the Mediterranean, of the sun and the sea, is unrelated to intellectual capacity and even life experience. In its essence, it is based on the ability of the sun to affect the human body sensually in the same way as it affects vegetation. The new Mediterranean culture that Camus envisioned in his 1937 lecture is based precisely on this principle: "These barbarians lounging on the beaches lying on the beaches give me the foolish hope that, perhaps without knowing it, they are modeling the face of a culture where man's greatness will finally discover its true visage."[68]

In *The Stranger*, Camus offers the most overwhelming representation of the sun's destructive yet revelatory impact on humans. The sun becomes Meursault's co-protagonist in the novel, as it appears in almost all the major scenes of the book (the mother's funeral, the meetings with Marie and Raymond, the trial, even in the prison where Meursault is awaiting execution). The epitome of its effect on Meursault comes in the intense and famously quoted scene where he kills the Arab (a completely absurd and incomprehensible act):

> I waited. The heat was beginning to scorch my cheeks; beads of sweat were gathering in my eyebrows. It was just the same sort of heat as at my mother's funeral, and I had the same disagreeable sensations— especially in my forehead, where all the veins seemed to be bursting through the skin. I couldn't stand it any longer, and took another step forward. I knew it was a foolish thing to do; I wouldn't get out of the sun by moving on a yard or so. But I took that step, just one step, forward. And then the Arab drew his knife and held it up toward me, athwart the sunlight.

---

[65] Camus, *Lyrical*, p. 83.
[66] Camus, *Notebooks*, p. 190.
[67] Camus, *Notebooks*, p. 79.
[68] Camus, *Lyrical*, p. 89.

A shaft of light shot upward from the steel, and I felt as if a long thin blade transfixed my forehead. At the same moment all the sweat that had accumulated in my eyebrows splashed down on my eyelids, covering them with a warm film of moisture. Beneath a veil of brine and tears my eyes were blinded; I was conscious only of the cymbals of the sun clashing on my skull, and, less distinctly, of the keen blade of light flashing up from the knife, scarring my eyelashes, and gouging into my eyeballs.[69]

Later, during the trial, Meursault struggles to explain the murder: "I tried to explain that it was *because of the sun*, but I spoke too quickly and ran my words into each other."[70] Once more, the sun is an amoral element, and does not induce a specific ideology but simply exerts its forceful influence on people. Feeling detached from a human sense of order (familial, social, judicial, and religious), Meursault is left to the mercy of a natural order that, having the sun at its center, is unbearably violent. As Alba Amoia correctly puts it, Meursault's "subjective will would like to aspire to a rational universe and a life that takes men into account, but objective realities impel him in the opposite direction."[71] It is for this reason that Meursault, in the novel's closing paragraph, opens his heart "to the benign indifference of the universe" and feels a close affiliation to it.[72] Eventually, Meursault is condemned to death, presumably not because he has killed the Arab but because he was unable to live within the confines of human order and expectations: because he smokes a cigarette and drinks coffee at his mother's wake, because he doesn't shed a tear at her funeral, because he begins his affair with Marie and goes to the cinema the day following the funeral, because he doesn't believe in God, because he does not have "those moral qualities which normal men possess...."[73] In his closing argument, the Prosecutor repeatedly states that such a man "has no place in the community."[74]

Whereas Camus constructs a philosophical system around the element of the sun, his relationship to the sea is described in more sensual terms. "I have always felt I lived on the high seas," he writes in *L'Eté*, "threatened, at the heart of a royal happiness."[75] In his conception of the Mediterranean, it is impossible however,

---

[69] Albert Camus, *The Stranger*, trans. Stuard Gilbert (New York: Vintage, 1946), p. 75.
[70] Camus, *Stranger*, p. 130. Emphasis added.
[71] Alba Amoia, *Albert Camus* (New York: Continuum, 1989), p. 46.
[72] Camus, *Stranger*, p. 154.
[73] Camus, *Stranger*, p. 127.
[74] Camus, *Stranger*, pp. 128, 129. Meursault's explanation of the Arab's murder is, of course, even more absurd (in the literal meaning of the word) if one approaches the text either historically or politically. Camus's attempt to express "the absurd" in the context of the French colonization of Algeria is complicated by his own vexed position as a Frenchman in Algeria. At the end of the book we are left with an Arab murdered by a French citizen *and the sun is blamed for the deed*. Elytis's position in Greece was certainly less complicated and his political disengagement safeguarded his poetry, for the most part, from such ambiguity.
[75] Camus, *Lyrical*, p. 181.

to perceive the sun as separate from the sea. In his essay "Nuptials at Tipasa," the unity of the two elements is described in relationship to its sensual impact on the human body:

> Yes, even here I know that I shall never come close enough to the world. I must be naked and dive into the sea, still scented with the perfumes of the earth, wash them off in the sea, and consummate with my flesh the embrace for which sun and sea, lips to lips, have so long been sighing....
>
> Here I understand what is meant by glory: the right to love without limits. There is only one love in this world. To clasp a woman's body is also to hold in one's arms this strange joy that descends from sky to sea.[76]

In *The Stranger*, Meursault's most sensual encounters happen in the presence of the sea. He meets Marie at the sea and spends his most pleasurable moments there with her. As in the "Nuptials," here too love and the sea become united under the Dionysian spell of the sun. In the sea Meursault and Marie fill their mouths with the foam and then spit it out against the sky: "But very soon my mouth was smarting with all the salt I'd drawn in; then Marie came up and hugged me in the water, and pressed her mouth to mine. Her tongue cooled my lips...."[77] Minutes before he kills the Arab, Meursault is again in the sea with Marie and, as she hugs him, he feels her legs twining round his, and his senses tingle.[78] These moments are scarce in the book. In the sea, Meursault no longer seems to be a "stranger" or an "outsider"; on the contrary, he feels a sense of balance and sensual completeness. He becomes acutely aware of this "wholeness" when he fires the first shot towards the Arab and hears a sound like the crack of a whip: "I knew I'd shattered the balance of the day, the spacious calm of this beach on which I had been happy."[79]

Camus's approach to the prevailing Mediterranean natural elements proposes an interesting tension between his perception of the sun and the sea. The sun is both unrelenting and merciful, it can rejuvenate and destroy, and it can arouse the senses to the point of Dionysian intoxication. The sea, by contrast, expresses a unity and a comfort and momentarily restores the unity of Self. "The unity Plotinus longed for" is expressed, in earthly terms, in the merging of the body with the sea.[80] For Camus, the tension between these two elements constitutes a natural philosophy that the ancients Greeks perceived and understood deeply. Natural beauty is oppressive because it increases the absurd condition of Man: "Everything that exalts life at the same time increases its absurdity. In the Algerian summer I learn that only one thing is more tragic than suffering, and

---

[76] Camus, *Lyrical*, p. 68.
[77] Camus, *Stranger*, p. 43.
[78] Camus, *Stranger*, p. 65.
[79] Camus, *Stranger*, p. 76.
[80] Camus, *Lyrical*, p. 90.

that is the life of a happy man. But this can also be the path to a greater life, since it can teach us not to cheat."[81]

In October 1933, when Camus was still mostly unknown to French literary circles, he wrote a short poem that captures well his youthful enthusiasm for Mediterranean sensation. The poem is entitled simply "Mediterranean" and foreshadows the central role nature and landscape will play, a decade later, in the formation of his thought:

> By you worlds are polished and made human
> By you we are restored and our pains made noble
>   Oh antiquity impelling us!
> Mediterranean, oh! Mediterranean Sea!
> Naked, alone, without secrets, your sons await death.
> Death will return them to you, pure at last, pure.[82]

It is perhaps coincidental, yet an event of extraordinary synchronicity, that a few months later, at the other end of the Mediterranean, Elytis would write his first poems, "Of the Aegean," similarly attempting to express sensation in a Mediterranean context.

Elytis met Camus for the first time in 1950, during his three-year stay in Paris (1948–1951). During this meeting, or during subsequent meetings, the two must have discussed their views on Mediterranean sensation since, in deciding to publish *Empédocle*, Camus and Char approached Elytis asking him to submit an article describing more or less what he was telling them in their meetings.[83] Elytis was certainly well familiar with Camus's work and was particularly interested in his lyrical essays, where his views on the Mediterranean sensation were expressed, as he writes, "with adamantine lucidity."[84] His 1992 essay collection includes, along with essays written in the period 1975–1995, a long passage from Camus's "Nuptials at Tipasa" translated into Greek under the title "The Mediterranean Man According to Albert Camus."[85] The affinity between Elytis's own essays and Camus's passage is remarkable, and highlights those elements Elytis finds particularly interesting in the French-Algerian thinker. The passage begins with the sensual exchange between the Mediterranean landscape and the human body, a theme that, as I have discussed above, is constantly present in Camus's vision of the Mediterranean:

> To clasp a woman's body is also to hold in one's arms this strange joy that descends from sky to sea. In a moment, when I throw myself down among the

---

[81] Camus, *Stranger*, p. 91.
[82] Albert Camus, *Youthful Writings*, trans. Ellen Conroy Kennedy (New York: Knopf, 1976), pp. 198–9.
[83] Elytis, *Ανοιχτά Χαρτιά*, p. 448.
[84] Elytis, *Ανοιχτά Χαρτιά*, p. 448.
[85] Odysseus Elytis, *Εν Λευκώ* (Athens: Ikaros, 1992), pp. 245–6.

absinthe plants to bring their scent into my body, I shall know, appearances to the contrary, that I am fulfilling a truth which is the sun's and which will also be my death's.[86]

Sensual pleasure is described here, as the interaction between Eros and the landscape, as an overwhelming sensation that unveils the truth of one's death. The connection between death and the sensual pleasure 'inherent' in the Mediterranean landscape has already been discussed in the context of Camus's perception of beauty's "oppressive qualities"[87] and in relation to his theory of the Absurd.[88] The remaining passage Elytis translates from Camus focuses on two important principles intrinsic to both Elytis and Camus's perception of the Mediterranean: a sense of optimism, or a coming to terms with the burden of existence, and the discovery of one's self:

> I love this life with abandon and wish to speak of it boldly: it makes me proud of my human condition. Yet people have often told me: there's nothing to be proud of. Yes there is: this sun, this sea, my heart leaping with youth, the salt taste of my body and this vast landscape in which tenderness and glory merge in blue and yellow. It is to conquer this that I need my strength and my resources. Everything here leaves me intact, I surrender nothing of myself, and don no mask: learning patiently and arduously how to live is enough for me, well worth all their arts of living.[89]

For Camus and Elytis, the Mediterranean offers a solar diaphaneity that is both sensual and unsympathetic. Stripped of the conventional understanding of life offered as consolation by religious or social conceptions, people are left, like Sisyphus, to face the burden of existence. In this radical aesthetisization of landscape, the Mediterranean is posited as a proud alternative that would liberate humans from any pre-imposed conceptions and allow them to discover their maskless and absurd self.

Before proceeding to place the Mediterranean landscape and its elements in the philosophical conception of Elytis, it is important to examine the context in which they appear. In essence, Elytis's theory of "Solar Metaphysics" represents a solid cosmological frame in which the powers once possessed by the Olympian gods are vested in the natural elements of the Aegean. The assertion becomes even more

---

[86] Camus, *Lyrical*, pp. 68–9.
[87] Camus, *Lyrical*, p. 148.
[88] The importance of the concept of death in Elytis's poetry has frequently been overlooked. In the subsequent discussion I will closely examine Elytis's complex perception of the Aegean seascape and landscape, which, as in Camus, is always fused with the totality of the human experience. Suffice it to say here that Elytis is concerned with the interaction between the forces of both Eros and Thanatos (in their Freudian meaning). The translation and inclusion in *Carte Blanche* of this passage from "Nuptials at Tipasa" points to Elytis's interest in this fusion of philosophy and aesthetics in approaching the Mediterranean.
[89] Camus, *Lyrical*, p. 69.

interesting if we consider Camus's perception of Greek tragedy. If the ancient Greeks knew despair in their experience of natural beauty and its oppressive qualities, then that same nature should be able to produce a similar effect in the modern Greek experience and should find an expression in the arts. Unlike some of his contemporaries, Elytis perceived ancient Greek myth as something that should be completely redefined in order to better express the experience of modern Greeks. In his interview with Ivar Ivask, Elytis explains his views on myth and its relation to modern Greek poetry:

> I have never employed ancient myths in the usual manner. No doubt it is advantageous for a Greek poet to employ ancient myths, because he thus becomes more accessible to foreign readers. A Greek poet who speaks of Antigone, Oedipus et cetera, moves in an area which is well known; through these mythical figures he can comment on contemporary events. This was done by Sikelianos and, above all, by Seferis. In the case of Seferis it was almost natural, because he was influenced not only by his own Greek heritage but also by the manner of Eliot. Ritsos too, especially in his latest period, employs from mythology and Greek tragedy. I have reacted against this, often quite consciously, because I thought all this was a bit too facile, yes, even in the theatre.... Since my chief interest was to find the *sources* of the Neo-Hellenic world, I kept the mechanism of myth-making but not the figures of mythology.[90]

The relationship of the thirties generation to myth was understandably an ambivalent one. They perceived Greek poetry as always trailing behind and imitating the Western European poets, from the establishment of the modern Greek State in the 1820s until the early twentieth century. The mythical method, the adaptation of myth in the Joycean manner to express the modern chaotic experience, which was passed along from Eliot to Seferis, did not have the same impact on Elytis. On the contrary, Elytis felt that the survival of ancient Greek ideas was simply another Western European achievement that played an instrumental part in how Europeans misperceived modern Greece. For Elytis, the Greek poet of the twentieth century found himself trapped within the confines of the nineteenth-century European misinterpretation of "Greekness." The following anecdote that concerns George Seferis's 1963 Nobel Prize in Literature gives us a better understanding of Elytis's categorical distance from ancient Greek myth. In his critique of Μέρες του 1945–1951 (Days of 1945–1951), Lawrence Durrell, who, along with Henry Miller, frequented Greek intellectual circles, commented on Seferis's use of myth:

> It was appropriate for Seferis to be honored with a Nobel Prize, because with him, Greek literature passed the great barrier and entered Europe, where it imprinted its solid right and became part of the European consciousness. This is not a deprecation of the great Greek poets of the last fifty years—on the contrary,

---

[90] Elytis, "On his Poetry," p. 639.

But the sensitivity of these poets remains Greek in its Balkan sense, and their work, *even though brilliant, is Greek in spirit*. Unlike Seferis, these poets were not essentially cosmopolitan souls....[91]

In response to this critique, Elytis wrote a short article where he sharply criticizes Durrell's perception of a difference between Greek-cosmopolitan poets and Greek-Balkan poets. This tension is also important in understanding the dichotomy between universality and locality. For Elytis, if modern Greek poetry, or any ethnic literature for that matter, can be instructive, it is in its ability to illustrate how it is different from mainstream literary conceptions (in this case, Western European literature). Commenting on the inability of Western intellectuals to approach modern Greek poetry outside the framework of ancient Greek conceptions, Elytis writes to Durrell:

> You continue, dear Larry, to have in mind the image of a Greece you were taught in your universities; that is why you always approach us through the laments of Antigone and Socrates' last words. Not that these don't exist today—they do exist. Only you will have to look for them on another scale and a different spiritual height. Because these people, that speak the same language and live in the same landscape, managed ... to shape their equivalences in their own vibrant reality and furthermore, to guide them to their original and natural truth.[92]

Elytis concludes his response to Durrell with the following emphatic proclamation: "Allow yourself to step down to the humble scale which is the alphabet of Neo-Hellenism; to initiate yourself in its primal and simple components: the fragrant herbs, the wave's brine, and the heat of the whitewashing lime."[93] The resistance to ancient myth in Elytis's poetry, then, constitutes a conscious attempt to create a modern mythological system that is equivalent to the ancient Greek on one hand, but with the components of contemporary Greece, on the other.

This is precisely what Elytis means by "mythopoesis" (mythmaking). The poem "Body of Summer," included in the collection *Sun the First*, serves as a good example of this mythopoetic process.[94] "It is the idea of summer," Elytis explains, "which is personified by the body of a young man":[95]

> Who lies on the upper beaches
> Supine puffing on smoke-silver olive leaves
> Cicadas warm themselves in his ears

---

[91] Elytis, *Εν Λευκώ*, p. 209. This is quoted and translated from the Greek text in Elytis's *Carte Blanche*. The emphasis is Elytis's.
[92] Elytis, *Εν Λευκώ*, p. 210. The open letter to Durrell was written in Greek but it was never published until its inclusion in *Carte Blanche*.
[93] Elytis, *Εν Λευκώ*, p. 211.
[94] In the interview with Ivask, Elytis himself refers to "Body of Summer" as a good example of the "mythopoesis" he often employs.
[95] Elytis, "On his Poetry," p. 639.

> Ants are working on his chest
> Lizards slide through his armpits' grass
> And through the seaweed of his feet a wave falls softly[96]

Elytis equates this personification with the process of myth-making. If ancient myths were essentially narratives in which forces became personified in mythical characters, Elytis keeps the mechanism of personification but reshapes the mythological character. Summer is given the body of youth, and it is in constant interaction with the elements of the Greek landscape (the sea, olive trees, cicadas, ants, lizards, the sun). This youthful body is also invested with the qualities of the Greek nature: it is "eaten away by oil and salt," it is as firm as a rock, and its curly pubis, which is "filled with little stars and pine needles," emits the aroma of basil. This is not simply a metaphor, where summer is likened to a youthful body. The body of Summer becomes a way of life that manages to overcome even the harshest winter: "The hills plunge into thick udders of clouds / Yet behind all these you smile carefree / And find again your immortal hour / As the sun finds you again on the beaches / As the sky finds you within your naked health." Elytis composed the poems included in the collection *Sun the First* during the Nazi occupation of Greece (1941–1944). The collection was published in 1942 in a time of oppression, famine, and the fierce resistance to the occupation. Under this light, "Body of Summer" could be seen as the poet's response to the forces that humiliate and oppress humanity. Beyond the apparent metaphor of overcoming the winter of history, Elytis turns the quest for freedom into a mythological motif, which is eternally inspired by the presence of summer and its interaction with people.

The personification of natural forces is one of the most repeated motifs in Elytis's poetry. "The Mad Pomegranate Tree" of *Orientations* is described as a young girl who "fights the world's cloudy skies."[97] In the "Orange Girl"[98] a young girl, drunk on the sun's juice, turns into an orange.[99] In "The Autopsy," the dissection of a young body reveals, instead of blood, veins and organs, elements of the Aegean landscape: "the olive root's gold" in "the leaves of his heart," a "strange heat" in his entrails, "the intense cyan-blue horizon line" beneath his skin, "a ruined echo of the sky" in his brain, "a little fine, sifted sun"

---

[96] Elytis, *Collected Poems*, p. 76. Ποιος είναι αυτός που κείτεται στις πάνω αμμουδιές / Ανάσκελα φουμέρνοντας ασημοκαπνισμένα ελιόφυλλα / Τα τζιτζίκια ζεσταίνονται στ' αυτιά του / Τα μυρμήγκια δουλεύουνε στο στήθος του / αύρες γλιστρούν στη χλόη της μασχάλης / Κι από τα φύκια των ποδιών του αλαφροπερνά ένα κύμα (Elytis, *Ποίηση*, p. 77).

[97] Elytis, *Collected Poems*, p. 71.

[98] In the subcollection "Variations on a Sunbeam" of *Sun the First*.

[99] We are reminded here of Camus's aforementioned description of Algerian boys and girls metamorphosed by the sun every summer.

in the conch of his left ear and "fireflakes on his groin."[100] In "Little Green Sea," the sea becomes a 13-year-old girl whom the poet wishes to adopt and send to school in Ionia "to study tangerine and absinthe."[101] The construction of a new mythology with the elements of the Greek landscape at its core is unprecedented, to this extent, in modern Greek poetry. The interaction of the human senses with the natural forces of the Aegean goes beyond these few examples, covering the entire spectrum of his poetry. As in Camus, the elements of the Mediterranean represent a complex philosophical system where the sun's interaction with the seascape and the landscape is a metaphysical experience. For both Elytis and Camus, this interaction cannot be dissociated from the sanctity it once possessed. Camus writes that the "Mediterranean is inhabited by gods and the gods speak in the sun and the scent of absinthe leaves, in the silver armor of the sea, in the raw blue sky, the flower-covered ruins, and the great bubbles of light among the heaps of stone."[102] For Elytis too, the sea and the sun are not disconnected from the white chapel on the steep hill, and the Byzantine icon can equally "frame" the Virgin and the nude girl, rendering nude beauty sacred.[103]

We have already examined the importance of surrealism in the early work of Odysseus Elytis, especially in the composition of *Orientations*. Surrealism's most important contribution to the young Elytis was the suggestion of a more open attitude towards the Greek language, that relieved him of traditional and conventional techniques of composition. At the same time, the revolutionary proclamations of the movement corresponded completely with his interest in the mysteries of nature. According to the young Elytis, the French surrealists placed in the foreground humanity's most important philosophical subjects: Eros, Death, and Nature. The fusion of these three concepts in the works of Elytis is remarkable, and spreads beyond his early collections and essays. In essence, his interest in these marks the conceptual space in which his entire oeuvre unfolds. In this frame, the interaction of the human body and its senses with the natural space offers a philosophical and an aesthetic riddle that only poetic language is capable of deciphering. Eventually, Elytis's understanding of this interaction converged into two main theories: the theory of Analogies and the theory of Solar Metaphysics.

Elytis's relationship with the Greek landscape and specifically the Aegean commenced at a very young age, when he would spend most of his summers on the island of Spetses. His fascination with the Aegean took on a magical quality in his childhood and solidified inside him what he calls his "personal myth." As myth explores the collective attempt to understand the mysteries of the human condition, "personal myth" is formed according to the idiosyncrasies and experiences of the individual in his/her natural surroundings. In other words,

---

[100] Elytis, *Collected Poems*, p. 195.

[101] In *The Light-tree and the Fourteenth Beauty*. Elytis, *Collected Poems*, p. 218.

[102] Camus, *Lyrical*, p. 65.

[103] Many of Elytis's collages place the female nude body in the classical Greek-Orthodox iconographic frame.

myth may be of collective or universal concern but it is expressed in the colors, scents, and sounds of a specific physical and natural space. In this sense, myth, as it becomes manifested in a particular geographical locus, is a unique and distinct expression. Elytis remembers his summer in Spetses as nothing less than a magical and mysterious interaction with nature:

> As kids we spent three quarters of the day in those well-built old Spetsian boats, with which we went to the opposite bay. There all the elements would take on a ritual function.
>
> In the morning we knew that the northWestern wind [μαΐστρος] blew and we set out with this wind. Around eleven the weather calmed and the sea became a little milkier. At noon you would see a blue line coming from Hydra and Ermioni, the northeastern wind that the locals called Grecolevante, on which we would return. In the afternoon again, at three, there was the arrival of the ship, which was an important affair for us, and in the evening we would go to the area of the Pebbles, where the schools are today.
>
> There were also the excursions, the festivals ... Saint Paraksevi's, Saint Marina's, and, most importantly, August 15. My father, I remember, organized masses at distant chapels and this has marked me tremendously because you would feel the incense getting mixed with thyme, a sensation that for me characterizes the combination of two elements: the natural and the metaphysical.[104]

In 1934, the 23-year-old Elytis also traveled extensively in mainland Greece in the old Chevrolet of a friend of his. "It was like sleeping for the first time with a woman whose body you had only imagined until then," he writes in "The Chronicle."[105] This journey coincided of course with an important moment in his life: his discovery of Éluard, Jouve, Ungaretti, and Cavafy, his first interest in surrealism, and, most importantly, the composition of his first poems, that would later be included in *Orientations*. Greek Nature came as an answer to his search for a new voice. In fact, in 1934 Elytis destroyed his old poems, primarily composed in imitation of Cavafy, and composed the "First Poems" of *Orientations*. "The way in which I viewed Nature," he writes in "The Chronicle," "went beyond Nature itself. From vision came a sensation and the sensation led, once more, to a vision."[106] Nature offered a space for the soul to move in and out of the changeless and the eternal.

---

[104] Elytis, *Αυτοπροσωπογραφία*, pp. 8–9. In his college years (1930–1936), along with surrealism Elytis discovered the Aegean islands of the Cyclades. "Here," he remembers, "there was also the architecture of the islands and their Ancient, Byzantine and Neohellenic inheritance" (Elytis, *Αυτοπροσωπογραφία*, p. 11). Around 1933 Elytis attended a lecture in Athens by Le Corbusier, who talked about Cycladic architecture and further explored, as I will later examine, the connection between nature and culture.

[105] Elytis, *Ανοιχτά Χαρτιά*, p. 325.

[106] Elytis, *Ανοιχτά Χαρτιά*, p. 237.

Gradually, Elytis's experience with the Greek landscape and seascape culminated, as in Camus, in the formation of a philosophy that centered on a metaphysical appreciation of landscape. Even though the interaction of the self with the natural elements of that landscape can be seen in his early poems, it was not until the publication of *The Axion Esti* that they became part of a more precise philosophical framework.[107] There, the Greek landscape is presented as a "Guardian of Tradition" to which the conscious man turns in solitude after confronting evil.[108] Similarly, in *The Light-Tree* the poet finds in the sea "Bits of stones the words of Gods / Bits of stones fragments of Heraclitus."[109] As in the case of Camus, the Mediterranean—here specifically the Aegean—is viewed as a cradle of meaning in its innate potential to influence thought. Modern Europeans, according to Elytis, excavated this landscape but they failed to unearth the significant concepts that produced the sites of that landscape.[110] The ideological convergence between Camus and Elytis on this point is clear; for both, the Mediterranean landscape evokes an *ethos* transferred from matter to spirit and, eventually, transposed to creation:

> From the pebble to the fig leaf and from the fig leaf to the pomegranate, as from Kouros the Charioteer and from the Charioteer to Athena.
>
> I dream of an Ethic that whose ultimate anagoge[111] would lead to the consubstantial and indivisible Trinity itself.[112]

Landscape is thus transposed to an *ethos* that mirrors the indivisibility of the Trinity. The process of transposition from matter to spirit is ultimately connected to Elytis's theory of Analogies. Before I proceed to the next chapter and examine the relationship between natural correspondences and poetic creation, two points need to be clarified.

---

[107] It is important to remember that Elytis started writing *The Axion Esti* after his return from Europe where he had met, among others, Albert Camus.

[108] This becomes evident from Elytis's notes on *The Axion Esti*, which were included in George Savides and Edmund Keeley's translation (see Keeley *The Axion Esti*, trans. Edmund Keeley and George Savidis. Pittsburgh: University of Pittsburgh Press, 1996, p. 80).

[109] Elytis, *Collected Poems*, p. 218.

[110] Elytis, *Εν Λευκώ*, p. 20.

[111] "Anagoge" (αναγωγή): in Greek, the word means to "lift up." The Oxford English Dictionary has two entries for the word: 1) "Spiritual elevation or enlightenment, esp., to understand mysteries"; 2) "Mystical or spiritual interpretation; an Old Testament typification of something in the New." Elytis applies the process of the mystical interpretation of the sacred texts to the interpretation of poetry.

[112] Elytis, *Collected Poems*, p. 455. Από το βότσαλο στο φύλλο της συκιάς κι από το φύλλο της συκιάς στο ρόδι, όπως από τον Κούρο στον Ηνίοχο κι από τον Ηνίοχο στην Αθηνά. / Ονειρεύομαι μιαν Ηθική που η εσχάτη αναγωγή της να οδηγεί στην ίδια ομοούσια και αδιαίρετη Τριάδα (Elytis, *Ποίηση*, p. 514).

Elytis's approach does not constitute a mere veneration of the Greek landscape. Like Camus, he perceived the sun, for example, as both punishing and benevolent. In *Open Papers* he writes: "how strange that in Greece light was always considered painless."[113] And in "Ode 6"of *The Axion Esti*, he presents the Sun as the source of an "oppressive Beauty":

> O sun of Justice in the mind * and you O glorifying myrtle
> do not oh I implore you * do not forget my country
>
> It has high mountains eagle shaped * and rows of vines on its volcanoes
> and houses very white * for neighboring the blue
>
> Though touching Asia on one side * and brushing Europe on the other
> it stands there all alone * in aether and in sea
>
> It's not a foreigners idea * nor is it any kinsman's love
> but everywhere a mourning * and light is merciless![114]

In Camus the sun illuminates the Absurdity of the world. The orientation of the Greek landscape in Elytis's poem is equally absurd: it is neither westward nor eastward, it is neither a "foreigner's idea" nor a "kinsman's love." The absurdity lies in the realization that "it stands there all alone" in the boundlessness of time.[115] The sun is "Just" because it is unconcerned with the plight of human history and human law. As Meursault in *The Stranger* points to the Sun to explain the murder of the Arab, Elytis here evokes the sun as an intelligible symbol of Justice that illuminates beauty despite man's presence in history.

---

[113] Elytis, *Ανοιχτά Χαρτιά*, p. 11.

[114] Elytis, *Collected Poems*, p. 155. *Της Δικαιοσύνης ήλιε νοητέ * και μυρσίνη συ δοξαστική / μη παρακαλώ σας μη * λησμονάτε τη χώρα μου! / Αετόμορφα έχει τα ψηλά βουνά * στα ηφαίστεια κλήματα σειρά / και τα σπίτια πιο λευκά *στου γλαυκού το γειτόνεμα! / Της Ασίας αν αγγίζει από τη μια * της Ευρώπης λίγο αν ακουμπά / στον αιθέρα στέκει να * και στη θάλασσα μόνη της! / Και δεν είναι μήτε ξένου λογισμός * και δικού της μήτε αγάπη μια / μόνο πένθος αχ παντού * και το φως ανελέητο!* (Elytis, *Ποίηση*, p. 150).

[115] Apart from Camus's conceptualization of the Mediterranean, the "oppressive qualities of beauty" are also central in Dionysios Solomos' *Free Besieged*, a poem that Elytis knew very well. The poem describes the siege of Messolongi by the Ottomans in the month of April. The beauty of the surrounding landscape falls as a merciless shadow on the enclaved Messolongians: "April and Eros dance and laugh / But as many flowers bloom and bear fruit, so many are the arms that besiege you" [my translation is from Yiannis Kokkinis, *Ανθολογία της Νεοελληνικής Ποίησης* (Athens: Estia, 1995), p. 626]. In the 1980 interview on National Greek television Elytis says: "if one of the modern Greeks was my teacher, that would of course be Solomos; I say this with awe because any comparison with him crushes me. Solomos was a great poet, and I believe if foreigners could read Greek, they would have placed him among the five or ten most important poets in the world, of all times" (Elytis, *Αυτοπροσωπογραφία*, p. 29).

Mediterranean Nationalism

Undoubtedly, Camus's Mediterranean is replete with the same stereotypes that characterize the earlier imaginary constructions outlined in the beginning of this chapter. His Mediterranean is a "barbaric" metaphysical space that can aid man in understanding his absurd position in (or in spite of) contemporary history. In this sense, it is also different from earlier fantasies of the Mediterranean. In Burton's Sotadic Zone theory or in Thomas Mann's *Death in Venice*, one senses, for example, the utter deprecation associated with the region's projected capacity to awaken homoerotic desire. In Camus, the barbarism associated with the awakening of the senses, the opposition to logic, the complete indifference of the "black" sun, are presented as qualities that can revitalize, or can be launched against, an anemic European civilization. His Mediterranean metaphysics waver between a dark exoticism and a romantic, yet tragic, imaginary construction. It was, perhaps, this revitalizing potential that Jacqueline Kahanoff saw in her reading of Camus and her reformulation of Levantinism as a positive hybrid space that Israelis should embrace and reconsider in a positive light. Instead of seeing Levantinism as a state of static in-between-ness she saw it as a concept informed by the constant negotiation between identities in the Levant. Yet, as Gil Hochberg writes, "while she seems alert to the similarities between the European colonialism she experienced as a child in Cairo and the interactions between Ashkenazi and Mizrahi Jews she recognizes in Israel, she fails to account for a similar colonialist violence between Jews and Palestinians."[116] The same striking omission is also present in the writings of Camus and his depiction of the Algerian geography as Mediterranean. As Edward Said writes, Camus's Mediterranean is as much about what is included in his writings as about what is excluded:

> The tendency is too often for readers rapidly to associate Camus's novels principally with French novels about France, not only because of their language and the forms they seem to take over from noble antecedents like *Adolphe* and *Trois Contes*, but because Camus's choice of Algeria seems incidental to the pressing moral material at hand. Almost half a century after their appearance, his novels are thus readily transmuted into parables of the human condition. True, Meursault kills an Arab but this Arab is not named and seems to be without a history, let alone a mother and father; true, Arabs die of plague in Oran but they are not named either, whereas Rieux and Tarrou are pushed very far forward in the action. So, we are likely to say (as, for instance, readers of Ben Jonson's poems are likely to say before reading *The Country and the City*) one ought to read the texts for the richness of what is there not for what, if anything, has been excluded. But I would insist, to the contrary and against the grain, that what is mainly in Camus's novels is what they appear to have been

---

[116] Gil Hochberg, *In Spite of Partition* (Princeton: Princeton University Press, 2007), p. 66.

cleared of—that is, the detail of that very distinctly French conquest begun in 1830 and continuing into the period of Camus's life and into the composition of his texts themselves.[117]

Camus's Mediterranean, Kahanoff's Levant, and Elytis's Aegean are all measured against the backdrop of European civilization: Kahanoff's Levantinism is posited as an antidote to the remnants of a colonial attitude that still poisons the relationship between people in the Eastern Mediterranean (and particularly between Jews in the newly formed State of Israel). Camus constantly compares Northern European logic to what he perceives as a more human Mediterranean sensation. And Elytis turns to the Aegean for an alternative formulation of Greekness, free from Western European assumptions and projections.

Once again, Said's description of Camus's novels as *French* is principally based on what they omit or what they silence. His Arabs are thus as nameless as Kahanoff's invisible Palestinians. What is even more significant is that both constructions are based on a hybrid view of the Mediterranean space and are posited against an exclusive regional nationalism. "To live in a monocultural ghetto—*that* seems to me like a negative and obsessive kind of loyalty: a compulsion almost a neurosis!" writes Kahanoff.[118] Camus would similarly declare that he loves his "country too much to be a nationalist"[119] and would emphatically "reject the principle of a Mediterranean nationalism" (confessing his faith only to "the nationalism of the sun").[120] Approaching Camus's novels from a similar angle, one could add that what they evoke is not simply an urban Frenchness but, rather, a cosmopolitan Frenchness. Mediterranean Humanism (or cosmopolitanism) functions here as a principle through which the rejection of national autonomy is justified—hence, Lord Cromer, the British Controller-General of Egypt from 1883 to 1907, would write: "the only real Egyptian autonomy, therefore, which I am able to conceive ... is one which will enable all the dwellers in *cosmopolitan* Egypt, be they Moslem or Christian, European, Asiatic, or African, to be fused into one self-governing body."[121] Camus would likewise declare that "there has never yet been an Algerian nation. The Jews, the Turks, the Greeks, the Italians, the Berbers would have just as much right to claim the direction of that virtual nation."[122] The Arab of *The Stranger* is nameless but if Meursault is French, it is only because he does not belong to a particular social or national system—he is, in other words, a cosmopolitan Mediterranean man.

---

[117] Edward Said, "Narrative, Geography and Interpretation," *New Left Review*, no. 180 (1990): 81–97, p. 88.

[118] Qtd in Gil Hochberg, *In Spite of Partition*, p. 51.

[119] Camus, *Lyrical*, p. 309.

[120] Camus, *Lyrical*, p. 190.

[121] Evelyn Baring Cromer, *Modern Egypt* (New York: Macmillan, 1916), p. 568. Emphasis added.

[122] Albert Camus, *Resistance, Rebellion and Death*, trans. Justin O'Brien (New York: Vintage, 1988), p. 145.

Elytis also rejects narrow constraints of nationalism. "Being minimally poetic," he writes echoing Camus, "I loved Poetry to the maximum in the same way that being minimally patriotic I loved Greece to the maximum."[123] His Aegean is a markedly Greek space that is inseparable from the language and the tradition that evolved in that particular geography. But his conception of the Greek geography is far from being cosmopolitan or even urban. And this is the second important difference that I would underline in comparing Camus and Elytis. Said reads Camus against the background of Raymond Williams' *The Country and the City*. More specifically, he sees Camus's misreading of the Algerian landscape as problematic (albeit not conscious) as the misreading of the country through the lens of the urban capitalist mode of production. As I have argued elsewhere, the most representative modernist Greek poets did not tend towards a description of the new cosmopolitan and chaotic urban space. Instead, Elytis and his contemporaries' work is characterized by a "drive to *decentralization*, a move away from the [urban] center and towards the [provincial] periphery."[124] Camus's provincialism is based on his description of Algeria as a postnational Mediterranean space. It strives to move away from the metropolis but it ends up replicating and embracing the totality of identity and the global Mediterranean subject. It is in this sense that his Algeria is depopulated and forcefully becomes a cohesive and antinational Mediterranean space. Elytis's depiction of the Aegean geography is admittedly provincial but it is also a cultural/ethnic space. His theory of Analogies, which is the focus of the next chapter, is an attempt to situate this metaphysical Greek geography outside the constricted limits of nationalism. To put it more clearly, for Camus the concept of a Mediterranean nationalism is a contradiction in itself; for Elytis, geography can only be described in cultural or local terms.

---

[123] Elytis, *Ανοιχτά Χαρτιά*, p. 17.

[124] Marinos Pourgouris, "Topographies of Greek Modernism," *The Avant-Garde and the Margin: New Territories of Modernism*, ed. Marinos Pourgouris and Sanja Bahun-Radunović (Cambridge: Cambridge Scholar's Press, 2006), p. 104.

Chapter 3
The Theory of Analogies

For whomever sea in sun is "landscape"—life seems easy and death too. But for whomever it is a mirror of immortality, it is "duration." A duration whose blindness alone does not let you conceive it.
—Elytis, *The Little Seafarer*

In contrast to the *automatism* that Breton advocated as the most essential literary device of surreal creation, Elytis's collections are strictly structured and his poems are meticulously edited. The most fundamental theoretical constructions of the poet are the theories of Analogies and of Solar Metaphysics, which strive to elucidate the complex relationship between form and content, poetic object and subject. This chapter examines Elytis's theory of Analogies—sometimes interchangeably used with the terms "correspondences" and "equivalences"—that he developed around the late 1940s. At the outset, we may generally describe the theory of Analogies as a poetical theory of object relations (i.e., the way a subject interacts with an object, and vice versa). In Elytis's case, these objects are usually objects of nature. On a deeper level, the theory comments on the inherent ability of the object to acquire and project emotional meaning.

One may fittingly argue that the theory belongs to the Neo-Platonic tradition of Fourierism that, as Donald Egbert writes, is based on the belief of a "universal unity" achieved through what Baudelaire called correspondences: "Fourier drew analogies between colors, sounds, curves, passions, and rights. He thereby extended the analogy between colors and sounds which played so important a part in the art theory of romantics and later symbolists."[1] Before proceeding to a more detailed discussion of the theory as it emerges from Elytis's essays, let us outline its principal claims:[2]

1. "Reality" is always perceived by a subject situated at a particular point of view. Consequently, the concept of reality lacks objectivity. Elytis distinguishes three states of reality:[3]

---

[1] Donald Drew Egbert, *Social Radicalism and the Arts: Western Europe* (New York: Knopf, 1970), p.134.

[2] The basic claims of Elytis's theory of Analogies were constructed here based on scattered references found in his two volumes of essays. The poet himself, however, never presented his views as a unified theory.

[3] As is the case with the theory of Analogies, the "three states of reality," too, were constructed here from scattered references in the poet's essays. Elytis himself does not explicitly connect these ideas in the form of a unified theory.

a. The first state of reality (πρώτη κατάσταση της πραγματικότητας): the reality that characterizes the apparent material substance of the object.
b. The second hyper-real state (δεύτερη υπερπραγματική κατάσταση): the reality of the subject's "subjective" emotional response to the object. In essence, the object is always evasive and resists the subject's gaze; it gazes back at the subject, stirring up an emotional response.
c. The third poetic state (τρίτη ποιητική κατάσταση): the reality that is reconstructed by poetry or art. The hundreds of *Natures Mortes* (fruits, vases, etc.) modern painters drew are nothing but an attempt to release the object from the bonds of its material existence and present it in its complete ontology.

2. Natural phenomena are also spiritual phenomena."[4] Each natural landscape has a particular impact on its inhabitants. The symbiotic relationship between man and nature has defined many of the idiosyncrasies and temperaments of the people of a region. Consequently, Elytis ascertains, landscape "is the projection of a people's soul on matter."[5]
3. Analogy is the process by which the relationship between landscape and art is expressed. Elytis gives the following example: "I have read that a great French architect said the line of a mountain near Athens is repeated in the pediment of the Parthenon. That is a perfect analogy!"[6]
4. Language is a semantic system born out of people's interaction with their environment. Its visual and acoustic qualities are parts of the landscape that gave birth to it; it can reveal to us "the particular radiance that natural phenomena assume in [a] specific region."[7]

The example of the relationship between the Parthenon pediment and the line of an Athenian mountain exemplifies the complicated relationship of the subject with the things/objects of the world. When Elytis speaks of analogies, he does not refer to a simple exchange between the object and the subject's emotional world. Rather, the analogy is one of direct correspondence: the subject is not *like* the object; as far as art is concerned, the subject *is* the object. Perhaps the theory can be better explicated

---

[4] Elytis, *Ανοιχτά Χαρτιά*, p. 407. This line appears in "The Chronicle of a Decade," which was published in its entirety in *Open Papers* (1974). However, the statement first appears in "Modern Poetic and Artistic Problems" (1944), with a minor alteration: "The phenomena of Nature are also phenomena of the spirit" (Elytis, *Ανοιχτά Χαρτιά*, p. 505). In this essay, Elytis attributes the statement to Paul Éluard.

[5] Elytis, *Εν Λευκώ*, p. 365.

[6] Elytis, "On his Poetry," p. 632. Elytis is probably referring to Le Corbusier when he speaks of a "French architect." However, the particular analogy more accurately belongs to Periklis Yiannopoulos who famously suggested, in *Η Ελληνική Γραμμή και το Ελληνικόν Χρώμα*, that the lines of the Parthenon are in perfect harmony with the surrounding landscape.

[7] Elytis, *Ανοιχτά Χαρτιά*, p. 28.

through painting. Let us, for instance, take Picasso's "La femme fleur" (1942), one of Elytis's favorite paintings, and examine the analogy between the woman and the flower. The analogy does not imply that the woman is *like* a flower or that the flower resembles the woman. Woman and Flower merge into one entity: the flower-woman. The subject perceives the painting with a preconceived idea of what constitutes a woman and a flower. Thus, the interplay is between the subject and a multitude of objects (the flower and the woman that the painting suggests, the subject's ideas of the flower and the woman, the newly formed image of the flower-woman, etc.). This intersubjective network is further complicated if one considers the subject's position (or point of view), the invisible presence of the painter, the material and colors used, the frame of the painting that "locks" the subject's gaze, and the semantic notation "Flower-Woman" that accompanies the painting and instructs the subject that "what you are seeing is a flower woman." Elytis's analogy between the line of a mountain and a Parthenon pediment reflects a correspondence between an object of nature and an architectural construction. Once more, the theory of Analogies does not simply suggest that the Parthenon pediment resembles the mountain but, rather, that the people surrounded by that particular landscape introjected its natural characteristics and then projected and incorporated them in their architecture, so that, in the end, the pediment "contained" the line of the mountain. As in the case of "La femme fleur," the interplay is between the subject and a number of objects. The Parthenon pediment possesses something of the people and the landscape: it is literally a part of Mount Pentelicon, where its marble was taken from; it has a particular functional and spiritual meaning (i.e., it is part of a religious temple dedicated to Athena); it depicts specific narratives that are also connected to natural or cosmic phenomena;[8] it is situated at a specific angle, and it interacts with the surrounding nature (i.e., the landscape, the sunlight, the hill of the Acropolis, etc.).

Elytis's assertion that a landscape "is the projection of a people's soul on matter" is better understood in this context. Art reveals the sublime relationship between man and nature, but examples of this relationship are also found in traditional artistry and architecture. Elytis sees the whitewashed houses of the Cycladic islands as an architectural example that combines functionality with aesthetic appearance. On the functional level, white lime reflects the intense light of the Mediterranean sun and keeps the house cool during the long summer months. On the aesthetic level, the white is combined with the blue of the sea and the colors of local flowers (geraniums, bougainvilleas, etc.); it becomes part of the memory as an assortment of colors, scents (of aromatic herbs), and sounds (the waves, the cicadas, the wind, the language, etc.).[9] The theory of Analogies, then, is an

---

[8] Examples of such phenomena are the contest of Athena and Poseidon for the loyalty of Athens, and the Birth of Athena from Zeus' head.

[9] This depiction constitutes, perhaps, the most stereotypical view of the Aegean—a depiction that is plastered on advertisement boards in order to entice tourists to visit the Greek islands. To read Elytis in this light, however, would be anachronistic. When the

attempt to transpose the intersubjective network of objects and subjects on the poetic realm through a *synaesthetic* process.[10]

Elytis's essays testify to a wide spectrum of influences that the poet incorporates into his own aesthetic theory. Five major influences are of particular interest in his conceptualization of the theory of Analogies: surrealism, Sigmund Freud, Pablo Picasso, Charles Baudelaire, and Gaston Bachelard. His attraction to the epistemological foundation of theory, particularly in the case of Breton, Freud, and Bachelard, is evident in Elytis's writings. In essence, these thinkers do not differentiate between what constitutes metaphysics and what constitutes empiricism: surrealism was rooted in the "scientific" discoveries of Freud by establishing a bureau of surrealist research ("centrale surréaliste"); Freud defined psychoanalysis as a mental science; and Bachelard, a distinguished physician, is as comfortable with the laws of physics as he is with metaphysics. Although the scientific credibility of these theorists has often been challenged, their influence in reevaluating empirical knowledge has been paramount (particularly for many modernist writers). They narrowed the gap between the physical and the metaphysical, the psychical and the somatic, reality and dream. Renato Poggioli writes that "the avant-garde thinker and artist is ... particularly susceptible to the scientific myth," and provides such examples as Rimbaud's "alchemy of the word," Ortega y Gasset's "algebra of the word," and the founding text of surrealism, co-written by Soupault and Breton, *Champs Magnétiques*.[11] The modernist obsession with language is part of the wider artistic "scientificism" and "experimentalism"[12] that attempted to place the word under the microscope, and dissect or deconstruct it into its fundamental essence.

Poggioli further asserts that the modernist spirit, contrary to popular belief, does not revolt against the techniques of science. Rather, it revolts "against this reduction of nonmaterial values to the brute categories of the mechanical and the technical."[13] Similarly, Elytis reacts categorically against the simplification and

---

generation of the 1930s was turning to the Aegean for inspiration, it still constituted an undeveloped space.

[10] The term "synaesthesia" is both a literary and a psychological term and is central to understanding both Elytis's analogies and Baudelaire's correspondences, which will be extensively discussed in subsequent sections. Psychologically, Synaesthesia [is] "the condition in which a sensory experience normally associated with one modality occurs when another modality is stimulated. To a certain extent such cross modality experiences are perfectly normal; e.g., low-pitched tones give a sensation of softness or fullness while high-pitched tones feel brittle and sharp, the color blue feels cold while red feels warm. However, the term is usually restricted to the unusual cases in which regular and vivid cross modality experiences occur, such as when particular sounds reliably produce particular color sensations." Arthur S. Reber, *The Penguin Dictionary of Psychology* (New York: Penguin, 1995), p. 779.

[11] Renato Poggioli, *The Theory of the Avant-Garde*, trans. Gerald Fitzgerald (Cambridge, Massachusetts: Belknap Press of Harvard University, 1968), p. 138.

[12] Poggioli's terms. Poggioli, *Avant-Garde*, pp. 131–40.

[13] Poggioli's terms. Poggioli, *Avant-Garde*, p. 138.

reduction that materialism, a scientific byproduct, brought to man's life.[14] At the same time, his poetry is characterized, as will become clear, by a distinct use of mathematical categories and an almost alchemical approach to the word in its acoustic, visual, conceptual, and etymological manifestations. In his essay "Dreams," he writes that, between the science of psychoanalysis and the popular dream-readers, he was looking for a third path, less scientific and less naïve at the same time.[15] The comment may be extended to describe the entire spectrum of his poetry. This third path was paved, on one hand, by the transposition of sublimated forces in an aesthetic form and, on the other, by the theory of Analogies. In other words, his poetry is described by formalization and ordering of those revolutionary forces that describe man and his spiritual relation to natural phenomena.

In his essays, Elytis also refers to a number of poets, painters, and philosophers who worked within a framework, similar to the theory of Analogies such as Periklis Yiannopoulos, Andreas Kalvos, Le Corbusier, Picasso, Blake, Shelley, Jouve, Heraclitus, and Democritus and the folk artists Theophilos and Henri Rousseau. I will concentrate here on those thinkers that Elytis refers to directly in the context of the theory: Bachelard, Baudelaire, Freud, and, to a lesser extent, Breton.

Gaston Bachelard and Poetic Imagination

Elytis had a life-long interest in aesthetic philosophy and particularly in Phenomenology, as it emerges in the works of Martin Heidegger and Gaston Bachelard. His reading of Bachelard can be traced to 1944 when, in his article "Luck-Art-Risk" [Τύχη-Τέχνη-Τόλμη] published in *Nea Grammata*, he refers to Bachelard's *Lautréamont* (originally published in 1939). In the 1975 interview with Ivar Ivask he reaffirms his interest in the French philosopher: "Since the sea means so much to me, you ask me whether I know Gaston Bachelard. Of course I know Bachelard; all of his works are on my bookshelf."[16] In *Open Papers* he refers to Bachelard in relation to the following concepts: the concept of Time in Poetry (in "Luck-Art-Risk"),[17] the exploration of matter's impact on the spirit ("The Girls"),[18] suprarationalism in Physics in relation to Bachelard's interest in surrealism ("Modern Poetic and Artistic Problems"),[19] and the aesthetics of Rhythm in Poetry ("Reevaluation and a New Beginning").[20] Elytis also mentions the French philosopher in the context of his early aspirations "to develop a theory based on a biological phenomenon": "[I aspired] to be precise, to reach

---

[14] c.f. Elytis, *Ανοιχτά Χαρτιά*, pp. 5–6 and pp. 33–4.
[15] Elytis, *Ανοιχτά Χαρτιά*, pp. 203–4.
[16] Elytis, "On his Poetry," p. 641.
[17] Elytis, *Ανοιχτά Χαρτιά*, p. 138.
[18] Elytis, *Ανοιχτά Χαρτιά*, p. 163.
[19] Elytis, *Ανοιχτά Χαρτιά*, p. 512.
[20] Elytis, *Ανοιχτά Χαρτιά*, p. 524.

the formulation of rules that have the same applicability on matter and the spirit, something that, later, Gaston Bachelard engaged in with success."[21] Three general conceptions seemed to have interested Elytis in Bachelard's phenomenology: a) his epistemological approach, which attributed the same validity to the laws of physics and aesthetics; b) the concept of Time in relation to the Poetical moment; and c) the laws that permeate the dream-state.[22] What is central in the discussion of the theory of Analogies is the scientific validation that Bachelard's philosophy gives to the adaptation of the theory on poetical imagination. As Richard Kearney suggests, for Bachelard "the world of possibility, at once invented and discovered by imagining, is the source of both scientific and poetic creation."[23]

Bachelard's philosophy approaches poetry through image and language and attempts to free matter from the constraints of form. From an Aristotelian point of view, matter is always dependent on form: the human spirit can only perceive matter when it is presented into a decipherable formation. But, as Colette Gaudin suggests, "for Bachelard, matter becomes the provocation of a basic relationship between subject and object, and the *'mother substance'* of all dreams."[24] Science alone is unable to examine a poetic image because it lies outside the realm of empirical rationalism. For Bachelard, what one imagines is still described by a material substance: imaginary elements "have idealistic laws that are just as certain as experimental laws."[25] He uses the term "material imagination" to emphasize the scientific foundation of this state: "Going beyond the seductive imagination of forms, [material imagination] thinks matter, dreams matter, lives in matter, or—what amounts to the same thing—*it materializes the imaginary.*"[26] Form is a seductive perception of things because it is based on the recognition of what is already familiar to the human mind. It poses no spiritual challenge, and its conception is based on past experience, memory, and conventionally ascribed language. Contrary to the conventional perception of form, however, material

---

[21] Elytis, *Ανοιχτά Χαρτιά*, p. 163.

[22] Elytis's interest in Bachelard's view of Time and the relationship between Matter and Spirit is expressed in direct terms. The influence of Bachelard on his discussion of dreams is more implicit: In "The Girls" he mentions that his interest in Bachelard coincided with his reading of Freud's *Interpretation of Dreams*; the concept of dream is extremely important in his essays and is coupled with the concept of Time in "Time Bound and Time Unbound" (Elytis, *Εν Λευκώ*, pp. 383–407).

[23] Richard Kearney, *Poetics of Imagining* (New York: Fordham University Press, 1998), p. 97.

[24] Colette Gaudin, "Introduction," in *On Poetic Imagination and Reverie*, trans. Colette Gaudin, ix–xxxvii (Putnam: Spring Publications, 1988), p. xxiii.

[25] Gaston Bachelard, *Air and Water: An Essay on the Imagination of Movement*, trans. Edith Farell and Frederick Farell (Dallas: Dallas Institute for Humanities and Culture, 1988), p. 7. Emphasis added.

[26] Bachelard, *Air and Water*, p. 7.

imagination allows for the creation of newly imagined forms: "Matter" Bachelard writes, "is the unconscious of form."[27]

Elytis's metaphysics share the same view of what constitutes poetic imagination. "It is the absence of imagination," Elytis writes, "that converts man into a handicap of reality."[28] The poet follows the path that is "deeply rooted in animate matter, passes from the world of completed forms, then to the world of possible [forms] (as in dreams), in order to settle in the continuously shining awareness of spiritual omnipotence."[29] In the same way that matter obeys natural laws, the poet "causes natural phenomena in the spirit;" he points to a direction that signals "a new order of things in the realm of objectivity."[30] For both Elytis and Bachelard, the laws that guide phenomena are not based on an empirical observation that is always subject to scientific validation. On the contrary, the "Cartesian method, so useful a tool for explicating the world, is inadequate when it comes to complicating experience—the true function of objective research."[31] Poetic images are mobile and dynamic, and their perpetual transformation resists logical analysis. College students, Elytis writes, can solve dazzling mathematical equations "with such ease that it makes you wonder: plus, minus, divided by, multiplied by—therefore ... Everything can be assembled and disassembled except for the poet's words."[32] But still, he adds, if we transpose our viewpoint we will be led to a "differently strict and differently validated mathematics" that is equally applicable to the realm of poetry.[33]

Poetry startles us because it perpetually seeks the redefinition of reality; it places us into a world where all previous knowledge is challenged and reassessed through what Elytis calls "the royal path of the senses."[34] In a similar tone, Bachelard asks: "How—with no preparation—can this singular, short lived event constituted by the appearance of an unusual poetic image, react on other minds and in other hearts, despite all the barriers of common sense, all the disciplined schools of thought, content in their immobility?"[35] The answer to the question lies in the fundamental nature of *correspondences*, a concept that Bachelard discusses extensively in relation to Poetic Imagination, and whose major principles form the foundation of Elytis's theory of Analogies.

As Elytis finds a close link between his theory of Analogies and nature, so does Bachelard point to the connection between metaphor and nature: "Metaphor,

---

[27] Gaudin, "Introduction," p. xxxi.

[28] Elytis, *Ανοιχτά Χαρτιά*, p. 9.

[29] Elytis, *Ανοιχτά Χαρτιά*, p. 183.

[30] Elytis, *Ανοιχτά Χαρτιά*, pp. 180–81.

[31] Gaston Bachelard, *New Scientific Spirit*, trans. Arthur Goldhammer (Boston: Beacon Press, 1984), p. 138.

[32] Elytis, *Εν Λευκώ*, p. 165.

[33] Elytis, *Εν Λευκώ*, p. 168.

[34] Elytis, *Ανοιχτά Χαρτιά*, p. 644.

[35] Gaston Bachelard, *The Poetics of Space*, trans. Maria Jolas (Boston: Beacon Press, 1994), pp. xviii–xix.

physically inadmissible, psychologically absurd, is, nevertheless, a poetic truth. It is because metaphor is a phenomenon of the poetic soul. It is also a phenomenon of nature, a projection of human nature on universal nature."[36] Bachelard devalues "those metaphors which simply replace one object for another, a thought for an image."[37] Instead, he understands metaphor as a system of *correspondences* in the Baudelairean sense of the term:

> Baudelairean correspondences are based on a profound harmony among material substances. They bring into being one of the greatest chemistries of sensations, which is from many points of view more coherent than Rimbaud's alchemy. A Baudelairean correspondence is a powerful locus of the material imagination. At this locus, all 'imaginary substances' commingle and fertilize one another's metaphors.[38]

Images dream of their materialization in the process of imagining. They carry within their essence archetypal forces that *correspond* to other objects, or to the human subject, bringing into being "the greatest chemistries of sensations." Elytis was certainly familiar with Baudelaire's famous sonnet "Correspondences," which he evokes in the same context as Bachelard's philosophy and Freud's *Interpretations of Dreams*; once more, he was reading these three at the time when he aspired "to form a philosophy based on a biological phenomenon" and, more specifically, to formulate rules "that would have the same applicability on matter and the spirit."[39] What he shares with both Bachelard and Baudelaire is their suggestion of an interplay between imagination and matter or, to use Baudelaire's term, symbols.

Of the four elements Bachelard approaches scientifically, phenomenologically, psychologically, and philosophically—namely fire, earth, air, and water—the latter two predominate in Elytis's poetry:

---

[36] Gaston Bachelard, *Water and Dreams: An Essay on the Imagination of Matter*, trans. Edith Farell (Dallas: Dallas Institute Publication, 1999), p. 183.

[37] Gaudin, "Introduction," p. xxxiii.

[38] Gaston Bachelard, *Air and Dreams: An Essay on the Imagination of Movement*, trans. Edith Farell and Frederick Farell (Dallas: Dallas Institute for Humanities and Culture, 1988), p. 50. Bachelard distinguishes between two categories of poetic imagination: the *material* and the *dynamic*. The former explores matter in its essence: correspondences in material imagination explore images that, despite their originality, are fixed and stir imagination only in their materialization as newly formed images. In the latter, correspondences continuously strive "to subject matter to motion.... One cannot imagine a sphere without having it turn, an arrow, without having it fly, a woman without having her smile" (Kearney, *Poetics of Imagining*, p.106). Bachelard further associates material imagination with Baudelairean correspondences and dynamic imagination with Shelleyan correspondences (see Bachelard, *Air and Dreams*, pp. 50–51).

[39] Elytis, *Ανοιχτά Χαρτιά*, pp. 162–3.

You well know there is no denying my Islander's side, and so the sea is also present.... Yes, I find even in the depths of the sea the kind of paradise which I seek! Water, consequently, may be my favorite element. Yet air is significant too, since there is always in my poetry a certain suspension, something which irresistibly desires to rise higher.[40]

For Bachelard, the four elements are complex loci of imagination that can engender and resolve contradiction. His elements of imagination can take a multitude of symbolic significations: water can be clear, running, narcissistic, deep, dormant, dead, heavy, maternal, feminine, pure, and violent; air is connected to wings and to dreams of flight, to the ascensional psyche and the imaginary fall, to the wind, to the blue skies as well as to clouds. Bachelard uses these elements to distinguish different types of poetic sensitivities: "Water, for example, has one set of symbolic correspondences in Melville's *Moby Dick* and quite another in Yeat's 'The Stolen Child.'"[41] In Elytis, water is frequently connected to the sea (η θάλασσα) and almost always acquires feminine characteristics. Air, on the other hand, is usually a masculine element (*ο αέρας, ο άνεμος*) and is connected to the poetic will to ascend. The most profound adaptation of the Bachelardian elements of imagination in Elytis is the collection *Maria Nephele*. The idiosyncrasies of the central character are clearly related to the element of wind and, specifically, to what Bachelard calls "the reverie of clouds": it is reverie without responsibility,[42] reverie of transformation and perpetual mobility;[43] it unveils "a world of forms in constant transformation" and "metereological forms of beauty."[44] Maria Nephele's last name literally means "cloud" and she is described by the poet as "a young woman, a modern radical of our age."[45] Her temperament is cloudy: she smokes, she is aloof; she remembers only dreams, rebels against the institutions of man, goes through a multitude of moods from poem to poem, curses the divine, and mocks the poets. At the same time, her constant transformation through a dynamic imagination acquires an abstract yet perceptible form; she is the other side of the poet: "we search basically for the same things" Elytis says, "but along different routes."[46]

Baudelairean Correspondences

Baudelaire's focus on language as a path that leads to "cosmic unity," as well as the grounding of his ideas within the boundaries of the modern city, has often

---

[40] Elytis, "On his Poetry," p. 641.
[41] Kearney, *Poetics of Imagining*, p. 104.
[42] Bachelard, *Air and Dreams*, p. 185.
[43] Bachelard, *Air and Dreams*, p. 189.
[44] Bachelard, *Air and Dreams*, p. 194.
[45] Elytis, "On his Poetry," p. 640.
[46] Elytis, "On his Poetry," p. 640. *Maria Nephele* will be extensively discussed in Chapter 5.

placed him, in many scholars' genealogies, at the root of European modernism.[47] No other poet has had such an impact on European literary history and no other poem of Baudelaire "has been more widely quoted or invoked" as his short sonnet "Correspondences."[48] The poem points to the discovery of a new language—the language of *symbols*—on which many poets in the beginning of the twentieth century would found their effort of deconstructing what they considered to be obsolete traditional expressions. The sonnet, published in 1857, proposes a *synaesthetic* appraisal of the world and is pivotal to the understanding of Baudelaire's philosophy of Nature:

> The pillars of Nature's temple are alive
> and sometimes yield perplexing messages;
> forests of symbols between us and the shrine
> remark our passage with accustomed eyes.
> Like long-held echoes, blending somewhere else
> into one deep and shadowy unison
> as limitless as darkness and as day,
> the sounds, the scents, the colors correspond.
> There are odors succulent as young flesh,
> sweet as flutes, and green as any grass,
> while others—rich, corrupt and masterful—
> possess the power of such infinite things
> as incense, amber, benjamin and musk,
> to praise the sense's raptures and the mind's.[49]

The implied metaphor between "Nature" and "temple" exemplifies Baudelaire's perception of Nature as a locus of signifiers that mark a spiritual center. The symbols of Nature "remark our passage" and "possess the power," as the last triplet indicates, "to praise the sense's raptures and the mind's." Nature *gazes* at the

---

[47] Cf. Allan Bullock, "The Double Image," in *Modernism: A Guide to European Literature 1890–1930*, ed. Malcolm Bradbury and James McFarlane, 58–70 (London: Penguin, 1991), p. 68, and George Hyde, "The Poetry of the City," in *Modernism: A Guide to European Literature 1890–1930*, ed. Malcolm Bradbury and James McFarlane, 337–48 (London: Penguin, 1991), p 337.

[48] F.W. Leakey, *Baudelaire and Nature* (Manchester: Manchester University Press, 1969), p. 197. Like Elytis, Baudelaire uses the term "correspondence" interchangeably "with the terms 'symbol', 'allegory', and 'analogy'" (Leakey, *Baudelaire and Nature*, p. 208).

[49] Charles Baudelaire, *Les Fleurs du Mal*, trans. Richard Howard (Boston: David R. Godine, 2000), p. 15. La Nature est un temple où de vivants piliers / Laissent parfois sortir de confuses paroles; / L'homme y passe à travers des forêts de symbols / Qui l'observent avec des regards familiers. / Comme de longs échos qui de loin se confondent / Dans une ténébreuse et profonde unité, / Vaste comme la nuit et comme la clarté, / Les parfums, les couleurs et les sons se répondent. / Il est des parfums frais comme des chairs d'enfants, / Doux comme les hautbois, verts comme les prairies, / Et d'autres, corrompus, riches et triomphants, / Ayant l'expansion des choses infinies, / Comme l'ambre, le musc, le benjoin et l'encens, / Qui chantent les transports de l'esprit et des sens (Baudelaire, *Les Fleurs*, p. 193).

passerby, and the decoding of this gaze is not taken for granted; as Leakey suggests, "whether he becomes aware of them or not, these voices are (in principle, at least) already and expectantly 'there.'"[50] One is reminded here of Kant's definition of the sublime object of Nature, "the representation of which determines the mind to regard the elevation of nature beyond our reach as equivalent to representation."[51] It is for this reason, Kant argues, that nature is simultaneously a source of pleasure and displeasure.[52] For Baudelaire too, there is a sublime quality in nature that raises it to the status of a mystical entity—the sonnet borrows religious symbols to emphasize the cosmic implications of nature's messages: "the pillars of Nature's temple," "symbols between us and the shrine," "deep and shadowy unison," the power of such infinite things / as incense, amber, benjamin and musk." Unlike Kant, however, who seems to place the sublime object of Nature beyond symbolic representation, Baudelaire believed, as Marcel Raymond affirms, that "the poet's task is to follow an intuitive sense with which he is endowed and to perceive analogies, correspondences, which assume the literary aspect of the metaphor, the symbol, the comparison, or the Allegory."[53] "Correspondences" certainly has an auditory quality to it—Nature *speaks* to the passerby with words (*paroles*) and echoes; what remains is for the poet / "seer" to decode its language. What is particularly important in the sonnet is Baudelaire's suggestion of a "synaesthetic" re-evaluation of the world. Nature's perplexing messages cause cross-modality experiences where "odors" become "succulent," are "sweet as flutes," and "green as any grass"; one can taste, see, and hear smells. For Baudelaire, such synaesthetic experiences can be recaptured in poetry, where phenomena become metaphors that can be then expressed in language.

The influence of Baudelaire's theory of correspondences on Elytis's poetic development is indisputable. For Elytis, the sonnet "Correspondences" pointed to a path in creation where sensation is condensed into a single eternal moment.[54] In Baudelaire the sharp division between the Natural and the Spiritual is bridged; the duality of the universe does not exist, since both concepts "are dependent on normal human perception" and thus "they resolve into a single incomplete reality."[55] Poetry makes this reality complete by capturing it in an eternal moment. Unity is perceived in the "symbol" whose essence compresses the synaesthetic moment, giving it form and projecting it onto reality. These symbols, in which opposites merge and unify,

---

[50] Leakey, *Baudelaire and Nature*, p. 206.

[51] Immanuel Kant, *Critique of Aesthetic Judgement*, trans. James Creed Meredith (Oxford: Clarendon Press, 1911), p. 119.

[52] Kant, *Critique of Aesthetic*, p. 106.

[53] Marcel Raymond, *From Baudelaire to Surrealism* (London: Methuen & Co., 1950), p. 12. It should be pointed out that Elytis was familiar with Marcel Raymond's studies on French literature. In his essays he cites the French critic in a short commentary on the work of the poet Pierre-Jean Jouve (Elytis, Ανοιχτά Χαρτιά, p. 622).

[54] Elytis, Ανοιχτά Χαρτιά, p. 162.

[55] Balakian, *Literary Origins*, p. 47.

are abundant in the poetry of Elytis: the sun is both punishing and benevolent, the sea is a little girl present and absent at the same time, Eros is a victory where one is defeated, the Moon beautifies sorrow; the light-tree, Elytonesos, Ioulita's Blue, Marina, Helen, Santorini, are condensed, multidetermined symbols that become incorporated in Elytis's broader mythopoetic system.

The poems of Baudelaire that Elytis chooses to cite in his essays are clear examples of the theory of correspondences. He quotes five such excerpts in his work in the original French:[56]

1. O toison, moutonnant jusque sur l'enclosure!
   O boucles! O parfum chargé de nonchaloir! (from "La Chevelure")[57]
2. Que diras-tu ce soir, pauvre âme solitaire
   Que diras-tu, mon cœur, cœur autrefois flétri
   A la très-belle, à la très-bonne, à la très-chère (from "Que diras-tu ce soir")[58]
3. Les parfums, les couleurs et les sons se répondent (from "Correspondances")[59]
4. Nous aurons des lits pleins d'odeurs légères (from "La Mort des Amants")[60]
5. L'homme y passe à travers des forêts de symboles (from "Correspondances")[61]

Elytis is particularly interested in Baudelaire's use of scent as a sense that interacts with objects and sentiments: the curls of the beloved smell of negligence, the lovers' death puts them in richly scented beds. In "Que diras-tu ce soir," Baudelaire speaks of the sacred fragrance that enrobes the beloved's flesh;[62] in "La Chevelure," the soul of the narrator slakes its thirst "for color, sound, and

---

[56] All of the excerpts from Baudelaire's poems, both in the original French and in the English translation, are quoted from Charles Baudelaire, *Les Fleurs du Mal*, trans. Richard Howard (Boston: David R. Godine, 2000).

[57] Baudelaire, *Les Fleurs*, p. 208. "Ecstatic fleece that ripples to your nape / and reeks of negligence in every curl" ("The Head of Hair" in Baudelaire, *Les Fleurs*, p. 30). In Elytis it appears in "The Method of Therefore" (Elytis, *Εν Λευκώ*, p. 182).

[58] Baudelaire, *Les Fleurs*, p. 224. "What will you say tonight, forsaken soul, / how will you speak, my long-since-withered heart, / to her, the loveliest and most beloved" ("What Will You Say Tonight" in Baudelaire, *Les Fleurs*, p. 47). In Elytis it appears in "The Notebook of a Lyrical" (Elytis, *Εν Λευκώ*, p. 232).

[59] Baudelaire, *Les Fleurs*, p. 193. "The sounds, the scents, the colors correspond" ("Correspondences" in Baudelaire, *Les Fleurs*, p. 15). In Elytis it appears in "The Notebook of a Lyrical" (Elytis, *Εν Λευκώ*, p. 235).

[60] Baudelaire, *Les Fleurs*, p. 327. "We shall have richly scented beds" ("The Death of Lovers" in Baudelaire, *Les Fleurs*, p. 149). It appears in Elytis's collection of poems *The Little Seafarer* (Elytis, *Collected Poems*, p. 444).

[61] Baudelaire, *Les Fleurs*, p. 193. "Forests of symbols … / remark our passage …" ("Correspondences" in Baudelaire, *Les Fleurs*, p. 15). It appears in Elytis's *The Little Seafarer* (Elytis, *Collected Poems*, p. 444)

[62] Baudelaire, *Les Fleurs*, p. 47.

smell";[63] and in "Correspondences," scents, colors, and sounds correspond in the forests of symbols.[64] In the prologue to a book on Yiannis Tsarouchis's paintings, Elytis uses, once more, Baudelairean correspondences to describe the painter's work: "according ... to the right of correspondences, granted to us by Baudelaire, I would say that ... if painting had a smell, Tsarouchis's paintings would smell of whitewashed walls...."[65] The synaesthetic implications of the metaphor are clear: the image of whitewashed walls produces a smell related to color.[66]

Elytis considered Baudelaire to be one of the most important European poets.[67] He placed him at the onset of a rebellious literature that combined its "worship of Evil with other pathologies of beauty": "hedonism in the forbidden, in guilt, and in remorse; the invocation of pain as a Virtue; the juxtaposition of the Artificial and the Natural; and the glorification of Hell over a bankrupt Paradise."[68] At the same time, he believed that after two World Wars in the twentieth century, the madness these poets proclaimed had become painfully real. The "total revolution" and the radical destruction of the much-too-logical world that the surrealists proclaimed—the surrealists who saw themselves as the inheritors of the rebellion heralded by Baudelaire—had taken place. The vicious forces they worshipped were unleashed for a second time in less than 30 years, leaving behind scores of dead bodies, leveled cities, gas chambers, and a disillusioned youth. For Elytis, these poets—part of a revolution that extended from Baudelaire, Rimbaud, and Lautréamont, to the surrealists—marked a necessary milestone. Truth, however, was to be sought elsewhere: in the other, equally significant, rebellion of Matisse, who produced his most colorful paintings during World War II, and in the perseverance of the human spirit that, despite adversities, fights back aligned with the forces of light:

>   Again I looked * like my country
> Mid stones I blos * somed and I grew
>   And I pay pack * murderers'
>   * Blood with light[69]

---

[63] Baudelaire, *Les Fleurs*, p. 30.

[64] Baudelaire, *Les Fleurs*, p. 15.

[65] Elytis, *Ανοιχτά Χαρτιά*, pp. 567–8.

[66] The most telling example of Elytis's interest in correspondences, as Baudelaire defined them, is the subcollection "Variations on a Sunbeam" of *Sun the First*. Seven colors are presented there that correspond to particular sensations and images that arise in the poet's interaction with the feminine.

[67] c.f. Odysseus Elytis, *Εν Λευκώ*, pp. 305, 311.

[68] Elytis, *Ανοιχτά Χαρτιά*, p. 442.

[69] From *Axion Esti*, Ode 10 (Elytis, *Collected Poems*, p. 169). Της πατρίδας μου πάλι * ομοιώθηκα / Μες στις πέτρες άνθισα * και μεγάλωσα / Των φονιάδων το αίμα * με φως / * ξεπληρώνω (Elytis, *Ποίηση*, p. 164).

Sigmund Freud and Dream Symbolism

Sigmund Freud's intellectual influence on the literature of the twentieth century is indisputable. Many writers and artists saw the publication of *The Interpretation of Dreams* in 1899 (dated 1900),[70] as a scientific validation of the aesthetic ideas that art and literature had been proclaiming for centuries:[71]

> Freud's greatest contribution to the natural history of the imagination is chapter 6 of *The Interpretation of Dreams*, and that has been powerful because it shows that the associative logic found in poetry is intrinsic to the human mind. His analysis of what is mainly clinical material has given a quasi-scientific status to the processes of the symbolic imagination—a partial re-establishment of poetry in the world from which it had withdrawn.[72]

For Freud, "there can be no doubt that our dreams are full of symbolism."[73] In decoding these symbolic elements of the dream-content he suggests that, to avoid arbitrary interpretations, the analyst must combine two techniques: a) free association on the dreamer's part, and b) good knowledge of symbols on the interpreter's part. These are in fact the techniques that, 25 years after the publication of *The Interpretation of Dreams*, André Breton would incorporate into the corpus of surrealist literary techniques. Free association paved the way for "automatic writing," and symbolic interpretation was in harmonious agreement with the surrealist attempt to redefine the symbols of the world by reaching beyond visible reality. Most importantly, Freud's theory was an affirmation that perversity is a common attribute of human experience. His interpretation subverted man's symbols, turning logic on its head with all kinds of sexual connotations: "the Eiffel Tower, rising suddenly from the Champ-de-Mars amid the neat boulevards, was, of course, a classic Freudian symbol."[74]

---

[70] Even though *The Interpretation of Dreams* is one of Freud's earliest works, he continued to revise it until the end of his life.

[71] Freud is often cited as having proclaimed: "The poets and philosophers before me discovered the unconscious. What I discovered was the scientific method by which the unconscious can be studied." However, this statement is nowhere to be found in Freud's writings. As Jeffrey Berman suggests, this quote was first quoted by Philip R. Lehrman in "Freud's Contributions to Science"—in the journal *Harofe Haivri* Vol. 1 (1940)—and then cited by Lionel Trilling in "Freud and Literature"—in *The Liberal Imagination* (1940). It is believed that Freud made the remark in 1928, to Professor Ernest Becker in Berlin. See Jeffrey Berman, *The Talking Cure: Literary Representations of Psychoanalysis* (New York: New York University Press, 1987), p. 304, n. 40.

[72] Richard Sheppard, "The Crisis of Language," in *Modernism: A Guide to European Literature 1890–1930*, 323–36 (London: Penguin, 1991), p. 328.

[73] Sigmund Freud, *The Interpretation of Dreams*, trans. James Strachey (New York: Avon, 1998), p. 388.

[74] Nahma Sandrow, *Surrealism: Theatre, Arts, Ideas* (New York: Harper and Row Publishers, 1972), pp. 11–12.

Freud points out that symbolic representation can be found, apart from dreams, in "folklore, and in popular myths, legends, linguistic idioms, proverbial wisdom and current jokes."[75] However, he warns against lumping together all such symbols; in many cases the relationship between symbol and representation is obvious, while in others it is concealed and puzzling. "It is precisely these latter cases," he notes, "which must be able to throw light upon the ultimate meaning of the symbolic relations." He concludes by opining that the disjuncture [in obscure symbolism] is due to the fact that "things that are symbolically connected today were probably united in the prehistoric times by conceptual and linguistic identity."[76] After cautioning against easy interpretations, Freud proceeds—in one of the most notorious segments of *The Interpretation of Dreams*, from a poetic standpoint—to produce a catalogue of typical symbolic representations of the dream-content. Here are a few examples:

1. All elongated objects, such as sticks, tree trunks, and umbrellas (the opening of these last being comparable to an erection) may stand for the male organ—as well as all long, sharp weapons, such as knives, daggers and pikes ...
2. Boxes, cases, chests, cupboards and ovens represent the uterus, and also hollow objects, ships, and vessels of all kinds.
3. Rooms in dreams are usually women (*Frauenzimmer*); if the various ways in and out of them are represented, this interpretation is scarcely open to doubt. In this connection interest in whether the room is open or locked is easily intelligible ...
4. Steps, ladders or staircases, or, as the case may be, walking up and down them, are representations of the sexual act.
5. Smooth walls over which the dreamer climbs, the façade of houses, down which he lowers himself—often in great anxiety—correspond to erect human bodies, and are probably repeating in the dream recollections of a baby's climbing up his parents or nurse ...
6. It is highly probable that all complicated machinery and apparatus occurring in dreams stand for the genitals ...
7. ... many landscapes in dreams, especially any containing bridges or wooded hills, may clearly be recognized as descriptions of the genitals ....[77]

---

[75] Freud, *Interpretation*, p. 386.

[76] Freud, *Interpretation*, p. 387. It is not surprising, then, that modernist poets and artists—many of whom were influenced by Freud's writings—approached the symbol from its primitive or archaic representation, which as Poggioli suggests, was based on *deformation* (Poggioli, *Theory of the Avant-Garde*, p. 176). Freud extensively discusses the (often misunderstood) idea of "primitivism" in *Civilization and its Discontents* and *Totem and Taboo*.

[77] Freud, *Interpretation*, pp. 389–91.

Again, these are only a few examples in a long list of typical symbolic representations in dreams, which Freud justifies by providing specific examples from his patients' experiences or his own. It is interesting to note that he kept expanding this catalogue of dream-symbols in each revision of his book and that these additions cover a period of over 20 years. Apart from the symbolic interpretation of the dream-content, Freud produces metaphors, or analogies, that are directly linked to psychical functions. In *The Interpretation of Dreams*, he draws analogies between psychical functions and myths or narratives: "wish fulfillment" is discussed in relation to the myth of Crassus and the Parthian Queen[78] as well as to the ghosts in the Underworld from *The Odyssey*, and the Titans.[79] The forgetting of dreams is related to Siegfried's cloak from Wagner's "Nibelungenlied,"[80] and "birth dreams" are explained in relation to the myths of Adonis, Osiris, Moses, and Bacchus.[81] Freud further redefines the psychological meaning of the myths of Moses and Oedipus, and even creates his own version of a primordial myth in *Totem and Taboo* (i.e., the famous primal horde theory).

If Bachelard achieved the bridging of the vast gap between physics and the imagination, Freud achieved a similar bridging of the gap between neuroscience and the imagination. It should be noted, however, that as influential as Freud was in scientifically substantiating the mechanism that describes imaginary functions (in his exploration of dreams, day-dreams, fantasies, jokes, slips of the tongue, etc.), and the power of unconscious over conscious functions, many modernist poets were still reluctant to employ his psychoanalytic theories. "Rilke refused to be analysed by Freud," Graham Hough writes, "Joyce refused to be analysed by Jung, and Lawrence thought he had refuted the whole psychoanalytic system."[82] The reason for this resistance on the part of the poets may be located in Freud's view of poetic creation as a process of sublimation. In his 1908 essay, "The Relation of the Poet to Day-dreaming," he argues that, whereas for most human beings daydreams and fantasies—being primarily egotistical and unsatisfied wishes—are repulsive and shameful, for the poet they become sources of pleasure. The poet achieves this by softening the "egotistical character of the day-dreams" and by placing it within an aesthetic framework; he manages to situate us, the readers, "into a position in which we can enjoy our own day-dreams without reproach or shame."[83]

---

[78] Freud, *Interpretation*, p. 609.
[79] Freud, *Interpretation*, p. 592.
[80] Freud, *Interpretation*, p. 553.
[81] Freud, *Interpretation*, p. 437.
[82] Graham Hough, "The Modernist Lyric," in *Modernism: A Guide to European Literature 1890–1930*, ed. Malcolm Bradbury and James McFarlane, 312–22 (London: Penguin, 1991), p. 318.
[83] Sigmund Freud, "The Relation of the Poet to Day Dreaming," in *Character and Culture*, ed. Philip Rieff, trans. Philip Rieff (New York: Collier, 1976), p. 43. Freud resorts to mainstream literature to justify this conclusion: to "the less pretentious writers of romances, novels, and stories, who are read all the same by the widest circles" (39–40). Even though

According to Freud, "sublimation of instinct is an especially conspicuous feature of cultural development."[84] Man is caught between the necessity of forming social constructions and his instincts that tend towards de(con)struction; the Freudian supposition clearly undermines any possibility for progress: as long as man remains a social being, in the interest of civilization, the instincts will inevitably remain suppressed.[85]

The major artistic movements of the early twentieth century, particularly in their revolutionary proclamations, have defined themselves within the parameters of these two poles: dadaism leaned towards complete deconstruction; surrealism—which, ironically, founded its principles on Freudian theory—attempted to combine total destruction and revolution with complete social change; and futurism leaned towards change that was in accord with technological advances. One could argue that modern poetry, in general, has principally been defined through the tension between construction and de(con)struction, which in turn deepened the tension between form and content, the individual and the collective, reality and imagination, social responsibility and free will. World War II marked the end of an entire literature, which vainly placed its bet on a revolution that would unleash the repressed energies of the human unconscious. The criticism of surrealism after the war might be justified on the basis of its absolute refusal to embrace "form": i.e., to offer a viable structure that could sustain the repressed and destructive unconscious energies.

Elytis's interest in Freud may be traced from around 1935, when he met Andreas Empeirikos.[86] He was particularly fascinated with Freud's *The Interpretation of*

---

modernist poetry tends towards eclecticism—in T.S. Eliot's description, it is "the voice of the poet talking to himself, or to nobody," or "an interior meditation ... regardless of any possible speaker or hearer" (qtd in Hough, *Modernist Lyric*, p. 313)—it still constitutes a reaction to personal and sociopolitical conventions and taboos.

[84] Sigmund Freud, *Civilization and its Discontents*, trans. James Strachey (New York: Norton, 1961), p. 51.

[85] The following anecdote, described by Matthew von Unwerth in *Freud's Requiem*, captures well another aspect of the modernist poets' resistance to psychoanalysis. When Rilke considered undergoing psychoanalysis, Lou Salome sent him a letter cautiously encouraging him to do so. Soon afterwards, however, she "sent Rilke a telegram, followed by a second letter, in which she retracted her approval and emphatically advised the poet against psychoanalysis. Rilke gratefully accepted her judgment. He told her that he feared that the palliative effects of analysis would come at the cost of his creativity ..." Matthew von Unwerth, *Freud's Requiem: Mourning, Memory, and the Invisible History of a Summer Walk* (New York: Penguin, 2005), p. 115.

[86] Empeirikos had returned from Paris, where he had been trained as a psychoanalyst and had undergone personal psychoanalytic treatment with the renowned psychologist René Laforgue. Some brief notes on Empeirikos's psychoanalytic interests testify to his Freudian training. In 1948, along with two Greek psychiatrists, Georgios Zabitsianos and Dimitrios Kouretas, and with the help of Princess Marie Bonaparte (Sigmund Freud's close friend), Empeirikos attempted to establish the Greek Psychoanalytic Association, the first of its kind in Greece. Although the Association did not succeed in

Dreams, which he always kept in his private library.⁸⁷ Like the French surrealists, Elytis saw Freud as the driving force in a revolution that challenged the Cartesian perception of the world by revealing the invisible reality of psychic functions. Unlike the French surrealists, however, who attempted a direct application of Freudian theory to poetic composition in the form of "automatic writing," Elytis completely rejected the notion that the unconscious can be directly approached through a random array of words. The surrealists incorporated Freud as part of the revolution that would unleash the repressed forces of the unconscious and would eventually, coupled with Marxism, upset man's corrupted institutions and conventions. Breton misread Freud by trying to mobilize, in his call for "total destruction," the very same forces that the latter attempted to bring to light through psychoanalysis. It is not surprising that Freud was indifferent to surrealism and that Breton expressed his disappointment with Freud when the two men met in 1921.

Contrary to the surrealist reading of Freud, Elytis perceived Freudian theory as a challenge to the blind worshipping of unconscious forces, so dominant in the late nineteenth-century European literature (for instance, in the poetry of Rimbaud, Lautréamont, and Baudelaire). World War II had proven the surrealists wrong: poetry could not align itself with those dark psychical forces responsible for the greatest catastrophe in modern history.⁸⁸ He further believed, like Freud, that the war reaffirmed that "one never reaches truth—alas—when they oppose the natural movements of their soul."⁸⁹ Instead, truth should be sought in what man ignores: "if there truly exists a secret message sent from the part of life that we ignore, I never happened to see it in the form of the boogeyman that goes

---

capturing the attention of scientific circles in Greece and abroad, it laid the foundations for the official recognition of the Greek Psychoanalytic Association in the late 1970s. In 1950, Empeirikos published his only complete psychoanalytic case study. It was entitled "Un cas de névrose obsessionnelle avec éjaculations précoces" ("A Case of Obsessive Neurosis with Premature Ejaculation") and it was published in *Revue Française de Psychanalyse*. (Andreas Empeirikos, "Un cas de névrose obsessionnelle avec éjaculations précoces," *Revue Française de Psychanalyse* 14, no. 3 [1950]: 331–66). The study is reminiscent of Freud's "Wolfman" and uses Freudian dream interpretation in order to uncover the patient's traumatic memories from the unconscious. A second psychoanalytic study entitled "A case of an unconscious Philomophylia" was found in the poet's personal manuscripts after his death. His devotion to the field of psychoanalysis led to his induction as a member of the Paris Psychoanalytical Association in 1950, and throughout his life, Empeirikos attended several of the organization's conferences (e.g., The International Psychoanalytical conference in Zürich, in 1949, and the International Psychoanalytical conference in Amsterdam, in 1951. See Andreas Empeirikos, *Μια Περίπτωσις Ιδεοψυχαναγκαστικής Νευρώσεως με Πρόωρες Εκσπερματώσεις και Άλλα Ψυχαναλυτικά Κείμενα* (Athens: Agra, 2001).

⁸⁷ Elytis used to say that ideally, he would like to live with, at most, a hundred books. Freud's *The Interpretation of Dreams* was one of the books he had in his private library. Ioulita Iliopoulou (personal communication).

⁸⁸ Elytis, *Ανοιχτά Χαρτιά*, p. 442.

⁸⁹ Elytis, *Ανοιχτά Χαρτιά*, p. 442.

around at midnight. I saw it in the moments when no hand could pull aside the trickster's sheet to reveal the deception."[90]

---

[90] Elytis, *Ανοιχτά Χαρτιά*, p. 443. Elytis provides some telling examples of these chance encounters that reveal the secret correspondence of the senses with the things of the world. More profoundly than any other passage in his essays, these elaborate moments revealed to the senses by chance—as in a dream—describe the raw material of a poetry that does not seek its justification in overthrowing visible reality but in illuminating invisible correspondences:

> The first time was in Olympia. A midday in late spring where chamomile and lilies covered the holy place with its fallen marble blocks .... Not a soul was around. And I was wandering alone, far toward the side of the river, near a rectangular space marked by the foundations of an unknown ... temple. Then, encouraged, a lizard, mystified by the absolute silence, came out of her hiding place and started running toward the center. It stopped as I began to move and waited, suspicious, for some time, and only when I managed to hold my breath it leaped with admirable speed and reached the center of the space precisely where a symmetrical square stone stood like a temple, higher than the rest, and where—I must add—by the chance of the moment, the only rays of the sun managed to penetrate the thick green foliage. There I saw it rising, after I lost it for a minute, and it started to move its head high and presenting its breast to the sun. It was a series of unbelievably charming little moves, a dancing system of a myriad little steps, a palindromic rhythm consisting of faint visible turns, joy coupled with awe in a prayer that reaches its destination ....
>
> The second time that I chanced to see something similar was in Spetses. The only window facing the "back small roof," as we used to call it, belonged to me. A noise coming from outside made me approach the blind and look through the cracks. It was little Eirini, the house's young girl, coming from the sea and wiping herself with a long colored towel. The drops of the sea fell from her hair to her eyebrows, immobilizing her lashes for a moment, then trembled and rolled down her cheeks. She chose a sunlit corner and, with a sudden move, spread her towel on the ground and lay down on her back with her legs half opened. Then, in a short while, she rose on her elbows, looked around to make sure no one was watching, stopped her glance at my window for some time (from inside I was holding my breath) and, relieved, she untied the top of her bathing suit and returned to her original position with her big uneven breasts perfectly exposed to the sun. A miracle. Across me there was the top of a lemon tree. Then the whitewashed wall of the roof. And closer to me, this naked body palpitating in the apotheosis of light. All this in an acoustic background consisting of the waves splashing and the tzi, tzi tzi [the sound of crickets], invisibly and omnipotently rising from the garden, from other gardens, from the olive grove nearby, from the entire island. Truly, I wondered, I could stay there for hours, like an angel in a mysterious photosynthesis.
>
> Then, I saw a colorful butterfly coming from afar. It passed near my widow, almost touched it—I remember that I managed to see the symmetrical black circles on its yellow wings. Then, at once and without hesitation, it went and sat gently on the girl's hair. It jumped about a bit and, there it was, with the last jump, on one of the two beautiful breasts that heaved in the rhythm of sleep. In the short span of time that it stayed there until it sprang up and left..." (Elytis, *Ανοιχτά Χαρτιά*, pp. 443–5).

Elytis places *The Interpretation of Dreams*, along with Baudelaire's correspondences and Bachelard's theory, at the foundation of his early interest in constructing a theory whose rules would have the same applicability in both matter and spirit.[91] Dream symbolism pointed to the scientific validation of the correspondences that exist between external objects (matter) and the human psyche. In dreams, an object becomes a metaphoric device that defines the very being of man. Elytis's most elaborate definition of the dream-state is presented in a long essay entitled "The Dreams," published in the volume *Open Papers*, where, after a short discussion on the characteristics of this state, he proceeds to present a series of 21 personal dreams.[92] His observations on the nature of dreams are clearly an amalgamation of Freudian and surrealist positions. A simple juxtaposition of Elytis's "Dreams," Freud's *Interpretation of Dreams*, and Breton's *Manifesto of Surrealism* (1924) illustrates the point well:

> It is no doubt true that we forget dreams more and more as time passes after waking; we often forget them in spite of the most painstaking efforts to recall them. But I am of the opinion that the extent of this forgetting is as a rule overestimated .... It is often possible by means of analysis to restore all that has been lost by the forgetting of the dream's content ... This demands a certain amount of attention and self discipline in carrying out the analysis .... (Freud)[93]

> From the moment when it is subjected to methodical examination, when, by means to be determined, we succeed in recording the content of dreams in their entirety (and that presupposed a discipline of memory spanning generations ...) we may hope that the mysteries which really are not will give way to the great Mystery (Breton).[94]

> Yes, Freud was right: a dream abandons you when you abandon it. Personally, in times when I happened to discipline myself on this matter, I managed to reconstruct, as an archaeologist pieces together the fragments of a vase, the entire object (in this case, the entire 'scenario' of a night ...). (Elytis)[95]

All three passages center upon the restoration of the dream content that has been repressed or censored in the waking state. There are obviously significant differences concerning the methods by which such restoration can be achieved, but what becomes clear in Breton and Elytis's use of Freud is the attempt to replace analysis with alternative processes (automatism or the collective archiving of dreams in the case of Breton, and a more individual poetic, or artistic, reconstruction of dream content in the case of Elytis). In fact, Breton and Elytis would go even further in the decontextualization of Freudian theory to construe a rebellious attitude based on the dream's amoral nature:

---

[91] Elytis, *Ανοιχτά Χαρτιά*, p. 163.

[92] Almost all of Elytis's formal divisions in his work are done in multiples of 7 (—in this case 7 × 3).

[93] Freud, *Interpretation*, pp. 555–6.

[94] Breton, *Manifestoes*, pp. 13–14.

[95] Elytis, *Ανοιχτά Χαρτιά*, pp. 204–5.

The mind of the man who dreams is fully satisfied by what happens to him. The agonizing question of possibility is no longer pertinent. Kill, fly faster, love to your heart's content. And if you should die, are you not certain of reawakening among the dead? (Breton)[96]

[In dreams] we act without commitments, without the sense of time, without shame. We go about unbuttoned, we urinate in front of others, we commit all sorts of indecencies—we even kill sometimes, stubborn against the entire police force of the world. (Elytis)[97]

Like Freud, Elytis presents his own dreams and divides them into categories: "Words and Dreams," "Dreams, People and Places," and "Dreams and Distance (Fragments of Dreams)." The dream-content varies: sometimes it is clearly related to sexuality (as in "The neighborhood of Evrota," or "The Dream of Preciosa"), sometimes to the imposing figures of his friends (Andreas Empeirikos in "The Girl with the Violet Spot," Angelos Sikelianos and George Seferis in "Poor Azakynthos"), and at other times to traumatic memories (his mother's death in "The Well," or the death of a close friend in "Dream of Giorgos Sarandaris"). Elytis presents the dreams without commentary and refrains from approaching them psychoanalytically. To reiterate his view on the utility of dreams once more: "Between the Freudian *Interpretation of Dreams* and the popular Dream-Readers I always hoped to find a third path, a way that is at the same time less scientific and less naïve; a way that would allow me to use the content of dreams independently of their psychoanalytic or their prophetic significations."[98] What Elytis attempts to disclose in his own dream-sequences are the basic functions of the dream process, which resemble the mechanism that drives the formation of the poetic image. This is certainly in agreement with Freud's suggestion that the poet plays with his daydreams like a child, and in the process of playing he creates poetry.[99] In dreams, as in poetry, "man ceases to recognize himself";[100] he faces a dimension of reality hitherto unknown—a dimension that utterly undermines the insistent perception of himself as a complete being.

This suggestion places poetry in the dubious position of being both a force of creation and of negation. Surrealism tried to bridge the gap between the Freudian view of the world—where the idea of progress becomes almost irrelevant—and the necessity for social and political change, by aligning itself with either Marxism or Trotskyism. This schism was the main cause of the disempowerment of the movement and its eventual demise, despite Breton's attempts to revive it, after World War II. Apart from a brief involvement in leftist politics in the

---

[96] Breton, *Manifestoes*, p. 13.
[97] Elytis, *Ανοιχτά Χαρτιά*, p. 204.
[98] Elytis, *Ανοιχτά Χαρτιά*, pp. 203–4.
[99] Sigmund Freud, "The Relation of the Poet to Day Dreaming," pp. 39–43.
[100] Elytis, *Ανοιχτά Χαρτιά*, p. 203.

early 1930s (while studying at the University of Athens), Elytis refrained from explicitly taking a political position. Yet, his poetry points to a certain vision of the future that is often connected to social and political change. The tension between the necessity and fallibility of "order," and the need for change is a constant theme in his poetry, where history (in its social and political implications) is measured against the individual.[101] Poetry, in its Freudian understanding as sublimation, perceives truth in its capacity to illuminate what is repressed, subjected to darkness, or placed in the periphery of consciousness. As it positions itself in the social realm, Elytis's poetry always aligns its potential energies with the weak, the invisible, and the suppressed. In a statement issued in 1951, he commented on the relationship between the poet and the public: "… I feel that the only way to see the absolute part of myself be validated is when I deprive it of its capacity as a personal case; when, in other words, I make it *public*."[102] In a subsequent statement published in 1961 he returned to the mission of the poet in relation to society: "I perceive poetry as a source of innocence full of revolutionary forces, and my mission is to guide these forces against a world that is unacceptable to my conscience, hoping, through continuous metamorphoses, to make it more agreeable to my dreams."[103] The description of poetry as a source of innocence seems to be reminiscent of Freud's comparison of the poet to the child. Poetry, like children, innocently discloses a truth that is revolutionary in its suggestion of an unconventional view of the world. The greatest influence of Freud on Elytis is precisely the disclosure of a world that lies beyond constructed reality.

The Development of the Theory of Analogies

Elytis first used the concept of analogies in a 1951 essay on Picasso, entitled "Equivalences chez Picasso." Teriade had already introduced Elytis to Picasso in 1948 and the two had spent some time together in Teriade's villa in Saint-Jean-Cap-Ferrat. The essay was written in French and was published in the surrealist magazine *Verve*, in an issue dedicated to the Spanish painter.[104] In describing Picasso's paintings, Elytis writes:

> In the same way that the severe lines of a bare mountain, suggesting simplicity and leanness, evoke equivalent actions on the moral plane, so do the lines of Picasso, as he has developed them across the astonishing trajectory of his work, teach us

---

[101] The tension between history and the individual, as it manifests itself in Elytis's poetry, is extensively discussed in Chapter 5, especially as it pertains to his collections *The Axion Esti* and *The Little Seafarer*.
[102] Elytis, *Εν Λευκώ*, p. 206.
[103] Elytis, *Εν Λευκώ*, p. 207.
[104] See Odysseus Elytis, "Equivalences chez Picasso," ed. E. Teriade, *Verve: revue artistique et littéraire* VII, no. 25–6 (1951), pp. 35–44.

the adventure and the enchanted discovery of the world and demand that we arrive at the realization of its poetical potential outside of all preconceived notions.[105]

What Elytis proposes here is evidently metaphysical: he argues that a bare mountain suggests simplicity and leanness and that the same "metaphorical" relationship exists between a work of art and the moral plane. This anthropomorphic transposition of the natural, or the artistic object, shatters, according to Elytis, all preconceived notions of reality. In the case of Picasso, the transposition is experienced in the presentation of the object in its multidimensional ontology: the viewer perceives the object of the painting from various angles, light and colors interact with the objects, and time is condensed to the single artistic moment when the object "is suddenly encircled, attacked from all sides, not knowing where to flee."[106] In the case of the natural object, i.e., the bare mountain, understanding how this transposition occurs is more difficult, and Elytis does not provide us, in "Equivalences chez Picasso," with a further clarification. One wonders, for example, which theoretical principles allow the poet to discern a specific "ethos" in the object of nature. The supposition is not only that human beings project meaning onto objects of nature, but that the objects of nature, too, may suggest a particular ethos; the interaction between man and nature is thus bi-directional. What we are presented with here are the first thoughts, the raw material, of the theory of Analogies that Elytis would crystallize, in later works, into a more precise and comprehensive philosophy.

In his interview with Ivar Ivask in March of 1972, Elytis reverts, once again, to painting in order to explain his use of the term "analogy":

> By "analogy" I mean here that, say, a line a painter draws is not limited to itself alone but has an "analogy" in the world of spiritual values. Seeing the mountains shaped this or that way must have an effect on the human spirit, must have its analogy.[107]

In the same way that Picasso's paintings do not simply mirror the external reality of the object, but rather reflect its internal essence, the specific shape of a mountain can have a similar effect on the human spirit.[108] Beyond the physicality of the

---

[105] Odysseus Elytis, "Picasso's Equivalences," *Books Abroad* 49, no. 4 (1975): 649–51, p. 650.

[106] Elytis, "Picasso's Equivalences," p. 649.

[107] Elytis, "On his Poetry," p. 632.

[108] In "Equivalences chez Picasso" Elytis describes the artist's studio in geographical terms: "Barely inside the refreshing shade of the Vallauris studios, one feels seized by the same gust of wind which, as often happens along the Mediterranean, makes the waters rise under a furious sun and fills up the deserted coast with all kinds of significant objects: an old basket, some bits of branches, an empty tin can, two half broken pitchers" (Elytis, "Picasso's Equivalences," p. 650). The description points to Elytis's belief in the inseparability of art and nature.

perceived object, be it mountains or paintings, Elytis is interested here in the reciprocal response between the object of nature and the perceiver. When one gazes at a bare mountain, the mountain gazes back. More precisely, the mountain was gazing at him before he had even laid his eyes upon it, since the physiognomy of a particular geographical space defines the parameters of experience to a considerable extent: before the perceiver gazed at it, the arid landscape, the scorching sun, the arctic snow, the green prairies had already defined his perception of nature and even his way of life. Furthermore, geography has influenced language—i.e., that system of signifiers, as Jacques Lacan puts it, through which humans enter into the world.[109]

The term "analogy" then refers to the ability of the human mind to transpose the physical or geographical phenomena onto spiritual values that are already inherent in their existence. The complicated relationship between nature and the human spirit fascinated Elytis from a young age. In *Open Papers* he describes his first exploration of Greek nature in the old Chevrolet of a friend in the early 1930s: "… the way in which I perceived nature resulted in a concept beyond nature. From vision came a sensation and the sensation led back to a vision. This movement was very important. I mean, the reciprocal movement of the soul, or, in a different way, the ceaseless movement within the Fixed and the Eternal."[110] In 1944, at the end of the German occupation of Athens, Elytis returned to this reciprocal movement between the subject and the object (of nature) in his essay "The Girls":

> Some verses and a space is what always remains from each poet. When you turn your lens toward them, what you perceived as trees, mountains, rivers, seem to move, change shape, dissolve, become what they were from the outset: simple, condensed sensations. This bay is a shudder, this shadow a lump in the throat, the running water is a solace. Sensation then is substituted by sentiment. Then—if the contemplation continues—sentiment is substituted by free associations with a plethora of images where the life of each person, without his knowledge, projects the life of other people. The metamorphosis of the "natural space" into "human" [space] is verified as in a theorem.[111]

Finally, in his 1995 *The Garden of Self-Deceptions*, the last collection of essays Elytis published before his death, he further comments on the relation between matter and mental phenomena:

---

[109] As we will soon examine, Edward Sapir goes to the extent of arguing that if we had at our disposal the complete thesaurus of a language, "we might to a large extent infer the character of the physical environment and the characteristics of the culture making use of it." Edward Sapir, *Selected Writings of Edward Sapir* (Berkeley and Los Angeles: University of California Press, 1951), p. 91.

[110] Elytis, *Ανοιχτά Χαρτιά*, p. 327.

[111] Elytis, *Ανοιχτά Χαρτιά*, p. 174.

Here, at this point, one can easily discern the dual essence of the material and mental phenomena. In the same way a part of matter partakes in another, or a thought partakes in the more general system of ideas that embodies it, so do both of these [Matter and Thought] partake interchangeably in one another.[112]

The theory is founded precisely on the ability of matter to influence and participate in thought.

Elytis explores the process by which this exchange is achieved: that is, the reciprocal movement between the perceiver's emotional world and the natural object. His description distinguishes three movements between the subject and the object. First, the subject perceives the object's gaze. This gaze evokes a particular emotional response that, in turn, leads back to a vision. This threefold movement between the subject and the object is intimately connected to Elytis's distinction between the "three states of reality."[113] The first state describes the existence of the object as part of a visual or representable entity. This is the visible reality that modernism, fueled in many instances by psychoanalysis, attacked on all sides. The second state describes the invisible reality of the object inherent in its ability to affect the subject. Elytis calls this a "hyper-real state" that is more real than the first[114] and he considers deviation from current reality as "the characteristic that describes the race of poets."[115] The third state is the poetic state and concerns the correspondence of language with the perceived natural object:

> The poetic state ... is a third state that is not subject to the contradictions and distinctions of every day life. It is a para-semantic [state] marked with words but interpreted in the psyche with vibrations whose impact reaches far ... into something that is completely unrelated to the original meaning of the words.[116]

In "The Chronicle of a Decade" he once more uses the term "para-semantic"[117] to describe the relationship between nature and language: "a landscape is not simply the sum of trees and mountains but a multi-signifying para-semantic; it is not simply the sum of a few words—symbols of objects—but a moral force mobilized by the human intellect ...."[118] Elytis regards nature as "embedded with secret messages," and views poetry as the "mechanism that deconstructs man and his relationship to objects."[119] In other words, poetry serves to unveil the "secret

---

[112] Elytis, *Εν Λευκώ*, p. 447.
[113] The three states of reality were summarized earlier in this chapter.
[114] Elytis, *Ανοιχτά Χαρτιά*, p. 117.
[115] Elytis, *Ανοιχτά Χαρτιά*, p. 10.
[116] Elytis, *Ανοιχτά Χαρτιά*, p. 11.
[117] "Para-semantic" (παρασημαντική): Elytis refers to the understanding of a word *beyond* (παρά) its conventional signification or meaning.
[118] Elytis, *Ανοιχτά Χαρτιά*, p. 328.
[119] Elytis, *Ανοιχτά Χαρτιά*, pp. 327–8.

messages," precisely by deconstructing and reframing man's relationship to the objects of nature. In its innermost essence, the theory of Analogies is a poetic effort in transposition that attempts to deconstruct, decode, and eventually reconstruct the world. The poem, the final product of this transposition, reveals a truth that is more "objective" than the object of nature itself. The subject merely perceives the form of the natural object. Poetry, by contrast, presents the material substance of this object at the moment it interacts with the subject's senses.

In his writings, Elytis often tries to offer concrete examples in order to clarify the theory of Analogies. In his 1979 Nobel address he argued that the only remaining common language among poets is that of the senses. "And when I speak of the senses," he continued, "I mean the 'analogies of the senses' to the spirit. All arts speak with analogies. A smell can be a swamp or purity. The straight line or the curve, the high or low pitch comprise translations of a visual or acoustic contact."[120] In his 1990 collection of essays *The Public and the Private*, he claims that the meaning of "innocence" is found most lucidly in "fragrant herbs"; "cleanliness" and "diaphaneity" in a "shining drop of water"; "purification"; and "spiritual candor" in "lime."[121] The senses in this process do not simply serve to construct percepts of natural objects; rather, they create certain impressions, which in turn lead to the formation of a particular ethos. The relationship between "innocence" and a "fragrant herb" is not a metaphorical one; the object is not a representation of its impression, but rather, the object contains the impression.[122] Similarly, it is the object's ability to carry the essence of an impression which, in the final analysis, infuses it with meaning. In this sense, the object becomes the instigator of meaning, albeit unbeknownst to the subject. It is precisely this secret aspect of nature as a carrier of meaning—which directly affects the subject—that the poet is trying to uncover.

In 1982 Elytis published the short collection *Three Poems Under a Flag of Convenience*, where each of the three poems focuses on a central theme. The title of each poem is a phrase, or word, repeated in each of the seven subsections of the poems.[123] "The Garden Gazes" is the collection's first poem and has the same title as one of Elytis's collages. The 1967 collage depicts a wide-open eye peering through an abstract arrangement of pink flowers, probably roses, which surround the eye and cover the entire canvas. At a closer look, however, one is able to discern a number of other eyes, or oval-shaped objects, also peering through the flowers, as well as two small abstract geometrical shapes at the point where a vertical and a horizontal line meet. An excerpt from the first section

---

[120] Elytis, *Εν Λευκώ*, p. 359.

[121] Elytis, *Εν Λευκώ*, p. 374.

[122] Elytis, *Ανοιχτά Χαρτιά*, p. 176.

[123] The three themes are: "The Garden Gazes" ("ο Κήπος Βλέπει"—Jeffrey Carson and Nikos Sarris translate this as "The Garden Sees"), "The Almond of the World" ("Το Αμύγδαλο του Κόσμου"), and "Ad Libitum" (the title is used in the original Latin and it means "At one's pleasure" or "as one wishes").

of the poem, composed 15 years after the creation of the collage, reveals the collage's close relation to the concept Elytis is exploring:

> reality
> doesn't care
> who has good use of the perishable part
> and who of the other
>
> tipped-down arrows and tipped-up arrows
> have never met
>
> *the garden sees*
>
> hears the sounds from the colors
> iridescence that a caress
> leaves
> on the naked body the moment
> myriad threads draw it
> aloft
> the messages rage
> what to do about it
> no one knows
>
> we remain like some wireless
> abandoned in the wilderness and out of action for centuries
> the waves struggling desperately to find a receiver [124]

In their most general understanding, both the collage and the poem represent a reaffirmation of the Baudelairean position of nature as a locus of secret messages or, in Baudelaire's own words, that there are "forests of symbols between us and the shrine [of Nature]." The gaze of the object, which appears as a constant theme in Elytis's work, also points to a much deeper concept: in both the collage and the poem, the signifying object, in this case the garden, gazes back independently of the subject's reception of the gaze. The image is playing an uncanny trick on the viewer: the incorporated hidden glances appear only if he looks closely enough. The poem echoes this position: the waves of the garden, these raging messages, desperately struggle to find a receiver.

In *The Four Fundamental Concepts of Psychoanalysis*, Jacques Lacan famously uses the example of Hans Holbein's painting "The Ambassadors" to

---

[124] Elytis, *Collected Poems*, p. 372. η πραγματικότητα / δεν ενδιαφέρεται / ποιος νέμεται το μέρος το φθαρτό / και ποιος το άλλο / τα βέλη προς τα κάτω και τα βέλη προς τα επάνω / δε συναντήθηκαν ποτέ / *ο κήπος βλέπει* / ακούει τους ήχους απ' τα χρώματα / τους ιριδισμούς που ένα χάδι / αφήνει / πάνω στο σώμα το γυμνό την ώρα / που το τραβούν μυριάδες νήματα / ψηλά / μαίνονται τα μηνύματα / τι να το κάνεις / δε νογά κανείς / μένουμε σαν ασυρματοφόρα / παρατημένα μες στην έρημο και αχρηστευμένα εδώ κι αιώνες / απελπιστικά παλεύοντας τα κύματα / να βρούνε δέκτη (Elytis, *Ποίηση*, p. 442).

describe the gazing force inherent in the image.[125] The two figures depicted in this painting "are frozen, stiffened in their showy adornments."[126] The peculiar blot in the lower center of the painting seems to escape the viewer's notice until he apprehends that, seen from a particular angle, this blot is in fact a skull. The "singular object floating in the foreground" Lacan says, "is there to be looked at, in order to catch, I would almost say, *to catch in its trap*, the observer, that is to say us."[127] This enigmatic object "reflects our own nothingness in the figure of the death's head."[128] Upon perceiving the skull the viewer finds himself in an uncanny state—the picture has fooled him, it has stripped him of his power over the object and voyeuristically gazed at him without his knowledge. It has made him aware of his inability to see the picture from the picture's standpoint, it has gained control of his power of vision and has brutally illustrated to him that he may see the image but he is missing the *gaze* of the object. As Lacan puts it, "The picture is certainly in my eye. But I am not in the picture."[129]

According to Lacan, we form a notion of our identity only through the *symbolic order*. The term is closely related to the Saussurean "signifier": the radical representation of the object (i.e., that which is possible to represent) as the subject perceives it (usually through language). Language provides the dynamic field in which the exchange between the "self" and the "other" can take place. The child enters the world through language and understands himself/herself only in relation to the other. *Reality* in this context is always subject to the limitations of our scopic field, and is nothing but an interplay between the subject and the symbolic order (what is in fact *Real* for Lacan is that which lies outside the symbolic order and is thus forever unattainable/unassimilated).[130] To repeat Elytis once more: "aloft / the messages rage / what to do about it / no one knows / we remain like some wireless / abandoned in the wilderness and out of action for centuries / the waves struggling desperately to find a receiver." What we encounter here is the other side of

---

[125] Elytis could have been familiar with, at least, the general framework of Lacan's ideas, since his mentor and good friend Andreas Empeirikos had attended several of Lacan's seminars. He was certainly very familiar with Sartre's philosophy, upon which Lacan builds his concept of "the gaze." In 1950 Elytis met Sartre in Paris.

[126] Jacques Lacan, *The Four Fundamental Concepts of Psychoanalysis (The Seminars of Jacques Lacan, Book XI).*, trans. Alan Sheridan (New York: Norton, 1998), p. 88.

[127] Lacan, *Fundamental Concepts*, p. 92.

[128] Lacan, *Fundamental Concepts*, p. 92.

[129] Lacan, *Fundamental Concepts*, p. 96.

[130] The Lacanian *Imaginary, Symbolic,* and *Real*: The *Imaginary* is the register of conscious and unconscious images (i.e., dreams, fantasies, or ego images); the *Symbolic* is connected to the Saussurean "signifier": the radical representation of the object (i.e., that which it is possible to represent) as the subject perceives it (usually through speech and language). The *Real* is the most complicated of these terms and it stands "for what is neither symbolic nor imaginary, and remains foreclosed from the analytic experience, which is an experience of speech" (Alan Sheridan, "Translator's Note," in *The Four Fundamental Concepts of Psychoanalysis*, trans. Alan Sheridan (New York: Norton, 1998), p. 280.

Baudelairean correspondences: the *garden gazes* but we fail to decode the messages. What remains after "social struggles stop when inventions / put themselves out of action when all demands are satisfied"—in short, when the symbols through which life attains meaning collapse—is the "void" [κενό] of the Real.[131] Still, Elytis's poem seems to suggest that it is in this Real, the space beyond which the symbolic seizes to exist, that Poetry struggles to find its own meaning.

Since the symbolic order consists in the exchange between the subject and the object through the medium of language, the poetic devices of *metaphor* and *metonymy* are central in the Lacanian schema. To illustrate what he means by metonymy Lacan provides the words "thirty sails" as an example, and draws the following conclusion: "… if the thing is to be taken seriously, we are left with very little idea of the importance of this fleet, which 'thirty sails' is precisely supposed to give us: for each ship to have just one sail is in fact the least likely probability."[132] If metonymy is based on a *word-to-word* connection, metaphor is based on the *one word for another* formula.[133] It is "the precise point at which sense emerges from non-sense…. [It] is at this frontier that we realize that man defies his very destiny when he derides the signifier."[134] Most significantly, Lacan proceeds to designate surrealism as the literary school that provided us with the most profound examples of the metaphoric function:

> It should be said that modern poetry and especially the surrealist school have taken us a long way in this direction by showing that any conjunction of two signifiers would be equally sufficient to constitute a metaphor, except for the additional requirement of the greatest possible disparity of the images signified, needed for the production of the poetic spark, or in other words for metaphoric creation to take place.[135]

In his 1945 "Assessment and a New Beginning," Elytis identifies the same point as one of surrealism's greatest contributions: "The capturing and expression of the pleasant or dramatic aspect of life through the means of the co-presence of two or more objects, distant from the conventional perceptions."[136] Although Lacan emphatically dismisses the term *analogy* as too simplistic, the correspondence between his description of the metaphoric function and Elytis's theory of Analogies is evident. Elytis's theoretical language is, as he admits, far from the epistemological fixed terminology achieved by Bachelard.[137] In fact, the term *analogy* (αναλογία) is often interchanged with *equivalence* (αντιστοιχία)

---

[131] Elytis, *Collected Poems*, p. 372.
[132] Jacques Lacan, *Écrits*, trans. Alan Sheridan (New York: W.W. Norton & Company, 1977), p. 156.
[133] Jacques Lacan, *Écrits*, pp. 156–7.
[134] Jacques Lacan, *Écrits*, p. 158.
[135] Jacques Lacan, *Écrits*, p. 156.
[136] Elytis, *Ανοιχτά Χαρτιά*, p. 518.
[137] Elytis, *Ανοιχτά Χαρτιά*, p. 163.

and *correspondence* (ανταπόκριση); the term metaphor, in its surrealist use as the greatest possible disparity between the signifying objects, is also used in the same context as analogy (i.e., "the ability to recreate the world literally and metaphorically").[138] Elytis also shares Lacan's distinction between metaphor and metonymy. In "The Girls," he comments that the poets who use the formula "this is *like* that" (in Lacanian terms a *word-to-word* connection) base themselves on a simplistic imposition of their thought on the reader.[139] On the contrary, modern poetry functions in a more complex arrangement of words, where the "correspondences between two objects, that appear to be foreign to one another, create a new instantaneous state."[140]

"Modern poetry," writes Renato Poggioli in *The Theory of the Avant-Garde*, "to a great extent, is a real and true *metaphysics of metaphor*."[141] Metaphor is used as a means of negating conventional perceptions of the image. In its very essence, it expresses agonistic and nihilistic impulses:

> The analogy upon which modern metaphor is based is a hermetic and occult affinity, dreamed up by some wee devil like Mallarmé's *demon of analogy*. In it, every interior link is eliminated by means of a fantastic process tending to confound dimensions and categories. In the course of this process ... the image often aims at making itself an emblem or hieroglyphic, cipher or seal—briefly, it aims at realizing what Ortega defines as the *algebra of the metaphor*.... The modern metaphor tends to divorce the idea and the figure, to annul in the last-mentioned any reference to a reality other than its own self.[142]

Poggioli describes this attempt to "elevate metaphor to symbol and myth" as the inheritance of symbolism and finds its first expression in the poetry of Mallarmé. In his own essays, Elytis also emphasizes the influence of Mallarmé on the surrealists and connects him with the attempt to compose *pure poetry*. The concept of *pure poetry* was as central to the modernist discourse in Greece as it was in France. As Poggioli observes, the modern idea of poetic purity must be distinguished from "the classical and neoclassical need for elegance and correctness"; rather, "the modern mystique of purity aspires to abolish the discursive and syntactic element, to liberate art from any connection with psychological and empirical reality...."[143] In their metaphysical applications, Rimbaud's *hallucinatory poetics*, Breton's *dream poetry*, Dali's *paranoia criticism*, Mallarmé's *hyperbolic symbolism*, and the majority of modernist movements, incorporate modern metaphor in order to "purify" poetry from its inherited conventionalisms and truisms.

---

[138] Elytis, *Ανοιχτά Χαρτιά*, p. 36.
[139] Elytis, *Ανοιχτά Χαρτιά*, p. 176.
[140] Elytis, *Ανοιχτά Χαρτιά*, p. 177.
[141] Poggioli, *Avant-Garde*, p. 196. The italics are Poggioli's.
[142] Poggioli, *Avant-Garde*, p. 197.
[143] Poggioli, *Avant-Garde*, p. 201.

The poet, said André Breton in a 1935 lecture given in Prague, has one tool to separate himself from the writer of prose: "he has for that purpose one tool, and one tool only, capable of boring deeper and deeper, and that is the *image*, and among all types of images, *metaphor*."[144] The surrealist object breaks with external reality, sets up new relationships with other elements, and defines a metaphysical sphere that transposes our perception of reality. In "The Crisis of the Object," Breton further cites Bachelard's statement that "there is more to be found in the hidden real than in the immediate known quantity," and goes on to state that the surrealist course instigated "a total revolution of the object."[145] This is precisely what Elytis also proposes in his theory of Analogies: a revolution that causes the metaphorical reconstruction of the world. What is particularly interesting in Elytis's conception is that language, with its metaphorical dynamism, is not discussed only through its psychological implications (as in the case of Lacan), or as an aspect that describes the surrealist objective in its totality. Language is intimately linked to geography and, consequently, the metaphoric dynamism differs from language to language. In other words, in the theory of Analogies, the sounds of phonemes, the shape of the letters, the poetic combinations of words based on their acoustic correspondences, differ from one linguistic system to another and are contingent on geographical factors. To put it simply, if perception is mediated through language, then each linguistic system shapes humans' relationship to their natural surroundings in different ways.

Interestingly, the importance of the human experience with language in relation to specific linguistic systems has not been adequately addressed either by Freud or Lacan, and has even been peripheral to Breton's surrealist politics, which attempted to move within the more universal parameters of Marxism and Trotskyism. The American linguists Edward Sapir and Benjamin Whorf are credited for propagating the now controversial theory of linguistic determinism in suggesting that one cannot think without language and that linguistic systems, to a large extent, emerged from the interaction of humans with their geographical surroundings. It is uncertain as to whether Elytis was familiar with the work of Whorf and Sapir, but he certainly was familiar with a similar undertone in Heidegger's philosophy.[146]

---

[144] Breton, *Manifestoes*, p. 268.

[145] Ibid., p. 86.

[146] Anthony Wilden suggests that Sapir's discourse is "correlative to Heidegger's philosophical development of a similar concept in his distinction between αἴσθησης and λόγος" (Anthony Wilden, "Lacan and the Discourse of the Other," in *The Language of the Self: the Function of Language in Psychoanalysis*, trans. Anthony Wilden, 157–311 [Baltimore: John Hopkins University Press, 1981], p. 202). The supposition here is that there is an unambiguous relationship between language (λόγος) and sensation (αἴσθησης); once spoken of, the object comes into being and has the capacity to act upon the subject. Elytis's extensive use of Heidegger in his essays is always connected to poetic language and to an attempt to perceive objects of nature through what he calls "the royal path of the senses" (Elytis, *Ανοιχτά Χαρτιά*, p. 644).

The basic claim of the Sapir-Whorf hypothesis is that language influences perception and thought; it is a system of signifiers that, depending on the subject's surrounding environment, defines and directs human perception. Two classic and much quoted examples are commonly used to clarify the hypothesis: the abundance of words referring to snow in the Eskimo language, and the Hopi Indian perception of time in a relativistic, as opposed to temporal, fashion.[147] These examples suggest, for Sapir and Whorf, that the subject's perception of nature depends on the vocabulary and structure of his/her language, or, as Stuart Chase explains, that "the picture of the universe shifts from tongue to tongue."[148] In "Language and Environment" (1912), Sapir further suggests that if we follow the reverse route, from language to nature, we could reconstruct a tribe's surrounding social and physical environment:

> It is the vocabulary of a language that most clearly reflects the physical and social environment of its speakers. The complete vocabulary of a language may be looked upon as a complex inventory of all the ideas, interests, and occupations that take up the attention of the community, and were such a complete thesaurus of the language of a given tribe at our disposal, we might to a large extent infer the character of the physical environment and the characteristics of the culture of the people making use of it.[149]

---

[147] In using the Sapir-Whorf hypothesis I certainly do not mean to return to the theory of linguistic determinism that has been abandoned since the 1960s. A number of scholars, as early as the 1950s and 1960s, have discredited the theory (most notably Roger Brown, Eric Lenneberg, Brent Berlin, and Paul Kay), which asserts that the cultural concepts inherent in a language affect the speaker's *cognitive* experience of the world. Steven Pinker writes: "People who remember little else from their college education can rattle off the factoids: the languages that carve the spectrum into color words at different places, the fundamentally different Hopi concept of time, the dozens of Eskimo words for snow. The implication is heavy: the foundational categories of reality are not "in" the world but are imposed by one's culture (and hence can be challenged, perhaps accounting for the perennial appeal of the hypothesis to undergraduate sensibilities). But it is wrong, all wrong …. [I]f thoughts depended on words, how could a new word ever be coined? How could a child learn a word to begin with? How could translation from one language to another be possible" (Steven Pinker, *The Language Instinct: How the Mind Creates Language* [New York: Perennial Classics, 2000] pp. 46–7). To be clear, then, what I am maintaining here in returning to the Sapir-Whorf hypothesis is their emphasis, as it will become obvious in my discussion, on the relationship between geography, culture, and language. In other words, in the context of Elytis's theories, I am interested in the striking similarities between their hypothesis and his repeated attempts to link geography and language and discover the ways in which such a relationship becomes manifested culturally (*not* cognitively). Needless to say, such a position is overtly metaphysical.

[148] Stuart Chase, "Foreword," in *Language Thought and Reality*, v–x (Cambridge, Massachusetts: MIT Press, 1978), p. vi.

[149] Edward Sapir, *Selected Writings*, pp. 90–91.

The Sapir-Whorf hypothesis has two implications: First, that the mapping of language reveals the particular characteristics of the physical environment and, second, that the nature of the language affects the people making use of it, defining their perception of the world. It is in this context that Sapir suggests that we could infer, apart from the landscape, the *character* of the culture. The hypothesis sees the translation from one language to another as an impossible task. Similarly, Elytis sees language as a force that goes beyond the duality signifier/signified and points to a particular ethos that differs from language to language. "We know you and you know us from the 20% or, at best, 30% that is left after translation," he told the audience at the Stockholm Academy during the Nobel ceremony.[150] He was further convinced that certain Greek poets, like Solomos and Kalvos, remain unknown to foreign audiences because of the difficulties in translating them.[151]

Even though "all arts speak with analogies,"[152] poetry holds a special position in the system of analogies since it makes use of language and thus, as the Whorfian hypothesis also suggests, has a closer connection with the objects of nature. As Elytis writes, language "baptized" natural phenomena in a phonetic, conceptual, and representational way following an unavoidably natural process:

> ... The mouths that spoke in this specific manner ... unconsciously obey the particular radiance that natural phenomena assume in this specific region....
>
> The day I realized that *in the Greek language there is no chiaroscuro*[153] I realized how reasonable is our inability to accept the Renaissance and I saw the last obstacle that prevented me from understanding the deeper unity of art in the Ancient Greek, Byzantine and Modern years, disappear. The phenomenon of the Greek language took, in my eyes, the characteristics of the 'unavoidable' that describes natural phenomena; it was in such degree that I came to believe firmly that the most dim and evasive foreign language, after a millennium in this region, would see its nature change, its sounds rising to the larynx and descending from the nose to the oral cavity, the words losing their superfluous syllables, wash out in the light and become rounded, their essence cleansed in a way, if not exactly the same, similar to the Greek.[154]

For Elytis, it is the projected ethos of the landscape as transmitted by language that unifies Greek art from antiquity to the present, and not the misplaced and misinterpreted representations of the Renaissance that sought a superficial re-adaptation of Greek myth, art, literature, and philosophy. The unity he finds in the Greek language is founded on the understanding that Greeks can relate to their

---

[150] Elytis, *Ανοιχτά Χαρτιά*, p. 355.

[151] There is an apparent tension in this suggestion, namely between the inaccessibility of language and the forces of globalization. Elytis discussed this tension in the context of Greece's position in the European Union.

[152] Elytis, *Ανοιχτά Χαρτιά*, p. 357.

[153] Italics are Elytis's emphasis.

[154] Elytis, *Ανοιχτά Χαρτιά*, pp. 28–9.

geographical surroundings through a linguistic system that, above and beyond the necessary changes it sustained, largely shared the same etymology and phonemes throughout its recorded history. Like George Seferis before him, he perceives a distinctiveness in the phenomenon of the Greek language, "in which objects have not changed possessors for thousands of years."[155]

The theory of Analogies approaches the relationship between Landscape and Language from an abstract metaphysical and phenomenological point of view. In the first stage, the impact of natural phenomena on people of a particular geographical region caused their constant naming and renaming through the prism of human perception and experience with them. In the second stage, this interaction between man and nature shaped the collective psyche of a people in an *introjective* process based on the ability of these phenomena to stir the sensory and emotional responses of humans. In the third stage, language made possible the *projection* of this emotional state onto the artistic level, where the deeper essence of these phenomena is revealed. It is from this angle that Elytis states the most emphatic metaphysical inference of the theory—namely, that a landscape is "the projection of a people's soul on matter,"[156] and that language often directs the concepts it expresses more than being directed by them.[157]

Language is discussed here in its visual, phonological, and signifying qualities. The "Aegean soil," Elytis writes in *The Public and the Private*, "has established an orthography where every omega, every upsilon, every accent, every subscript, is nothing more than a bay, a slope, a vertical rock on the curve of a ship's stern, wavy vineyards, lintels of churches, red or white, here and there from pigeon lofts and geranium pots."[158] He speaks of the close association of the Greek language with what he calls "first meanings"[159] and affirms his interest "in the mystery of the birth of things through that rejoicing of the soul which is the vocal sound."[160] Unlike Ezra Pound who, influenced by the work of Ernest Fenollosa, developed the *ideogrammic method* based on the relationship between image and meaning in Chinese calligraphy, Elytis is more interested in the association between the ontology of the word (i.e., the complex relationship between its visual image, sound, and meaning) with the emotional response it stimulates in the subject.

---

[155] Elytis, *Εν Λευκώ*, p. 469.
[156] Elytis, *Εν Λευκώ*, p. 365.
[157] Elytis, *Ανοιχτά Χαρτιά*, p. 329.
[158] Elytis, *Εν Λευκώ*, pp. 365–6.
[159] Elytis, *Εν Λευκώ*, p. 329.
[160] Elytis, *Εν Λευκώ*, p. 441. The inability to discern a clear pattern between the phonetic composition of a word and the value or meaning it represents, places any discussion of the subject in the metaphysical realm. One should note that Sapir explores this relationship in at least five papers: "Language" (1933), "Sound Patterns in Language" (1925), The "Psychological Reality of Phonemes" (1933), "A Study in Phonetic Symbolism" (1929), and "The Concept of Phonetic Law as Tested in Primitive Languages by Leonard Bloomfield" (1931).

Undoubtedly, Elytis's poetry is characterized by a distinctive visual and acoustic strictness particularly related to the phonetic experience. The combination of words is often determined by their phonetic value: e.g., the sounds of "ρ" and the accented "ά" in "το τετράφυλλο δάκρυ" (*Axion Esti*, Psalm E);[161] the sounds of "μ" and "ρ" in "Μακρινή Μητέρα Ρόδο μου Αμάραντο" (*Axion Esti*, Psalm I);[162] the sounds of "θ" and "σ" combined with open vowels in "Γι' αυτό θρυλούσε η θάλασσα" (*The Light Tree*, "Delos");[163] the consonants "ρ" and "κ" combined with the vowel "α" and the endings "η" and "ω" in "Μικρή πράσινη θάλασσα δεκατριώ χρονώ" (*The Light-tree*, "Little Green Sea").[164] In other instances, Elytis uses abstract combinations of letters to imitate sound. The following excerpts from "Three times the truth," from *The Light-tree*, illustrate Elytis's use of sound and voice in connection with meaning and the aesthetic order of words:

> The wild bird transposed the truth pit pit among the boulders   It kept nibbling tlip tlip at the briny water in the rock pools
> [...]
> I lived on nothing   Only the words didn't suffice me   In passing air   my ears spinning out an otherworldly voice   *fchia fchiu fchiou*   I thought up so many things   What handfuls of polished stones   what baskets of fresh bees and what water jugs where you hear the captive air thunder *vvvv*
>
> [...] I reached the point of imprinting the waves from the tongue to the hearing
> —Hey black poplars I cried and you blue trees what do you know of me?—*thoi thoi thmos*—Hey? what?—*Arieo ethymos thmos*—I didn't hear   what is it?— *Thmos Thmos adhysos*
>
> Until at the end I felt   and let them call me crazy   that from nothing comes Paradise."[165]

The declaration "I reached the point of imprinting the waves from the tongue to the hearing," demonstrates Elytis's use of language in both its phonetic and signifying qualities. The analogy between sound, phonetic sequence and meaning

---

[161] "The four leaf tear-drop" (Elytis, *Collected Poems*, p. 153).
[162] "My distant Mother * Rose Unwithering" (Elytis, *Collected Poems*, p. 169).
[163] "And this sea was legending" (Elytis, *Collected Poems*, p. 209).
[164] "Little Green Sea thirteen years old" (Elytis, *Collected Poems*, p. 218).
[165] Elytis, *Collected Poems*, pp. 211–12. Μετατόπιζε το αγριοπούλι πιτ πιτ πάνω στους βράχους την αλήθεια Μες στις γούβες τ' αρμυρό νερό τλιπ τλιπ όλο τσιμπολογούσε [...] Μ' ένα τίποτα έζησα   Μονάχα οι λέξεις δε μου αρκούσανε   Σ' ενός περάσματος αέρα ξεγνέθοντας απόκοσμη φωνή τ' αυτιά μου   φχια φχιου φχιου   εσκαρφίστηκα τα μύρια όσα   Τι γυαλόπετρες φούχτες   τι καλάθια φρέσκες μέλισσες και σταμνιά φουσκωτά όπου άκουγες ββββ να σου βροντάει ο αιχμάλωτος αέρας [...] Έφτασα κι αποτύπωνα τα κύματα στην ακοή απ' τη γλώσσα / – Ε καραβάκια μαύρα   φώναζα   κι εσείς γαλάζια δέντρα τι ξέρετε από μένα;– Θόη θόη θμός – Ε, τι; – Αρίηω ηθυμώς   θμος- Δεν άκουσα   τι πράγμα;– Θμός θμός άδυσος / Ώσπου τέλος ένιωσα   κι ας πα' να μ' έλεγαν τρελό   πως από 'να τίποτα γίνεται ο Παράδεισος. Elytis, *Ποίηση*, pp. 208–9.

in this poem exemplifies his perception of language as a vast system of phonetic combinations that poetry deconstructs in the process of redefinition. Abstract sounds are often followed by words of the same letter [αγριοπούλι, πιτ τιτ, πάνω, or ββββ, βροντάει (wild bird, pit pit, among, or vvvv, thunder)];[166] the sound *vvvv* is connected to both the "fresh bees" and the "captive air"; the indecipherable sounds "thoi," "thmos," "ethymos," and "adhysos" point to other approximations in the Greek language, the most apparent of which is "adhysos" (άδυσος), which sounds like "abyssos" (άβυσσος, abyss). Finally, the rhyme of "Adhysos" with the last word of the poem, "Paradise" (Παράδεισος), further creates a tension in the binary "Paradise-Abyss," and is connected to the more general search for truth that the poem seeks to attain.[167]

Another technique that Elytis uses is anagrammatism, which is employed in order to capture things at the moment of their birth and give an aura of mystery to the discovery of the word. In the "Genesis" of *The Axion Esti*, six anagrams are used in capital letters: ROES, ESA, ARIMNA, NUS, MORILMATITY, YELTIS.[168] Their decoding reveals the sequence: Eros, Sea, Marina, Sun, Immortality, and Elytis.[169] These are all central concepts that Elytis explores not only in *The Axion Esti*, but also throughout his work. In Greek, they also point to playful approximations that reinforce their signifying value: ROES (ΡΩΕΣ) sounds like "flow" or "stream" (ροή) and apart from "Eros" it could also be decoded as "hours" (ΩΡΕΣ); ESA (ΑΛΑΣΘΑΣ) approximates the beginning of the word "inerrable" (Αλάνθαστος);[170] ARIMNA (ΑΡΙΜΝΑ), a name (Marina) that Elytis always associates with the sea since its *etymological meaning* is "of the sea," approximates the word "stern" (πρύμνα); MORILMATITY (ΑΪΑΣΑΝΘΑ) combines two words: the first half sounds like "eternally" (αεί); the second half of the word approximates "blossoms" (άνθη). The significance of these words in the context of "Genesis" in *The Axion Esti* is paramount. Emulating a biblical tone, the section begins with the birth (genesis) of things in the poet's perception and his eventual discovery of the world through the creative process.[171] These anagrams deconstruct the world in order to rediscover it. The world exists because the poet

---

[166] Of course, the phonetic play with words in the original Greek cannot be conveyed in the English translation.

[167] For further examples of this technique see the following poems: "Yellow" (in "Variations on a Sunbeam" of *Sun the First*), "The Red Horse" and "The Two of the World" (in *The Light-Tree*), and "Helen of Crete" (in *Stepchildren*).

[168] Elytis, *Collected Poems*, p. 128.

[169] One should recall that the name "Elytis" is also a self-coined term.

[170] In *Maria Nephele* Elytis writes in an epigraph: "A wrong sea cannot be."

[171] "Genesis" begins with the following lines: "In the Beginning the light And the first hour / when lips still in clay / taste the things of the world." For another interesting example of anagrammatism in Elytis's poetrym, see "The Presence" in *Maria Nephele*, where the anagram "ARIMNA EPHE EL" appears.

perceives it, or, as Elytis writes, citing Martin Heidegger, "only poetically, man inhabits the world."[172]

Artistic analogies always imply a deciphering process. Apart from these three techniques, Elytis employs other methods where meaning is associated with the deciphering of language. Poem 11 of *The Little Seafarer* imitates the appearance of Classical inscriptions; it appears only in capital letters and has no spaces or punctuation. The implications of the technique are multiple: the reader is put in the position of examining the poem as an archaeologist who has discovered an ancient papyrus. The order of words in the poem can take on a different meaning according to where the reader chooses to place punctuation marks. In the same collection, Elytis lists all the words that the Seafarer carries in his traveling bag in alphabetical order. These are words that Elytis finds aesthetically and phonetically attractive. Each word, in this case, bears the weight of its own meaning without having been incorporated into a poetic system. In poem 2, Elytis delves further into the deconstruction of language, citing seven letters and describing the associations they produce based on their sound or appearance: "Lambda" is wet, "R" is child-like, "E" is all wind, etc. Put together, the letters make the word "ALGREUS," which can have several other approximations in Greek (i.e., salt, chase/hunt, farm/field, pain).[173] These playful correspondences bring to mind Rimbaud's poem "Voyelles" where, in a similar process, vowels are associated with colors and images.[174] Finally, Elytis often subjects language to mathematical formulations. Poem XIV of *The Little Seafarer*, for example, consists of seven mathematical formulas from "the school of the sea."[175] Also, the poems in the collection

---

[172] Elytis, *Εν Λευκώ*, p. 174.

[173] Jeffrey Carson suggests three associations in his footnote to the translation of the poem: "salt" (als), "chase hunt" (agra), and "farm-field" (agros). Another association is the word "algos," which is an Ancient Greek word that means "pain."

[174] A noir, E blanc, I rouge, U vert, O bleu: voyelles, / Je dirai quelque jour vos naissances latentes: / A, noir corset velu des mouches éclatantes / Qui bombinent autour des puanteurs cruelles [A black, E white, I red, U Green, O blue: vowels, / One day I will tell you of your latent birth: / A, black hairy corset of shining flies / Which buzz around cruel stench]. Arthur Rimbaud, *Complete Works, Selected Letters*, trans. Wallace Fowlie (Chicago: University of Chicago Press, 1966), pp. 120–21.

[175] Here are some examples:
- "If you take Greece apart, in the end you will see remaining to you an olive tree, a vineyard, and a ship. Which means: with just so much you can put her back together."
- "Where fig trees are is Greece. Where the mountain extends beyond the word mountain is the poet. Sensual pleasure is no subtrahend."
- "Every progress on the ethical level can only be in inverse proportion to the ability of power and number to determine our fate." From *The Little Seafarer*, Poem XIV, Elytis, *Collected Poems*, p. 457.

Maria Nephele are accompanied by short epigraphs of mathematical precision.[176] In assuming the structure of mathematical formulae, the poems are offered as true, or objective, correlations; analogies are presented as proven equations.

Even after the reformation of Greek Grammar in the 1980s, when the complex accents, breath marks, and iota subscripts of ancient Greek were omitted as unnecessary (except for the sign indicating the principal accent), Elytis kept using all of these, and also many of the endings of Ancient Greek. In his short essay "For the Optics of Sound" he launches into a caustic critique of the omission of the breath marks and the final "ν" [n] in modern Greek as well as of the use of foreign words on the signs of Athenian stores. As odd as this may sound for a poet with surrealist influences, it points to the fact that Elytis was interested in the complete experience of language, where the appearance of the word cannot be neglected. "My apologies, but you never allow your underwear to show. But still, you wear it," he writes in a sarcastic tone, and proceeds to make an analogy with a eunuch who frequents the Sultan's harems with pride, even if he is missing something.[177]

Matei Calinescu argues that modernism tends towards radicalism "in both political thinking and aesthetics":

> ... politically independent artists, and even some of the staunchest defenders of purist doctrines, were often tempted to borrow terms from the language of radicalism and use them in condemning the "official" culture of their time, with all its aesthetic and other taboos. Thus towards the end of the nineteenth century, some of the most significant artistic statements contained notions directly derived from the vocabulary of politics. The most convincing example is perhaps Mallarmé's view, expressed in an important interview with Jules Huret (1891), that the modern poet is, simply and emphatically, "on strike against society."[178]

Modernist movements such as dadaism and surrealism continued this polemic against the "official" culture even more emphatically, by rejecting official language

---

[176] Here are some examples:
- "Superstition brought to a mathematical clarity would help us perceive the deeper structure of the world." From *Maria Nephele*, Elytis, *Collected Poems*, p. 313.
- "One 'makes' the truth exactly as one makes the lie." Elytis, *Collected Poems*, p. 332.

[177] Elytis, *Εν Λευκώ*, pp. 318–19. Careful planning and a strict structural presentation characterize all of Elytis's poetry collections. The number of poems included in these collections is always a multiple of seven; they are usually accompanied by the paintings of well-known artists (Tsarouchis, Moralis, Ghika, Pownall) or photographs. The most characteristic indication of Elytis's meticulousness was the delay of the publication of *Ποίηση*. As was mentioned earlier, according to the poet's companion, Ioulita Iliopoulou, Elytis wanted his complete poems to be a small publication—small enough to fit in the school bag of a young girl. The collection was eventually published in 2002 and numbers close to 700 pages, but it is remarkably compact.

[178] Calinescu, *Five Faces*, pp. 107–8.

as a conventional construct of a dying aristocratic world; hence, writes Richard Sheppard, "the Modernist poet ceases to be the manipulator of fixed *quanta* and attempts to liberate the repressed expressive energies of language."[179] Metaphor, in this context—in its Baudelairean and Symbolist use—allows for the reconstruction of the world and makes poetry possible at a time when language, in its official use, deemed it impotent.

In the case of Greece, this conflict between traditional, or official, language and modern poetic language created an even more dichotomous tension. Modern Greek poets did not reject tradition to the same extent that their French counterparts did; in fact, even the most adamant supporters of surrealism in Greece, in the 1930s, insisted on the potential of the movement to reenergize Greek tradition. Suffice it to say that Elytis spoke, in the 1940s, of surrealism's capacity to utilize the animate elements of Greek tradition and rebaptize them through modern means of expression, and that Empeirikos—the forerunner of Greek surrealism—favored and used *katharevousa* instead of the demotic language. At the same time, Greek modernist poets maintained their harsh polemic against the established literary traditions and pledged their loyalty to the revolutionary ideas of surrealism.[180] The disparity between tradition and modernity is evident in Elytis's poetry, which centers on the theme of "Greekness" but uses the linguistic tools of modern poetry. In the 1980 National Greek Television documentary dedicated to his work, Elytis extensively discusses this disparity:

> In many people's eyes, my dedication to "Greekness," on one hand and to a modern revolutionary movement on the other seemed like a contradiction. But deep down it wasn't.
>
> At the precise moment ... when we were looking to find the true face of Greece, to purge it from the distortions brought about by the Renaissance, the revolutionary inheritors of the Renaissance emerged and attacked the negative part of their inheritance. This was certainly of great help to us.
>
> In this way we managed to better see our true identity. And we must understand this well. That is, what we admire in Classical Greek art is not that which the Westerners continued in the metopes of their palaces. It is this: Greekness as a way of seeing and constructing things was continued exclusively by our folk tradition. I mean to say that the courtyard of a house, with its stone steps, with the whitewashed walls, with the geraniums in the tin cans, or the yard of a

---

[179] Richard Sheppard, "The Crisis of Language," p. 329.

[180] In the decade 1935–1945, Elytis openly attacked many conservative academicians and opened several dialogues with established poetic circles: he attacked E. Liakakos, Napoleon Lapathiotis, Ch. Levantas, and Michael Rodas as ignorant, and Leuteris Alexiou, Yiannis Sfakianakis, Vas. Dedousis, and P. Stasinopoulou as paranoid. He launched a caustic critique against N.P. Papas and Markos Avgeris, and attempted to answer Angelos Sikelianos and Takis Papatzonis's reservations towards surrealism. Finally, he opened productive dialogues, in the form of open letters, with Theotokas, Papanoutsos, and Tsatsos.

monastery with the well, the cells, and the arches, is closer to the spirit that gave birth to Apollos and Nikes or Theometors [Blessed Virgins] and Saints than the pastoral scenes and the pink little angels made by the Renaissance masters.[181]

The attempt to understand national identity is certainly a rare occurrence in the evolution of European modernism; few modernist poets in the West were interested in adopting modernist tools to explore the concept of ethnicity. At the same time, as Malcolm Bradbury suggests, to speak of modernism as a collective term independently of the cities in which it developed, overlooks the importance of the traditional elements vibrant in the cultural exchange of modernist cities.[182] The cultural diversity of Paris, New York, Zürich, Berlin, and Vienna did not exist to the same degree in the more homogeneous Athens, where the vast majority of artists and writers were Greek and where the dominant language of expression was also Greek. One may argue that the fixation of Greek modernism on national identity was an immediate result of a peripheral culture trying to recognize, or authenticate itself. This claim, however, would be neglecting the revolutionary nature of Greek modernism, which used a similar polemic as its European counterpart. Foreign critics have been perplexed, according to Elytis, with the fact that Greek poets, "independently to which generation or period they belong, are always concerned with their land [τόπος]."[183] Greece, for Elytis, is a symbol always explored in the linguistic ethos (in its metaphorical or metaphysical essence), a symbol that reveals particular sensations, perceptions, images, and always points to the ever-present locus of Greek nature.

The "Greekness" often ascribed to his poetry has made Elytis uneasy, to say the least, since it was accompanied with an oversimplification of the deeper ideas and metaphysical qualities in his thought. The setting to music of *The Axion Esti* by Mikis Theodorakis in 1964, and the awarding of the Nobel Prize in 1979, added to Elytis's popularity, raising him to the status of a "national poet." During the 1967–1974 dictatorship, the songs from *The Axion Esti* (especially "A Solitary Swallow" and "O Sun of Justice in the Mind") were often sung as a form of resistance to the fascist regime. To this date, children and youth choirs sing these songs in Greek schools as an important part of musical and literary history. Astonishingly, even the political and religious establishments quote Elytis's poetry, ironically neglecting the poet's evident dismissal of politics as corrupt, and his intrepid use of icons and religious texts. His incorporation in popular culture is even more astounding when one considers the difficulty of his texts; it is hardly possible to think of a similar case in world literature where a poet of surrealist influence and using such abstract language has been incorporated, to this extent, into the public sphere. The greatest affliction that Elytis's poetry has suffered has certainly been the stereotypical characterizations of the poet as an "optimist" (neglecting the fact

---

[181] Elytis, *Αυτοπροσωπογραφία*, pp. 21–2.
[182] Bradbury, "Cities of Modernism," pp. 95–8.
[183] Elytis, *Ανοιχτά Χαρτιά*, p. 330.

that the concept of death permeates his poetry), or as "the poet of the Aegean" (neglecting the fact that Elytis's Greece is a metaphysical abstract locus of ideas unrelated to ethnocentric themes).

Throughout his life, Elytis adamantly defended his poetry against easy interpretations. Three passages, the first from an interview with Ivar Ivask, the second from "The Chronicle of a Decade," and the third from "First Things First—Poetry," reveal Elytis's disdain for stereotypical characterizations and his attempt to clarify his use of the Greek language and landscape:

> I would like to discuss another matter with you, namely, my Greekness. This is for me not a national or local thing. I have never been a chauvinist in any way. Greece represents for me certain values and elements which can enrich universal spirits everywhere. Being Greek, I try to present precisely these values on a universal level. It is not a nationalistic bent which animates me to do this. To understand all this better I have developed a theory of Analogies.[184]

> I have never been a patriot or a nature-lover and I was perplexed when I saw these characterizations attributed to me; I was as perplexed as someone who, in older times, inferred the existence of electricity by observing storms, and people around him called him an 'Autumn Romantic' would be. I was incapable, it seems, of detaching the sense from its object and presenting all its derivatives in the realm of the spirit.[185]

> In literature, and especially in modern poetry, such a mentality—so elementary that it can only distinguish things as black or white—has managed, as in an identical mold, to issue a plethora of replicas: if you don't whine then you are eudaemonist or blissful; if you don't recount your sorrow you don't have any, you are carefree; if you speak about Greece, you are a provincial, you don't possess a universal spirit; if you care about your language, you are backward, outside the pulse of your time; finally, if you ask to make something solid, you are a formalist and an esthete.[186]

Elytis proposes the theory of Analogies as an answer to his being characterized as a nature lover, a provincial, and a nationalist. It is important to remember that his comments come as a response to a rapidly globalizing postwar Europe, when the future of minor languages, like Greek, was being threatened by the practical necessity for a European lingua franca. Poets concerned with the themes of Nature, landscape, and local language seemed out of touch with the pulse of the times. The concern for nature belonged to the eighteenth- and nineteenth-century European tradition; language was an issue the Greek poets had already resolved at the turn of the twentieth century, with the triumph of the popular demotic over the

---

[184] Elytis, "On his Poetry," p. 632.
[185] Elytis, *Ανοιχτά Χαρτιά*, p. 328.
[186] Elytis, *Ανοιχτά Χαρτιά*, p. 8.

purist *katharevousa*. To be concerned with the landscape of your country implied ignorance at one of the most important periods in the history of mankind.

For Elytis, the term "country" cannot be distinguished from the term "language." Political and historical definitions of what constitutes a nation, as Michel Foucault aptly pointed out, are bound to repress vital aspects of memory in order to represent a comprehensive and common identity of the nation. But, as Sapir claims, language contains a register of words that can present a more objective idea of identity. Elytis often points to the gap that exists between official definitions of the "nation" (as proposed, say, by politicians and historians) and the identity of the people that, he believes, could be more accurately explored through language (and, consequently, literature). In the essay *The Public and the Private*, he recalls returning home late at night and finding Mrs. Evgenia, who had prepared food for him, listening with religious devotion to some political leader speaking on the radio. "I am not sure she understands," he writes, "not because she is uneducated but because the speech does not have the required essential structure."[187] The language of politicians serves a political aim: it expresses a "point of view," where repetitions, omissions, generalizations, clichés, abstractness etc., are deliberately placed in a superficial framework. In other words, the structure of political language is unable to explore the deeper potential of language. Elytis continues,

> ... I feel like stepping out on the balconies and shouting: Nothing of the things they circulate in schools, churches, and political rallies, takes a passport for the soul unless it has the necessary conceptualization by the means of expression. The laws of art are also the laws of life.[188]

Elytis also points to the tension that exists between the origins of language and the academic rules formulated much later in order to appropriate it. People created and used language "until we came with our diplomas and our rules to help them. And we almost vanquished them," he notes.[189] On the one hand, the necessary formulation of grammatical rules creates a consensus of communication, but on the other it makes language rigid and substantially diminishes those creative forces that originally gave birth to it. Many contemporary Greek poets and writers, reverted to "dialect" in order to rediscover the vibrant elements of language: Seferis, for example, found this long-lost vitality in the Cypriot dialect, Kazantzakis in the dialect of his native Crete, and, more recently, Michalis Ganas in the language of folk songs. Similarly, Elytis makes use of the Aegean islands' dialects and also takes the liberty to coin new words such as *fotodentro*, *Elytonesos*, *oksopetra*, and *katarkythmevo*.[190]

---

[187] Elytis, *Εν Λευκώ*, p. 376.
[188] Elytis, *Εν Λευκώ*, p. 376.
[189] Elytis, *Εν Λευκώ*, p. 366.
[190] Elytis, *Collected Poems*, pp. 205, 283, 508, 534.

Greek Literature in the Era of Multinational Capitalism: Analogy, Allegory

Fredric Jameson's "sweeping hypothesis" that "*all* third-world texts are *necessarily* ... allegorical" has long been met with suspicion and has been rejected on various grounds. As Elliot Colla suggests,

> Critics rightly pounced on the essentialisms in Jameson's essay: his problematic definition of the "Third World," his blanket generalizations about life in the Third World, his comments about the mature form of the modernist novel and the anachronistic feel of literature from the formerly colonized world, his Fourth International assumptions about the innately progressive revolutionary character of anticolonial national liberation movements.[191]

Rey Chow further adds to the list of problems with Jameson's essay his stereotypical assumption that the split between the personal and the public that characterizes the West is not applicable when reading third world texts. This commensurable relationship between the individual and the collective allows Jameson, according to Chow, to make several stereotypical assumptions: i.e., that individual works of literature mimic the collective and that "third world productions are *all alike.*"[192] At the same time, both Colla and Chow might be cautious about Jameson's "sweeping hypothesis" but they find merit in several of its methodological suggestions. For Colla, in some third world texts the personal and the collective are indeed negotiated through national discourse. For Chow, Jameson's text openly asserts such "stereotyping as a viable method of reading."[193]

What I have been arguing in this chapter is that Elytis's use of Analogies is primarily an attempt to explain that his Greekness is not motivated by "a nationalistic bent."[194] Although Greece does not quite fit the stereotypical category of the "third world," I find that a comparison between the term "allegory," as Jameson uses it, and the term "analogy" in Elytis is useful in sorting out some of the generalizations ascribed to Jameson's argument. While personal observations may not constitute a legitimate line of argumentation, I will add my own experience of growing up in a divided Cyprus and educated in the public school system there. It is fair to say that the greatest part of our standard curriculum, which was identical to the Greek, was comprised of texts that could and were interpreted as national allegories. These texts educated students on such subjects as the poet's love for the nation, the depiction of the nation's geography, the anxieties of the nation in particular historical moments, etc. Literature, in this context, becomes a means of mapping the nation. Stereotypical as it might be, instead of perceiving such mapping in the current theoretical environment as too

---

[191] Elliott Colla, *Conflicted Antiquities: Egyptology, Egyptomania, Egyptian Modernity* (Durham: Duke University Press, 2007), p. 269.

[192] Chow, *Protestant Ethnic*, p. 98.

[193] Chow, *Protestant Ethnic*, p. 99.

[194] Elytis, "On his Poetry," p. 632.

narrow, conservative, or suspiciously constructed, what I would suggest is that it points to the function of national literature as a means of negotiating between the official national narrative and the literary constructions of ethnicity that emerge, to begin with, in the constant reiterations of identity in a particular cultural context. Elytis's analogies differentiate between Greekness as an official category sanctioned by the state—with citizens, symbols, commemorations, a national calendar, etc.—and an alternate Greekness as marked by the experience of identity in a particular culture: the language that people speak, the geography that surrounds them, their traditions, and, most importantly in the case of Elytis, the relationship between these categories of experience. The potential that such negotiations make possible, should not be seen as exclusive or exceptionalist. In fact, the same libidinal investments, as Jameson would have it, are present in more recent works of Greek literature that attempt a negotiation between ethnicity and the experience of immigration in Greece. To put it simply, collections like Elytis's *Axion Esti* or Ritsos's *Romiosyni*, tell us something about the anxieties of affirming one's identity when that identity continuously confronts the forces (both internal and external) that situate it in a specific hierarchical system. Contrary to the conventional description of nationality (or national allegories) as rigid, such collections expose the pliant and phantasmagorical matter that defines ethnicity. They present ethnic identity as a concept that is in perpetual discovery of itself but, at the same time, it is *rooted* in those natural elements that surround it. It is at this point where I find Jameson's theory still useful in understanding how third world literatures (and I would add, literatures that perceive themselves as belated or hierarchically less privileged than the first world), might tell us something about ethnicity. Even in those poems where the subject-matter is concerned with the absent beloved, or existential ruminations (such as death)—even in poems where the subject-matter is expressively *personal*—Elytis frames the poem within the Greek geocultural context. Thus, the absent beloved in *The Monogram* is absent only in relation to the overwhelming presence of the Greek nature: the sea, the island, the mountain, the fragrant herbs, etc. The imaginary Greece that the poet constructs in *The Little Seafarer* comes "from the other, the real one, as the dream comes from the fact of [his] life."[195] And the Greek world that is praised as "worthy" in *Axion Esti* is described precisely as a negotiation between the public and the private as well as between what is permanent and what is ever-changing in the continuous (re)discovery of ethnicity: "Now the Gods' humiliation Now the ashes of Man / Now now the zero / and Forever the world the small the great!" (190).[196]

If what Jameson suggests is that the categories of the personal or the individual should always be seen as substitutions for the collective or the national, Elytis's analogies remind us that such collectivities are themselves diverse and in constant negotiation with the personal experience of one's surroundings. In the

---

[195] Elytis, *Collected Poems*, p. 424.
[196] Elytis, *Collected Poems*, p. 190.

remaining chapters, what I will be arguing is that these negotiations are not simply discernible in the subject-matter of the poem but also in its form. In fact, one of Elytis's most profound contributions to the development of modernism in Greece is the attention he gives to the generally neglected poetic form. In the theory of Solar Metaphysics, and its related category of Architectural Poetics, Elytis attempts to present a poem or a collection's structure, as reflective of the poem's content, creating yet another (hidden) layer of meaning.

Chapter 4
Solar Metaphysics

> Thus often when I am speaking of the sun, a huge crimson rose gets tangled in my tongue. But it is not possible for me to be silent.
>
> —Elytis, *Sun the First*

We have examined thus far Elytis's notion of natural objects as possessing a certain *ethos* that varies according to the geographical region and language within which they are represented: a bare mountain may suggest simplicity and leanness, fragrant herbs may suggest innocence, a shining drop of water may be expressive of "cleanliness" and "diaphaneity," and lime may suggest "purification" and "spiritual candor." These correspondences precede the poetic metaphor, as they have been projected onto the experience of language and have been appropriated by the idiosyncrasies of the people (i.e., lime is experienced in the whitewashed houses of the islands, the clear drop of water in the diaphanous Aegean sea, fragrant herbs in their religious or ritualistic use). The "Sun," as well as its derivative concepts (light, fire, heat), is one of the most frequently used and most complex elements in Elytis's poetry. At least three of his collections are shaped around this concept (*The Light-tree and the Fourteenth Beauty*, *Sun The First*, and *The Sovereign Sun*), and almost all his collections explore a certain aspect of his "solar ethos." The poem "Laconic," from *Six and One Remorses for the Sky*, exemplifies the importance of this concept in Elytis's poetry:

> Anguish of death so inflamed me, that my glow returned to the sun.
> It sends me now into a perfect syntax of stone and aether,
> So, he whom I sought, *I am*.[1]

---

[1] Elytis, *Collected Poems*, p. 200. Ο καημός του θανάτου τόσο με πυρπόλησε, που η λάμψη μου επέστρεψε στον ήλιο. / Κείνος με πέμπει τώρα μέσα στην τέλεια σύνταξη της πέτρας και του αιθέρος / Λοιπόν, αυτός που γύρευα, *είμαι* (Elytis, *Ποίηση*, p. 195). The line "he whom I sought, *I am*" may also bring to mind the story of "Moses and the Burning Bush" of the Old Testament. The associations are indeed many: in both images, truth or enlightenment appears in the form of fire (the sun, the burning bush). In the Old Testament story, an angel appears to Moses as a flame in a burning bush ("the bush was burning, yet it was not consumed," Exodus 3.2). When Moses turns to see this "great sight" he hears the voice of God, who instructs him to guide his people out of Egypt. "Then Moses said to God, "If I come to the people of Israel and say to them, 'The God of your fathers has sent me to you,' and they ask me, 'What is his name?' what shall I say to them?" God said to Moses, 'I AM WHO I AM'" (Exodus 3.13–14). Psalm V of *The Axion Esti* also refers to the story of "Moses and the Burning Bush": "My foundations in the mountains / and the peoples bear the mountains on their shoulder / and on them memory burns / neverburnt bush" (Elytis, *Collected Poems*, p. 149).

The sun appears here as an essential element of the poet's existential pursuit. As in Camus, it is connected to death, the ultimate existential mystery. It also sends the poet into a "perfect syntax of stone and aether"; it is the guiding force, the center, of the poetic quest.

Elytis's theory of Solar Metaphysics attempts to establish the "perfect syntax" of the modern poetic form based on the symbol of the sun. Whereas the theory of Analogies is concerned primarily with the *content* of the poem, Solar Metaphysics is linked to the *form* or structure of the entire poetic presentation. The formation of the theory dates approximately to 1950, when Camus and Char asked Elytis to write an essay for their new magazine *Empédocle*. The essay, titled "Pour un lyrisme d'inventions architecturales et de métaphysique solaire" ["For a lyricism of architectural inventions and of Solar Metaphysics"], was drafted but was never published, as the publication of the magazine was short-lived. Elytis returned to his attempt to present a comprehensive theory that would unite his ideas of correspondences and of Solar Metaphysics in 1951 while staying at Royaumont (France). As he writes in the "Chronicle of a Decade," he was consumed, at the time, with the idea of forming a theory on the relationship between aesthetics and meaning in contemporary poetry. By the time he left France, later in the same year, he had written a manuscript entitled "Seven Letters from Royaumont" (Εφτά Επιστολές από το Royaumont); reminiscent of Rilke's "Letters to a young Poet," the work presented his ideas in a series of seven letters addressed to a young Greek poet. Elytis gives us in the "Chronicle" a brief description of the issues he was concerned with in these letters:

> The difficulty of adaptation between the Western and Eastern spirit; the misinterpretation of the deeper Greek spirit by foreigners, that made communication between us difficult and for which we were also responsible; the mission of poetry in our age; the metaphysical need outside of any religious typology; the importance of language and its correspondence with other phenomena of nature and the spirit; the reappearance of the problem of form in modern poetry; the example of visual arts—all these would constitute the nuclei for many more letters and, in a way, the codification of my conclusions. The "Seven Letters From Royaumont" were completed in the summer of 1951....[2]

Unfortunately, the manuscripts of the "Seven Letters From Royaumont" were lost during Elytis's return journey to Athens. What is particularly interesting, in relation to the lost manuscripts of the "Letters" and the unpublished article of *Empédocle*, is "the reappearance of the problem of form in modern poetry." In fact, it becomes evident that Elytis's post-1950 collections, particularly the longer ones, are characterized by a much stricter architectural structure, both schematically and conceptually.

The modernist attempt to liberate language from conventional poetic adaptations introduced a tension between the form of the poem and its content.

---

[2] Elytis, *Ανοιχτά Χαρτιά*, p. 454.

A primary concern of modernist creation was to address the confines of meter, rhyme, and form. Thus, in the late nineteenth and early twentieth century, poetic experimentation aimed to define a new modern space in which this relationship would unfold. Poggioli suggests that modernist experimentation went so far as to perceive the arts as "interchangeable and mutually correspondent."[3] Apollinaire, for example, attempted to combine poetic meaning with image, creating what he called *visible lyricism*.[4] Understandably, Poggioli describes Apollinaire's *visible lyricism*, as well as Reverdy's *plastic lyricism* and Mallarmé's *typographical emphasis*, as "extreme and absurd extravagancies" that resulted from the "desperate and sleepless search for individual expression."[5] He also claims, however, that it is this kind of avant-garde experimentation that led to Joyce's *Ulysses*, which is almost classically stylized despite its Dionysian tensions. Contrary to the achievements of the novel, Western poetry sought novelty either by moving in the direction of the prose poem, which is characterized, as Clive Scott suggests, by "its accidental nature" and "its *uncontrollable* novelty,"[6] or in newly imported Eastern genres such as the Japanese Haiku. The tendency of the poem towards condensed meaning on the one hand, and the appropriation of formless free verse on the other, caused the crisis of form in modernism to manifest itself more explicitly in poetry than in any other genre.

Even though Elytis's *Orientations* (1939), *Sun the First* (1941), and *Song Heroic and Mourning* (1945) indicate his early interest in structuring his poems, it was not until the early 1950s that the question of form acquired a clear theoretical framework in his works. It was, in fact, the publication of *The Axion Esti* (1959), composed in the period 1950–1959, that exemplified Elytis's use of architectural and conceptual schematization. The theory of Solar Metaphysics represents, perhaps, the most comprehensive attempt to address the issue of form in western poetry. In constructing the theory, Elytis writes that he ventured to unite two seemingly uncompromising aspects of poetic modernism—namely, the morphology of the poem and its ideological content—in such a way so that "the elements of one would become the natural and unavoidable consequence of the other."[7] The poem compresses a specific meaning, an epiphany, into a single instance. Elytis argues that this poetic moment needs to be expressed within a mirroring chronotope:

---

[3] Poggioli, *Avant-Garde*, p. 134.

[4] Apollinaire's "The Carnation" is famously shaped like a flower and his "It's Raining" depicts words in diagonal lines (imitating rain). Also see the poems "Aim" and "Heart and Mirror." Guillaume Apollinaire, *Selected Writings*, trans. Roger Shattuck (New York: New Directions, 1971), pp. 169, 171, 173, 167.

[5] Poggioli, *Avant-Garde*, p. 135.

[6] Clive Scott, "The Prose Poem and Free Verse," in *Modernism: A Guide to European Literature 1890–1930*, ed. Malcolm Bradbury and James McFarlane, 349–68 (London: Penguin, 1991), p. 351.

[7] Elytis, *Ανοιχτά Χαρτιά*, p. 449.

> ... in order [for the poem] to assume a 'body' and to emulate effectively the position of the sun, as well as its highest mission in the system of images and meanings it entails, this meaning must be developed incessantly and in conjunction with a symbolic transcription into rhythmic and strophic features, analogous to those that render time sensible to human cognition.
>
> Forgive me for this complicated sentence. I will attempt to express it in a different way: The process of formulating a calendar of celebrations, or the mutual transubstantiation of natural and imaginative elements in a mythology, should resume working from the collective to the personal scale and with *one medium, the one and only medium of lyrical energy*. And this, in other words, means: the specific development and appropriation of concepts should dictate a specific development and appropriation of parts and, at the same time, such development and appropriation of parts should constitute the *sine qua non* of the wholeness of the result.[8]

It is important that structure is not forced on the poem. Instead, it should be "the natural and unavoidable consequence" of meaning; it must be a natural expression of a meaning that compliments or mirrors the poem's content. In his Nobel lecture Elytis attempts, once more, to define the basic premise of the theory:

> What interested me, obscurely at the beginning, then more and more consciously, was the edification of that material according to an architectural model that varied each time. To understand this, there is no need to refer to the wisdom of the Ancients, who conceived the Parthenons. It is enough to evoke the humble builders of our houses and of our chapels in the Cyclades, finding on each occasion the best solution: their solutions. Practical and beautiful at the same time, so that in seeing them Le Corbusier could only admire and bow.
>
> Perhaps it is this instinct that woke in me when, for the first time, I had to face a great composition like *The Axion Esti*. I understood then that without giving the work the proportions and perspective of an edifice, it would never reach the solidity I wished.[9]

Northrop Frye suggests that "the term structure which we have used so often, is a metaphor from architecture, and may be misleading when we are speaking of narrative, which is not a simultaneous structure but a movement in time."[10] Elytis, on the other hand, views architectural aesthetics as inextricably linked to poetic form. In order to understand the theory of Solar Metaphysics, which is, in its essence, a theory of architectural poetics, it is important to examine Elytis's view of modern architectural aesthetics, particularly as influenced by the Swiss architect Le Corbusier. Before proceeding to do so, however, I will first concentrate on the

---

[8] Elytis, *Ανοιχτά Χαρτιά*, p. 450.
[9] Odysseus Elytis, *Nobel Lecture*, December 8, 1979, http://nobelprize.org/nobel_prizes/literature/laureates/1979/elytis-lecture-e.html (accessed August 27, 2006).
[10] Northrop Frye, *The Great Code: The Bible and Literature*, p. 63.

importance of the sun as a conceptual and structuring force in Elytis's thought. I have already attempted a similar reading in comparing Camus and Elytis's use of the sun as a multidetermined symbol in the Mediterranean context. What is more significant in this discussion, is the perception of the sun as a gravitational force that provides the space in which content and structure unfold and interact with one another.

Sun-Symbolism, Heraclitus, Plotinus

One could certainly argue that Elytis's utilization of the sun as a symbol came as a natural resistance to the dark clouds of pessimism that characterized much of Greek poetry in the 1920s. At the same time, his first poems are well balanced between a youthful and vibrant presentation of sunlit concepts, and melancholic meditations on death. But if we must distinguish a recurring natural element in *Orientations*, it would be that of the sea; it is not coincidental, after all, that the 24-year-old Elytis writes in his poem "Anniversary": "I brought my life this far / to this spot that struggles / Always near the sea."[11] In his second collection, *Sun the First*, however, the sun undoubtedly becomes the central poetic motif. It is, of course, significant that the collection was published during the German occupation of Athens and after Elytis's nearly fatal experience in World War II. In this context, the sun appears as an important symbol of resistance utilized, in his poetry, during one of the darkest historical periods in Greece.

"Poetry exists," Derek Walcott writes, "in spite of history."[12] Similarly, Elytis perceives poetry's most essential mission, during dark historical times, to be its alignment with the forces of light. "In the years of Buchenwald and Auschwitz," he writes in "The Chronicle," "Matisse painted the most succulent and the most raw, the most enchanting flowers or fruit ever made, as if the miracle of life found the way to compress itself within them forever."[13] Elytis wrote his most sun-centric poems during some of Greece's most devastating historical periods: *Sun the First* during the Nazi occupation of Greece and both, *The Light-Tree* and *The Sovereign Sun*, during the fascist rule of the Generals (1967–1974).

Sun-symbolism takes a wide spectrum of correspondences in his poetry. Often, it encapsulates Dionysian energy: it throbs in the teeth of tomboys,[14] it is found

---

[11] Elytis, *Collected Poems*, p. 18. In "Anniversary" Elytis also cites Swinburne: "… even the weariest river winds somewhere safe to sea" (from Swinburne's "The Garden of Proserpine").

[12] Derek Walcott, *The Antilles: Fragments of Epic Memory*, December 7, 1992, http://nobelprize.org/nobel_prizes/literature/laureates/1992/walcott-lecture.html (accessed October 10, 2007).

[13] Elytis, *Ανοιχτά Χαρτιά*, p. 406.

[14] Elytis, *Collected Poems*, p. 81.

between the legs of boys,[15] it gets the young girls drunk,[16] "it bursts within us and we hold our mouths in terror."[17] It guides humans, or humans guide *it*: sometimes we revolve around the sun,[18] and at others "it takes a lot of work to make the sun turn round."[19] It is at once a force of rejuvenation and destruction, of consolation and absence, of construction and deconstruction; it is punishing in the summer and warm in the winter; it is the primordial energy of "both light and death."[20] It does not represent a monolithic symbol of correspondences but rather a multireferential element that can be more accurately approached through the poet's construction of a metaphysical system around it.

Elytis perceives the sun as the central unifying element of both the solar and the poetic systems:

> From there on, we can say that the position of the sun in the ethical world plays the same role as in the nature of things; the poet is the blade between the ethical and the real. The portion of darkness diffused in him by conscience is measured by light, a light that is reflected back to him, making his image—the human image—more transparent.[21]

The sun is seen as a fundamentally ethical concept that can become, in this metaphysical transposition, the bedrock of human conscience. Camus's perception of the "New Mediterranean Culture" is based on the same principles that Elytis admits had fueled his own formation of this concept.[22] The projected Mediterranean ethos of both thinkers revolves around the placement of the region in an "exact moment," that renders it vastly different from the countries of Northern Europe.

When Char and Camus asked Elytis in 1950 to write the essay on Solar Metaphysics—or more precisely, to put in writing the ideas he had discussed with them in private conversations[23]—the eventual failure of the magazine, as he admitted later, "rescued [him] ... from a certain impasse."[24] We may assume that the theory of Solar Metaphysics was still, in the early 1950s, in its formative stages. The influence of Camus certainly helped Elytis towards the gradual crystallization of the theory, but at the same time, we can easily discern Elytis's general interest in Solar Metaphysics before his meeting with Camus. Elena Koutrianou suggests that his fascination with the sun could be traced back to his childhood and the reading

---

[15] Elytis, *Collected Poems*, p. 87.
[16] Elytis, *Collected Poems*, p. 100.
[17] Elytis, *Collected Poems*, p. 454.
[18] Elytis, *Collected Poems*, p. 480.
[19] Elytis, *Collected Poems*, p. 148.
[20] "Both Light and Death" is a line from Andreas Kalvos's poem "To Death." Elytis uses this as the title of a section in *The Little Seafarer*.
[21] Elytis, *Ανοιχτά Χαρτιά*, p. 452.
[22] Elytis, *Ανοιχτά Χαρτιά*, p. 453.
[23] Elytis, *Ανοιχτά Χαρτιά*, p. 448.
[24] Elytis, *Ανοιχτά Χαρτιά*, p. 449.

of "Books for young Greek Children" ("Βιβλία για τα Ελληνόπουλα").[25] She also points to other possible sources that Elytis read as an adult: N.G. Politis' studies on the sun in Greek Tradition, and the poetry of Angelos Sikelianos, Kostis Palamas, Andreas Kalvos, and George Seferis.[26] While these poets, particularly Kalvos, Seferis, and Sikelianos, certainly had a strong impact on Elytis, especially in their depiction of Greek tradition, the theory of Solar Metaphysics goes far beyond the poetic utilization of the sun as an important symbol of the Greek experience. The metaphysical conceptualization of the theory and its eventual incorporation in Elytis's mythopoetic system can be more accurately traced to the philosophies of Heraclitus and Plotinus.

Elytis's interest in Heraclitus was, in some ways, we might say, inevitable: here was an ancient Greek philosopher that Breton and Aragon exalted as a surrealist in dialectics.[27] In a similar spirit, Elytis sees Heraclitus' philosophy as an illumination of the hidden nature of things and the realm of fantasy.[28] He further classifies him among the few sharp spirits that had unknowingly heard the surrealist voice.[29] Heraclitus is indeed remarkably modern, at least in his attempt to synthesize opposites. On the one hand, he adheres to empirical observation and, on the other, he persistently describes that which is unapparent or obscure; while his universe is constructed within unchanging physical boundaries, he presents human existence within the frame of a constant metaphysical flux. His influence on Elytis in relation to the theory of Solar Metaphysics concentrates on three major themes: the existence of an alternative reality, the synthesis of opposites, and the view of the sun as an ethical symbol. The following fragments of Heraclitus are divided according to these themes:[30]

On the existence of an alternative—unapparent—reality:

> Men have been deceived with regard to their knowledge of what is apparent in the same way as Homer was—and he was the wisest of the Greeks. For some children who were killing lice deceived him by saying: 'What we saw and caught we leave behind, what we neither saw nor caught we take with us' [B56].

> Unapparent harmony is better than apparent [B54].[31]

---

[25] As Koutrianou explains, the series includes the well-known book "The Alphabet of the Sun" ("Το αλφαβητάρι του Ήλιου").

[26] Elena Koutrianou, Με Άξονα το Φως. Η Διαμόρφωση και η Κρυστάλλωση της Ποιητικής του Οδυσσέα Ελύτη (Athens: Idryma Kosta kai Elenis Urani, 2002), p. 157.

[27] Nadeau, *Surrealism*, pp. 35, 140.

[28] Elytis, *Ανοιχτά Χαρτιά*, pp. 130, 557.

[29] Elytis, *Ανοιχτά Χαρτιά*, p. 340.

[30] All quotes are from Jonathan Barnes, *Early Greek Philosophy* (New York: Penguin, 2001). The references in the brackets refer to the corresponding fragments.

[31] Elytis quoted this fragment in his Nobel lecture.

Most do not understand the things they meet with—not even when they have learned them do they know them; but they seem to themselves to do so [B17].

On the synthesis of opposites:

The path up and down is one and the same [B60].

Wisdom is one thing: to grasp the knowledge of how all things are stirred through all Combinations—wholes and not wholes, concurring differing, concordant discordant, from all things one and from one all things [B10].

Cold things become hot, hot cold, wet dry, parched moist [B126].

The same things, there are present, living and dead, the awake and the sleeping, young and old; for the latter change and are the former and again the former change and are the latter [B88].

On sun, light, fire:

Fire will come and judge and convict all things [B66].

The Thunderbolt steers all things [B64].[32]

You will not find the limits of the soul although you travel all the path—so deep is its account [B45].

The world, the same for all, neither any god or any man made; but it was always and is and will be, fire ever-living, kindling in measures and being extinguished in measures [B30].

Time is an orderly motion, with measures and limits and periods. Of these the sun is overseer and guardian, defining and arbitrating and revealing and illuminating the changes and the seasons which bring all things [B100].

The sun will not overstep its measures; otherwise the furies, ministers of justice, will find it out [B94].[33]

If the sun did not exist it would be dusk [B99].

---

[32] Elytis uses this quote twice in his poetry: in *Three Poems Under a Flag of Convenience* ("The Garden Sees," Elytis, *Collected Poems*, p. 4) and in *Maria Nephele* ("Thunderbolt Steers," Elytis, *Collected Poems*, p. 314).

[33] Elytis quoted this fragment in his Nobel lecture.

In a long section of his Nobel address, Elytis explains how these three themes are connected. Heraclitus, he says, is among those spirits that realized the existence of an alternative or a second reality (*seconde réalité*). History deems this second reality, which resides in the realm of imagination, secondary. Elytis then quotes Hölderlin's question "Wozu Dichter in dürftiger Zeit" ("what are poets for in destitute times?"),[34] from the famous elegy "Bread and Wine," and responds:

> Unfortunately, times were always *dürftig* for mankind. But poetry has also always functioned. These two phenomena are destined to accompany our earthly fate, one counterbalancing the other. How else? If the night and the stars are perceptible to us it is because of the Sun. The difference is that the sun, according to the ancient sage, cannot surpass its bounds lest it becomes hubris (ύβρις). For life to be possible, we have to keep a correct distance to the ethical Sun, just as our planet does from the natural Sun.[35]

His response echoes Heidegger's answer to the same question and his definition of *dürftig*: "Not only have the gods and the god fled, but the divine radiance has become extinguished in the world's history. The time of the world's night is the destitute [*dürftig*] time, because it becomes ever more destitute. It has already grown so destitute, it can no longer discern the default of god as a default."[36] For Heidegger, poetry traverses the world's night—it experiences and endures it, making the turning into the "openness of being" possible. For Elytis, the sun becomes the symbol that illuminates consciousness in the world's night. It is at this juncture that Heraclitus' philosophy becomes most relevant: the ethical sun marks the correct distance at which life can be sustained. Such a view of the sun is far from a Romantic utopia that launches whatever power it possesses against the history and technocracy of destitute times. On the contrary, it is a balancing force that cannot surpass its bounds (otherwise, the furies, ministers of justice, will find out). As Heraclitus suggests, the sun is the "overseer and guardian" of Time—even destitute time.[37]

Heraclitus' linking of the Sun and Justice is echoed in Elytis (as well as in Heidegger, to a certain extent) through the idea that the mechanism that mobilizes Art is identical to the mechanism of Justice. The triadic theme of Sun—Justice—Poetry is, in fact, a recurring one in Elytis's work. In "Chronicle of a Decade" he writes:

---

[34] I use Albert Hofstadter's translation of *dürftig as destitute times* (from the translation of Heidegger's *Poetry, Language, Thought*). See Martin Heidegger, *Poetry, Language, Thought*, trans. Albert Hofstadter (New York: Perennial Classics, 1971).

[35] Elytis, *Εν Λευκώ*, pp. 349, 351.

[36] Heidegger, *Poetry*, p. 89.

[37] Elytis further explains that, "in healthy times [the antithesis of destitute times], Beauty [κάλλος] was identified with Good [αγαθόν], and Good with the Sun" (Elytis, *Εν Λευκώ*, p. 347). It should be noted that, for Ancient Greeks, the word "Good" [αγαθόν] did not carry the moral connotations that it has acquired in the Judeo-Christian belief system; rather, it was more related to a state of excellence.

If there exists a humanistic view for Art's mission, it can only be understood, I believe, in these terms: As an invisible process identical with the mechanism of Justice. Of course, I am not referring to the Justice of the courts but to the other, constituted slowly and painfully through the teachings of humanity's great mentors, through political struggles for social liberty, through the highest poetical achievements. From such great effort, drops of light slowly fall every now and then in the soul's great night, as drops of lemon fall on polluted water.[38]

And in the short "Statement of 1951" he proclaims: "I believe in the return of justice, which I associate with light, in the world. And with a glorious ancestor of mine I take pride in shouting in the face of our times: no, I do not love the gods whose worship is performed in darkness."[39] The same idea is repeated, almost verbatim, 15 years later, in the "Statement of 1966": "I believe … in a justice that is associated with absolute light. I am an idolater that, without wanting to, happened to touch Christian sainthood on the other side.[40] The presentation of poetry as an expression of justice and a safeguard of consciousness is at least as old as Homer. The Homeric epics offer abundant examples of what constitutes both human and divine law—thus, in *The Odyssey*, the hospitable Phaeacians, as well as Nestor and Menelaus, are contrasted to the unruly and unjust suitors and the Cyclops. By the fifth century, B.C., however, the relationship between justice and poetry shifts to such an extent, that Plato famously bans all poets from his ideal Republic on the premise that they are falsifiers. If we accept Freud's general assertion that the creative artist sublimates what is socially, or legally, in this case, inappropriate, then we can see that poetic expression has unmistakably evolved as a resistance to current reality. It is *because* politics reside in current reality, and often define it, that poetry exists in constant friction with political practice. For Elytis, justice is constituted "through the teachings of humanity's great mentors, through political struggles for social liberty, through the highest poetical achievements." The attempt to universalize justice necessitates a degree of personal responsibility, and poetry provides the space in which conscience can be awakened. The poet's intent is not to create a world where strife is purged; on the contrary, as Heraclitus suggests, strife *is* justice: it is the point of constant friction in the ever-present "destitute times."

The concept of justice implies a process of structuring: it can only exist within a frame of commonly accepted rules. "I feel," Elytis writes, "that the only way to see the absolutely personal part of myself be verified, is when I deprive it from the capacity of the personal; when, in other words, I render it *public*."[41] The theory of Solar Metaphysics provides the structure within which the poetic idea of justice,

---

[38] Elytis, *Ανοιχτά Χαρτιά*, p. 452.

[39] Elytis, *Εν Λευκώ*, p. 206. This "glorious ancestor" is Heraclitus.

[40] Elytis, *Εν Λευκώ*, p. 207. The two statements essentially "frame" the years of composition of *Axion Esti*—Elytis had begun working on it in 1950 and completed it in 1959 but it was not published until 1960.

[41] Elytis, *Εν Λευκώ*, p. 206.

as Elytis defines it, can exist, at the space within which it can become public. At this point, we can see the resemblance of the theory's general claim to Plotinus' thought; Like Heraclitus, Plotinus presents "light" as the divine manifestation of justice. In his spiritual cosmology, all existence stems from the triadic hypostasis of the One, the Intelligence and the Soul. His metaphysics, as presented in *The Enneads*, is structured around this hypothesis. The structural division of Plotinus's work into nine treatises (hence the title *The Enneads*) seems to interest Elytis, who, in *The Axion Esti*, refers to "the nine steps Plotinus climbed."[42] Apart from the scattered references to the Neoplatonic philosopher in his essays, Elytis published, in *Carte Blanche*, a free translation of a short section in *The Enneads* under the title "The Divine Light According to Plotinus."[43] What interests Elytis more than Plotinus' divine metaphysics, however, is his elaboration of the concept of "light" in its sensory and mental perceptions:

> It is not a light like the one the eye captures from the outside. It is a different light, brighter, that belongs to the eye itself; that even at night, in the darkness, it leaps up and spreads out in front of you. That even if you lower your glance because you do not want to see anything, it will still shine. That even if you firmly close your eyes, again you will see it, since it immanently exists in you [....]
>
> You wonder where it came from: from the inside or the outside world. Then, when it disappears, you say: it was from the inside. And yet, no—it was not from the inside. Nor do you need to wonder where it came from. There is no starting point. It comes from nowhere and it is not directed anywhere. It only appears and disappears.[44]

Plotinus claims that the divine light does not move towards Man—it is not inside or outside: it simply *is*. Echoing Plato's concept of Forms (είδος), he suggests that the sun is merely an image of this light.[45] Light is perceived here as a primordial element that becomes "visible" to man only in certain moments. The "Genesis" that commences *The Axion Esti* begins with this presupposition: "In the beginning was light." The original "logos" of John's Gospel is replaced here with "light." One does not acquire a consciousness of the justice Elytis links with light through an imposed *Logos* but through the epiphanic qualities of *luminosity* and *diaphaneity*: "I am not speaking of one's natural capacity to perceive objects in all their details but of the metaphorical capacity to retain their essence and to guide them towards a purity that expresses their metaphysical significance as in a revelation."[46]

---

[42] Elytis, *Collected Poems*, p. 188.
[43] Elytis, *Εν Λευκώ*, pp. 311–12.
[44] Elytis, *Εν Λευκώ*, pp. 311–12. It is important to stress the fact that Elytis takes many liberties in translating Plotinus's text.
[45] Elytis, *Εν Λευκώ*, p. 312.
[46] Elytis, *Εν Λευκώ*, p. 343.

Plotinus's deification of light (φως)—a light that is frequently contrasted to darkness (σκότος)—is a common metaphor in the Gospels. In Genesis, after creating the heaven and the earth, God creates light. Describing the Logos that became flesh, John writes: "In him was life and the life was the light of men. The light shines in the darkness, and the darkness has not overcome it." John further claims that his testimony bears witness to "the true light that enlightens every man."[47] According to John, Christ used the same metaphor to describe himself: "I am the light of the world; he who follows me will not walk in darkness, but will have the light of life."[48] In Ephesians, Paul uses light as a metaphor of accepting God: "when anything is exposed by the light it becomes visible, for anything that becomes visible is light."[49] Light also appears as a divine symbol in two of the most significant incidents of the New Testament. On his way to Damascus, Saul is suddenly blinded by a divine light, an encounter that enlightens him and converts him into "Paul"; and John, turning to see the voice that dictated the Apocalypse to him, sees a face "like the sun shining in full strength" ("και η όψις αυτού ως ο ήλιος φαίνει εν τη δυνάμει αυτού").[50] As an important element of Elytis's mythopoetic system, light possesses a similar function in his poetry. In the "Genesis" of *The Axion Esti*, written in an apocalyptic tone, the poet is beckoned by "the whole many-rayed sun with its axle" inside him, to "read and try / and fight."[51] In the similarly apocalyptic poem "Revelation," in *Maria Nephele*, Elytis described the voice of an old man that summoned the Antiphonist to "prophesy over many people and nations and tongues and kings"[52] and then, "giving off white flames he merged with the sun."[53] As it has become evident, Elytis associates the concept of light (φως) with justice (δικαιοσύνη) and with the awakening of consciousness (συνείδηση). He concluded his Nobel address with these three themes:

> To hold the sun in one's hands without being burned, to transmit it like a torch to those following, is a painful act but, I believe, a blessed one…
>
> One day the dogmas that hold men in chains will be dissolved before a consciousness so inundated with light that it will be one with the Sun, and it will arrive on those ideal shores of human dignity and liberty.[54]

---

[47] John 1:1–9.
[48] John 8:12.
[49] Ephesians 5:13.
[50] Revelation 1:16.
[51] Elytis, *Collected Poems*, p. 123.
[52] Revelation 10:11.
[53] Elytis, *Collected Poems*, p. 307.
[54] Odysseus Elytis, *Nobel Lecture*, December 8, 1979, http://nobelprize.org/nobel_prizes/literature/laureates/1979/elytis-lecture-e.html (accessed August 27, 2006).

Le Corbusier: From Architecture to Poetry

The theory of Solar Metaphysics is principally a theory of structural, or architectural poetics. In his early twenties, Elytis became strongly interested in architecture and, specifically, in the works of Le Corbusier:

> I remember that in those years, 1933 if I am not mistaken, Le Corbusier had come to Athens. At the time I was enthralled with architecture and I admired Le Corbusier because he truly was the father of modern architecture.
>
> When I heard him speak about the folk artisans and builders that constructed the Cycladic houses, when I heard him speak and explain the way in which they had found solutions that accommodated man and were at the same time aesthetically beautiful, it made a great impression on me. It also solved a great contradiction in me: I could admire aspects of tradition and modernity equally. The seeming antithesis between them did not exist.[55]

Elytis is probably remembering here Le Corbusier's 1933 lecture at the National Metsovio Polytechnic of Athens in the context of the Fourth C.I.A.M. conference (Congrès Internationaux d'Architecture Moderne). It was entitled "Air – Sound – Light" and it concentrated on how to construct cities that combined architectural aesthetics with functional aims (i.e., cleaner air, less noise, and utilization of light). Even though Elytis was only 22 at the time, and still relatively unknown in Greek poetic circles, he would later form strong friendships with many individuals that were either close to Le Corbusier or who were familiar with his ideas on Cycladic architecture: apart from Stratis Eleftheriades Teriade, he would meet Léger in 1949 and Christian Zervos in 1948. He would also form a close relationship with the painter Nikos Hadjikyriakos Ghikas, one of Le Corbusier's closest Greek acquaintances, who later offered one of his paintings to adorn Elytis's "Stepchildren" (1974). Elytis found in Le Corbusier a kindred spirit who understood Mediterranean aesthetics and offered ways in which they could be applied to architecture. It is not coincidental, perhaps, that the theory of Solar Metaphysics took its first form after the meeting with Camus, who was already familiar with Le Corbusier—the two men met for the first time in 1935 in Algiers, at a time when Le Corbusier was deeply interested in Algeria.[56]

The Swiss architect visited Greece twice. In 1911, departing from Germany at the age of 24, he traveled through Bohemia, Serbia, Romania, Bulgaria, Turkey, Greece, and Italy.[57] Towards the end of the summer he arrived in Greece and visited Mount Athos, Thessaloniki, Athens, Itea, and Delphi. His impressions from

---

[55] Elytis, *Αυτοπροσωπογραφία*, pp. 11–12.

[56] Le Corbusier had attended a conference in Algiers in 1931 and became interested in providing a plan for the city. In the decade that followed, he produced many plans for the city, all of which were rejected.

[57] Le Corbusier, *Κείμενα για την Ελλάδα*, trans. Leda Pallantiou (Athens: Agra, 1992), p. 176.

the journey, recorded in detail in his journals, indicate a strong interest in classical Greek architecture, particularly the Acropolis. His subsequent articles in *L'Esprit Nouveau* and his first major publication *Towards a New Architecture* (*Vers une Architecture*, 1923) reveal his long-lasting enthrallment with the Parthenon:

> There has been nothing like it anywhere or at any period. It happened at a moment when things were at their keenest, when a man, stirred by the noblest thoughts, crystallized them in a plastic work of light and shade. The mouldings of the Parthenon are infallible and implacable. In severity they go far beyond our practice, or a man's normal capabilities. Here, the purest witness to the physiology of sensation, and to the mathematical speculation attached to it, is fixed and determined: we are riveted by our senses; we are ravished in our minds; we touch the axis of harmony.[58]

Le Corbusier further uses the Parthenon as an example of a "standard" that shaped much of the architecture in Classical Greece, and offers an equivalent example in the modern design of automobiles; competition allows for the evolution of a "standard" that will revolutionize automobile design: "Let us display, then, the Parthenon and the motor car so that it may be clear that it is a question of two products of selection in different fields, one which has reached its climax and the other is evolving."[59] Elytis's poem "The Alpha Romeo" in the *Rhos of Eros* proposes an equally radical and playful comparison between the Parthenon and the automobile:

> I marveled at the Parthenon
> and in its every column
> I found the golden rule
> But I say it today
> I find the good and beautiful
> In a sport Alpha Romeo[60]

Giorgos Theotokas, whose book *Free Spirit* (Ελεύθερο Πνεύμα) became the manifesto of the generation of the 1930s, presents a similar analogy: "An airplane in the sky of Greece, above the Parthenon, brings forth a new harmony that no one has captured yet."[61]

Beyond their playfulness, both images are obvious commentaries on the attempt to harmonize modernity and tradition, as well as on the newly discovered

---

[58] Le Corbusier, *Towards a New Architecture*, trans. Frederick Etchells (New York: Dover Publications, 1986), pp. 219–20.

[59] Le Corbusier, *New Architecture*, p. 140.

[60] Translated by Marinos Pourgouris. Θαύμασα τον Παρθενώνα / και στην κάθε του κολόνα / βρήκα τον χρυσό κανόνα / Όμως σήμερα το λέω / βρίσκω το καλό κι ωραίο / σε μια σπορ Alpha Romeo (Elytis, *Ποίηση*, p. 292).

[61] Giorgos Theotokas, *Το Ελεύθερο Πνεύμα* (Athens: Ermis, 1986), p. 69.

love for speed.⁶² In the case of Elytis, the comparison of the car with the Parthenon also suggests an architectural analogy: the "golden rule" found in the columns of the Parthenon can also be found in the Alpha Romeo. Le Corbusier suggests that the inventors of great ocean liners, airplanes, and cars far surpassed the architects; aided by competition, the former achieved the development of a unique style, whereas the latter remained lazily fixed on past models. These "machines," he proposes, hail the dawn of the "New Spirit" (l'esprit nouveau) in Architecture: "A house is a machine for living in. Baths, sun, hot-water, cold-water, warmth at will, conservation of food, hygiene, beauty in the sense of good proportion. An armchair is a machine for sitting in and so on."⁶³ The harmony ascribed to the Parthenon is comparable, for Le Corbusier, to the building of ocean liners, airplanes and cars: Natural law (aerodynamics, gravity, friction, etc.) is combined with human aesthetics, directing the creation of form and style. The "New Spirit" also becomes important in Elytis's Solar Metaphysics, where Poetic form, or structure, is defined by the "nature" of the poem (content, voice, emotion, etc.).

Le Corbusier discovered on the islands of Greece a fusion of tradition with modernity in the same way that he had perceived the harmony ascribed to the Parthenon in the advances of modern engineering. His journal entries that describe the impressions from his journey in 1911 reveal his deep fascination with Classical and Byzantine architecture. In 1933 he would travel, for the first time, to the Greek islands. Between August 5 and 8, following an invitation by the Greek archaeologist Anastasios Orlandos, the participants at the C.I.A.M. conference visited the Aegean islands, joined by Fernand Legér, Maurice Raynal, Paul Gauguen, Gaston Bonheur, and Amédée Ozenfant.⁶⁴ Le Corbusier's essays written prior to this journey already reveal his praise of Mediterranean sensation and the creative potential inherent in its geography. In "Certitude" (1932) he wrote about the cathartic quality of the Mediterranean sun, and in "Esprit grec, esprit latin, esprit gréco-latin" (1933), he described the Mediterranean as a space in which one could "act within light and harmony, with a feeling of responsibility and pleasure."⁶⁵ Six years after his visit to the Cyclades, Le Corbusier compared his two visits to Greece:

---

⁶² Although some Greek poets of the 1920s and 1930s embraced machines and speed, futurism did not manage to exercise a wide influence in Greece. Such attitudes are not contradictory. By embracing technology, the poets did not attempt to replace nature with modern technology; they were simply reacting to the burden of "ancient Greece" since the mythical subtext dominated both Greek and much of the western literary creation. They were searching for a way to harmonize modern Greece, as they understood and experienced it, with the symbols of classical Greece (in this case, the Parthenon).

⁶³ Le Corbusier, *New Architecture*, p. 95.

⁶⁴ Le Corbusier, *Κείμενα*, pp. 19, 20. Interestingly, they all traveled on a ship owned by Empeirikos's father (about one and a half years before Elytis met Empeirikos).

⁶⁵ Le Corbusier, *Κείμενα*, p. 130.

> In the space between the first and the second journey to Greece I understood that the Mediterranean was an inexhaustible source of information useful to our history. Yet, I ignored the fact that the Cycladic houses, those white flowers, reaffirmed to us, in great consolation, that they were still in bloom.... Contrary to our gestures that had become clumsy—gestures of a mechanized civilization sinking at that time in confused disappointment—movements here did not need but a soft touch of the spirit to turn into movements of modest or impetuous heroes for which no one speaks today except for the poets....
>
> Of what utility could this theorization of life be for the people of modernity—a life that is perpetuated in today's landscapes, the villages, the houses and the Greek customs? It reaffirms the human scale!
>
> Returning from the islands and Greece, the architect cannot separate his actions from the archetype of these human and decisive values.[66]

Le Corbusier's experience of the islands was nothing short of an epiphany. Unlike the nineteenth-century Romantics such as Byron and Shelley, who saw the rebirth of the Greek nation as a reenactment of past glory, Le Corbusier, like the Greek poets of the thirties generation, discovered a Greece that is "harmonious with modern times."[67] The Aegean islands and the Acropolis are equally part of a rebellion that motivates man towards an "alive and pleasant action."[68] The misinterpreted image of Greece is ascribed to the falsehoods of Western academics: "After 2,000 years they marked Greece with false characteristics: static, philosophizing philosophy, stripes of Corinthian rhythm, white eyes, cold body, aristocratic veil and raised arm under the columns, apathy or fossiled drama...."[69] "The Academies were lying" and their assessment of Greece offered nothing but "anachronistic dusts of the West."[70] On the contrary, Le Corbusier argues, Greece teaches rebellion: it is "the testimony of a heroic, creative, and vibrant age." "Any man who loves life," he concludes, "must board the ship in Marseilles and set sail towards Greece. That is the point of departure for our West."[71]

Interested as he was in architecture in the 1930s, Elytis was certainly familiar with Le Corbusier's ideas on Greece. Most of the Swiss architect's essays were published in Greek periodicals of the time (e.g., *Τεχνικά Χρονικά, 20ός Αιώνας*) or in books and magazines that Elytis undoubtedly read (e.g., *Le Voyage en Grèce*, Christian Zervos's *L'Art en Grèce*). In the "Chronicle of a Decade" he describes how the impressions of Le Corbusier and of other participants in the Fourth C.I.A.M. conference influenced his own thought:

---

[66] Le Corbusier, *Κείμενα*, pp. 161–2.
[67] Le Corbusier, *Κείμενα*, p. 150.
[68] Le Corbusier, *Κείμενα*, p. 153.
[69] Le Corbusier, *Κείμενα*, p. 148.
[70] Le Corbusier, *Κείμενα*, p. 151.
[71] Le Corbusier, *Κείμενα*, pp. 152–3.

The words some of the most famous modern architects uttered in interviews, when they came to Athens in 1934 for their fourth conference were still fresh in my mind. I admired how, with a glance at our landscape, they captured the special problems that it posed; what is more, they related these problems to solutions proposed by "modern art" in its attempt to emancipate itself from the tyranny of the bad heritage that was the Renaissance. Painters like Léger or poets like Reverdy spoke even more specifically, through Petros Apthoniatis's periodical *Voyage en Grèce*, about that which should have come out of our own eventual aesthetic position, out of a reevaluation of the fundamental Greek values.[72]

Le Corbusier perceived Greece as the "point of departure for [our] West." This *eastwards* movement was, of course, a wider modernist phenomenon; apart from the Eastern Mediterranean, European poets looked for inspiration in the philosophy, art, religion, and literature of the Far East. For the Greek poets of the thirties, the turn to the Eastern borders of the nation amounted to a rediscovery of identity. As Vangelis Calotychos suggests, "in his first collection, Elytis announces this orientation to the east, by conferring upon, in the title Προσανατολισμοί or Orientations, a word which, once broken down, gives us the words προς and ανατολή (towards the east)."[73] His chronotope is defined temporally with a move away from classical myth, and spatially with a transposition of the (lost) center to the Aegean islands.

West vs. East, North vs. South, and the Rediscovery of Tradition

In reevaluating "the fundamental Greek values," Elytis juxtaposes two ideological forces: *East vs. West* and *North vs. South*. Like Camus, who sees Northern and Central Europeans as "buttoned up to the neck," Elytis compares them with the people of the Mediterranean: the "deformed monsters" of the Northern European mythologies gradually take "a human shape" as they move southward towards the Mediterranean.[74] Unlike Southern Europe, the north has become asynchronous with nature and has fallen victim to the plight of technocracy. Elytis's mapping of modernist tension is primarily founded on differences of temperament: Mediterranean sensitivity is contrasted with Northern European austerity. In a 1946 review of the iconographies of General Makriyiannis and the paintings of the folk artist Panagiotis Zografos, Elytis suggests that the lack of "a sensitive measure" in Greek art, in the century following liberation from the Ottomans, is due to the overwhelming influence of the West:

> It is certain that such an absence is due to our not nearly complete absorption by the West, to the expense, to be more precise, of our great counter-support

---

[72] Elytis, *Ανοιχτά Χαρτιά*, p. 389.

[73] Vangelis Calotychos, *Modern Greece: A Cultural Poetics* (Oxford: Berg, 2003), p. 168.

[74] Elytis, *Ανοιχτά Χαρτιά*, p. 452.

that has always been the East. That is why we feel the need to defend the role of the East today, not simply concerning painting but our civilization in general; that is why we find more natural, more beneficent, for our youth to be influenced by a Matisse, for example, who represents an in-depth antithesis to the monodogmatic Europeanism, than a Lytras or an Iakovides,[75] painters who, despite their possible personal merits, are victims of the North.[76]

The East/West juxtaposition is more historically grounded and partakes in the general frustration of European artists with the central role assumed by the so-called Western civilization. The reaction of the Romantics and the Symbolists against the values that the West came to represent had turned to total rebellion by the end of World War I. "It was the destructiveness of the war itself," Eric Cahm writes, "which finally undermined the fabric of the national past, and led the way into the total cultural nihilism of the dadaists and the total political and social transformation envisaged by the 1917 Russian Revolution."[77] The reaction to the national past directed the modernist orientation eastwards (politically, culturally, and artistically).

Contrary to the Western modernist trend, Greek modernism did not combine its turn eastwards (towards the Aegean, Asia Minor, Cyprus) with the undermining of traditional values. In fact, the eastward orientation of the thirties generation aimed to recover the national center that had been lost under the impact of the Renaissance. The relatively young modern Greek nation (about 100 years old in the 1930s) still lived in the shadows of Classical Greece. Elytis's critique, launched against both the West and the Greek intellectuals who continued to imitate the classical models, is characteristic of this tension: "A stilted truth regarding Greece, for example, is its history as the official Greeks present it to us; another, also stilted, is its history as the Europeans present it to us."[78] And elsewhere: "In our days, there are those who continue to play that ungrateful role of the old Humanists who, dressed in black, copied copies, prayed at the Acropolis, and added editorial observations to the orators, with an insensitivity that literally thrust away the true Greece to the antipodes."[79] In essence, the Greek modernist rebellion amounted to a rediscovery of tradition. In the case of Elytis, this dichotomy between the embracing of modernist rebellion and the attempt to define the modern face of Greece is perhaps the most puzzling in the poets of his generation. He did not adopt T.S. Eliot's ideas on the utilization of tradition, particularly through the use of the mythical

---

[75] Nikiforos Lytras (1832–1904) and Giorgos Iakovides (1853–1932) were Greek painters who followed in the tradition of the Munich school (i.e., German Romantic painters that gathered in Munich in the second half of the nineteenth century).

[76] Elytis, *Ανοιχτά Χαρτιά*, pp. 548–9.

[77] Eric Cahm, "Revolt, Conservatism and Reaction in Paris 1905–25," in *Modernism: A Guide to European Literature 1890–1930*, ed. Malcolm Bradbury and James McFarlane, 162–71 (London: Penguin, 1991), p. 163.

[78] Elytis, *Ανοιχτά Χαρτιά*, p. 18.

[79] Elytis, *Ανοιχτά Χαρτιά*, pp. 190–91.

subtext, but rather shared Seferis's fascination with the rediscovery of the new (more "authentic") face of Greece. His fascination with surrealism and his early encounter with Le Corbusier's ideas played a central role in the crystallization of his position on tradition and modernity. He perceived the surrealist rebellion as a total rejection of the Renaissance inheritance, which he blamed for the misrepresentation of "Greekness." In contrast to George Seferis, who found an amalgamation of the classical and the modern Greek identity through the use of Eliot's *mythical method*, Elytis turned to geography, nature, and the vibrant folk tradition of the islands.

To a certain extent, the literary activities in Athens, in the 1930s, resembled much of what was happening in other European cities: new meeting places, new periodicals, a surrealist exhibit, controversial lectures, and a continuous clash between the established academia and the young artists. At the same time, however, the quest for a spiritual center was relocated according to each artist's idiosyncrasies: Elytis and his friend Nikos Gatsos found a truer face of Greece on the islands; Kazantzakis, writing in the 30s and 40s, found a spiritual locus in his native Crete, and Seferis recovered a vibrant dialect on the island of Cyprus.[80] Regardless of their different individual orientations, the generation of the 1930s attempted a redefinition of Greek culture by transposing the center from the much-too-classical Athens to the island periphery. As Calotychos writes, they "undertook the definition of a new transcendental ethos of Hellenism no longer defined in terms of territory or politics, but through culture."[81] What is interesting about this attempt at redefinition was the fact that it simultaneously took place within and contrary to the modernist spirit. On the one hand, the poets of the 30s were adamant supporters of the modernist poetic project but on the other, they resisted the modernist tendency towards a global poetry. The tension between modernity and the establishment of a new tradition is, Matei Calinescu writes, a general modernist characteristic: "It has become almost a truism ... to describe the modern artist as torn between his urge to cut himself off from the past—to become completely "modern"—and his dream to found a new *tradition*, recognizable as such by the future."[82] In the case of Elytis and the generation of the thirties, the urgency to resolve this tension was even greater, as it wavered between modernization and the redefinition of modern Hellenic ethos.

---

[80] When Seferis went to Cyprus for the first time (while serving as a diplomat in the Greek embassy of Beirut) he sent a letter to his friend Nanos Valaoritis about his impressions of the island: "It was the first time that I saw this island. I was deeply moved and embarrassed, in a way, for not suspecting that so much Greece was so near me (an hour by plane from Beirut).... You speak, in a letter of yours, about the 'primordial lesson.' There in Cyprus you will find it if you have eyes to look for it. These people are closer to the roots than we are—I don't think they know it and perhaps it's better that they don't." In Nanos Valaoritis, *Μοντερνισμός, Πρωτοπορία και "ΠΑΛΙ"* (Athens: Kastaniotis, 1997), pp. 82–3.

[81] Calotychos, *Modern Greece*, p. 158.

[82] Calinescu, *Five Faces*, p. 67.

The paradox of Greek modernity further resided in the already existing tension that Gregory Jusdanis describes as modern art's "paradoxical position in simultaneously mediating identity and reflecting on it from a distance."[83] It is important, then, to stress the fact that the "Greekness" often ascribed to the generation of the thirties was not, in most cases, an attempt to define a national narrative. In fact, they criticized the nineteenth-century attempt to project such narrative of continuity between ancient and modern Greece. What these poets achieved was not so much a definition of the Hellenic ethos but rather the creation of a personal microcosm with macrocosmic reverberations. Certainly, "Greekness" was not defined politically or territorially; neither was it defined historically or out of the collective consciousness of its people. For Elytis, the relationship between "the real Greece" and the "other Greece" is the same as the relationship between life and dream:

> I resided in a country that came from the other, the real one, as the dream comes from the facts of my life. I too named it Greece and I drew it on paper so I could look at it. It seemed so little; so elusive.
>
> As time went by I kept trying it out: with certain sudden earthquakes, certain old thoroughbred storms. I kept changing the position of things to rid them of all value. I studied the Vigilant and the Solitary[84] so that I might be found worthy of making brown hillcrests, little Monasteries, fountains. I even produced an entire orchard full of citrus trees that smelled of Heraclitus and Archilochus. But the fragrance was so strong I got scared. So I very slowly took to setting words like gems to cover this country I love. Lest someone see its beauty. Or suspect that maybe it does not exist.[85]

What is particularly interesting in Elytis's description is the concurrent tendency towards deconstruction and reconstruction. The poet acts as a Creator (a position

---

[83] Jusdanis, *Belated*, p. 48.

[84] "I studied the Vigilant and the Solitary ..." (Μελετούσα τ' Ακοίμιστα και την Ερημική): Elytis is connecting here his view of Greece with poetic experience. This "other" Greece is constructed *because* the poet is vigilant (or sleepless: α-κοίμιστος) and solitary (Ερημικός). In essence, this creation is as personal as a "dream."

[85] From *The Little Seafarer*, Poem II. Elytis, *Collected Poems*, p. 424. Κατοίκησα μια χώρα που 'βγαινε από την άλλη, την πραγματική, όπως τ' όνειρο από τα γεγονότα της ζωής μου. Την είπα κι αυτήν Ελλάδα και τη χάραξα πάνω στο χαρτί να τηνε βλέπω. Τόσο λίγη έμοιαζε· τόσο άπιαστη. / Περνώντας ο καιρός όλο και τη δοκίμαζα: με κάτι ξαφνικούς σεισμούς, κάτι παλιές καθαρόαιμες θύελλες. Άλλαζα θέση στα πράγματα να τ' απαλλάξω από κάθε αξία. Μελετούσα τ' Ακοίμιστα και την Ερημική ν' αξιωθώ να φκιάνω λόφους καστανούς, μοναστηράκια, κρήνες. Ως κι ένα περιβόλι ολόκληρο έβγαλα γιομάτο εσπεριδοειδή που μύριζαν Ηράκλειτο κι Αρχίλοχο. Μα 'ταν η ευωδία τόση που φοβήθηκα. Κι έπιασα σιγά σιγά να δένω λόγια σαν διαμαντικά να την καλύψω τη χώρα που αγαπούσα. Μην και κανείς ιδεί το κάλλος. Ή κι υποψιαστεί πως ίσως δεν υπάρχει (Ο Μικρός Ναυτίλος, II, Elytis, *Ποίηση*, p. 497).

that the poet also assumes in the "Genesis" of *The Axion Esti*) but also challenges, and tests his creation with "sudden earthquakes" and "thoroughbred storms." In other words, he resists a superficial assessment of his "Greece" by testing its validity—the view of the historical nation is challenged and defined through the destructiveness of history (war, political turmoil, social injustice, etc.); in the poetic construction, it is nature (earthquakes and storms) that becomes the testing-ground of the imaginary nation.

Elytis's *dream nation*[86] comes into being through a process of deconstructing what is nationally real. In this sense, the regional character of Greek modernism is not a contradiction: in order to recover the suppressed "other" (the elusive ethos of the idea that is Greece) the poet must deconstruct the national, "real," narrative. This deconstruction of reality, an idea that Elytis embraced from his early surrealist years, leads to a *codification* of the dream nation. *The Little Seafarer* is perhaps Elytis's most explicit attempt, along with *The Axion Esti*, to define "Greekness" in terms similar to dream symbolism: "If you take Greece apart, in the end you will see remaining to you an olive tree, a vineyard, and a ship. Which means: with just so much you can put her back together" (*The Little Seafarer*, Poem XIV).[87] The tension between the historical and the dream nation is further emphasized in *The Little Seafarer* by the inclusion of brief descriptions ("Spotlights") of betrayal in Greek history beginning from Antiquity to the present.[88] In "Spotlight ii" for instance, we hear of Miltiades's condemnation by the court, Aristides's ostracism, Phidias's imprisonment and death, Socrates's execution, Alexander's execution of Parmenion, and Phocion's death sentence.[89] The dream nation is the other side of Greek history—it is what history represses and neglects but it is as real as dreams.

Following Teriade's advice, in 1935 Elytis went to Mytilini, along with Andreas Empeirikos, in order to collect the paintings of the unknown folk artist Theophilos Hadjimichael. They went around the island collecting any object that Theophilos had drawn on: oil paintings, wall paintings, drawings on wood, even

---

[86] The term "dream nation" is used by Stathis Gourgouris in *Dream Nation: Enlightenment, Colonization, and the Institution of Modern Greece* (Stanford: Stanford University Press, 1996). Gourgouris explains: "As form, the Nation is fundamentally unintelligible. Or more precisely: *a nation cannot be read as a text; even if it were to make sense, we would distrust it*. This is why it is decisive to perceive the formal nature of the nation as akin to that of a dream.... The emphasis must shift from nation-as-text to nation-as-dream, which is to say that those texts bearing the nation's mark may ultimately be seen as descriptions of the nation's dream thoughts, thus figural transcriptions (prone to disguise and occultation-secondary revision) of the nation's dream-work" (p. 30). I use the term here in a slightly different way. Both the dream nation and the poet's dream *of* the nation are imaginary constructions, but the relationship between them, in Elytis's case, can be hostile (hence his distinction between the "real Greece" and the "other Greece").

[87] Elytis, *Collected Poems*, p. 457. Also see, in *The Little Seafarer*, poems III, XI, XXV, XXVI.

[88] For further discussion on the structural division of *The Little Seafarer* see Chapter 5.

[89] Elytis, *Collected Poems*, p. 447.

paintings on tin cans. By 1936, Teriade presented some of the findings to his circle of acquaintances in Paris, which included Giacometti and Le Corbusier. The latter published an article the same year, in *Le Voyage en Grèce* about the folk artist:

> An indigenous painter of the Greek landscape and the Greek ethos.... An authentic character of a tender and lucid Greece, rid of all artificiality, of the older Greece which is still ever-present outside the cities of "commerce and industry."

> Through Theophilos, we see the people and landscape of the Greeks: rosy soil, pine and olive trees, the sea and the mountains of the gods, people bathing in a dangerous serenity that offers itself to the sudden exaltations of the soul. We find ourselves at the basis, the beginning, we see ourselves illuminated, informed, and moved in front of this material world that is golden and prepared for an unfathomable brilliance.[90]

For Le Corbusier, Theophilos was an "indigenous" example of what is vibrant and alive in modern Greece. As in his impressions from his second journey to Greece, particularly to the islands, here too he perceives a Greek ethos that is rooted in the surrounding landscape. Elytis shared Le Corbusier's suggestion of a continuity embedded not in the aesthetic imitation of the classical model but in a diachronic ethos inherent in the relationship of the people with the landscape (an idea that Camus also embraced).

In a subsequent monograph that Elytis published on the artist (*Theophilos*, 1973),[91] he further places the painter at the "antipodes of Western art" and "closer to the Byzantine perception."[92] Quoting Élie Faure's commentary on Monet's influence by Japanese lithographs, he compares the eastern and western artist:

> 'The modern European painter, the impressionist, struggles to extract from an instance in his painting the thousands of impressions that it is possible to encompass. On the contrary the artist of the East, the more schematic artist, concentrates in an instance of his painting the thousands of impressions that he has gathered inside him out of the thousands of other analogous moments of his life.' Let us not forget that Theophilos is in his largest part an Easterner: thus his difficulty in adapting to the dimension of depth, his love for light colors, and his sensitivity towards small natural paradises.[93]

---

[90] Le Corbusier, "Θεόφιλος," *Η Λέξη* 172 (Nov–Dec 2002): 968–9, p. 968. Translated by Marinos Pourgouris.

[91] Elytis, *Ανοιχτά Χαρτιά*, p. 298. An excerpt from the book was originally published in 1947 in the periodical *Αγγλοελληνική Επιθεώρηση* [English-Greek Review] (Vol. 3, no 1, May 1947) under the title "Η αισθητική και συναισθητική καταγωγή του Θεόφιλου Χατζημιχαήλ." ["The aesthetic and synaesthetic descent of Theophilos Hadjimichael"].

[92] Elytis, *Ανοιχτά Χαρτιά*, p. 284.

[93] Elytis, *Ανοιχτά Χαρτιά*, p. 298.

The brilliance of Theophilos resides, for Elytis, in his autodidactic techniques influenced by Byzantine iconography, which emphasized the use of color and mystical emotion over depth and reality of depiction. Most importantly, Theophilos belongs to the folk tradition that became the unconscious carrier of the Hellenic ethos. "Greekness" for Elytis, is "a way of seeing and doing things" and, as such, "it was continued exclusively by the folk tradition."[94] Juxtaposing the Renaissance depiction of "Greekness" that produced "pastoral scenes and pink angels" with the Greek folk tradition, with its "whitewashed houses" and "the geraniums in the tin can," he finds the latter to be closer to the spirit that gave birth to an Apollo or a Winged Nike.[95] As a representation of the internal other, Elytis's dream nation is constructed by revitalizing the suppressed elements that survived in the folk tradition of the islands. The turn eastwards is not coincidental; the West had much to do with this suppression by appropriating and projecting the image of a classical Greece that loomed over and overshadowed the Greek tradition.

Architecture, Landscape, Poetry

"The business of Architecture," writes Le Corbusier, "is to establish emotional relationships by means of raw material."[96] Emotional relationships are further contingent on the architect's "mood:" "Your mood has been gentle, brutal, charming or noble. The stones you have erected tell me so. You fix me to the place and my eyes regard it. They behold something which expresses a thought." Roman architecture, he continues, is indicative of Rome's will "to conquer the world and govern it"; it was an empire governed by order and the "desire for domination and organization."[97] His admiration of the Cycladic houses is rooted in the same principle: "returning from the islands and Greece the architect can not ignore the archetype of the human and determinative value that he finds there."[98] In both cases, architecture is presented as an *ethopoetic art* or a mirror of cultural values.

Elytis's Solar Metaphysics is founded on a similar principle; it constitutes, in essence, the transposition of this architectural premise to the realm of poetic aesthetics. In the same way that the steeples of Chartres would be "irreconcilable

---

[94] Elytis, *Αυτοπροσωπογραφία*, p. 21.

[95] Elytis, *Αυτοπροσωπογραφία*, p. 22. As was discussed in Chapter 1, Elytis also criticized the Western representation of "Greekness," reminiscent of the Renaissance, in a letter that he sent to Lawrence Durrell in response to the latter's description of Seferis as a "European poet" (see Elytis, *Εν Λευκώ*, pp. 209–11). The simultaneous turn to the East and the discovery of folk tradition was certainly not limited to the case of Theophilos. During his visit in Cyprus, Seferis speaks of the native folk artists with admiration and regrets the slow decline of their trade; Ritsos composed one of his best known collections of poetry, *Epitafios*, drawing from the language and structure of traditional lament rituals.

[96] Le Corbusier, *New Architecture*, p. 153.

[97] Le Corbusier, *New Architecture*, pp. 154–6.

[98] Le Corbusier, *Κείμενα*, p. 162.

in the sky of Aegina," the Greek sense of the sea cannot be conveyed in the form of the sonnet.[99] As a Doric temple captures "the deeper spirit of paganism," or the dome "the essence of orthodoxy," the elements of the poem (images, concepts, metaphors, etc.) must be apportioned in a form that renders them the "sine qua non of the total result."[100] Such theorization places genre within a particular cultural and historical context.

"Landscapes ... provide physical shape; they picture the nation."[101] Through language, as Sapir notes, one can reconstruct the culture and geography of a people. Similarly, Elytis maintained that both culture and geography are expressive of a particular ethos—they are part of an ethical locus that poetry (i.e., language) makes visible, both schematically and conceptually. In the context of modernity, the theory seems to be an anachronistic return to a kind of morpholatry. Elytis, however, avoided the use of such terms as "form" or "formalism" and preferred to describe his technique as architectural poetics.[102]

To understand the distinctiveness of Solar Metaphysics in this respect, and to distinguish it from preexistent notions of form, further clarifications are necessary. Firstly, Elytis applied the theory only to his longer collections; more specifically, *The Axion Esti*, *Maria Nephele*, and *The Little Seafarer*. His architectural poetics is not applied to his shorter collections, since the content can sustain meaning without having the need for structure. Secondly, structure is perceived as the architectural foundation instigated by, and in constant exchange with, content. It is not, in other words, a pre-assigned formula, as in the case of a sonnet. Thirdly, the architecture of the poem can be discerned in a number of ways: the use of specific line numbers, the use of a specific number of words, the drawing of mathematical relationships between each poem of a collection, the division into conceptual schemata, etc. Fourthly, the structure of the poem must not be forced on the reader: "the reader must be absorbed by the meaning. The scheme and architecture are needed to give solidity to the work."[103] In the same way that Valéry supported the use of rhyme as an instigator of content, since it determined the direction of a poetic line, here structure is intricately connected to the content.[104]

What remains to be discussed, apart from a specific application of the theory to Elytis's work, is its characterization as "solar" and "metaphysical." During his

---

[99] Elytis, *Ανοιχτά Χαρτιά*, p. 451.

[100] Elytis, *Ανοιχτά Χαρτιά*, pp. 450–51.

[101] Stephen Daniels, *Fields of Vision: Landscape, Imagery and National Identity in England and the United States* (Princeton: Princeton University Press, 1993), p. 5.

[102] Elytis, *Αυτοπροσωπογραφία*, pp. 31–2.

[103] Elytis, *Αυτοπροσωπογραφία*, p. 33.

[104] Interestingly, both Elytis and T.S. Eliot used the example of Valéry to indicate the relationship between Form and Content. See Elytis, *Αυτοπροσωπογραφία*, p. 33 and Eliot's "Reflections on Vers Libre," in Thomas Stearns Eliot, *Poems and Prose* (New York: Knopf, 1998).

interview on National Greek Television (ERT), Elytis attempted to explain this transposition of architectural poetics to the metaphysical realm:

> When I speak of Solar Metaphysics, I mean the Metaphysics of Light, and this is a difficult subject that one cannot simplify. In any case, I use the term "solar" to point to the nuclear formation of the poem, something that concerns not simply the content but also the technique.
>
> Philosophers can speak freely on a theoretical level but the poet must coordinate theory with action. In other words, the poet's theory must be manifested and illustrated in the work.
>
> If one imagines conscience in the place of the sun, on one side and, on the other, all the factors that contribute to poetic expression—images, similes, metaphors, thoughts—in the place of the planets, he will see that the movement of this system assumes the same nature as that of a solar system. That is why I referred to the nuclear formation of the poem.
>
> Thus, light, as the beginning and end of every apocalyptic phenomenon, is expressed with the achievement of a growing visibility; an eventual diaphaneity in the poem that allows you to see through matter and through the soul. In my opinion, that is also the final aim of the poem.[105]

One can argue that Joyce's *Ulysses* achieves a similar diaphaneity in creating an intimate relationship between schematics, concepts, and content. In his case, structure is largely dependent on and guided by the mythical subtext. Furthermore, it is expressed in shifts from style to style (popular romance novel, the historical narrative, dream sequence, etc.), and it is not restricted by the aesthetics of poetry. The most important difference, however, is the way the two writers approach reality—Joyce claimed that if Dublin were wiped off the face of the earth, it could be reconstructed through *Ulysses*. His use of structure leads to a reconstruction of reality through a stream of consciousness. Elytis, by contrast, uses structure as a means of transposing reality and creating a hyper-reality: one can certainly not reconstruct the Greek islands through his poetry, but rather, metaphysically speaking, the ethos of the landscape and the language.

It is important to note that Elytis does not use the terms Solar Metaphysics and architectural poetics interchangeably. Structure, in a simplified form, is present in the totality of his work. The theory of Solar Metaphysics was conceptualized in the 1950s and took years to crystallize. In his interview with Ivar Ivask for *Books Abroad*, Elytis characterizes it as a central theory in the third period of his poetry and offers as examples his collections *The Light-Tree* and *Maria Nephele*.[106] Solar Metaphysics centers around the notion of diaphaneity (διαφάνεια), which is related

---

[105] Elytis, Αυτοπροσωπογραφία, pp. 34–5.

[106] "In my first period nature and metamorphoses predominate (stimulated by surrealism, which always believed in the metamorphosis of things). In my second period,

to Martin Heidegger's use of the term *alētheia*. According to Heidegger, *alētheia*, a Greek word for "truth," is not linked with correctness, as Plato suggested, but rather with the process of uncovering [*Verborgenheit*].[107] Poetry, or the work of art, acts as a negotiating force between the concealing earth and the apparent cosmos: "The happening of truth results in the work's reposing-in-itself between earth and world. This repose is the unity that results from the struggle or inter-play between earth's self-concealing nature and the self-disclosing nature of world."[108] Thus, "when truth sets itself into the work, it appears."[109] What is distinctive about Elytis's application of the Heideggerian understanding of *alētheia* is its association with (the Greek) landscape. Elytis equates the concept of "diaphaneity" with "luminosity," both of which are revealing of truth, and perceives them as the qualities that characterize the Greek space, the Greek landscape and the need for expression. In his Nobel address he alludes to the revelatory qualities of these concepts: "I am not talking about the natural ability to perceive things in all their details but about the metaphorical ability to hold their essence and lead them to such clarity that simultaneously denotes their metaphysical significance as in a revelation."[110] It is the revealing essence of landscape that makes language possible: from its embedded secret messages, words are formed, then phrases whose "decodification brings you closer to the deepest truth [vérité, αλήθεια]."[111]

---

including *The Axion Esti*, there is greater historic and moral awareness, yet without the loss of the vision of the world which marks my first period" (Elytis, "On his Poetry," p. 640).

[107] In *Being and Time* Heidegger describes the concept of truth as a process of discovery: "To say that a statement is *true* means that it discovers the beings in themselves. It asserts, it shows, it lets beings "be seen" (*apophansis*) in their discoveredness. The *being true* (*truth*) of the statement must be understood as *discovering*. Thus, truth by no means has the structure of an agreement between knowing and the object in the sense of a correspondence of one being (subject) to another (object)." Martin Heidegger, *Being and Time*, trans. Joan Stambaugh (Albany: State University of New York Press, 1996), p. 201. The italics are Heidegger's. Etymologically, *alētheia* if formed from the privative affix "α" and the verb "λήθω" (to be mistaken). In his *Dictionary of the Ancient Greek Language*, Stamatakos renders "αληθής" as "ο μη κεκρυμμένος ή μη αποκρυπτόμενος, άρα πραγματικός" [the non hidden or noncovered, thus real]. Ioannis Stamatakos, *Λεξικόν Αρχαίας Ελληνικής Γλώσσης* (Athens: Vivliopromitheutiki, 1999), p. 61. In this sense, Heidegger's suggestion shifts the focus from truth as an absolute fact, to truth as a process of uncovering what is hidden—truth, in other words, can only be defined as the opposite of what is covered or concealed.

[108] Gilbert J. Shaver, "Rev. of Poetry, Language, Thought, by Martin Heidegger," *Boundary 2: A Journal of Postmodern Literature* 1 (1973): 742–9, pp. 744–5. Shaver continues to say: "Heidegger is not just switching terms on us. Earth is not mere content nor is it only matter, like stone or paint. It is the origin to which every thing returns, hence it is self-concealing. World is not mere form. It is 'the self disclosing openness of the broad paths of the simple and essential decisions in the destiny of a historical people'" (Shaver, "Heidegger," p. 745).

[109] Martin Heidegger, *Poetry*, p. 81.
[110] Elytis, *Ανοιχτά Χαρτιά*, p. 343.
[111] Elytis, *Ανοιχτά Χαρτιά*, p. 345.

Elytis's interest in the architectural construction of the poem can be traced back to his first poems. After discovering the poetry of Éluard and Jouve, Elytis reportedly destroyed his first poems, which were written in imitation of Cavafian verse, and composed the "First Poems" of *Orientations*. A brief example from this collection will suffice in illustrating his early attempt to "frame" the poem in a distinct pattern. This is, in fact, the first published poem of *Orientations*, and it exemplifies Elytis's atypical position between surrealism and structured verse:

> Eros
> The Archipelago
> And the prow of its foams
> And the gulls of its dreams
> On its highest mountain the sailor waves
> A song
>
> Eros
> Its song
> And the horizon of its voyage
> And the echo of its nostalgia
> On her wettest rock the betrothed awaits
> A ship
>
> Eros
> Its ship
> And the nonchalance of its summer winds
> And the jib of its hope
> On its lightest undulation an island cradles
> The coming[112]

The most obvious observation, in terms of structure, is the length of the poem's lines: each seems to loosely expand from the first to the fifth line and contract with the final word (in other words, the number of words in each line increases, with the exception of the third and fourth at the center of each stanza, which remain the same). Furthermore, the three stanzas of the poem constitute grammatical mirrors of each other. The word "έρωτας" ["eros"] is repeated in each first line; each second line is always a neutral noun related to Eros; each third and fourth line uses the conjunction "and" (κι), and is in the genitive. Each fifth line is the longest and most intricate: it always uses a superlative (πιο), a combination of adjective/noun, a second noun, and the only verb of each stanza. The sixth line is the noun that the verb acts upon: the sailor waves *a song*, the betrothed awaits a *ship*, the island

---

[112] Elytis, *Collected Poems*, p. 5. Ο έρωτας / Το αρχιπέλαγος / Κι η πρώρα των αφρών του / Κι οι γλάροι των ονείρων του / Στο πιο ψηλό κατάρτι του ο ναύτης ανεμίζει/ Ένα τραγούδ / Ο έρωτας / Το τραγούδι του / Κι οι ορίζοντες του ταξιδιού του / Κι η ηχώ της νοσταλγίας του / Στον πιο βρεμένο βράχο της η αρραβωνιαστικιά προσμένει / Ένα καράβι / Ο έρωτας / Το καράβι του / Κι η αμεριμνησία των μελτεμιών του / Κι ο φλόκος της ελπίδας του / Στον πιο ελαφρό κυματισμό του ένα νησί λικνίζει / Τον ερχομό (Elytis, *Ποίηση*, p. 11).

cradles *the coming*. Each stanza weaves itself into the next, as the last line of each stanza becomes the second line of the next (with the only difference being the change from an indefinite to a definite article).

As Mario Vitti observes, the poem creates a web of associations: Eros, the Archipelago, the song, and the ship are semantically linked, and the omission of such obvious similes as "like" creates further connections between the nouns: "the sea-gulls *are* dreams."[113] This web of associations certainly points back to Elytis's surrealist influence, and the supposition that the random association between previously uncombined words creates a new dynamic for poetry. In this case, however, the words are far from being random: they are carefully chosen and correspond with the central notion of Eros in the island setting (the archipelago, the ship, the sea-gulls, the prow of the foam, the wet rock). Vitti further suggests that the poem is an apt illustration of Elytis's effort to break conventional or traditional rules of composition and, at the same time, replace them with new ones.[114] Eros, in this sense, is placed in both a conceptual (the island) and a structural space (the poem). Structure may give a sense of solidity to the poem, but it also turns against itself in creating a dynamic pattern of repetition that remains suspended: it suggests to the reader that this movement has begun before the first stanza and it continues after the last (we already know the first and last line of the invisible previous stanza and the first and second line of the one that follows the poem's ending). This "suspension" works well with the poetic image: the sailor waves a song, the betrothed awaits a ship and an island cradles the coming. Erotic desire is described in terms of dream and nostalgia suspended in hope of "the coming."

It is important to understand the first poems of *Orientations* as a discovery of style for the 23-year-old Elytis. A brief examination of the collection's structural component further underlines Elytis's interest in combining the influence of surrealism with structure, which the movement lacked:

1. Groups of Seven: Most of the poems in *Orientations* are divided into groups of seven or multiples of seven: "Seven Nocturnal Heptastichs" (seven poems), "Windows toward the Fifth Season" (seven poems), "Orion" (seven poems), "Dionysos" (seven poems), "Clepsydras of the Unknown" (seven poems), "Clear Skies" (21 poems), "The Concert of Hyacinths" (21 poems), "In the Service of Summer" (14 poems).
2. Number of Lines in each stanza:
    a. Many of the poems are divided into stanzas of identical lines: e.g., "Anniversary" (15 X 4), "Blissful Donna" (6 X 4), "Beautiful Girl in the Garden" (6 X 5), "The Mad Pomegranate Tree" (6 X 6).
    b. The poems of "Seven Nocturnal Heptastichs" are always seven lines long.

---

[113] Vitti, *Οδυσσέας Ελύτης*, p. 24.
[114] Vitti, *Οδυσσέας Ελύτης*, p. 23.

3. Mirroring: In the case of "Seven Nocturnal Heptastichs," the arrangement of lines in each poem creates a distinct "mirroring" structure. All poems are seven lines long and each stanza is divided into a specific number of lines giving us the following structure:

Poem I:	4 + 3
Poem II:	4 + 3
Poem III:	3 + 4
Poem IV:	7
Poem V:	4 + 3
Poem VI:	4 + 3
Poem VII:	3 + 4

The structure of the first three poems is identical to that of the last three; at the center is the only poem with no line-breaks. In the third and last poem in "Of the Aegean" this mirroring (or reflection) is accomplished in a framing of the poem with the key words/concepts: there are two stanzas (each is five lines long); the first line of the first stanza begins with the word "Sea surf" and ends with the word "Eros"; the last line of the last stanza reverses the order: it begins with the word "Eros" and it ends with "sea surf."

4. Repetition: Many of the poems achieve an internal structure through a repetition of specific words or phrases. A telling example is "Anniversary," whose four stanzas begin with the line "I brought my life this far"; in "Beautiful Girl in the Garden" each of the five stanzas includes the line "oh how lovely you are." The sense of a more abstract structuring is maintained in the frequent use of repetitive phrases or words—primarily conjunctions—that give a certain fluidity to the poem (see, for example, "The Mad Pomegranate Tree," "Birth of Day," "Image of Boeotia," and "Age of Glaucous Memory").

Even in these early attempts, Elytis associates poetic content and poetic form. In other words, structure is used as a foundation that supports meaning. At the same time, Elytis's early poetic structures can only be understood as the experimentations of a young poet who was concerned with finding his own voice. His reluctance regarding the publication of these early poems is clearly expressed in "The Chronicle of a Decade;" it was, in fact, Giorgos Katsimbalis who "forced" him to publish the first poems in the eleventh issue of *Nea Grammata*.[115] His uncertainty about publishing his work was further intensified by his family's discomfort with his poetic explorations (thus, the assumption of the pen name "Elytis") as well as by his ambivalent position: wanting to write poetry, on the one hand, and wanting

---

[115] When Elytis entrusted Katsimbalis with some poems, the latter went to the printer and returned with the first printed draft of what he suggested should be included in the periodical. Elytis reluctantly agreed. See Elytis, *Ανοιχτά Χαρτιά*, pp. 361–2.

to study law, on the other. Eventually his poetry would move towards the antipode of the impulsiveness that characterizes his first poems.[116] Nevertheless, what makes these early attempts at structuring the poem important in our exploration of Elytis's metaphysics is the effort to set the amorphous surrealist creation within a tangible frame. Mario Vitti suggests that "Dionysos" and "The Clepsydras of the Unknown" (in *Orientations*) are "evidence of Elytis's approach to a 'nucleus' of surrealist poetry."[117] But even in these most "automatic" poems of the collection we perceive an emphatic tendency towards structure.

Beginning with *Orientations*, where mathematical and structural experimentation is scattered and inconsistent, Elytis often employs the number seven as a structuring principle. The choice of the number is, of course, not coincidental; it most prominently appears in St. John's Apocalypse, one of Elytis's most beloved works, as well as in other Biblical passages, which he often uses as a subtext in his poetry.[118] A numerological examination of his collections, especially following *Sun the First*, reveals the significance of the number seven to the creation of a solid mythical system around it. Consider, for example, the structure of his poetry collections in respect to the number of poems they include:

Song Heroic and Mourning:	14 poems
The Axion Esti	
The Genesis:	7 free verse hymns
The Gloria:	quatrains + triplets, seven couplets
Six and One Remorses for the Sky:	7 poems
The Light-Tree and the Fourteenth Beauty:	21 poems
The Monogram:	7 poems
Stepchildren	
First Series:	7 Poems
Second Series:	7 Poems
Maria Nephele	
Part A:	14 Poems
Part B:	14 Poems
Part C:	14 Poems
The Eternal Wager:	7 Sections
Three poems under a Flag of Convenience	
The Garden Sees:	7 Poems
The Almond of the World:	7 Poems
Ad Libitum:	7 Poems

---

[116] Elytis, *Αυτοπροσωπογραφία*, p. 29.

[117] Vitti, *Οδυσσέας Ελύτης*, p. 49.

[118] The Apocalypse is clearly structured around the number seven. We have for example: *The Seven Seals*—once the seventh is opened, *seven* Angels stand before God, who gives them *seven trumpets*. As the seventh angel sounds the seventh trumpet, *seven bowls* are poured into the land, the sea, the rivers, the sun, the throne of the beast, the river Euphrates, and into the air. There are also the seven churches, spirits, stars, dooms, etc. Elytis translated John's *Apocalypse* into modern Greek. See Odysseus Elytis, trans., *Η Αποκάλυψη του Ιωάννη*, trans. Odysseus Elytis (Athens: Ypsilon, 1985).

Diary of an Invisible April:	49 poems
The Little Seafarer	
Spotlights:	7 entries in four sections
To Anoint the Past:	7 prose poems in four sections
With Both Light and Death:	7 poems in three sections
The Elegies of the Jutting Rock:	14 poems
West of Sorrow:	7 poems[119]

Apart from the overall structure of his collections, the number seven appears in other divisions within specific poems: The "Gloria," of *The Axion Esti*, for example ends with a repetition of "Now" and "Forever" seven times; "Seven Days for Eternity," of *Six and One Remorses for the Sky* is divided into seven sections (one for each day); the lines of each of the seven poems of *The Monogram* are always a multiple of seven. Sometimes, the number also appears in specific textual references: "the 24-hour life" (*Maria Nephele*), "the Seven Axes" (*Axion Esti*), "the seven wise men" (*The Light-Tree*), "the seven olive trees" (*Maria Nephele*, "Revelation"). The recurrence of this symbolic number in Elytis's work embodies the attempt to create both a mystical and a structural frame for his poetry. Numerology in the Bible aims to create a similar effect; it further emphasizes the "perfect structure" and sanctity of a divine universe. In Elytis, it is ultimately connected with the creation of a space that can sustain poetic meaning. In essence, it constitutes a mystical canonization and "sanctification" of a personal mythopoetic system. The final chapter will examine some of Elytis's larger collections in the context of their structure. That is, it will attempt to demonstrate how structure functions, not simply to sustain the poem, but also to construct an architectural design that can reflect poetic meaning in itself.

The Structure of the Poem Resembles Architecture

In this chapter, I provided a general description of Elytis's theory of Solar Metaphysics, which attempts to relate the content of the poem with its overall structure. For Elytis, the individual poem and, more importantly, longer collections of poetry, need to achieve a certain cohesiveness. Such structuring might be imperceptible to the reader but it gives the text a structural body (its "rhythmic and strophic features") that interacts seamlessly with its content (its "system of images and meanings"). Since the theory is principally based on the utilization of the sun as a central symbol in Elytis's work, I proceeded to consider the influence that Heraclitus and Plotinus's descriptions of the sun and, more specifically, its importance in their philosophy. This brief diversion from the chapter's central theoretical concern also aimed at positioning the sun conceptually in the overall structure of meanings that the theory suggests. One is reminded here of Cleanth

---

[119] The more elaborate structures of *The Axion Esti*, *The Little Seafarer*, *Maria Nephele*, as well as *The Monogram*, are extensively discussed in Chapter 5.

Brooks's seminal essay "The Heresy of Paraphrase" where he claims that "the essential structure of a poem (as distinguished from the rational or logical structure of the 'statement' which we abstract from it) resembles that of architecture or painting: it is a pattern of resolved stresses.... It is a pattern of resolutions and balances and harmonizations, developed through a temporal scheme."[120] Elytis, as I have discussed, also imagines the reader's experience of the poem's structure as akin to the human perception of time (i.e., perfectly structured yet imperceptible). What Brooks means when he refers to structure, however, is not really *form* but rather "a structure of meanings, evaluations, and interpretations; and the principle of unity which informs it seems to be one of balancing and harmonizing connotations, attitudes and meanings."[121] Elytis's theory extends the structure of meanings to include form—Brook's structure of meanings is also linked, in this way, to a corresponding structure of forms. The intimate correspondence between the two is explored in more depth in the fifth chapter.

In this chapter, I also examined the influence of Le Corbusier on Elytis and, more specifically, his theories on the unity between aesthetics and practicality as they are expressed in traditional Cycladic architecture. Solar metaphysics, I argued, is simultaneously a modern and a traditional construction. It may be compared to T.S. Eliot's mythical method in the sense that it attempts to structure history's "immense panorama of futility and anarchy." Consequently, it relies on tradition and it turns to the East, the Aegean, for the rediscovery of Greekness. Finally, I explored the usual forms that architectural poetics takes in Elytis's poetry. The repeated use of the number seven and its multiples becomes, for Elytis, a way of sanctifying, and of providing a metaphysical yet meaningful shape, to the poem; if the projected centers of existence have foundered in modernity (i.e., religion, tradition, morality), then the poem must be able to create its own sustainable structures.

With these investigations in mind, I would like to close this chapter by returning briefly to my introductory discussion on poststructuralism and the position of ethnic literatures. One could argue that Elytis's preoccupation with tradition, poetic structure, and nationality, makes his poetry rather obsolete in the current theoretical environment. His work doesn't strictly fit the categories of cosmopolitanism or postcolonialism; the fact that his work is comparative— that is to say that it is in constant dialogue with other thinkers—may not, for some critics, evade the fact that, in its essence, it constitutes a hellenization of the European modernist tradition. But the challenge here is not to establish that Elytis's theory of Solar Metaphysics, or his interest in Greekness, is in accord with the poststructural reading of poetry. Rather, the point is to establish that the modernist project in the case of Greece, Poland, Romania, or Egypt amounts to a reconfiguration of national identity, tradition, or history. As I have argued in the

---

[120] Cleanth Brooks, *The Well Wrought Urn: Studies in the Structure of Poetry* (New York: Harcourt, 1947), p. 203.

[121] Brooks, *Wrought Urn*, p. 195.

previous chapter, Elytis's turn to the Aegean and Greek tradition does not signify a flawed construction of collective Greek identity—it is as much a construction as it is a deconstruction.

Solar Metaphysics should be understood in this context: it is the search for unity or coherence in the *absence* of it. I will elaborate this point further since, I often find, it is at the center of several misreadings of Elytis's poetry today. The most obvious example that points to the construction of an imperceptible (i.e., not immediately recognizable) pattern in Elytis's poetry collections is *The Monogram*, where the architectural structure of the work, which I will explore in detail in the next chapter, frames the landscape of absence. The collection is essentially a work of mourning for the absent beloved—Solar Metaphysics here can only be understood in the context of loss: the structure of meaning and the architecture of the poem revolve around the absent center constituted by the loss of the beloved. The same is true when one examines Elytis's collections that explore the subject of Greekness more explicitly. In *The Little Seafarer*, the poet sets forth to traverse the cultural topography of this constructed Greekness, only to declare, in the end: "and here I am: unable to learn what I give, what they give me, and left over is injustice...."[122] As I have already discussed, the same feeling of failure and loss is present in some of the collection's poems as well. Here too, the strict, yet imperceptible, structure of the collection should be understood as an attempt to frame what is ultimately a personal construction of Greekness that fails in relation to the outside (to what *they* give as the poet writes). *Maria Nephele* is similarly structured around poetic exile and, like *The Axion Esti*, ends with a prophetic vision—a hopeful vision that remains unrealized. This obsession with the structure of failure or loss is an intricate part of the modernist project. Eliot's suggestion of myth as a structuring device, Breton's insistence that the unconscious is organized and that automatic writing can reveal its hidden order, or Joyce's profoundly meticulous structuring of *Ulysses*, testify to the persistent efforts of many modernists poets and writers to come up with ways to give order to what was otherwise perceived as chaotic, painful, or flawed, be it national identity (as in the case of Elytis and Joyce), history (especially in the case of Eliot), or, more generally, loss, absence, and impossibility.

---

[122] Elytis, *Collected Poems*, p. 508.

Chapter 5
Architectural Poetics

> If you have never made love with mathematics you will never be able to prove that what you write resembles them.
> —Elytis, *From Nearby*

> Superstition brought to a mathematical clarity will help us perceive the deeper structure of the world.
> —Elytis, *Maria Nephele*

Matei Calinescu writes that "[a]lthough its pursuit is not that of truth in a logical or scientific sense, the poet's mind has to be as disciplined as that of a scientist. Poetry and mathematics are inherently related—a belief that Baudelaire shares with Novalis and other German Romantics ...."[1] Elytis's theory of Architectural Poetics pushes the relationship between poetry and mathematics to its most extreme manifestation. It is, perhaps, his most innovative contribution to the resolution of the modernist crisis of form. It is also interesting to consider that the theory was developed in the context of the more general preoccupation of modernist Greek writers with the reconciliation between European modernism and local or traditional cultural expressions. In this chapter, I attempt two things: first, an exploration of the theory of architectural poetics as it emerges in Elytis's poetry and, second, an examination of the relationship between poetic form and content. More specifically, I will be discussing four of Elytis's collections: *The Monogram*, *The Axion Esti*, *The Little Seafarer*, and *Maria Nephele*. The choice of the last three is not arbitrary; all of Elytis's long poems, as he discloses in his ERT interview, revolve around a structural nucleus.[2] *The Monogram* is included here because it constitutes, in my opinion, the most lucid introduction to his Architectural Poetics (though it is considerably shorter than the rest).

The order in which these poems are presented is not chronological. I begin with *The Monogram* since the function of structure there is more readily perceptible. I then continue with *The Axion Esti* and *The Little Seafarer* due to their conceptual proximity; generally, we can say that both poems explore the tension between the individual and the collective, or the poetical and the historical, and both are attempts to define the aesthetics of Greekness. *Maria Nephele* is discussed at the end because it constitutes an exception; it is the most private and, by far, the most vernacular of Elytis's works. Finally, in order to exemplify the relationship between Architectural Poetics and the content of the poems, I examine these collections in the context of three theories: *The Monogram* in relation to Freud's theories on Mourning and Melancholia, *The Axion Esti* and *The Little Seafarer* in

---

[1] Calinescu, *Five Faces*, p. 57.
[2] Elytis, *Αυτοπροσωπογραφία*, pp. 31–2.

relation to Michel Foucault and Friedrich Nietzsche's views of history, and *Maria Nephele* in relation to C.G. Jung's archetype of the *anima*. Since Elytis was well acquainted with Freud and Jung, their theories may also be seen as a theoretical subtext of the aforementioned collections. The reading of the poems' content through the lens of these theories is by no means exclusive. The reason I chose these is because, first, with the exception of Foucault, Elytis was familiar with the work of these thinkers. Second, because they are also theories of structure: Freud and Jung's theories attempt a certain mapping of unconscious processes, Foucault and Nietzsche's theories amount to an unveiling of the often illusory function of historical structures. Finally, I wish to provide the reader with possible approaches to Elytis's poetry as a way to understand and expand these theories beyond their limited applications to western literatures. I hope such investigations would add to the rich possibilities an exploration of the relationship between content and form can present to the students and scholars of modernism.

Undoubtedly, part of the discussion here may seem too overtly structural, numerological, and perhaps even tiresome to the reader. One does not expect to engage in the solution of what appear to be mathematical equations when reading poetry. If I may be permitted to use a hyperbolic analogy as an excuse for this structural reading, I would say that the pleasure derived from solving Elytis's structural riddles is similar to the satisfaction a cosmologist might get from discovering a certain order in the structure of the universe; an equation among many, perhaps, that makes such expansive and distant world a little more comprehensible to us. As in the case of Joyce's *Ulysses*, one can certainly read these works without the help of the author's schemata. What is certain is that, like Joyce, Elytis has "put in so many enigmas and puzzles" in these collections, "that it will keep the professors busy for centuries arguing over what [he] meant."[3]

The Monogram: When the Shadow of the Object Falls Upon the Ego

Although the occurrences of the same number in Elytis's poetry speaks for a framing of his entire work, architectural poetics becomes essential only in his lengthier collections;[4] architectural construction is central in *The Axion Esti*, *Maria Nephele*, and *The Little Seafarer*. It is perhaps easier, before proceeding to an architectural analysis of these three, to briefly examine *The Monogram*, because, though it is a much shorter collection, it exemplifies the strong connection between content and form as Elytis perceived it. The collection consists of seven poems. The most obvious observation concerns the length of each poem's lines, that "ascend" in multiples of seven, reach a peak at the central poem (49 lines or 7 X 7), and then descend again in the same increments:

7   21   35   49   35   21   7

---

[3] Richard Ellmann, *James Joyce* (Oxford: Oxford University Press, 1982), p. 521.
[4] Elytis, *Αυτοπροσωπογραφία*, p. 31.

The line increments/decrements from one poem to the next are always 14: i.e., 7+14=21+14=35+14=49-14=35-14=21-14=7. As Kimon Friar suggests, this arrangement creates an intelligible symmetry:[5]

```
                        7

                  7     7     7

            7     7     7     7     7

      7     7     7     7     7     7     7

            7     7     7     7     7

                  7     7     7

                        7
```

Each poem imitates this ascending/descending pattern in the division of stanzas (the first poem, for example begins with a stanza of three lines, then continues with one, then three again). As I will demonstrate, this ascending/descending pattern is linked to the poetic content and, more specifically, it reflects the work of mourning: the initial lamentation that reaches its peak at the collection's center (Poem IV) leads to its eventual dissipation that signals a certain coming-to-terms with loss. The overall schematization of stanza/line division is as follows:

POEM I			3	1	3		
POEM II		3	4	7	4	3	
POEM III	1	7	5	9	5	7	1
POEM IV	11	1	7	11	7	1	11
POEM V	7	4	3	7	3	4	7
POEM VI		6	4	1	4	6	
POEM VII			2	3	2		

Not only do the poems correspond in terms of line-length, they also reflect one another in the division of stanzas (Poems I and VII consist of three stanzas, Poems II and VI of five, Poems III and V of seven). However rigid this structure may be,

---

[5] Kimon Friar, "Introduction," in *The Sovereign Sun: Selected Poems*, trans. Kimon Friar, 3–44 (Newcastle: Bloodaxe, 1990), p. 40.

Elytis claims that it would be a mistake if it was obvious enough for the reader to discern.[6] Its aim is simply to give an unconscious coherence to the entire work.

The numerological foundation of *The Monogram* emerges as a riddle whose solution is in accord with the poetic content. The association of the "riddle" with the poem is certainly not unintentional: the poem already tends towards a "hidden reality" that resides in an obscure space. Elytis was extremely meticulous in providing the necessary space within which content and meaning could be sustained most effectively. Apart from structural concerns, all of his collections are characterized by a careful choice of font, cover, and accompanying images. The cover of *The Monogram* depicts two letters, M and K, arranged in a reflective pattern; it is a monogrammed seal that was designed by the poet himself. The same "reflective pattern" is suggested with the inclusion of an image in the collection: an ancient bronze mirror that depicts two lovers facing each other in identical postures. Mario Vitti connects the initials M and K with an "unfortunate affair" Elytis had in 1955, 16 years before the composition of the collection.[7]

The cryptographic nature of the collection is also in accord with the Heideggerian perception of the "work of art" as a negation of a superficial material understanding of the world; the work, in this sense, negates formal perceptions and reveals the deeper essence of truth (*alētheia*). Elytis further attempts a structural recreation of the world based on a more metaphysical understanding of matter. The absent beloved in *The Monogram*, or, more precisely, the space that sustained Eros, is literarily reconstructed. Truth, or *alētheia*, is "uncovered," in a Heideggerian sense, by the reader who is simultaneously ask to solve the riddles of poetic content and form.

The Monogram begins with an epigraph that signals the mood of the collection: "I shall mourn always—hear me?—for you alone, in Paradise."[8] This is indeed a collection of mourning—of lamenting the loss or absence of the object of desire. Before proceeding to analyze the psychoanalytical implications of this "mourning"—an analysis that adds to my exploration of the collection's structure—I will briefly outline the conceptual structure of *The Monogram*.[9] For now, suffice it to say that the text attempts what we can call a schematization of both loss and its overcoming. I have concentrated, thus far, on the purely formal, or mathematical structuring of the collection, as exemplified, most notably, in its reflective arrangement. A similar "reflection" is also achieved in terms of content, and emerges in three distinct ways: firstly, the beginning and ending of most of

---

[6] Elytis, *Αυτοπροσωπογραφία*, p. 33.

[7] Vitti, *Οδυσσέας Ελύτης*, pp. 314–15. Vitti further writes: "Despite this observation, that we owe to the poet himself, I doubt that there is a need to connect the conception of the poem with a specific biographical occasion."

[8] Elytis, *Collected Poems*, p. 241.

[9] In *The Monogram* Elytis chooses the word "πένθος" (mourning) as opposed to "λύπη" (sadness), a word thath is used extensively in *Maria Nephele*, or "μαράζι" (heartache) used directly in relation to μελαγχολία (melancholy) in the poem "Melancholy of the Aegean" (in *Orientations*).

the poems linguistically resemble each other; secondly, the poetic images place mourning in a geographical space constituted by the elements of the Greek landscape, extending, in this way, the reflective relationship between the "body of the text" and the "body of land;" thirdly, those poems with an equal number of lines also share a conceptual correspondence.

The first observation is also the most evident: Poem II begins with the line "*I mourn* the sun and I mourn the years that come," and ends with "*I mourn* the garment that I touched and the world came to me";[10] Poem III begins with "Thus I *speak of you and me*" and ends with "To *speak of you and me*";[11] Poem IV begins with "It's too early yet in the world, *hear me*?" and ends with "I love you, I love you, *hear me*."[12] In Poem VII Elytis returns to the same reflective pattern we have seen in *Orientations*: it begins and ends with the words "*In Paradise*."[13] The second observation is also apparent: the experience of mourning is placed in the geographical space of the Mediterranean. Mourning unfolds amidst and in relation to jasmine flowers, waves, boats, harbors, beacons, vine arbors, rosebushes, pine trees, fishermen, cypress trees, stone walls, mushrooms, bays, hills, shores, volcanic soil, etc. At the same time, it is placed within the locus of the Greek tradition; we read of stone statues, miracles of icons emitting tears, the eggs of resurrection, and the Goddess of Samothrace. The third observation, concerning the conceptual outline of the collection, is more evasive. Once more, the line length of each poem produces the following sequence: 7, 21, 35, 49, 35, 21, 7. The collection can be divided into two identical parts that meet at an independent center (namely, the fourth and longest poem of 49 lines). Such division, emphasized by the reflective qualities of the two parts, invites a comparison between the poems of an equal line-length. Indeed, the reflective poems generally correspond conceptually with one another: Poem III, for example, begins with the line "Thus I speak of you and me" and Poem V—its equivalent in line length—begins with "of you I have spoken in olden times." This "reflection" continues throughout the two poems.[14]

What is more significant, perhaps, is not what makes these poems similar but rather, the way in which the poetic concepts progress from one poem to the next. The first three poems are intimate recollections of the relationship as it was

---

[10] Elytis, *Collected Poems*, p. 243.

[11] Elytis, *Collected Poems*, p. 244.

[12] Elytis, *Collected Poems*, pp. 245–6.

[13] Elytis, *Collected Poems*, p. 248. All the italics here are mine (to emphasize the repetitive patterns).

[14] Compare, for example, the following lines:

Poem III	Poem V
– The waves have heard of you	– And no one had heard of you
– High in the house with the vine arbors	– High on the roof or behind the yard's flagstones
– The half-closed window shutter you, I the wind that opens it	– I who don't want love but the wind

experienced in the specific landscape and as it was prophetically foretold in the first poem. The poet recalls, in mourning, the absent beloved:

> The Bodies spoken to and the boats strumming sweetly
> The guitars flickering underwater
> The "believe me" and the "don't" there
> Once in the music, once in this air.[15]

> The waves have heard of you
> How you caress, how you kiss
> How you say in a whisper the "what" and the "eh"
> Around the neck around the bay
> Always we the light and shadow.[16]

In the fourth poem, which is at the center of the collection, mourning becomes heart-wrenching lament. The repetition of the question "hear me?" further stresses the absence of the beloved and imitates a state of grief (we may imagine here, in other words, the narrative voice in the process of being interrupted by weeping); sentences are interrupted with the constant interjection of the question/invocation "hear me"; the transition of images or ideas is continuous, and phrases often refer to both the preceding and following lines:

> The day will come, hear me
> The enormous lianas and the lava of volcanoes
> Will bury us and thousands of years later, hear me
> They'll make us luminous fossils, hear me
> For the heartlessness of men to shine, hear me
> Over them
> And throw us away in thousands of pieces, hear me
>
> In the waters one by one, hear me
> I count my bitter pebbles, hear me
> And time is a great church, hear me
> Where sometimes the figures, hear me
> Of Saints
> Weep real tears, hear me.[17]

---

[15] Elytis, *Collected Poems*, p. 243. Μιλημένα τα σώματα και οι βάρκες που έκρουσαν γλυκά / Οι κιθάρες που αναβόσβησαν κάτω από τα νερά / Τα «πίστεψέ με» και τα «μη» / Μια στον αέρα, μια στη μουσική (Elytis, *Ποίηση*, p. 253).

[16] Elytis, *Collected Poems*, p. 244. Ακουστά σ' έχουν τα κύματα / Πως χαϊδεύεις, πως φιλάς / Πως λες ψιθυριστά το «τι» και το «ε» / Τριγύρω στο λαιμό στον όρμο / Πάντα εμείς το φως κι η σκιά (Elytis, *Ποίηση*, p. 254).

[17] Elytis, *Collected Poems*, p. 245. Οι πελώριες λιάνες και των ηφαιστείων οι λάβες / Θα 'ρθει μέρα, μ' ακούς / Να μας θάψουν, κι οι χιλιάδες ύστερα χρόνοι / Λαμπερά θα μας κάνουν πετρώματα, μ' ακούς / Να γυαλίσει επάνω τους η απονιά, μ' ακούς / Των ανθρώπων / Και χιλιάδες κομμάτια να μας ρίξει / Στα νερά ένα ένα, μ' ακούς / Τα πικρά μου βότσαλα

In the remaining three poems the tone changes completely, as the poet comes to a more essential understanding of the nature of mourning. The absent beloved is projected into and identified in the surrounding landscape and in "what one loves."[18] Mourning is a process of overcoming, and though it leads to the painful realization and acceptance of absence, it also identifies Eros as a source of inspiration and creativity. The last two poems are indicative of this progressive transformation in the poet. The same voice that was refusing to accept separation in the fourth poem, saying, "I go nowhere, hear me / Either no one or we two together, hear me," now comes to a different understanding:

> Go, go even if I've been lost
> Alone, and let the sun you hold be a newborn babe
> Alone and let me be the homeland that mourns
> Let the world I sent to hold the laurel leaf for you be
> Alone, the wind strong and alone the very round
> Pebble in the blink of the dark depths
> The fisherman who lifted up and cast back again into time Paradise![19]

It is precisely this progressive understanding—this *working through* of mourning—that makes Freud's "Mourning and Melancholia" a likely subtext for *The Monogram*. In his 1917 essay, Freud argues that the permanent loss of an object, [be it] "a loved person or ... some abstraction ... such as one's country, liberty, an idea and so on,"[20] can result in either a state of mourning or melancholia:

> Reality-testing has shown that the loved object no longer exists and it proceeds to demand that all libido shall be withdrawn from its attachments to that object. This demand arouses understandable opposition—it is a matter of general observation that people never willingly abandon a libidinal position, not even, indeed, when a substitute is already beckoning to them. This opposition can be so intense that a turning away from reality takes place and a clinging to the object through the medium of a hallucinatory wishful psychosis.[21]

μετρώ, μ' ακούς / Κι είναι ο χρόνος μια μεγάλη εκκλησία, μ' ακούς / Όπου κάποτε οι φιγούρες / Των Αγίων / Βγάζουν δάκρυ αληθινό, μ' ακούς (Elytis, *Ποίηση*, pp. 255–6).

[18] "What one Loves": The title of a section in *The Little Seafarer*. Elytis borrows the line from Sappho.

[19] Elytis, *Collected Poems*, pp. 247–8. Πήγαινε, πήγαινε και ας έχω εγώ χαθεί / Μόνος, και ας είναι ο ήλιος που κρατείς ένα παιδί νεογέννητο / Μόνος, και ας είμ' εγώ η πατρίδα που πενθεί / Ας είναι ο λόγος που έστειλα να σου κρατεί δαφνόφυλλο / Μόνος, ο αέρας δυνατός και μόνος τ' ολοστρόγγυλο / Βότσαλο στο βλεφάρισμα του σκοτεινού βυθού / Ο ψαράς που ανέβασε κι έριξε πάλι πίσω στους καιρούς τον Παράδεισο! (Elytis, *Ποίηση*, pp. 258–9).

[20] Sigmund Freud, *Mourning and Melancholia*, Vol. XIV, in *The Standard Edition of the Psychological Works of Sigmund Freud Vol. XIV* (1914–1916), trans. James Strachey, 237–58 (London: Hogarth Press, 1957), p. 243.

[21] Freud, *"Mourning,"* p. 244.

"Normally," Freud continues, "respect for reality gains the day."[22] In the case of mourning, after a certain lapse of time, "each single one of the memories and expectations in which the libido is bound to the object is brought up and hyper-cathected, and detachment from the libido is accomplished in respect of it."[23] In melancholia, however, the ego establishes an *identification* with the abandoned object; in other words, the libido is not displaced onto a new object but withdraws into the ego. "Thus the shadow of the object falls upon the ego, and the latter could henceforth be judged by a special agency, as though it were an object, the forsaken object."[24] In *The Ego and the Id* (1923), Freud modified his early theory on the nature of mourning and melancholia with respect to *identification*. "At that time" he writes, "we did not appreciate the full significance of the process and did not know how common and how typical it is."[25] Revising his initial view of the ego's identification with the object as an exclusive characteristic of melancholia, he now claims: "it may be that this identification is the sole condition under which the id can give up its objects."[26]

Freud asserts that "by taking flight into the ego, love escapes extinction."[27] *The Monogram*'s first poem foretells the reader: "time will consent for a moment / how otherwise, since men love each other."[28] Poem II constitutes a recollection of the experience, in which the poet refuses to abandon the memory of the absent beloved; instead, he internalizes or introjects the lost object, identifying it, temporally and spatially, with his own ego; time can only be perceived in relation to the dyad "us":

> I mourn the sun and I mourn the years that come
> Without us and I sing the others that have passed
> If that is true.[29]

In a Freudian reading, the ego cannot distinguish itself from the object: it is as if it only existed, and will exist, within the temporal space of a dyadic identification with the object. In the third poem, the internalization progresses to such a degree that the "you" (the lost object) and the "I" (the Ego) become a synergetic unity:

> Always you the little star and always I the dark boat
> Always you the harbor and I the beacon on the right
> The wet dockwall and the gleam on the oars
> High in the house with the vine arbors

---

[22] Freud, "*Mourning*," p. 244.
[23] Freud, "*Mourning*," p. 245.
[24] Freud, "*Mourning*," p. 249.
[25] Sigmund Freud, *The Ego and the Id*, trans. James Strachey (New York: Norton, 1960), p. 23.
[26] Freud, *The Ego and the Id*, p. 24.
[27] Freud, "*Mourning*," p. 257.
[28] Elytis, *Collected Poems*, p. 243.
[29] Elytis, *Collected Poems*, p. 243. Πενθώ τον ήλιο και πενθώ τα χρόνια που έρχονται / Χωρίς εμάς και τραγουδώ τ' άλλα που πέρασαν / Εάν είναι αλήθεια (Elytis, *Ποίηση*, p. 253).

The bound-up rosebushes, the water that feels cold
Always you the stone statue and always I the lengthening shadow
The half-closed window shutter you, I the wind that opens it.[30]

The aesthetic unity of space exists only in relationship to the merged "you" and "I." The "flight into the ego" reaches here its most desperate state that, before revising his theory, Freud initially perceived as the state of melancholia. Clearly, the depiction of the absent beloved as a "stone statue" and the "I" as "the lengthening shadow" is reminiscent of Freud's description of identification as a process in which "the shadow of the object falls upon the ego."[31] The poem is abundant with such images/concepts of identification:

Thus I speak of you and me (III, line 1)[32]

Always we the light and the shadow (III, line 13)[33]

To cry out of you and so my own voice strikes me
To smell of you and so men turn wild (III, lines 30–31)[34]

Since Freud later recognized internalization and identification as "common" and "typical" processes, the distinction between mourning and melancholia must be sought in the subject's ability, or inability, to "master the loss" of the object. Already in "Mourning and Melancholia" Freud presents the two states as remarkably similar, and the reconceptualization of *identification* as a common aspect of mourning in *The Ego and the Id* renders the distinction between the two even more elusive; in fact, melancholia is generally described as "pathological mourning."[35] The key element that eventually differentiates the two is "the ambivalence in love relationships":

> Where there is a disposition to obsessional neurosis the conflict due to ambivalence gives a pathological cast to mourning and forces it to express itself in the form of self reproaches to the effect that the mourner himself is to blame for the loss of the loved object, i.e. that he has willed it.[36]

---

[30] Elytis, *Collected Poems*, p. 244. Πάντα εσύ τ' αστεράκι και πάντα εγώ το σκοτεινό πλεούμενο / Πάντα εσύ το λιμάνι κι εγώ το φανάρι το δεξιά / Το βρεμένο μουράγιο και η λάμψη επάνω στα κουπιά / Ψηλά στο σπίτι με τις κληματίδες / Τα δετά τριαντάφυλλα, το νερό που κρυώνει / Πάντα εσύ το πέτρινο άγαλμα και πάντα εγώ η σκιά που μεγαλώνει / Το γερτό παντζούρι εσύ, ο αέρας που το ανοίγει εγώ (Elytis, *Ποίηση*, p. 254).

[31] Freud, "*Mourning*," p. 249.

[32] Έτσι μιλώ για σένα και για μένα.

[33] Πάντα εμείς το φως κι η σκιά.

[34] Να φωνάζω από σένα και να με χτυπά η φωνή μου / Να μυρίζω από σένα και ν' αγριεύουν οι άνθρωποι.

[35] Freud, "*Mourning*," p. 250.

[36] Freud, "*Mourning*," p. 251.

Unlike the mourner, the melancholic "knows *whom* he has lost but not *what* he has lost in him."[37] Thus, "in mourning it is the world which has become poor and empty; in melancholia it is the ego itself."[38] In *The Monogram* there is no ambivalence in the memory of the absent beloved; in recollecting and representing the relationship, poems II and III are an account of what was lost, or, more precisely, *what the poet mourns for*. What makes the collection "a text of mourning" rather than of melancholia is the progressive mastering of loss as it is presented in the last three poems.[39] The poet does not remain trapped within the strong identification between the ego and the object, but rather manages to recognize the loss of the object without negating the ego.[40] Before proceeding to examine how such an understanding unfolds in *The Monogram*, it is important to consider the way in which "loss is mastered" or, to use a Freudian term, how a "working through" of mourning is achieved.

In *Beyond the Pleasure Principle*, Freud presents what is probably the most famous example of such "mastering." He describes his one-and-a-half year-old grandson playing the "first game" he invented: the young boy holds a "wooden reel with a piece of string tied round it" and throws it away until it disappears exclaiming an "expressive 'o-o-o-o'" (which Freud associates with the German word *fort* [gone]):

> He then pulled the reel out of the cot again by the string and hailed its reappearance with a joyful '*da*' ['here']. This, then, was the complete game— disappearance and return. As a rule one only witnessed its first act, which was repeated untiringly as the game itself, though there is no doubt that the greater pleasure was attached to the second act.[41]

Freud argues that, in essence, the child is coming to terms with the constant disappearance/reappearance of the mother. What is vital here is that the child achieves the mastering of loss, or absence, through a game of reenactment and creative repetition. Freud then proceeds to explain that "a compulsion to repeat"[42] is a fundamental tendency of the unconscious and then connects this compulsion with the definition of instinct as "an urge ... to restore an earlier state of things."[43]

---

[37] Freud, "*Mourning*," p. 245.

[38] Freud, "*Mourning*," p. 246.

[39] We must remember that the poems of the collection are reflective (the first three imitate the last three in line length). The structure of *The Monogram* reaffirms the common ground between mourning and melancholia. If we were to use a structural metaphor here we could say that mourning is the other side of melancholia.

[40] According to Freud, the negation of the ego occurs because of the "narcissistic identification" of the ego with the object. In other words, the lost object becomes part of the ego and as a result it can be hated, debased, and forced to suffer.

[41] Sigmund Freud, *Beyond the Pleasure Principle*, trans. James Strachey (New York: Norton, 1961), p. 14.

[42] Freud, *Pleasure Principle*, p. 24.

[43] Freud, *Pleasure Principle*, p. 43. In his 1914 essay "Remembering, Repeating and Working Through," Freud also stresses the importance of repetition in the form of

In relation to the pleasure principle, repetition has a dual function: on the one hand, it can lead to a healthy mastering of loss and, on the other, it can be the main force of resistance, since it is connected with the instinct of *thanatos* (the restoration of "an earlier state of things"). In this sense, by introjecting the lost object, both the melancholic and the mourner tend to return to an earlier state of being (or time) and in doing so "save love [or the object] from extinction." Perhaps the fundamental difference between melancholia and mourning is that, in the case of the former, the experience of loss is rigidly repeated, whereas in the latter, it might be *creatively* reenacted and hence mastered, as in the child's *fort-da* game.

In his essay "Repetition and Repetition Compulsion," Hans Loewald stresses the importance of approaching repetition from the viewpoint of both its pathological and creative potential. He distinguishes between what he calls "passive repetition" and "active repetition":

> Psychoanalysis has always maintained that the life of the individual is determined by his infantile history, his early experiences and conflicts; but everything depends on *how* these early experiences are repeated passively [...] and to what extent they can be taken over in the ego's organizing activity and made over into something new—a re-creation of something old as against a duplication of it. In such re-creation the old is mastered, where mastery does not mean elimination of it but dissolution, and reconstruction out of the elements of destruction. We may thus distinguish between repetition as reproduction and repetition as re-creation, the passive and active form.[44]

It is important, then, that the child who engages in the *fort-da* game—his "first game," according to Freud—masters the mother's loss by creative invention and active repetition.

It is hardly necessary to emphasize the importance of such conceptualization in the field of literature. One readily sees, for example, the fundamental role of mimesis as an aspect of ordering and memorization in the function of the Homeric

---

"acting out": the patient may not remember "that he used to be defiant and critical towards his parents' authority" but he acts it out by "behaving that way to the doctor" (Sigmund Freud, "Remembering, Repeating and Working Through," in *The Standard Edition of the Psychological Works of Sigmund Freud, Vol. XII (1911–1913)*, trans. James Strachey, 145–56 [London: Hogarth Press, 1958], p. 150). In this sense, repetition becomes an important component of the psychoanalytical work, through which the patient may master what is repressed. After all, it is on the basis of repetition that the concept of "transference"—one of the most important components of psychoanalytic treatment—was founded.

[44] Hans W. Loewald, "Some Considerations on Repetition and Repetition Compulsion," in *Papers on Psychoanalysis* (New Haven: Yale University Press, 1980), p. 90. One cannot help but notice that Hans Loewald's argument is strikingly similar to Percy Shelley's view of poetry's function: "[Poetry] creates anew the universe, after it has been annihilated in our minds by the recurrence of impressions blunted by reiteration." Percy Bysshe Shelley, "A Defence of Poetry," in *Criticism: Major Statements*, ed. Charles Kaplan and William Anderson (New York: St. Martin's Press, 1991), pp. 332–3.

formulae or traditional folk songs. In the case of Homer and folk poetry, however, repetition works towards the greater attempt to sustain tradition and the culture's "sacred universe." Modernity, with its resistance to tradition and the conventional techniques of expression, unveiled an unsustainable world, or, in T.S. Eliot's words, an "immense panorama of futility and anarchy." One can perceive, in this sense, Eliot's "mythical method"—a way to give order to the futility of modern history—as an attempt to actively repeat myth in an effort to reconstruct the world "out of the elements of destruction"; Joyce's *Ulysses* is, according to Eliot, the most profound example of such an attempt.[45]

Repetition is at the very heart of poetic creation in its relation to meter, rhyme, assonance, consonance, alliteration, and even metaphor. In that sense, modern poetry had to negotiate between its resistance to duplication and its desire to aesthetically reconstruct the world. Modernism may have rejected formal poetic structures, such as ballads and sonnets, but it certainly absorbed many of the poetic techniques grounded in repetition. Valéry embraced rhyme, Dylan Thomas extensively used assonance, and Kazantzakis wrote his 33,333-line-long *Odyssey* in 17-syllable meter. At the same time, modernist poetry is characterized by the increasing use of line-repetition as a means of structuring the poetic space.[46]

The most noteworthy example of such line-repetition is perhaps Federico García Lorca's "Lament for Ignacio Sánchez Mejías," where Lorca inserts in every other line Lorca inserts the phrase "at five in the afternoon":[47]

---

[45] T.S. Eliot, *Selected Prose of T.S. Eliot*, ed. Frank Kermode (New York: Harvest, 1975), p. 177. Many of the great modernist debates centered on subjects related to repetition. T.S. Eliot's defense of tradition and Valéry's defense of rhyme are two such instances.

[46] The repetition of lines in modern poetry is in fact a widespread phenomenon. Examples of extensive line-repetition are of course abundant; in this discussion, I am more interested in those cases where the poem is "conscious" of this repetition (where it is not used in isolated moments). Another noteworthy example would be Eliot's "Ash Wednesday" and, most importantly, *The Wasteland*, where the poet attempts, as Loewald would say, a reconstruction "out of the elements of destruction."

[47] I turn to Lorca here for a number of reasons. Elytis admired Lorca's poetry and translated his "Romancero Gitano" for the volume of translations Δεύτερη Γραφή. But Lorca's popularity in Greece goes beyond his influence on Elytis and it constitutes a remarkable phenomenon in the context of cross-cultural reception. Simply consider the following: since 1948 when Karolos Koun first staged a performance of *Blood Wedding*, the play has been performed a total of 39 times and in five different Greek translations; *The House of Bernarda Alba* has been performed 36 times and in eight translations; *The Shoemaker's Prodigious Wife*, 20 times; *Yerma* and *Love of Don Perlimplín and Belisa in his Garden*, 14 times; *Doña Rosita the Spinster*, nine times; it's also telling that almost all of Lorca's plays have been preformed, at some point, in Greece. In total, Lorca's plays have been performed over 150 times since the 1940s. And since the 1980s, *Blood Wedding* has been performed almost every single year in Greece. The first translations of Lorca's poetry appeared in the April and September issues of the periodical *Kyklos* in 1933. They were translated by Nikos Kazantzakis after his visits to Spain in the late 1920s. Since then, some of Greece's leading poets and writers have translated the Spanish poet; among

At five in the afternoon.
It was five at sharp in the afternoon.
A young boy brought the white sheet,
at five in the afternoon.
A basket of already waiting lime,
at five in the afternoon.
The rest was death and only death,
at five in the afternoon.[48]

By the end of the first poem the repetition reaches its utmost state of despair: "At five in the afternoon. / Oh, what a terrible five in the afternoon! / It was five on every one of the clocks! / It was five in the shade of the afternoon!"[49] This constant repetition of the precise moment of Sánchez Mejía's death can be seen as an attempt to come to terms with the emptiness left behind by his loss.[50] The poem is temporally and spatially situated at the moment of trauma—the moment of his death—in order to master the loss. The last poem of the "Lament for Ignacio Sánchez Mejías," entitled "An Absent Soul," is an example of the painful but creative mastery that characterizes the state of mourning as I have described it:

Nobody knows you. No. But I will sing of you.
I sing of your profile and grace for a later time.

---

them: Odysseus Elytis, Nikos Gatsos, Klitos Kyrou, Takis Varvitsiotis, Aris Diktaios, Manolis Anagnostakis, Kosmas Politis, Nikos Engonopoulos, and many others; over 68 different translations of Lorca's poems have appeared in more than 30 books. One of the most interesting expressions of the Lorca phenomenon in Greece is the setting to music of his poems by Mikis Theodorakis, Manos Hadjidakis, Stavros Xarhakos, Giannis Glezos, Christos Leontis, Nikos Mamagkakis, and Giorgos Kouroupós. The reason for Lorca's popularity in Greece may be sought in the Mediterranean sensibility that many Greek poets found in Lorca as well as in his persistent use of the Andalusian tradition as a subtext. As Elytis writes, Lorca's poetry was "more lightning-bright, closer to our aesthetic and more familiar to our Mediterranean idiosyncrasy" and it "arrived right when, for different reasons, we too opened our windows to demotic rhythms and traditional echoes" (Elytis, *Ανοιχτά Χαρτιά*, p. 398). For more on Lorca's reception in Greece see Virginia López Recio, *Το Φεγγάρι, το Μαχαίρι, τα Νερά: Ο Λόρκα στην Ελλάδα* (Athens: Ekdoseis ton Philon, 2006).

[48] Federico García Lorca, *Ode to Walt Whitman and Other Poems*, trans. Carlos Bauer (San Francisco: City Lights, 1988), p. 51.

ᴬ las cinco de la tarde. / Eran las cinco en punto de la tarde. / Un niño trajo la blanca sábana / *a las cinco de la tarde.* / Una espuerta de cal ya prevenida / *a las cinco de la tarde.* / Lo demás era muerte y sólo muerte / *a las cinco de la tarde* (Lorca, *Ode*, p. 50).

[49] Lorca, *Ode*, p. 53. The same technique is used in the second poem of the "Lament for Ignacio Sánchez Mejías" where the phrase "I do not want to see it" is repeated throughout the poem.

[50] As Lorca's translator Oscar Bauer writes, "Igancio Sánchez Mejías had been a hero to a generation of poets because he was the prototype of that rare individual who could fuse into one complex personality the man of action and the contemplative man of letters" (Lorca, *Ode*, p. vii).

Of the renowned maturity of your knowledge.
Your appetite for death, and the taste of its mouth.
Of the sadness your joyous bravery once possessed.

A long time will pass before being born, if ever,
an Andalusian so open, so very rich in adventure.
I will sing of his elegance with words that wail,
and recall a sad breeze through the olive-trees.[51]

The four poems that make up the "Lament for Ignacio Sánchez Mejías" move towards a progressive realization of loss, similar to that in *The Monogram*. The comparison is not coincidental: Elytis admired Lorca's work and translated his *Romancero Gitano* into Greek.[52] About seven years after Lorca's publication of the "Lament for Ignacio Sanchez Mejías," Elytis began his composition of *Song Heroic and Mourning for the Lost Second Lieutenant of the Albanian Campaign* (1945). The two poems certainly share a great deal: they are both founded on historical events, both recall the bravery of a specific individual, and both progressively transubstantiate his loss into song. Most importantly, they have conceptual affinities:

In Lorca's "Lament":[53]	In Elytis's "Song Heroic and Mourning":[54]
1. No, I never want to see it!	1. O do not look at the point
	Whence his life fled. Do not say how
Tell the moon to come quick,	Do not say how dream's smoke ascended high
for I never want to see Ignacio's	And then one moment And thus one
blood there upon the sand	And thus one moment abandoned the other,
	And the eternal sun thus,
No, I never want to see it!	abandoned the world
2. That stone is now his forehead where dreams lie moaning	2. Now he lies on his scorched greatcoat With a stopped wind in his quiet hair[55]
3. For the sea, too, shall die.	3. Sun weren't you eternal?
4. death laid its tiny eggs in the wound at five in the afternoon	4. Suddenly the moment misfired and found its courage

---

[51] Lorca, *Ode*, p. 67. No te conoce nadie. No. Pero yo te canto. / Yo canto para luego tu perfil y tu gracia. / La madurez insigne de tu conocimiento. / Tu apetencia de muerte y el gusto de tu boca. / La tristeza que tuvo tu valiente alegría. / Tardará mucho tiempo en nacer, si es que nace, / un andaluz tan claro, tan rico de aventura. / Yo canto su elegancia con palabras que gimen / y recuerdo una brisa triste por los olivos (Lorca, *Ode*, p. 66).

[52] The poems were published in the *Second Writing* and were translated in 1947. Elytis also makes specific reference to the "Lament for Ignacio Sánchez Mejías" in his essay "The Method of Therefore."

[53] All excerpts are from Federico García Lorca, *Ode*, pp. 51–67.

[54] All excerpts are from Elytis, *Collected Poems*, pp. 107–17.

[55] Elytis *repeats* the line "He lies on his scorched greatcoat"; Lorca repeats the line "Now upon that stone lies Ignacio."

What both poems share with *The Monogram* is the use of repetition to "work through" the experience of loss. All three poems mourn a loss—the loss of youth, love, and friendship. In all three, the death/absence of the object is concurrent with a loss of something in the poet's self.

What makes *The Monogram* more relevant to our current discussion is the close relationship between repetition, structure, and the "working through" of loss. As I have argued, in both the *Second Lieutenant* and *The Monogram*, repetition is coupled with a progressive movement that corresponds, textually, to "the work of mourning." Each poem begins, literally or conceptually, where the previous one ends. In *The Monogram* this progression also works schematically. Considering that Elytis's schemata are always different in each collection—they are only comparable in their use of repetition—it is important that the structure of the collection is both reflective and progressive. The underlying poetic narrative is vivid and clear: the poet's despair is intensified as we move from the first to the third poem, reaches the point of a lament in the central poem, and "deflates" as it progresses towards the end (Poems 5–7). In terms of structure, this progression is comparable to the popular tradition of ritual laments, which provide the appropriate "space" for the expression and overcoming of grief; mourning, in other words, is placed in a recognizable traditional form.[56] It is also comparable to Freud's perception of the creation of the appropriate "ceremonial"[57] setting for the work of psychoanalysis.

In "Remembering, Repeating and Working Through," Freud writes: "the patient does not *remember* anything of what he has forgotten and repressed, but *acts* it out. He reproduces it not as a memory but as an action; he *repeats* it, without, of course, knowing that he is repeating it."[58] *Acting out* becomes possible because the patient is able to transpose traumatic memories (through the medium of *transference*) to his relationship with the analyst.[59] By its very nature, the "work of art" already constitutes *acting out*, inasmuch as it is a transposed action. Coincidentally, in the first poem of *The Monogram* Elytis uses precisely the verb "to act out" [παραστάνω]:

> Fate will turn elsewhere the lines
> Of the palm, like a switchman
> Time will consent for a moment

---

[56] For the structure of ritual laments in Greek tradition see Margaret Alexiou's *The Ritual Lament in Greek Tradition*. Cambridge: Cambridge University Press, 1974.

[57] Freud uses the word "ceremonial" in relation to the utilization of "the couch" in psychoanalysis. Of course, the ceremonial or structuring aspects of psychoanalysis can also be traced in the arrangements concerning time and money. See Sigmund Freud, *On Beginning the Treatment (Further Recommendations on the Technique of Psychoanalysis)*, trans. James Strachey, Vol. XII (London: Hogarth Press, 1958).

[58] Freud, "Remembering," p. 150.

[59] Freud here gives a brief example: "For instance, the patient does not say that he remembers that he used to be defiant and critical towards his parents' authority; instead he behaves in that way to the doctor" (Freud, "Remembering," p. 150).

How else, since men love each other

The sky will *act out* our innards
And innocence will strike the world
With the sharpness of the black of death[60]

This reflection between what we can call traumatic memory ("our innards"—σωθικά) and the cosmos (the sky—ουρανός) is at the center of the collection's progression: memory is gradually transposed, or *cathected*, to use a Freudian term, onto nature, enabling the poet to perceive love as a cosmic phenomenon. At the same time, the poet views innocence as an apocalyptic force that, like thunder, "will strike the world." In the second poem, this reference becomes more lucid, as the poet writes: "To smell of you and so men turn wild / Because men can't endure the untried / The brought form elsewhere and its early, hear me / It's too early in the world my love / To speak of you and me."[61] Whether Elytis refers to a violation of a specific morality (such as age difference, an extramarital affair, etc.), or the general resistance of people to love, his image invokes the surrealist proclamation of the dream's revenge: innocence will take revenge for the social repression of such concepts as dream and love. As a product of sublimation, the work of art is the poet's revenge on the world, and structure makes its *action* possible.

When the "work of mourning" reaches the last poem, the tone is completely different. Having progressed through the ritual of mourning, the poet can now say: "I've seen much and the earth to my mind seems more beautiful," or, "Thus I have looked at you and that's enough / For all time to become innocent."[62] The concluding poem reaffirms the power of creativity that manages to reconstruct the erotic locus, but it also expresses the understanding of the gap between current reality and imagination:

In Paradise I've marked an island out
Identical to you and a house by the sea

With a big bed and a little door
I've cast an echo into the bottomless deeps
To see myself each morning when I arise

To see half of you pass in the water
And half for which I weep in Paradise.[63]

---

[60] Elytis, *Collected Poems*, p. 243. Θα γυρίσει αλλού τις χαρακιές / Της παλάμης, η Μοίρα, σαν κλειδούχος / Μια στιγμή θα συγκατατεθεί ο Καιρός / Πώς αλλιώς, αφού αγαπιούνται οι άνθρωποι / Θα *παραστήσει* ο ουρανός τα σωθικά μας / Και θα χτυπήσει τον κόσμο η αθωότητα / Με το δριμύ του μαύρου του θανάτου (Elytis, *Ποίηση*, p. 253).

[61] Elytis, *Collected Poems*, p. 244.

[62] Elytis, *Collected Poems*, p. 247.

[63] Elytis, *Collected Poems*, p. 248. Στον Παράδεισο έχω σημαδέψει ένα νησί / Απαράλλαχτο εσύ κι ένα σπίτι στη θάλασσα / Με κρεβάτι μεγάλο και πόρτα μικρή / Έχω

The placement of "weeping" in paradise synthesizes two antithetical notions; the construction of a poetic space, literally and metaphorically, that withholds love does not amount to an escape from reality, since the poet is still able to weep even within that imaginary space. Yet, the poem is full of energy, with a clearly erotic reference to "a big bed and a little door," the description of a morning awakening, and the creative ability to identify the island with the beloved. Most importantly, the absent object is perceived as a reflection *outside* of the ego: the poet is able to see himself *and* a semi-reflection of his creation.

The concept of "mourning," in its psychoanalytic implications and poetic manifestations, occupies an important position in Elytis's other works as well. It constitutes part of the synthesized opposites that the poet applies most effectively in the *Axion Esti* and through his "Theory of the One Point" (Η Θεωρία του ενός Σημείου).[64] In other words, the poet's central concepts are not simply, as it has often been suggested, "Eros" or "Light," but rather the point where these merge with their opposites (in this case "Death" and "Darkness"). Mourning, in this context, is indicative of the ability of life to go on despite loss, or, as Camus would say, of the necessity to imagine Sisyphus happy despite his endless suffering.[65] This synthesis of opposites in "mourning" is expressed most emphatically in such

---

ρίξει μες στ' άπατα μιαν ηχώ / Να κοιτάζομαι κάθε πρωί που ξυπνώ / Να σε βλέπω μισή να περνάς στο νερό / Και μισή να σε κλαίω μες στον Παράδεισο (Elytis, *Ποίηση*, p. 259).

[64] As Vitti claims, we learn of the "theory of the One Point" from the poet's personal notes on the *Axion Esti* (Vitti, *Οδυσσέας Ελύτης*, p. 237). Elytis directly refers to this concept in "The Genesis" of *The Axion Esti*: What is good? What is evil? / A point A point / and on this you balance and exist / and beyond it trepidation and darkness / and behind it the grinding teeth of angels / A point A point / and on it you can infinitely proceed / or else nothing else exists anymore (Elytis, *Collected Poems*, p. 130).

[65] I find the comparison between Camus and Elytis on this point very useful. According to Camus, "if the descent [of Sisyphus] is thus sometimes performed in sorrow, it can also take place in joy.... When the images of earth cling too tightly to memory, when the call of happiness becomes too insistent, it happens that melancholy arises in man's heart: this is the rock's victory, this is the rock itself. The boundless grief is too heavy to bear. These are our nights of Gethsemane. But crushing truths perish from being acknowledged. Thus, Oedipus at the outset obeys fate without knowing it. But from the moment he knows, his tragedy begins. Yet at the same moment, blind and desperate, he realizes that the only bond linking him to the world is the cool hand of a girl. Then a tremendous remark rings out: 'Despite so many ordeals, my advanced age and the nobility of my soul make me conclude that all is well.' Sophocles' Oedipus, like Dostoevsky's Kirilov, thus gives the recipe for the absurd victory. Ancient wisdom confirms modern heroism" (Camus, *Sisyphus*, pp. 121–2). One easily discerns the relationship between Camus's perception of "sorrow" and "joy" and Freud's distinction between mourning and melancholia. Sisyphus *identifies* with the rock in the Freudian sense but at the same time he overcomes the crushing truth of this by acknowledging it (i.e., by bringing it forth to consciousness).

epigraphs in *Maria Nephele*[66] as "in the village of my language Sadness is called the Radiant Lady,"[67] or "Sorrow gets pretty because we look like her."[68]

Elytis's attempt to synthesize opposites has often been misunderstood; popular criticism has always depicted Elytis merely as an optimist, the poet of Eros or of the Aegean,[69] and even serious critics saw, in such collections as *West of Sorrow*, *Diary of an Unseen April*, and *The Elegies of the Jutting Rock*, poetic litanies, or meditations, on Death.[70] The application of the term "mourning," in its Freudian conception, offers a much more appropriate prism through which these collections can be approached. It provides a template reflective of the poet's effort to negotiate between creativity and the "modern condition," which is essentially a condition of loss.

The Axion Esti: Erasing History With One's Heel

> Think now
> History has many cunning passages, contrived corridors
> And issues, deceives with whispering ambitions,
> Guides us by vanities.
>
> T.S. Eliot, "Gerontion"

The Axion Esti is, by far, the most popular of Elytis's works; it received the 1959 Greek National Poetry Award,[71] it was cited by the Nobel Academy in 1979 as "one of twentieth-century literature's most concentrated and richly faceted poems," and it was put to music in 1964 by Mikis Theodorakis, making it one of the most recognizable collections in the history of modern Greek Literature. The songs of *The Axion Esti* were often used as a form of resistance in tense historical periods such as the Generals' junta and the ongoing occupation of

---

[66] These epigraphs were published separately under the title *Book of Signs* [*Σειματολόγιον*].

[67] Elytis, *Collected Poems*, p. 309.

[68] Elytis, *Collected Poems*, p. 314.

[69] In reference to these popular misreadings of Elytis, Nikos Dimou, writes: "they tried to imprison him in clichés—to eliminate him with stereotypes: the Aegean, the young sailor, the sea, nostos." Nikos Dimou, *Οδυσσέας Ελύτης: Δοκίμια Ι* (Athens: Nefeli, 1992), p. 157.

[70] For an account of such misreading see Mario Vitti's excellent article "Εισαγωγή: Το Εργο του Ελύτη και η Ελληνική Κριτική," in *Εισαγωγή στο Εργο του Ελύτη*, ed. Mario Vitti (Heraklion: Panepistimiakes Ekdoseis Kritis, 2000).

[71] The granting of the National Award to *The Axion Esti* was quite controversial. Because its publication was delayed, Elytis submitted it to the National Library in 1959 though the book was eventually published in March 1960. In 1960 the Periodical *Nea Poreia* (of Thessaloniki) published several articles arguing that the book did not meet the 1959 deadline and the prize should, thus, not have been awarded to it. The Ministry of Education responded supporting its decision to award Elytis the prize (See Dimitris Daskalopoulos, "Χρονολόγιο Οδυσσέα Ελύτη (1911–1986)," *Χάρτης* 21–3 (1986): 261–80, pp. 270–71.

Cyprus by Turkish forces.⁷² The implications of this collection's popularity are many: there are very few instances in poetic modernism in which poems became culturally appropriated to such an extent, and there are even fewer instances in which this cultural appropriation was expressed in a historical context. The use of the text in this context is not surprising since, in many ways, *The Axion Esti* is a metahistorical text—it challenges the "official" Greek narrative by juxtaposing it with the poet's perception of "Greekness" or, better yet, by literally mapping the "dream nation" (as opposed to the "official nation"). For Elytis, as we have already seen, the official Greek narrative was a western re-importation and an unfortunate result of the Renaissance's misreading of what constitutes "Greekness." As the creator-poet declares in "The Genesis," he essentially "set(s) off for a clearing … erasing history with [his] heel."⁷³ But the dream nation is not without history—it is, to recall Elytis's words from *The Little Seafarer*, as alive as "the real one."⁷⁴

As I have already discussed, much of the intense modernist debate of the 1930s centered on the disparity between what is imported, as an ideology imposed on Greece by the West, and what is local, or a more authentic part of the Greek experience. The tension between East and West permeated the historical, social, and political spheres and, in some ways, shaped the outlook of the 1930s generation of poets and writers. As Gregory Jusdanis writes, "opposition to the West had a long history. The Church itself had been militantly antiwestern since the sack of Constantinople by the Crusaders in 1204."⁷⁵ The rise of the "Megali Idea," which envisioned a resurrection of the Byzantine Empire, looked eastward, to Asia Minor for its realization. The linguistic problem—that is, the tension between the demotic and the *katharevousa*—was principally about accepting the vernacular Greek, spoken by the majority of people, or maintaining a puristic made-up language that appealed to Western Grecophiles. The search for an authentic Greek identity was concomitant with a search for historical "origins" and an anti-Western attitude propagated by many of the leading intellectuals in the early twentieth century.

In the search for the lost Greek memory, Byzantium offered a convenient alternative to Ancient Greece; the latter was widely adopted by the West (politically, culturally, architecturally, and literarily), whereas the former was a historical locus of resistance to the West.⁷⁶ Jusdanis explains:

---

⁷² Apart from Grigoris Bithikotsis, the original singer, the songs of *The Axion Esti* were also performed by many popular Greek performers such as Giorgos Dalaras, Maria Farantouri, Yiannis Kotsiras, Yiannis Parios, and many others.

⁷³ Elytis, *Collected Poems*, p. 125.

⁷⁴ "I resided in a country that came from the other, the real one, as the dream comes from the facts of my life" (Elytis, *Collected Poems*, p. 424).

⁷⁵ Jusdanis, *Belated Modernity*, p. 115.

⁷⁶ I should stress here that the resistance to the classical tradition was not a general phenomenon. Three examples are of particular interest: Angelos Sikelianos, who attempted a reestablishment of the Ancient Delphic Festivals; Yiannis Ritsos, who combined his leftist beliefs with mythological subtexts; and George Seferis, who adhered to T.S. Eliot's use of the mythical method.

The resurgence of Hellenism quite often involved a return to popular practices traced back to Byzantium. Tradition for many writers usually represented Byzantine inheritance as transmitted through the Orthodox Church and the scholars living under Ottoman rule. Against the hegemony of the West these critics proposed the culture of the East. By the East they meant the culture of Orthodoxy rather than the Orient, for the Orthodox Church had defined itself as Eastern, a characteristic inherited from the Byzantines, who constituted the Eastern Empire, in contradistinction to Rome and the Western Empire.[77]

Two of the most vociferous supporters of this eastern relocation of the lost center were Periklis Yiannopoulos (1870–1910) and Ionas Dragoumis (1878–1920). Both were fiercely anti-Western and attempted a rediscovery of Greece through a reexamination of both history and tradition. Yiannopoulos's writing is a mix of ethnocentric beliefs and Romantic views of Greek nature.[78] The magazine *Nea Grammata*, which introduced Elytis's poetry, aligned itself with many of Yiannopoulos's aesthetic beliefs, particularly those pertaining to the rediscovery of Greece through its natural setting.[79] Similarly, Dragoumis maintained that "the worst calamity befalling Greeks was ... their imitation of European culture, which extinguished their demotic and Byzantine traditions. Modernization initiated two tendencies: *xenolatria* and *archeolatria*—the worship of the foreign and the ancient."[80] Even though both Yiannopoulos and Dragoumis were writing at the acme of the "Megali Idea," their ethnocentric ideas would later prove paramount in the exploration of Greekness by the generation of the 1930s.[81]

By the 1930s the "Megali Idea" had completely foundered, with the loss of Asia Minor in 1922; the writings of Dragoumis and Yiannopoulos, as Elytis would later write in "The Chronicle of a Decade," seemed like "nearby hills that a sudden flood [had] turned into distant and uninhabited islands."[82] Yet, he proceeds to write,

> Or, at least, that is what I thought then. It was too early for me to distinguish, behind the former's political shape and behind the latter's hyperbole, the eternal and healthy part of their views, which a 'modernizing' study performed by a brilliant and bold fellow thinker at that time could have illuminated and restored to its fertilizing potential.[83]

---

[77] Jusdanis, *Belated*, p. 115.

[78] Yiannopoulos committed suicide shortly before Elytis was born.

[79] See, for example, Yiannopoulos's *Η Ελληνική Γραμμή και το Ελληνικόν Χρώμα* which was published in *Nea Grammata* in 1938. Perikles Yiannopoulos, "Η Ελληνική γραμμή και το Ελληνικό Χρώμα," *Τα Νέα Γράμματα* 4, no. 13 (Jan–March 1938): 117–24, 132–9, 213–14.

[80] Jusdanis, *Belated Modernity*, p. 113.

[81] In his *Generation of the Thirties* [Η Γενιά του Τριάντα], Mario Vitti briefly discusses the influence of Dragoumis on Giorgos Theotokas; Theotokas was one of the leading figures of what came to be known as the 1930s generation.

[82] Elytis, *Ανοιχτά Χαρτιά*, p. 354.

[83] Elytis, *Ανοιχτά Χαρτιά*, p. 354. Yiannopoulos's influence on Elytis's theory of analogies is indisputable. For a more substantial discussion on this influence see Pantelis Voutouris's "Odisseas Elitis-Periklis Ghiannopulos. Dalla linea greca al neoclassicismo surrealista."

On the one hand, Elytis seems to understand the writings of Dragoumis and Yiannopoulos as hyperbolic and ethnocentric, while on the other, he believes in the "fertilizing potential" of these same ideas. Most importantly, the statement illustrates the traditional character of Greek modernity; if Greek modernism is an interesting case in the wider context of European modernism, it is because it demanded a negotiation between the "modern" and the "traditional" by constructing the former with the material of the latter.[84] Elytis negotiated between the two by relating the "essence" of the work of art to the "local," and its "form" to the modern aesthetics.[85] For him, and for many poets in the thirties, modernism constituted a revolutionary force that could be launched against the false image projected by the West's misreading of Greekness. "Such an attitude," he writes, "helped the 'moderns' to look at their own place with a clearer eye and to turn their attention to the neglected, until then, values of the East."[86]

With *The Axion Esti*, Elytis broke a silence of about 13 years after the publication of *Song Heroic and Mourning* in 1945.[87] In terms of structure, the work had been the most ambitious undertaken by the poet, and it would prove to be one of the most unique poetic compositions of Greek modernism. Elytis writes:

> From there on, what remained was the technique, that I purposely attended to since I felt that the time had come for someone in Europe to show—from what I know no other European poet had attempted such a thing until now—that it is possible for the modern experience to go through its classical period, not with a return to the old limitations, but with the creation of new limitations that the poet himself makes in order to overcome them and, thus, to achieve, once more, a solid construction.[88]

---

[84] I will not get into a more elaborate discussion here on the tensions between tradition and modernity. I will quote, however, the following interesting passage from Jusdanis's *Belated Modernity*: "[T]hough I must refer to terms such as modernity and tradition, I do not imply that they are antithetical.... The split between tradition and modernity has been, as I argue earlier, a function of the modernization project, which assumes that modern societies have completely eradicated traditional elements and, conversely, that traditional societies have no modern features. I would like to see these concepts as continued rather than separate, dialectically related rather than diametrically opposed...." And Jusdanis goes on to state: "'Belated' societies, however, exhibit an uneasy fit between traditional and modern constructs" (Jusdanis, *Belated*, pp. xv–xvi).

[85] Elytis, *Ανοιχτά Χαρτιά*, p. 497. In his 1944 essay "Contemporary Poetic and Artistic Problems."

[86] Elytis, *Ανοιχτά Χαρτιά*, p. 497.

[87] Parts of the longer poem "Goodness in the Wolf-Passes" [Η Καλωσύνη στις Λυκοποριές] were published in the 1947 New Year's edition of the magazine *Mikro Tetradio* [Μικρό Τετράδιο]. Elytis decided not to publish this poem again. It is significant that he began its composition after returning from his three-year-long trip to Paris where he met, among others, Reverdy, Breton, Éluard, Tzara, Jouve, Char, Mirò, Ungaretti, Eliot, Picasso, Léger, Matisse, and Camus.

[88] Qtd in Vitti, *Οδυσσέας Ελύτης*, p. 235. It is significant that Elytis situates himself within the European poetic tradition. We see here the way in which Europe simultaneously

The Axion Esti achieves this solidity both structurally and conceptually. Let us begin with the more apparent structural divisions of the collection. As Jeffrey Carson and Nikos Sarris note, "Axion Esti means 'worthy it is' and it is found in a hymn to the Virgin from the Byzantine liturgy and in a Good Friday encomium to Christ."[89] It also refers to the famous "Axion Esti" icon of the Virgin, on Mount Athos; the icon depicts the Virgin with Jesus as a child holding a scroll.[90] This reference becomes significant from the beginning of the poem when a voice—the voice of "he who I truly was He many aeons ago"—tells the poet "Your commandment ... is this world / written in your viscera / Read and try / and fight...."[91] The collection introduces itself as a canonical work—an icon or a holy text—and the poet puts himself in the position of a Christ-like messenger of the Word/Logos. In the introductory epigraph we further read a passage from Psalms 129:2: "Much have they afflicted me from my youth up; But they have not prevailed against me."[92] Once again, the Biblical subtext is important, as the Psalm is a thanksgiving to God for rescuing Israel:

> "Sorely have they afflicted me from my youth," let Israel now say—"Sorely have they afflicted me from my youth, yet they have not prevailed against me. The plowers plowed upon my back; they made long their furrows." The LORD is righteous; he has cut the cords of the wicked. May all who hate Zion be put to shame and turned backward! Let them be like the grass on the housetops, which withers before it grows up, with which the reaper does not fill his hand or the binder of sheaves his bosom, while those who pass by do not say, "The blessing of the LORD be upon you! We bless you in the name of the LORD!"[93]

The psalm is a sort of a counter-narrative of resistance spoken by an oppressed people. In his interview on national Greek television, Elytis gave a similar explanation of how *The Axion Esti* was composed:

> As strange as it may sound, my stay in Europe made me see the drama of my country more clearly; there the injustice that befell Greece and the poet alike leapt up more vividly. Little by little these two were equated in me. I repeat, it may sound strange but I clearly saw that the fate of Greece between other nations was similar to the fate of the poet between other men—I mean, of course, the people of money and power. That was the first spark, the first discovery. And the need I felt for an invocation [δέηση] gave me the second discovery. To give, in

---

functions as both a locus of identification for him, and many other poets of his generation, and a hauntological point of reference that he measures against his own poetic theories.

[89] Elytis, *Collected Poems*, p. 119.

[90] Yiannis Moralis's painting that adorns the cover of the book depicts an anthropomorphic winged sun hovering over the sea, and an Orthodox icon (the frame points to its Orthodox origin). The actual image on the icon is a vague mermaid-like figure divided symmetrically.

[91] Elytis, *Collected Poems*, p. 123.

[92] Elytis, *Collected Poems*, p. 119.

[93] Psalm 129.

other words, to this protest of mine against injustice the form of an ecclesiastical liturgy. That is how *The Axion Esti* was born.[94]

As Elytis saw it, the "injustice that befell Greece" at the time he was writing *The Axion Esti* came from several directions: Greece was misread by the West; it was marginalized by the great nations of Europe that saw more in its ancient glory than in its present deplorable state; and, most importantly, it had undergone a long civil war, which was largely orchestrated and fueled by the Great Powers.[95] Elytis situates the poet in the same position as the marginalized nation and in opposition to the official historical narrative—a narrative that is constructed and manipulated by those in power. The first part of the collection, "The Genesis," is structured around the restoration of the status of the poet and of his "dream nation," and concludes: "This then I am / and the world the small the great!"[96] In "framing" the work in the Orthodox tradition, Elytis resorts to what he sees as eastern rather than western structures. This framing goes far beyond subtextual references and is most vividly represented in the actual structural division of its three parts.

The three parts that make up the collection are "The Genesis," "The Passion," and "The Gloria." Each of these is further divided into corresponding segments. A general schematization of the three parts would yield the following correspondences:

A. "The Genesis"
7 hymns with a similar refrain at the end

B. "The Passion"
Psalm A—Psalm B	Psalm G—Psalm H	Psalm M—Psalm N
Ode I—Reading 1—Ode II	Ode V—Reading 3—Ode VI	Ode IX—Reading 5—Ode X
Psalm C—Psalm D	Psalm I—Psalm J	Psalm O—Psalm P
Ode III—Reading 2—Ode IV	Ode VII—Reading 4—Ode VIII	Ode XI—Reading 6—Ode XII
Psalm E—Psalm F	Psalm K—Psalm L	Psalm Q—Psalm R

C. "The Gloria"
Section i	6 quatrains + 1 triplet + 6 quatrains + 1 triplet+5 quatrains+7 couplets 6 quatrains+1 triplet
Section ii	+6 quatrains+1 triplet+6 quatrains +1 triplet+5 quatrains+7 couplets
Section iii	6 quatrains+1 triplet+6 quatrains +1 triplet+5 quatrains+7 couplets

There are several intricate correspondences in the collection: Edmund Keeley suggests that, "according to the poet's commentary, each 'paragraph' [in "The Genesis"] corresponds to a stage of the Creation, of the Ages of Man, of the hours

---

[94] Elytis, *Αυτοπροσωπογραφία*, pp. 19–20.

[95] Great Britain and the United States supported the national forces; the communist rebels turned to Tito (Yugoslavia) and Stalin (Soviet Union) for support. The fifth reading of "The Passion" (The Courtyard of the Sheep) in *The Axion Esti* directly refers to the Greek Civil War.

[96] Elytis, *Collected Poems*, p. 133.

from dawn to midday."[97] In "The Passion," which comprises the greater part of the collection, the lines of each Ode are italicized and divided by an asterisk (*) and in each Psalm, every other line is indented (beginning with the first).[98] The narrative style of the Readings borrows from both the Bible and the biblical tone of General Makriyiannis's diaries.[99] The indented/nonindented sequence is also followed in "The Gloria," where each triplet is a reference to objects of the Greek experience[100] and each couplet in the three sections begins with the same word.[101]

If "The Genesis" represents the creation of the "dream nation" and the "awakening" of the poet, "The Gloria" embodies the now-matured poet's glorification of his creation. But it is in the central part of "The Passion" that the tension between memory and counter-memory, fantasy and reality, and ultimately the historical nation and the "dream nation" emerges. The poet's detailed personal notes provide a clear outline of the collection's conceptual structure:[102]

A. CONSCIOUSNESS FACING TRADITION

Psalm A	Poet and Consciousness	
Psalm B	Poet and Language	Vehicles of Freedom

Birth and sanction of the concepts

Ode A	Liberty and Language	
Reading 1	The Confrontation of Evil	
Ode B	Fortitude	

Concepts which demand virtues such as

Psalm C	Frugality	The Pillars of the
Psalm D	Pride and Rebellion	Native Land

With full awareness of the consequences, which are:

Ode C	Solitude	
Reading 2	Struggle	
Ode D	Sacrifice	

---

[97] Odysseus Elytis, *The Axion Esti*, p. 79.

[98] Elytis never used the terms "Psalm" and "Ode." He simply used lower case Greek letters (where "Ode" is used here) and capital case Greek letters (where "Psalm" is used here). The headings "Ode" and "Psalm" were introduced by Elytis's translators.

[99] Yiannis Makriyiannis (1794–1864) is one of the most celebrated generals of the 1821 revolution. What is interesting about his diaries is the fact that Makiyiannis was uneducated and, thus, uses a mixture of vernacular and biblical styles. He kept a diary from approximately 1829 to 1850.

[100] In the presented order: the names of eight winds, nine Aegean islands, nine flowers, nine girls, nine boats, nine mountains, and nine trees.

[101] The first set of couplets begins with "Hail," the second with "he," and the third with an interchange between the words "Now" and "Forever."

[102] Elytis made these notes available to his English translators George Savidis and Edmund Keeley. See Odysseus Elytis, *The Axion Esti*.

And which make the conscious human to turn to deeper elements, that is:

Psalm E	The Mountain	The Guardians of tradition
Psalm F	The Sea	

B. CONSCIOUSNESS FACING DANGER

Psalm G	The Enemy	The External Danger
Psalm H	The "Protectors"	

Who seek to alter human authenticity and lead to:

Ode E	The Quest for the Soul
Reading 3	The Heroic Deed
Ode F	The Invocation of Justice

And to the Intelligible Sun, so that the consciousness may rise over those who are:

Psalm I	The Erring Bourgeois	Internal Danger
Psalm J	The Decadent Youth	

Who constitute the image of the present world, which is made equally of:

Ode G	Beauty and Misery
Reading 4	Greatness and Martyrdom
Ode H	Elation and Tears

The present world of perverted Western Christian civilization which must be exorcised by new weapons:

Psalm K	The Gospel of Pure Water and Poetic Speech	The Natural Greek Symbols
Psalm L	The other Cross consisting of the Trident and the Dolphin	

C. CONSCIOUSNESS SURPASSING DANGER

Psalm M	The Beatification of the Senses	Physical Metaphysics
Psalm N	The Reinstatement of the Senses	

Which for another future, emerge as:

Ode I	Oracles from the Barren Rock
Reading 5	Teachings from the Fires of Destruction
Ode J	Voices from the Blood of Love

And which reach:

Psalm O	The Comparison with the Deity	The Surpassing of Death
Psalm P	The Denial of Fate	

Through the vehicle of the one who is:

Ode K	The Poet as Monk of Bodily Vigor
Reading 6	The Poet as Modern Prophet
Ode L	The Poet as Evangelist of a Transcendental Country

	Which is the present country reached after the fulfillment of the "void" of sacrifice and which has been realized through:	
Psalm Q	The Mutual Compensation of Good and Evil	The Absolute Reality of the Spirit, Glory of the Poet and of Greece
Psalm R	The Reidentification of Beauty with Justice	

What becomes apparent in this elaborate schematization of "The Passion," is that the central theme that permeates its three sections is that of Consciousness. David Rosen claims that, "modern Poetry after Eliot is a poetry of consciousness," as opposed to the premodern poetry of "imagination."[103] As hyperbolic as the claim may sound, it is certainly correct in assuming that the modernist revolution—be it political, social, or artistic—aimed at filling history's void through an attempt to restore man's consciousness. In this sense, the creative writer is not merely sublimating personal desires but also performing a revelation of truth. When Camus writes, for example, that the myth of Sisyphus is tragic only "because its hero is conscious," he is suggesting that consciousness leads to the realization of the world's absurdity; true happiness, according to Camus, is possible only in the consciousness of the absurd.[104] Similarly, Elytis argues (in a 1951 statement made around the same time he started the composition of *The Axion Esti*) that the aim of his mythopoetics is "to restore the individual to the collective and consciousness to the 'command high above' [άνωθεν εντολή]."[105] Modernism had confined consciousness to the individual psyche, and poetry was left to negotiate its role as both a personal creation and a collective force.[106] Since consciousness cannot be sustained in an institutional, metaphysical, historical, or Romantic context, poetry must make an effort to sustain it as a "command high above"; to be conscious is to realize the existence of a world beyond the reality proposed by history. The first poem of "The Passion," which Elytis's notes mark as "Poet and Consciousness," is precisely an attempt to negotiate between the poet's consciousness and the collective position:

> Each with his own weapons, I said:
> At the Passes I shall open my pomegranates
> At the Passes I shall post the Zephyrs as guards
> I shall unleash old kisses my longing consecrated!
> Wind lets loose the elements and thunder assails the mountains
> Fate of the innocent you are my own Fate![107]

---

[103] David Rosen, "T.S. Eliot and the Lost Youth of Modern Poetry," *Modern Language Quarterly: A Journal of Literary History* 64, no. 4 (Dec 2003): 473–94. p. 481.

[104] Camus, *Sisyphus*, pp. 121–2.

[105] Elytis, *Εν Λευκώ*, p. 206.

[106] Elytis's position verifies Peter Bürger's description of the modernist anxiety to bridge the gap between aesthetics and the "praxis of life."

[107] Elytis, *Collected Poems*, p. 137. Ο καθείς και τα όπλα του, είπα: / Στα Στενά τα ρόδια μου θ' ανοίξω / Στα Στενά φρουρούς τους ζέφυρους θα στήσω / τα φιλιά τα παλιά θ'

If consciousness becomes a fundamental structuring concept, it is because it is at the antipode of the surrealist attempt to capture, through the use of automatism, that which resides outside of consciousness, namely the unconscious. Furthermore, Elytis does not map consciousness in a global schema but rather as part of the Greek experience—an experience, which—like the "fate of the innocent"[108] and the fate of the poet—is at the periphery of the so-called western system of Christian values. Consciousness is placed next to tradition, danger, and the overcoming of danger in an attempt to restore and revitalize what the poet understands as the marginalization of Greece. The complex structure of the collection can be seen, then, as a mapping of the homeland made possible by a "revealing" or "uncovering" of truth (*alētheia*) in the Heideggerian sense or, more simply, as a genealogical mapping of the history of Greek consciousness.

Foucault's distinction between "origins" and "genealogy" provides an appropriate lens through which we can examine the structure of *The Axion Esti* as a metahistorical attempt—as opposed to a nationalistic one—to define "Greekness." Foucault writes:

> However, if the genealogist refuses to extend his faith in metaphysics, if he listens to history, he finds that there is 'something altogether different' behind things: not a timeless and essential secret, but the secret that they have no essence or that their essence was fabricated in a piecemeal fashion from alien forms.... What is found at the beginning of things is not the inviolable identity of their origin; it is the dissension of other things. It is disparity.[109]

The pursuer of origins believes in the metaphysical moment when the nation, or the idea, was born; the genealogist is neither interested in origins nor in "restor[ing] an unbroken continuity."[110] On the contrary, he "seeks to reestablish the various systems of subjections: not the anticipatory power of meaning but the hazardous play of dominations."[111] And history's aim is not to "discover the roots of our identity but to commit itself to its dissipation."[112]

Such an approach to history appears, at first, to be in complete antithesis to Elytis's attempted "mapping of the nation." The Axion Esti, however, is not concerned with the tracing of origins; a similar "tracing of origins" was constantly attempted, from the 1821 revolution against the Ottomans to the disastrous defeat of the Greeks in Asia Minor, and it proved to be a futile assessment of history.

απολύσω που η λαχτάρα μου άγιασε! / Λύνει αέρας τα στοιχεία και βροντή προσβάλλει τα βουνά. / Μοίρα των αθώων, είσαι η δική μου η Μοίρα! (Elytis, *Ποίηση*, p. 134).

[108] Elytis, *Collected Poems*, p. 137.

[109] Michel Foucault, "Nietzsche, Genealogy, History: Selected Essays and Interviews," in *Language, Counter-Memory, Practice*, ed. Donald Bouchard, trans. Donald Bouchard and Sherry Simon, 139–64 (Ithaca: Cornell University Press, 1977), p. 142.

[110] Foucault, "Nietzsche," p. 146.

[111] Foucault, "Nietzsche," p. 148.

[112] Foucault, "Nietzsche," p. 162.

Korais's attempt to enforce a language that resembled ancient Greek, Koletis's preaching of the "Megali Idea" [Great Idea], the West's perception of Greece as an ancient site, and the resurgence of nationalism, were all impositions that pointed to a moment of birth and a place of origins. The Renaissance traced the inception of Greece in Antiquity, Korais in the fixed structures of language, Koletis in the birth and rise of Byzantium, and nationalism was invested in the ever-present glory of both the Byzantines and the Ancient Greeks. Elytis is more interested in the disparity and "uncovering" of what Foucault calls the "non place of dominion."[113] Structure should not be confused with an attempt to map what is historically assumed to be true. On the contrary, *The Axion Esti* confronts history as well as the conventional perceptions of "Greekness." Like Nietzsche, Elytis traces disparity in the rise of a perverted Christian civilization that construed a fallacious historical narrative.[114] As the beatification of pity constitutes for Nietzsche a Judeo-Christian attempt to control power, Elytis sees in the Western Christian civilization a corruption of the meaning of Greekness that only served the West's claim to an inherited Hellenic Idea. As Foucault argues, "the success of history belongs to those who are capable of seizing these rules, to replace those who had used them, to disguise themselves so as to pervert them, invert their meaning, and redirect them against those who had initially imposed them."[115] What Elytis recovers in The Axion Esti is not the past glory of the ancient Greeks or the Byzantines, but that which has managed to survive despite the suppression of history, by incorporating itself in the folk tradition, the geography, and the language.

The exploration of Greece as a peripheral nation is concomitant in Elytis's work with the recovery of what has been suppressed in the course of history. The turn to the East is an attempt to return to the moment of historical disparity, or "dissipation," and reaffirm the existence of Greece by relocating it outside Western geography. The view of Greece as the marginalized "other" is understood both as a personal poetic resistance to the official or imposed historical narrative, and as an effort to illuminate what is suppressed or neglected, and make it public. In the third Ode of *The Axion Esti* we read:

> In spite of earthquakes * and of famines
> In spite of enemies* in spite of my
>   Kith, I resisted * I held out was heartened was strengthened
> Once and twice * and thrice
> I founded my house on * memory alone

---

[113] Foucault, "Nietzsche," p. 150.

[114] Just like Elytis believed that the West had misread modern Greece, Nietzsche also believed that Western scholars had completely misread the ancients. In "Homer's Contests," one of his earliest essays, Nietzsche writes: "we would shudder if we were ever to understand [the Greeks] in Greek." Friedrich Wilhelm Nietzsche, *The Portable Nietzsche*, trans. Walter Kaufmann (New York: Penguin, 1976), p. 33.

[115] Foucault, "Nietzsche," p. 151.

> I took my halo and * wreathed myself alone
> The wheat that I pro * claimed I scythed alone![116]

History is reconstructed in the memory or, to use the Foucauldian term, in the *counter-memory* of the poet, and resistance is directed internally (my Kith) and externally (the enemies). At the same time, resistance is made possible by the use of such public loci as language and geography. Language is by its very nature a force of resistance, as it carries within it (in etymology, grammar, metaphor, proverbs, myths) the *counter-memory* of the culture. Similarly, geography resists official history by imprinting itself on language. The poet moves in and out of the two loci, restructuring reality and reclaiming what has been oppressed.[117] The use of structure allows for the oppressive historical narrative to be exorcised by the invention of a new order.

Foucault sees the body as "the inscribed surface of events." He situates genealogy "within the articulation of the body and history. Its task is to expose a body totally imprinted by history and the process of history's destruction of the body."[118] Elytis's construction of the meta-historical poetic space is similarly situated "within the articulation of the body and history." The body's interaction with history is violent, as it is especially emphasized in the Readings of *The Axion Esti*: the soldiers marching to the Front "furiously scratch themselves for a long time"[119] until they bleed or "hit the ground face down on the scrap" during a bombardment.[120] In the third reading, we see "young men with swollen feet" and "the men and women and the wounded with their bandages and crutches";[121] in the fourth, a young man is shot "straight through the ear."[122] In the fifth reading, Greece is described as "the courtyard of sheep" and the wind herds "the corpses

---

[116] Elytis, Collected Poems, p. 145. Στο πείσμα των σεισμών *στο πείσμα των λιμών / Στο πείσμα των εχτρών *στο πείσμα των δικών / Μου, ανάντισα κρατήθηκα *ψυχώθηκα κραταιώθηκα / Μία και δύο *και τρεις φορές / Θεμελίωσα τα σπίτια μου * στη μνήμη μόνος / Πήρα και στεφανώθηκα *την άλω μόνος / Το στάρι που ευαγγέλισα *το 'δρεψα μόνος! (Elytis, Ποίηση, p. 142).

[117] We are reminded here of Elytis's description of nature as an interaction with the immobile and the eternal.

[118] Foucault, "Nietzsche," p. 148. In *The Gay Science*, Nietzsche writes: "I have asked myself whether, taking a large view, philosophy has not been merely an interpretation of the body and a *misunderstanding of the body*. Behind the highest value judgments that have hitherto guided the history of thought, there are concealed misunderstandings of the physical constitution—of individuals or classes or even whole races." Friedrich Wilhelm Nietzsche, *The Gay Science*, trans. Walter Kaufmann (New York: Vintage, 1974), pp. 34–5.

[119] Elytis, *Collected Poems*, p. 140.
[120] Elytis, *Collected Poems*, p. 146.
[121] Elytis, *Collected Poems*, p. 154.
[122] Elytis, *Collected Poems*, p. 159.

of the slain."[123] Only in the sixth reading, the last before "Gloria," is the body restored and dreams take their revenge on history.[124]

The body does not only interact with the violence of history. It is the only locus the poet has in order to "read" the world and reconstruct it.[125] The poet resists history by reassessing the material substance of reality. In other words, he confronts history by placing it next to other "real" experiences such as landscape, language, and the body. Such reassessment of reality does not constitute a utopian escape from history, but what Foucault calls "effective history."[126] The poet's notes, for example, indicate that Psalm M is structured around the theme of the "beatification" of the senses:

> Take my guts, I have sung!
>   Take my sea with its white northwinds,
> the wide window filled by lemon trees
>   the many bird songs, and the one girl
> whose joy though I only touched her was enough for me
>   take them, I have sung!
> Take my dreams, how could you read them?
>   Take my thought, where could you say it?
> I am pure from end to end.
>   Kissing with my mouth I enjoyed the virgin's body.
> Blowing with my mouth I colored the sea's hide.
>   I enriched all my ideas with islands.
> On my consciousness I dripped lemon.[127]

In his Nobel lecture (1992), the Caribbean author Derek Walcott stated: "the fate of poetry is to fall in love with the world, in spite of History."[128] The statement comes as a sharp contradiction to Theodore Adorno's famous declaration that "to

---

[123] Elytis, *Collected Poems*, p. 168.

[124] "And dreams shall take revenge, and they shall sow generations forever and ever!" (Elytis, *Collected Poems*, p. 74).

[125] In the "Genesis" we read: "Your commandment is this world ... read it and try and fight" (Elytis, *Collected Poems*, p. 123). And in "Psalm X" the "Young Alexandrians" (decadent youth) mock the poet for "trusting only in his own body" (Elytis, *Collected Poems*, p. 157).

[126] Foucault, "Nietzsche," p. 153.

[127] Elytis, *Collected Poems*, p. 165. Πάρετέ μου τα σπλάχνα, τραγούδησα! / Πάρετέ μου τη θάλασσα με τους άσπρους βοριάδες / το πλατύ το παράθυρο γεμάτο λεμονιές / τα πολλά κελαηδίσματα, και το κορίτσι το ένα / που και μόνον αν άγγιξα η χαρά του μού άρκεσε / πάρετέ μου, τραγούδησα! / Πάρετέ μου τα όνειρα, πώς να διαβάσετε; / Πάρετέ μου τη σκέψη, πού να την πείτε; / Καθαρός είμαι απ' άκρη σ' άκρη. / Με το στόμα φιλώντας εχάρηκα το παρθένο κορμί. / Με το στόμα φυσώντας χρωμάτισα τη δορά του πελάγους. / Τις ιδέες μου όλες ενησιώτισα. / Στη συνείδηση μου έσταξα λεμόνι (Elytis, *Ποίηση*, p. 159).

[128] Derek Walcott, *The Antilles: Fragments of Epic Memory*, December 7, 1992, http://nobelprize.org/nobel_prizes/literature/laureates/1992/walcott-lecture.html (accessed October 10, 2007).

write poetry after Auschwitz is barbaric."[129] In the case of Elytis and Walcott, historical violence is exorcised by a juxtaposition with the experience of the body in geography and language. Facing the beauty of the Caribbean landscape, "the sigh of history dissolves."[130] At the end of *The Axion Esti*, natural beauty, as in Camus, is identified with a new system of Justice. As the poet declares, "In whitewash I now enclose my true Laws. / Blessed, I say, the strong who decipher the Immaculate."[131] Since, as Foucault claims, "the body manifests stigmata of past experience,"[132] the study of the body can lead to more effective study of history. For Elytis, the term "body" expands to include, apart from the human body, the body of land and the body of language.[133] It is in these loci, in this interconnected network of material, real constructs, that human experience is recorded *genealogically*.

A genealogical approach to *The Axion Esti* clarifies many of the misconceptions regarding its "national" foundation. Its eastern structure does not signify an attempt to return to Greece's Byzantine origin, but rather a resistance to the western misreadings of "Greekness." At the same time, the collection does not claim an objective approach to history, as the Foucauldian study of descent does. "The Gloria," after all, raises the constructed "dream-nation" above the threat of history; by the end of "The Passion" the poet marches to a "sinless" and "unwrinkled" country.[134] Elytis started the composition of *The Axion Esti* six years after the end of the German occupation and in the immediate aftermath of the Greek Civil War. The eastward orientation of the collection, its biblical or apocalyptic language, the very nature of the historical narratives presented (all spanning the period from World War II to the Greek Civil War), propose a specific meta-historical narrative; the text *resists* a history that had proven itself brutal and violent.

Elytis would attempt, once more, to place the "dream nation" in a specific poetic locus in *The Little Seafarer*, published in 1985. However, by then Greece was in a very different sociopolitical and historical position. The Civil War and the Generals' Junta were relatively distant memories (though still contested historical moments). Democracy had been restored since 1974 and the country had joined the European Union in 1981.

---

[129] Theodore Adorno, *Prisms (Studies in Contemporary German Social Thought)*, trans. Shierry Weber Nicholsen (Cambridge, MA: MIT Press, 1983), p. 22.

[130] Walcott, "The Antilles."

[131] Elytis, *Collected Poems*, p. 177.

[132] Foucault, "Nietzsche," p. 148.

[133] For an example of an approach to history through landscape see Psalm V: "My foundations are in the mountains / And the peoples bear the mountains on their shoulders / And on them memory burns / Neverburnt bush/ Memory of my people they call you Pindus and call you Athos" (Elytis, *Collected Poems*, p. 149). For an example of an approach to history through language see Psalm II: "I was given the Greek language; a poor house on Homer's shores" (Elytis, *Collected Poems*, p. 138).

[134] Elytis, *Collected Poems*, pp. 176, 177.

The Little Seafarer: Time Bound, Time Unbound

Elytis's little seafarer takes his journey literally, stylistically, historically, and geographically. The stylistic progressions may be described as similar to James Joyce's use of multiple writing styles in *Ulysses*. The overall schematization of the collection in terms of structure and style is as follows:

Section	Style
ENTRANCE	
SPOTLIGHT I	History [Scenes of historical brutality from Antiquity to modernity]
To Anoint the Repast (I–VII)	Prose Poems
With Both Life and Death (1–7)	Verse Poems
What one Loves (The Traveling Bag)	A list of "items" (paintings, lines from poems, music, etc.) that the little seafarer carries with him.
SPOTLIGHT II	History [Scenes of historical brutality in ancient Greece]
To Anoint the Repast [VIII–XIV]	Prose Poems
With Both Light and Death [8–14]	Verse Poems
What one Loves (Aegean Route)	A list of words (mostly related to the sea and to the island dialects) that the little seafarer carries with him.
SPOTLIGHT III	History [Scenes of historical brutality in Byzantine Greece]
To Anoint the Repast [XV–XXI]	Prose Poems
With Both Light and Death [15–21]	Verse Poems
What one Loves (Snapshots)	A list of sensual photographic 'snapshots' of geographical locations and girls.
SPOTLIGHT IV	History [Scenes of historical brutality in Modern Greece]
To Anoint the Repast [XXII–XXVIII]	Prose Poems
EXIT	

Like *The Axion Esti* and *The Monogram*, the four repeated sections of *The Little Seafarer* can be arranged in a reflective pattern:

Entrance – SA / LW / SA / LW / SA / LW / SA – Exit[135]

Once more, we have a structural pattern that emerges in seven parts. The implications of this arrangement are multiple. The poem moves in and out of history, metaphysics, and poetry. The spotlights are narrated in an impersonal *historical* voice. The prose poems are all narrated in the first person, and their meaning is more accessible. The verse poems are more evasive (some are written in ancient Greek, others, in

---

[135] Spotlight (S), To Anoint the Repast (A), With Both Light and Death (L), What one Loves (W).

the style of classical papyri, with no spaces), and though they maintain the personal tone of the prose poems, they seek an interaction with an "other."[136] The long lists of the items the little seafarer carries with him are not accompanied by any explanations. If we consider the sequence in which these sections are presented, we clearly perceive a movement from the impersonal and descriptive, to the personal and condensed. In other words, there is a movement from historical reality to the more accessible reality of the prose poem, to the more evasive realm of poetry, and finally to the condensed sensation of the word or the image.

The concept of Time is central in this progression. The historical segments move chronologically, with the first spotlight recapitulating this movement: it begins at an open court in ancient Athens, and then moves to Byzantine Constantinople, to nineteenth-century Nauplion, and finally to contemporary Athens. The choice of place is not coincidental: all the cities were once centers of the historical Greek "nation."[137] The historical progression of time is ruptured by poetic time. The verse poems are written in a language that transgresses historical time: Elytis uses ancient, biblical, and modern Greek. The geographical references in "What one Loves" are not concerned with political borders shaped by history: the little seafarer travels freely from Crete, to the Aegean, to Etruria, Cordoba, Palermo, Aix-en-Provence, and elsewhere, and does not remain confined within the borders of Greece.

The juxtaposition of historical time with poetic time renders history—repeated history—obsolete. Elytis had already discussed the relationship between history and time in relation to *The Axion Esti*, when he wrote of "an eternally repeated scene in the history of the nation to point where the concept of time ceases to exist."[138] This statement echoes Nietzsche's concept of the Eternal Return: since matter is limited and time is unlimited, we are forever caught in a cycle of endless repetition.[139] Nietzsche convalesces from the nausea of this realization by projecting meaning onto the eternal "moment." Elytis similarly condenses time into an instantaneous expression. Apart from the obvious condensation of the moment in an image, or in a single word (in "What one Loves"), the progression of time in history is contrasted with the fixed time of the poem, i.e., the poem is literally time-less and time-unbound:

---

[136] Most of them are addressed to "you" (second person plural or singular).

[137] Athens was/is the historical center of ancient and contemporary Greece, Constantinople of the Byzantine Empire, and Nauplion was the first capital of Greece following the War of Independence (1821). Athens became the capital in 1834.

[138] The statement is from a note of Elytis that was eventually published in 1995 by Giorgos Kehalioglou in the periodical *Ποίηση*. See Giorgos Kehalioglou, "Ένα ανέκδοτο υπόμνημα του Ελύτη για το Αξιον Εστί," *Ποίηση* 5 (Spring 1995), p. 54.

[139] Nietzsche discusses the concept in the following works: *The Gay Science* (Section 341), and *Thus Spoke Zarathustra* ("On the Vision and the Riddle" and "The Convalescence").

If there were a way for someone to be, at the same time, before and after[140] things, he would understand to what a degree time's opening, that simply devours events, loses its meaning, exactly as in a poem. And then—since the poem is an expansion of the instantaneous, or, contrarily, a contraction of the unending—he can win his freedom without any recourse to gunpowder.[141]

It is only in our one-sidedness, our "fixed" position in time, that history becomes significant. Historical time "devours events" because it is unable to stand before *and* after them; it merely follows them. Time ceases to exist precisely because history is a repetitive devouring and an eternal return of a trauma.

Psychoanalyst André Green goes as far as to describe the claim of "historical truth" in terms of "compulsive repetition":

> Historical Truth can thus be defined by a typical sequence: *an event (traumatic) inscribed on very early and barely differentiated raw material which, consequently, is not accessible to memory; repression; distortion; a return in the form of compulsive repetition having the power of actualization which only gives a transformed image of what once existed, but is based on a nucleus of truth that is both inescapable and unknowable as such.*[142]

Along similar lines, Nietzsche writes: "there is a degree of insomnia, of rumination, of historical sense which injures every living thing and finally destroys it, be it a man, a people or a culture."[143] As a traumatic event, history is forgotten, repressed, distorted, and returns in the form of "compulsive repetition." Elytis lists a total of 28 historical events, some of which are lost in that immense panorama of futility that is history (to use Eliot's phrase) and others which are deliberately unspecific. The following are some examples:

> Before an old and empty lot, in contemporary Athens, a crowd with priests and bishops jostles to throw a stone, "the stone of anathema" (Spotlight i, sixth scene).[144]

---

[140] Elytis, *Collected Poems*, p. 503. Jeffrey Carson and Nikos Sarris's translation is slightly different. Instead of "before and after things," which I use here, they translate the original "μπρός και πίσω απ' τα πράγματα" as "before and behind things."

[141] Εάν υπήρχε τρόπος να βρίσκεται κανείς, την ίδια στιγμή, μπρος και πίσω απ' τα πράγματα, θα καταλάβαινε πόσο το άνοιγμα του χρόνου, που καταβροχθίζει απλώς γεγονότα, χάνει τη σημασία του· όπως, ακριβώς, μέσα σ' ένα ποίημα. Και τότε—αφού είναι μια ανάπτυξη του ακαριαίου ή, αντίστροφα, μια σύμπτυξη του ατέρμονος το ποίημα—να κερδίσει την ελευθερία του χωρίς να καταφύγει σε κανενός είδους πυρίτιδα (Elytis, *Ποίηση*, p. 542).

[142] André Green, *Time in Psychoanalysis*, trans. Andrew Weller (New York: Free Association, 2002), p. 30. Italics are André Green's.

[143] Friedrich Wilhelm Nietzsche, *On the Advantage and Disadvantage of History for Life*, trans. Peter Preuss (Indianapolis: Hackett Publishing Company, 1980), p. 10.

[144] Elytis, *Collected Poems*, p. 420. Μπρος από 'να παλιό και άδειο οικόπεδο, στη σύγχρονη Αθήνα, ένα πλήθος ανάκατο με παπάδες και δεσποτάδες συνωστίζεται για να ρίξει μια πέτρα, «τον λίθον του αναθέματος» (Προβολέας α, σκηνή έκτη). Elytis, *Ποίηση*, p. 496.

Alexander the Great, outside his tent, gives the order to exterminate his devoted general Parmenion (Spotlight ii, sixth scene).[145]

At Christmas matins, Michael the Stutterer, helped by six other conspirators, kills his benefactor Emperor Leo V (spotlight iii, sixth scene).[146]

The enumeration of such events, narrated in a distant "objective" tone, exposes the compulsively repetitive nature of history. At the same time, Elytis enumerates his own list of "events"—the items, words, and impressions in "What One Loves"—which, we can say, claim an unhistorical assessment of reality based on sensation. What, then, is the difference between historical and poetic truth? If we return to André Green's description of historical truth, we can postulate the following: historical truth claims a return to the singular event in time and in doing so is doomed to failure, since "it is not accessible to memory"; poetic truth seeks to expose or, in Heidegger's expression, to "uncover" truth by exposing the sequence in which history represses, distorts and compulsively repeats an event.[147]

Apart from facilitating the constant moving in and out of historical and poetic time, the structure of *The Little Seafarer* constitutes an explicit attempt to map the poet's "dream nation":

---

[145] Elytis, *Collected Poems*, p. 447. Ο Μέγας Αλέξανδρος, έξω από τη σκηνή του, δίνει διαταγή να εξοντώσουν τον αφοσιωμένο του στρατηγό Παρμενίωνα (Προβολέας β, σκηνή έκτη). Elytis, *Ποίηση*, p. 511.

[146] Elytis, *Collected Poems*, p. 473. Στον εωθινό των Χριστουγέννων, ο Μιχαήλ Τραυλός, βοηθημένος από άλλους έξι συνωμότες, σκοτώνει τον ευεργέτη του αυτοκράτορα Λέοντα τον Ε' (Προβολέας β, σκηνή έκτη). Elytis, *Ποίηση*, p. 527.

[147] I find it interesting that both Nietzsche and Elytis approach remembrance and forgetting in their relation to history, time and consciousness using the same example of the animal that lacks consciousness. Nietzsche writes: "Consider the herd grazing before you. These animals do not know what yesterday and today are but leap about, eat, rest, digest and leap again; and so from morning to night and from day to day, only briefly concerned with their pleasure and displeasure, enthralled by the moment and for that reason neither melancholy or bored.... Man may as well ask the animal: why do you not speak to me of your happiness but only look at me? The animal does want to answer and say: because I always immediately forget what I wanted to say—but then it already forgot this answer and remained silent; so that man could only wonder" (Nietzsche, "On the Advantage," p. 8). In the first prose poem of *The Little Seafarer* Elytis writes: "One day the life I had lost I found in the eyes of a young calf, who looked at me with devotion. I realized that I had not been born by accident. I set myself to rake through my days, to turn them upside down, to search.... If there is no way even for time to vanquish falsehood, then for me the game is up" (Elytis, *Collected Poems*, p. 423). Both Elytis and Nietzsche approach human existence and the burden of history in relation to animals. The herd and the calf become the "other" through which human beings reflect on their position in history.

> I resided in a country that came from the other, the real one as the dream comes from the facts of life. I too named it Greece and I drew it on paper so I could look at it.[148]

> ... to conceive and to utter another, second world that always comes first within me.[149]

> My bones will appear later phosphorescing an azure
> Which the Archangel carries in his arms and lets trickle
> As with great strides he traverses the second Greece of the upper world.[150]

> A complete, self sufficient and coherent world that responds to me and to which I respond and we enter together as one body into the danger and the miracle.[151]

Despite its existence in the time-unbound poetic realm, this "other" Greece is not a utopia for Elytis. On the contrary, the material substance that the poetic imagination claims is found in the raw ingredients of history; both use language, claim territories, and interact with the body. As in *The Axion Esti*, the interaction of history with the body in *The Little Seafarer* is violent: we read in the "spotlights" of the cutting of noses, hands, and feet, of strangulations,[152] slaughter, plunder, poisoning,[153] executions, and assassination attempts;[154] the body exposes the violence of history.

The resistance to the nation's historization is thus concomitant with a resistance against that which rejects the body. Poetic imagination, on the other hand, attempts a restoration of bodily sensual pleasure:

> From early childhood they stuffed my head with an image of a death hooded in black, who held life like a mousetrap and offered it to us, and in it the lure of sensual pleasure. Permit me to laugh. He who chewed bay leaf said something else. And it is not by chance that we revolve around the sun.

> The body knows.[155]

---

[148] Elytis, *Collected Poems*, p. 424. Κατοίκησα μια χώρα που 'βγαινε από την άλλη, την πραγματική, όπως τ' όνειρο από τα γεγονότα της ζωής μου. Την είπα κι αυτήν Ελλάδα και τη χάραξα πάνω στο χαρτί να τηνε βλέπω (Elytis, *Ποίηση*, p. 497).

[149] Elytis, *Collected Poems*, p. 427. ... να συλλάβω και να πω έναν άλλο, δεύτερο κόσμο, που φτάνει πάντα πρώτος μέσα μου (Elytis, *Ποίηση*, p. 499).

[150] Elytis, *Collected Poems*, p. 433. Θα φάνουν αργότερα τα οστά μου φωσφορίζοντας ένα γαλάζιο / Που το πάει αγκαλιά ο Αρχάγγελος και στάζει με τεράστιους / Διασκελισμούς διαβαίνοντας την Ελλάδα τη δεύτερη του επάνω κόσμου (Elytis, *Ποίηση*, p. 500).

[151] Elytis, *Collected Poems*, p. 505. Ένας πλήρης, αυτάρκης και συγκροτημένος κόσμος που μου ανταποκρίνεται και του ανταποκρίνομαι και εισχωρούμε μαζί σαν ένα σώμα στον κίνδυνο και στο θαύμα (Elytis, *Ποίηση*, p. 543).

[152] Elytis, *Collected Poems*, p. 473.

[153] Elytis, *Collected Poems*, p. 447.

[154] Elytis, *Collected Poems*, p. 498.

[155] Elytis, *Collected Poems*, p. 480. Από μικρό παιδί μου γεμίσανε το κεφάλι με την εικόνα ενός θανάτου κουκουλωμένου στα μαύρα, που κρατά τη ζωή σαν φάκα και μας την

"Truths of the imagination," Elytis writes, "decay with much more difficulty. Rimbaud survived the Commune the way Sappho's moon will survive Armstrong's moon."[156] The structure of *The Little Seafarer* maps out the imagination in the time-less moment of poetry. Thus, the truths of the imagination are rendered in a specific shape. Depending on our position or, rather, on our distance from the historical event, we can either say that the shape of history is linear, cyclical, or simply a chaotic vortex. Modernism certainly rejected a linear reading of history and, fueled by the theories of Nietzsche and Freud, commonly reverted to a cyclical or chaotic conceptualization of it. Elytis's presentation of history in the *Little Seafarer* is characterized by repetition: names, places, and time-periods may change, but history is guided by the same motivations (power, betrayal, self-interest, etc.). At the same time, he does not propose an alternative schema for the material imagination. After all, what characterizes poetry's claim of truth, for Elytis, is this constant movement in and out of historical time and its resistance to contemporary reality. His use of poetic architecture rejects both a nostalgic return to the past and an eschatological mapping of a utopia. Its function may be more effectively approached through the genre of music, where mathematical structure leads to a certain sensation. Mozart's music, Elytis writes, "changes the dimensions of reality" and "realistically" captures, through "the methodology of externalization ... the second and more real life, purified and impervious."[157] It is precisely this "second life," which Elytis perceives as real as the first, that is schematized in the architectural poetics of *The Little Seafarer*.

On the one hand, with The *Little Seafarer*, Elytis returns to the territory he had mapped out in *The Axion Esti*. Both collections juxtapose historical truth with the truth of the imagination, and the political nation with the dream nation. On the other hand, they are immensely different: *The Little Seafarer* is much more polyphonic, is not grounded in the Byzantine tradition, and confronts a very different history. In the 25 years that had elapsed between the publication of

---

προτείνει ανοιχτή, με το δόλωμα της ηδονής στη μέση. Αφήστε με να γελάσω. Κάτι άλλο έλεγε κείνος που μασούσε τη δάφνη. Και δεν είναι τυχαίο που γυρίζουμε όλοι μας γύρω απ' τον ήλιο. / Το σώμα ξέρει (Elytis, *Ποίηση*, p. 529). How does the body know? Elytis answers the question in a small epigraph from *The Book of Signs*: because "a naked body is the only extension of the imaginary line that unites us with the mystery." As we have seen, this "mystery" is not a form of escape from the nightmare of history but a reassessment of the body's relationship with what Bachelard calls "material imagination." I have also examined the proximity between the ideas of Camus and Elytis in relation to the body's interaction with the Mediterranean world; here, too, the sun and the body are loci of that truth which unites us with a metaphysical "mystery."

[156] Elytis, *Collected Poems*, p. 554. In the posthumous collection *Εκ του Πλησίον* [From Nearby], Elytis writes: "Do not listen to Armstrong. The moon's smell must be something between a kiss and the fragrant oil of cypress trees" (Elytis, *Ποίηση*, p. 601). All excerpts from *Εκ του Πλησίον* are translated by Marinos Pourgouris.

[157] Elytis, *Εν Λευκώ*, p. 252.

The Axion Esti in 1959 and *The Little Seafarer* in 1985, democracy was restored (1974), Greece had joined the European Union (1981), and globalization was the most controversial topic in political debates.[158] Richard Clogg summarizes the divisiveness of the Greeks regarding the accession of the country to the European Union through the declarations of the two leading political figures of the time:

> Konstantinos Karamanlis (ND): "Greece belongs in the West"
> Andreas Papandreou (PASOK): "Greece belongs to the Greeks"[159]

Elytis's relationship with political practice ranged from indifference to hostility. When Karamanlis's New Democracy Party offered to make him a senator following the fall of the junta in 1974, he refused; he similarly rejected the invitation by the Academy of Athens to make him a permanent member in 1976. At the same time, he did not remain apathetic to the larger implications concerning globalization and materialism. In a speech at the University of Rome, in the early 1980s, he expressed the concern that "the practical dimensions of the [European Union] ideal ... will not be realized or endure, if they are not supported by a spiritual substratum."[160] A similar concern was expressed earlier, in his prologue to the *Open Papers*, where he saw the influence of globalization as detrimental to the cultures of small nations: "young and small nations, full of impulsive energies, are forced, in one way or another, to align with the strong and powerful, who have lost all sap and sustain themselves with pre-manufactured rules of civilization."[161]

The position of man in the modern technologically advanced and materialistic system guided by the strong and the powerful, is more aptly described in a pantomime metaphor: Elytis imagines an actor who desperately tries to position his body in a way that, fixed in single spot, he would be able "to breathe, defecate, make love, and watch television without moving."[162] In doing so, the actor is desperately trying to keep pace with a "complex machine" constructed after "many years of research." Freud would, perhaps, argue that this is in accord with the death instinct—"the instinct to return to the inanimate state."[163] Materialism is precisely this regressive force—it aims "to restore an earlier state of things" and constitutes, we may argue, a return to the womb, where its complex mechanism sustains the infant in a state characterized by the least possible movement.[164]

---

[158] Two major political parties in Greece, namely PASOK and KKE, disagreed with the accession of Greece to the Union. The New Democracy Party fervently supported it.

[159] Clogg, *Συνοπτική Ιστορία*, p. 191.

[160] Elytis, *Εν Λευκώ*, pp. 302–3.

[161] Elytis, *Ανοιχτά Χαρτιά*, p. 24. The "strong and powerful" know small nations, Elytis argues, only through the imperfect tool of translation, which leads to "squinting values."

[162] Elytis, *Ανοιχτά Χαρτιά*, p. 33.

[163] Freud, *Pleasure Principle*, p. 46.

[164] Nathaniel Hawthorne's short story "Wakefield" is an excellent example of a similar positioning of man in a fixed spot. I will summarize it here for the reader's consideration. The main character, Wakefield, decides one day to take a short journey. He bids farewell

In *The Little Seafarer*, Elytis describes both the imagined nation and its consequent effect on the poet's ethos. In other words, the ethos of frugality, or "littleness," that Greek landscape exemplifies, finds a correspondence in the life of the poet. Consider, for example, the following two prose poems:

> Well then, I went all about my country *and I found its littleness so natural*, that I thought, this can't be, it must be that this wooden table with the tomatoes and the olives by the window is on purpose. So that this feeling drawn from the plank's squareness with its few vivid reds and many blacks, may go straight out into icon-painting. And icon-painting, rendering a true image, may spread itself with a blissful light above the sea until the *real grandeur of this littleness is revealed*.[165]

> Lower the chest in which I have laid all my possessions: two pairs of trousers, four shirts, some underwear. Next to it, the chair with the huge straw hat. On the ground, on the black and white tiles, my two sandals. By my side I also have a book.

> I was born to have just so much. Extravagant speech makes no impression on me. *From the least thing you get there sooner*. Only it is harder.[166]

---

to his wife and sets off. Upon his return he becomes curious about his wife's life during his absence. Thus, he delays his return and hides near the house, observing his wife. Days go by, months, years. He sees a doctor and a priest going into the house. Wakefield finds it difficult, after the passage of some time, to return. He may have left the house but the house has left him as well (Nathaniel Hawthorne, *Tales* [New York: Norton, 1987], p. 81). Hawthorn concludes the story as follows: "Amid the seeming confusion of our mysterious world, individuals are so nicely adjusted to a system, and systems to one another, and to a whole, that, by stepping aside for a moment, a man exposes himself to a fearful risk of losing his place for ever. Like Wakefield, he may become, as it were, the Outcast of the Universe" (82–3).

[165] Elytis, *Collected Poems*, p. 425. Emphasis added. Λοιπόν τριγύριζα μέσα στη χώρα μου κι έβρισκα τόσο φυσική τη λιγοσύνη της, που 'λεγα πως, δε γίνεται, θα πρέπει να 'ναι από σκοπού το ξύλινο τούτο τραπέζι με τις ντομάτες και τις ελιές μπρος στο παράθυρο. Για να μπορεί μια τέτοια αίσθηση βγαλμένη απ' το τετράγωνο του σανιδιού με τα λίγα ζωηρά κόκκινα και τα πολλά μαύρα να βγαίνει κατευθείαν στην αγιογραφία. Και αυτή, αποδίδοντας τα ίσα, να προεκτείνεται μ' ένα μακάριο φως πάνω απ' τη θάλασσα εωσότου αποκαλυφθεί της λιγοσύνης το πραγματικό μεγαλείο (Elytis, *Ποίηση*, p. 498).

[166] Elytis, *Collected Poems*, p. 451. Πιο χαμηλά την κασέλα όπου έχω αποθέσει όλα μου τα υπάρχοντα: δυο παντελόνια, τέσσερα πουκάμισα, κάτι ασπρόρουχα. Δίπλα, η καρέκλα με την πελώρια ψάθα. Χάμου, στ' άσπρα και μαύρα πλακάκια, τα δυο μου σάνταλα. Έχω στο πλάι μου κι ένα βιβλίο. / Γεννήθηκα για να 'χω τόσα. Δε μου λέει τίποτε να παραδοξολογώ. Από το ελάχιστο φτάνεις πιο σύντομα οπουδήποτε. Μόνο που 'ναι πιο δύσκολο (Elytis, *Ποίηση*, p. 512). This exaltation of "littleness" or, "the least thing," characterizes much of Elytis's poetry. "From nothing comes Paradise" he writes in *The Light-Tree* (Elytis, *Collected Poems*, p. 212) and in the posthumous collection,

The first prose poem describes the "littleness" of the imagined nation, and the second the ethos of "littleness" as the poet applies it to his own life. One senses here Elytis's dual attitude towards *materiality*, an attitude that describes much of modernist poetry in general. On the one hand, modernist poetry claims a rebellion that dreams of becoming an action; it is thus dependent and founded upon matter. On the other hand, as Poggioli suggests, modernism is a reaction against the "reduction of nonmaterial values to the brute categories of the mechanical and the technical."[167] This duality also explains Elytis's ambivalent attitude towards the idea of a united Europe. If supported by a cultural infrastructure—one that allows the space for the expression of local cultures—it could become a positive model of multiculturalism. But it could also become an instrument of that complex mechanism that fixes man, like the pantomime actor, in a position of immobility, inaction and, eventually, extinction.

The elaborate structure of "The Passion" in *The Axion Esti* is a mapping out of history and the poet's reaction to it. Historical tensions there can lead to the heroic deed, greatness, and martyrdom. By contrast, in *The Little Seafarer*, the poet's perception of the world and his view of history are kept separate. All the historical events of the "spotlights" lead to injustice, murder, betrayal, and brutality. The structure of history here is not as elaborate: the historical events are simply presented chronologically, linearly, until, at the end, they nullify themselves in the understanding that history is a never-ending cycle of violence. Once again, the poet moves in and out of history briefly but resides, overwhelmingly, in his own world, where the body interacts with reality through its own senses. The greatest difference between the two texts is the way in which they resolve the tension between history and poetry: while *The Axion Esti* concludes with the glorification of the "other" Greece, as the poet perceives it (in "Gloria"), *The Little Seafarer* returns to an assessment of the journey he undertook. In the "Entrance," the poet explains why he sets out on this journey:

> I shall leave. Now. With whatever: travel bag on my shoulder; guidebook in my pocket; camera in my hand. Deep into the earth and deep into my body I shall go to find out who I am. What I give, what they give me and left over is injustice.[168]

Historical or social injustices are thus measured against the poet's perception of the world. Upon the conclusion of the journey the poet reassesses his experience:

Εκ του Πλησίον [From Nearby], he similarly writes, "the distance between 'nothing' and 'the least' is greater than between 'the least' and 'a lot'" (Elytis, *Ποίηση*, p. 622).

[167] Poggioli, *Avant-Garde*, p. 138.

[168] Elytis, *Collected Poems*, p. 419. Είπα θα φύγω. Τώρα. Μ' ό,τι να' ναι: το σάκο μου τον ταξιδιωτικό στον ώμο· στην τσέπη μου έναν Οδηγό· τη φωτογραφική μου μηχανή στο χέρι. Βαθιά στο χώμα και βαθιά στο σώμα μου θα πάω να βρω ποιος είμαι. Τι δίνω, τι μου δίνουν, και περισσεύει το άδικο (Elytis, *Ποίηση*, p. 495).

Far into the body and far into the earth that I tread I went to find out who I am. I stored up small happinesses and unexpected meetings, and here I am; unable to learn what I give, what they give me and left over is injustice.[169]

The poet confronts history by exploring his body and the earth but, in the end, it is historical reality, not poetic imagination, that takes precedence over human experience; thus "left over is injustice." In both the "Entrance" and the "Exit" Elytis interlaces his own narration with lines from Dionysios Solomos's *Free Besieged*,[170] and the inclusion of these lines further exemplifies the impossibility of escaping history's claws. Solomos's poem refers to the people of Messolongi who, though besieged by the Ottomans, refused to surrender, and chose to live within the confines of their city. Eventually, the siege of Messolongi, in Solomos's poem, ends with the death of its inhabitants, while, ironically, nature is still in bloom. The "Golden wind of life" is unable to intervene in history's brutality. In *The Little Seafarer* it is not simply history that intervenes: the "Golden wind of life" beckons the eyes but they remain helpless: "… Incomprehensibility / no one hears…. The voice was turned elsewhere and the eyes remained unmiracled."[171] The poet's perception remains a personal creation, caught between the realms of the private and the public. "I remain an inconsolable private citizen that has not managed to belong anywhere, to any community, not even that of the Poets," Elytis wrote in his 1990 collection of essays *The Public and the Private*.[172] If the poet comes to an understanding at the conclusion of *The Little Seafarer*, it is that of Poetry's inability to direct the world towards collective change. Like Freud, whose theory did not conceive the world as striding towards a progressive elimination of the unconscious—such suggestion would have been absurd—Elytis perceives poetry as "full of revolutionary forces" directed against a world unacceptable to the poet's conscience.[173] As the structure of *The Little Seafarer* suggests, this tension between history and poetry, the external and the internal, the public and the private is ongoing and irreconcilable.

---

[169] Elytis, *Collected Poems*, p. 508. Μακριά στο σώμα και μακριά στο χώμα που πατώ πήγα να βρω ποιος είμαι. Τις μικρές ευτυχίες και τ' αδόκητα συναπαντήματα θησαύρισα, και να με: ανήμπορος να μάθω τι δίνω, τι μου δίνουν και περισσεύει το άδικο (Elytis, *Ποίηση*, p. 545).

[170] In the "Entrance": "Golden Wind of Life"; in the "Exit" "Helpless are the eyes."

[171] Elytis, *Collected Poems*, p. 508.

[172] Elytis, *Εν Λευκώ*, p. 379.

[173] Elytis, *Εν Λευκώ*, p. 207.

Maria Nephele: On the Other Side I Am the Same[174]

> Car *Je* est un autre[175]
> A. Rimbaud

In a 1972 interview, Elytis told Ivar Ivask that the first draft of his new collection *Maria Nephele* was finished but he was not satisfied with it yet.[176] It would take him approximately six more years to complete the work, which was eventually published in 1978. In the same interview, excited as he was with his new poetic project, he revealed to Ivask the general structural and conceptual framework of the collection:

> It is a strange kind of poem. In it a girl speaks. Her words are on the left side of the page and the poet's recreation is on the right. Yet it is not a dialogue, but two monologues side by side. *It will be my first poem which takes place in an urban environment.*[177]

> It is approximately the same length as *The Axion Esti*, but its structure is even more complex than that of the latter. I am aware that the average reader is not interested in the design underlining the poem. I, however, set up difficulties expressly in order to be able to overcome them, in order to restrain myself, to make myself operate within set limits. It is for this reason I speak of "architectural invention."[178]

Maria Nephele is indeed a "strange kind of poem." Elytis's language here is more colloquial than in his other collections and the parallel monologues do not unfold in the foreground of the Greek islands, but rather, in a city setting with museums, bars, high buildings, electronic music, etc. The main body of the text is divided into three sections, each encompassing 14 poems; in each section, seven of the poems are spoken by Maria Nephele and seven by the poet, or the "Antiphonist." The collection is introduced with "The Presence" where the two characters engage in a dialogue over the course of which, however, they rarely address each other directly; rather, they talk about each other except for a brief moment when the conversation becomes more intense.[179] Section A is followed by "The Song of Maria Nephele," which is a rhyming poem of five quatrains. Section B is followed by "The Song of the Poet,"

---

[174] This is the epigraph at the beginning of *Maria Nephele* (Elytis, *Collected Poems*, p. 289). It also appears in "The Concert of the Hyacinths" (Elytis, *Collected Poems*, p. 49).

[175] "For *I* is another." Rimbaud's now famous exclamation in a letter to Paul Demeny. (Rimbaud, *Complete Works*, p. 304).

[176] Elytis, "On his Poetry," p. 640.

[177] Elytis, "On his Poetry," p. 638.

[178] Elytis, "On his Poetry," p. 640. Emphasis added.

[179] There, frustrated with Maria Nephele's misperceptions, the Antiphonist tells her: "As for you, you'll never hold a bird—you are not worthy." The "bird" he is referring to is from an ancient Greek grave stele. This is in fact a recurring image in grave steles: mourning is expressed in the image of a seated kore who holds a bird in her palm.

which is also a rhyming poem of ten couplets; both poems, then, have an equal number of lines (i.e., 20). The collection concludes with "The Eternal Wager," which consists of seven numbered triplets. We can already see, in these interceding sections, Elytis's attempt to synthesize the two voices into a dyad: Maria Nephele expresses herself in quatrains, the Antiphonist in couplets, and the "uniting" poem—"The Eternal Wager"—in which the poet addresses a feminine "you," is in seven triplets, where the number seven reflects once more a "structuring" instrument in Elytis's poetry.

But what exactly makes this collection more complex, as Elytis says, than the already structurally dense *The Axion Esti*? A simple outline of the titles and the overall structural division will illustrate the complexity of the poem:

The Presence
Section A

Maria Nephele says:	*And the Antiphonist*:
1. The Forest of Men	1. The Map-Fix
2. Nephele	2. Nephelegeretes
3. Patmos	3. The Revelation
4. Disquisition on Beauty	4. The Waterdrop
5. Through the Mirror	5. Aegeis
6. Thunderbolt Steers	6. Hymn to Maria Nephele
7. The Trojan War	7. Helen

The Song of Maria Nephele
Section B

The Antiphonist says:	*And Maria Nephele*:
1. Pax San Tropezana	1. The Planet Earth
2. The Dagger	2. Each Moon Confesses
3. Ancestral Paradise	3. Paper Kite
4. Eau de Verveine	4. Disquisition on Purity
5. Upper Tarquinia	5. Eye of the Locust
6. Hymn in Two Dimensions	6. Declaration of Responsibility
7. The Holy Inquisition	7. St. Francis of Assisi

The Song of the Poet
Section C

Maria Nephele says:	*And the Antiphonist*:
1. Bonjour Tristesse	1. Morning Exercises
2. The Poets	2. That Which Persuades
3. The Twenty-Four-Hour Life	3. The Lifelong Moment
4. Disquisition on Justice	4. Nude Study
5. Electra Bar	5. Parthenogenesis
6. Djenda	6. Ich Sehe Dich
7. Stalin	7. The Hungarian Uprising

The Eternal Wager

What becomes immediately apparent in this outline is the alternating pattern in which the monologues are presented. In the first section, Maria Nephele speaks and the Antiphonist "responds," in the second the order is switched, and in the third we return to the first arrangement. The poet is not simply responding to Maria Nephele, but rather the two are trying to reach a mutual understanding in expressing their world-view.

The most important structural device is the correspondence between the poems of the three sections. Let us take, for example, the fourth poem of each section. In each of these, Maria Nephele is presenting a "Disquisition" (on Beauty, Purity, and Justice). The corresponding poems of the Antiphonist are: "The Waterdrop," "Eau de Verveine," and "Nude Study." All three are built around the theme of water.[180] The corresponding monologues of Maria Nephele and the Antiphonist approach similar themes but along different routes: when she speaks of "Beauty" in relation to fear, he speaks of the poetic world as "a water-drop above the chasms"; when he speaks of his poetic purity, she describes purity as "what the swallows impute to us";[181] and when she speaks of the deceptive nature of human justice ("even when a snake is blameless– you'd wipe it out")[182] he poetically describes justice as "a smooth young naked body."[183] The conceptual structure becomes even more complex if we compare all six poems with one another. If we were to connect the central themes in each poem as they are narrated by the two characters separately we would arrive at the following sequences: Maria Nephele: beauty—purity—justice; and the Antiphonist: poetic life (waterdrop)—life of purity (eau de verveine)—justice (naked body).[184]

---

[180] The water theme is more apparent in the first poem but is more implicit in the other two. In French, "Eau," of course, means "water." At the same time, Elytis may be thinking of a popular French perfume of the 1970s by Guerlain: *Eau de Verveine*. The word "Verveine" has many connotations: it is a plant of the *verbena* species. The OED also gives us the following entry under the word: "A perfume obtained from the leaves of vervain." The assumption that Elytis is playing with a perfume brand here is supported by the poem's opening lines: "I said: I am clean / washed with essence of verveine" [Είπα καθαρός είμαι / πλυμένος με το απόσταγμα βερβένας] (Elytis, *Collected Poems*, p. 334). Etymologically, "verveine" comes from "verve" which, apart from carrying the meaning of "zest" or "vigor," may also refer to the periodical *Verve*, with which Elytis was very familiar, since it was edited by Teriade, and his essay on Picasso was also published there. Finally, "Nude Study" is the only one of the three poems that does not refer to the concept of "water" in its title. It is built, however, on this very theme: nudity is explored, or studied, by "sailing around / a smooth young naked body" (Elytis, *Collected Poems*, p. 355).

[181] Elytis, *Collected Poems*, p. 335.
[182] Elytis, *Collected Poems*, p. 354.
[183] Elytis, *Collected Poems*, p. 355.
[184] As it becomes clear here, the Antiphonist's language is more evasive—he uses symbolic correspondences (for example, a naked body = justice) more openly than Maria Nephele, who is more direct in her monologues. In fact, the entire poem is built on such word-associations. As Elytis told Ivask in discussing *Maria Nephele*: "the success of a poem's language depends on the way in which it combines certain words" (Elytis, "On his Poetry," p. 638).

Finally, the two characters use a *consistent language*. In section A ("The Waterdrop"), the Antiphonist says: "… everything a drop of beauty trembling on the eyelashes";[185] the "eyelash" as a symbol is used again in section C ("Nude Study") where he says: "… the eyelashes lower / quivering with so much truth."[186] Thus, the symbolism created in the first poem is extended through the third, creating a complex symbolic network where "beauty" is connected to "truth." Similarly, Maria Nephele uses the invocation "Ladies and Gentlemen" in her fourth poem in all three sections:

> Das Reine Ladies and Gentlemen
> kann sich nur darstellen im Unreinen
> (Disquisition on Beauty, Section A)[187]

> Because Ladies and Gentlemen
> what the swallows impute to us
> —the spring we did not bring—
> is exactly our purity
> (Disquisition on Purity, Section B)[188]

> I am sorry my disquisition's manner
> Is not what suits our day
>   Ladies and Gentlemen
> (Disquisition on Justice, Section C)[189]

The use of a consistent language gives the two characters the attributes of actors with distinct personalities. After all, "characters" are formed by repetition or, better yet, one reaches an understanding of oneself, or one's character, through recurring psychic patterns, as they are expressed in dreams, linguistic patterns, or forms of interpersonal exchange.[190] Furthermore, such an arrangement creates what we can call a complex network of structured signifiers. The signifier "Purity," for instance,

---

[185] Elytis, *Collected Poems*, p. 309.

[186] Elytis, *Collected Poems*, p. 355.

[187] Elytis, *Collected Poems*, p. 308. Das Reine Κυρίες και Κύριοι / kann sich nur darstellen im Unreinen (Λόγος περί Κάλλους, Μέρος Α). Elytis, *Ποίηση*, p. 376. As Geoffrey Carson and Nikos Sarris note, this line comes from a 1798 letter from Hölderlin to Christian Ludwig Neuffer. They translate the line as follows: "The pure / can reveal itself only in the impure."

[188] Elytis, *Collected Poems*, p. 335. Επειδή Κυρίες και Κύριοι / κείνο που μας προσάπτουνε τα χελιδόνια /—η άνοιξη που δεν φέραμε – / είναι ακριβώς η αγνότητά μας. (Λόγος περί Αγνότητος, Μέρος Β). Elytis, *Ποίηση*, p. 400.

[189] Elytis, *Collected Poems*, p. 354. Λυπούμαι αν η τροπή του λόγου μου δεν είναι αυτή / που αρμόζει στις ημέρες μας / Κυρίες και Κύριοι (Λόγος περί Δικαιοσύνης, Μέρος Γ). Elytis, *Ποίηση*, p. 422.

[190] It is not coincidental, of course, that when Elytis first published *Maria Nephele* he gave it the subtitle "A Stage Poem" [Ένα Σκηνικό Ποίημα].

appears in Maria Nephele's "Disquisition on Purity" but it is also central in her recitation of Hölderlin's lines in the "Disquisition on Beauty" (i.e., "das Reine"); in both poems, purity appears in a specific instance, namely with the invocation "Ladies and Gentlemen" in the fourth poem of each of the three sections.

These structural correspondences are constant throughout the entire collection. Apart from establishing the two characters' personas and forming parallel conceptual associations, they also exemplify Elytis's claim that the two "search basically for the same things but along different routes."[191] To further stress this point, I will briefly consider the sixth poem of both characters in all sections. The linguistic, conceptual, and structural correspondences in these poems are most prominent in their concluding lines:

	Maria Nephele says:[192]	*And the Antiphonist:*[193]
Section A	Κάθε καιρός κι ο Τρωικός του πόλεμος. [Each time with its Trojan War.]	Κάθε καιρός κι η Ελένη του. [Each time with its Helen.]
Section B	*The Antiphonist says*: Κάθε καιρός κι η Ιερή του Εξέταση. [Each time with its Holy Inquisition.]	*And Maria Nephele*: Κάθε καιρός κι ο άγιος Φραγκίσκος της Ασσίζης του. [Each time with its St. Francis of Assisi.]
Section C	*Maria Nephele says*: Κάθε καιρός κι ο Στάλιν του. [Each time with its Stalin too.]	*And the Antiphonist*: Κάθε καιρός κι η Ουγγρική του Εξέγερση. [Each time with its Hungarian Uprising too.]

Once more, the linguistic correspondence is clear; all six poems conclude with variations on the same sentence. The progression from section to section is significant: we proceed from the realm of myth to religion and, eventually, to history. At the same time, the suggestion of a chronological progression (from antiquity to the medieval times to the twentieth century) is undermined by the very

---

[191] Elytis, "On his Poetry," p. 640.

[192] The three excerpts by Maria Nephele are quoted from Elytis, *Collected Poems*, pp. 318, 342, 364, respectively (in English) and from Elytis, *Ποίηση*, pp. 386, 411, 432, respectively (in Greek).

[193] The three excerpts by the Antiphonist are quoted from Elytis, *Collected Poems*, pp. 319, 343, 365, respectively (in English) and from Elytis, *Ποίηση*, pp. 387, 410, 433, respectively (in Greek).

claim of these sentences: i.e., these events recur in every time period.[194] It is also apparent that the corresponding events/individuals are linked thematically and chronologically.[195] Finally, every historical/mythological (i.e., collective) event is juxtaposed with a reference to an individual: the Trojan War vs. Helen, the Holy Inquisition vs. St. Francis, and the Hungarian Uprising vs. Stalin.[196]

What remains to be addressed is how these pairings simultaneously constitute "difference" and "sameness." For Maria Nephele, Stalin is not historically unique; on the contrary, he is a condensed model of "the many" Stalins of history—in fact, he is merely an expression of the One: "Before the One can up and make me alter / before He's able to impose a "new order" / I say it again and so long— I am off to jail: / a moon belongs to America—but a soul / that's not for sale—to Matala[197] or Katmandu."[198] Apparently, Maria Nephele includes America, along with Stalin, in that historical pattern—of the oppressive One—recurring in "each time." Her reaction is understandable: Armstrong's landing on the moon and the famous planting of the American flag came to symbolize, for Elytis, the rise of a materialistic society where objects exist only when they are conquered.[199] Furthermore, Elytis was writing *Maria Nephele* during and immediately after the Junta rule (1967–1974), which the American government had explicitly aided.[200]

---

[194] These poems stress the circular nature of history: e.g., "Maria Nephele / goes forward redeemed from the revolting meaning of history" (Elytis, *Collected Poems*, p. 319), "The brand new world is also the oldest / world in reverse" (Elytis, *Collected Poems*, p. 343).

[195] The correspondence between Helen and the Trojan War needs no further explanation. The second pair, St. Francis-Holy Inquisition is more implicit. St. Francis died in 1226 around the time when the Inquisitions were established. Finally, Stalin died in 1953, three years before the Hungarian revolution was crushed by Russian troops.

[196] The parallelism between the individual and the collective is central in the last set of poems. In "Stalin," Maria Nephele argues that "the many counterfeit the One" (Elytis, *Collected Poems*, p. 364), while in "The Hungarian Uprising," the Antiphonist reverses the order: "You heard the virgin's words: *the One counterfeits the many*" (Elytis, *Collected Poems*, p. 365).

[197] "Matala" (Μάταλα): "village on Crete's southern coast, whose caves in the 1970s were as popular with hippies as was Katmandu" (Jeffrey Carson and Nikos Sarris's note, Elytis, *Collected Poems*, p. 364).

[198] Elytis, *Collected Poems*, p. 364.

[199] We have already seen two examples of Elytis's view regarding Armstrong and the moon in our discussion of *The Little Seafarer*: 1) "Truths of the Imagination decay with much more difficulty…. Sappho's moon will survive Armstrong's moon" (Elytis, *Collected Poems*, p. 454), and 2) "Do not listen to Armstrong. The moon's smell must be something between a kiss and the fragrant oil of cypress trees" (from the collection *Εκ του Πλησίον*, Elytis, *Ποίηση*, p. 601).

[200] When the American president Bill Clinton visited Greece in 1999 he was greeted with massive demonstrations due to America's involvement in the bombardment of Yugoslavia. During his short stay, he gave the first official apology for the US collaboration with the dictatorial regime of 1967–1974. The following is a short excerpt from the British Broadcasting Corporation's coverage of Clinton's statement: "When the junta took over in

The Antiphonist, on the other hand, offers an example of the unique "many" that defy the One. The Hungarian uprising is an instance of youth resisting the theories that force the unity of "the Army's body and Man's body" into One; the One that is "the Supreme Archon / ... / advancing with gunbarrels / and caissons in the name of the Party and the People."[201]

Maria Nephele begins with the epigraph, "On the other side I am the same." The poet's "other" is a young girl who drinks, smokes, listens to records, wears "wide pants and an old trenchcoat," and is possessed by melancholy.[202] Elytis aligns his world-view with those of a rebellious young girl in the 1970s. Around the time he was writing *Maria Nephele*, he wrote the essay "First things First— Poetry," as an introduction to the volume *Open Papers*. In the same way he had once seen the fate of the poet as analogous to the fate of a peripheral Greece (as in *The Axion Esti*), here he views the poet's world-view as comparable to that of a disenchanted and defiant youth:

> I feel obliged to take into serious consideration some typical symptoms of "rage," "revolt" and "anarchy" which characterize today's youth—especially now that they are in their disinterested phase, that is they haven't managed to be channeled in camps that seek other kinds of profit—to understand and applaud them, as they truly deserve.[203]

In fact, this attempt is what makes *Maria Nephele* completely different from anything else Elytis had published until then. In the first pair of poems, Maria Nephele challenges the Antiphonist to abandon the safety of the world he had constructed through his poetry and follow her: "Poet my abandoned cicada / no one has noon anymore; / extinguish Attica and come near me / I'll take you to the forest of men...."[204] The poet hears her call but in order to descend to the "forest of men" he has to abandon the elevated language that describes his world: "Poetry O my holy Lady—forgive me / but I must stay alive to cross the other bank."[205] When the collection was published, many critics received it with

---

1967, the United States allowed its interests in prosecuting the Cold War to prevail over its interest, I should say its obligation, to support democracy, which was, after all, the cause for which we fought the Cold War," he added. "It is important that we acknowledge that," he told a gathering of business leaders in Athens, who responded with applause. The president's remarks were aimed at defusing anti-American sentiments that spilled into the streets of the Greek capital on Friday, when demonstrators set businesses ablaze to express their contempt for Mr. Clinton's visit." British Broadcasting Corporation, *Clinton: US failed Greek Democracy*, November 20, 1999, http://news.bbc.co.uk/2/hi/world/europe/ 529932.stm (accessed December 8, 2007).

[201] Elytis, *Collected Poems*, p. 365.
[202] Elytis, *Collected Poems*, p. 291.
[203] Elytis, *Ανοιχτά Χαρτιά*, pp. 32–3.
[204] Elytis, *Collected Poems*, p. 296.
[205] Elytis, *Collected Poems*, p. 297.

skepticism, reservation and doubt.[206] Elytis's language is indeed uncharacteristic of his previous collections, not only when Maria Nephele speaks, something that could be "excused" in his use of a persona, but also when the Antiphonist/Poet speaks. Instead of high language and sonorant word-combinations, critics were faced with a youthful vernacular and slang:

> Head left keep turning it:
> all is shit.
> Head right keep turning it:
> all is shit.
> Position one. Conclusion none.
> Break off, dismissed, no more cuts or curls.
> Kiss the girls.[207]

To "cross the other bank" the poet challenges himself as he has never done before; he challenges his language and style, his appropriation as an official literary figure, his belonging to a "different generation," and all the etiquettes that assigned a particular role to him (i.e., the national poet, the poet of Eros, of the Aegean, of Greece, etc.).

The greatest challenge in this "crossing" is a more personal one. Elytis's "other" is not merely an alter ego—she is of a different age, sex, and character, and her relationship with the poet is a complex one: it wavers between Eros and admiration, she guides him and influences him, she mocks him and agrees with him. She is what C.G. Jung would call his *anima*.

ARIMNA EPHE EL: The Poet and his Anima[208]

In Jungian psychoanalysis, the anima is an archetype of the collective unconscious. Steven Walker describes it as "the unconscious female element in a man" whose role is to "compensate for his conscious masculinity."[209] In discussing the archetype in relation to Maria Nephele, we should keep in mind that the anima, as all archetypes for that matter, has, for Jung, a complex psychic function whose relationship with consciousness is simultaneously defined by individual experience and preexisting constitutional factors. The following typical characteristics are what make the anima *collective*, but at the same time each man's relationship to it is defined according to his own personal experience with the feminine. As Walker writes, the anima can express itself in the form of a *femme fatale* ("an archetypal temptress

---

[206] Vitti, "Εισαγωγή," p. 25.

[207] Elytis, *Collected Poems*, p. 349. Στροφή της κεφαλής αριστερά: / όλα είναι σκατά. / Στροφή της κεφαλής δεξιά: / όλα είναι σκατά. / Εις θέσιν – εν! Συμπέρασμα κανέν- /α. Τους ζυγούς λύσατε. / Τα κορίτσια φιλήσατε (Elytis, *Ποίηση*, pp. 415–16).

[208] Ioulita Iliopoulou confirms Elytis's knowledge of C.G Jung's theories adding that the poet had many of Jung's books in his personal library (personal communication).

[209] Steven F. Walker, *Jung and the Jungians on Myth* (New York: Routledge, 2002), p. 45.

or deceiver") and it can also be represented, in mythology, "as a group: sirens, Rhinemaidens, dancing fairies, swan maidens, or water nymphs…."[210] A singular representation of an anima, as opposed to a group representation, is contingent on psychological maturity.[211] The anima can have "both negative and positive" qualities: "she can be the delusion-making and fatal factor in a man's life, but she can also be a helpful figure, his companion in his exploration of the psyche."[212]

Walker cites Flaubert's alleged statement "Madame Bovary, c'est moi," as an example of the author's fascination and identification with the anima archetype.[213] Clearly, a similar identification can be seen in Elytis's epigraph "on the other side I am the same." These statements perceive the self as a male-female syzygy.[214] In other words, the masculine "I" (i.e., moi, είμαι) is not separate from its female projection (i.e., Madame Bovary, άλλη όψη). On the one hand, Maria Nephele may be rebellious and moody (she has a "cloudy" temperament), but on the other, there is no doubt that her role is to guide the poet—the mature poet—in the exploration of his psyche. However, as she warns him in her first poem, this journey he is about to undertake is not going to be an easy one: "I shall guide you / and rush upon you; my fingernails will enter your flesh / the truth—don't they say?— is painful."[215] Like Circe, who tells Odysseus, "you must travel down to the House of Death"[216]—a piece of advice that "crushes" his heart—the Antiphonist is similarly "crushed," but he accepts the challenge because, as he says, he "must stay alive": "Farewell O Paradises and unclaimed gifts / I live I go straight to me / far away where I am. / The moment came. Maria Nephele / take my hand—I shall follow you."[217]

Apart from the epigraph that adorns *Maria Nephele*, there are other references in the collection that may indicate Elytis's conscious use of the anima archetype. It is well-known that the Italian director Federico Fellini, also an admirer of Jung's theories, makes a subtextual reference to the anima archetype in what is, perhaps, his most profound film, *8½*. In the film, a female cousin reminds the main character, Guido, of a magic spell, a word game, they used in their childhood; the cryptic phrase is none other than "asa nisi masa," which, when decoded, by removing the second syllable from each word, gives us the word "anima." Similarly, in the "Presence," Maria Nephele and the Antiphonist are arguing about an inscription on a grave stele. Whereas he doesn't recall that there was anything written on the stele, she clearly recalls a vague sentence:

---

[210] Walker, *Jung*, p. 48.

[211] Walker, *Jung*, p. 48.

[212] Walker, *Jung*, p. 49.

[213] Walker, *Jung*, p. 49.

[214] Jung connects the male-female syzygy with the anima representation. Carl Gustav Jung, *The Archetypes of the Collective Unconscious*, 2nd ed. Bollingen Series XX, trans. R.F.C. Hull (Princeton: Princeton University Press, 1990), p. 70.

[215] Elytis, *Collected Poems*, p. 296.

[216] Homer, *The Odyssey*, trans. Robert Fagles (New York: Penguin, 1996), 10: 539–46.

[217] Elytis, *Collected Poems*, pp. 297, 299.

M.N.	*ARIMNA ... as if I could still see the carved letters in the light ... ARIMNA EPHE EL ...*
A.	She was missing. The whole upper part was missing. There were no letters at all.
M.N.	*ARIMNA EPHE EL ... just on the EL the stone had been cut and broken. I remember it well.*[218]

The anagram "ARIMNA EPHE EL" can be read in a number of ways. First and foremost, it is an anagram of her name (something, we may add, that the Antiphonist fails to see). ARIMNA can be further decoded into a female name, "Marina," "Ephe" is the name of a girl, and "El" may refer to two more female names: "Eleni" (Helen) or "Eleftheria" (Freedom). The fact that the Antiphonist and Maria Nephele are disagreeing about a phrase written on a grave stele that depicts a "kore" further emphasizes the suggestion that the poet is exploring a feminine force: Maria Nephele clearly perceives the female name written on the grave stele—after all, the anima can be a deadly force—but the Antiphonist, at least at this early point, cannot see anything. As Elytis's translators suggest, the word "Ephe" (Εφη) is also the verb "to say" in Ancient Greek, and the broken "El" may be referring to "Elytis," thus constructing the phrase: "Marina says Elytis."[219]

Furthermore, an alternative anagrammatism gives us the French verb "Ranima" (the past tense of "ranimer"), which bears the meaning of "to resurrect" or "to revive." From a Jungian viewpoint this re-animation would be equivalent to a "bringing to consciousness." The grave stele is thus a condensation of multiple feminine forces: the seated maiden, Ephe, Marina, El(eutheria), El(eni), and, most importantly, Maria Nephele, who reads this ambiguous phrase to the Antiphonist. The challenge he is asked to confront is an encounter with his anima (the locus of multiple feminine forces). Initially, he "resists" (in a psychological sense) an understanding of the mysterious phrase, insisting that "the whole upper part [of the stele] was missing," that "there were no letters at all," and that Maria Nephele "saw it in her dreams."[220] Eventually, overcoming his resistances, he asks Maria Nephele to take his hand and pronounces that he will follow her. First, however, he asks Poetry—the "Holy Lady," as he calls her—for forgiveness ("forgive me but I must stay alive / to cross the other bank"). If Elytis's works are characterized by an elevated and elegant poetic language, in *Maria Nephele* his anima exposes him to the raw and sharp vernacular of youth. Inevitably, the poet's encounter with his anima has to be an encounter with a language different than his own.

---

[218] Elytis, *Collected Poems*, p. 292. M.N.: ΑΡΙΜΝΑ ... σαν να τα βλέπω ακόμη χαραγμένα τα γράμματα μέσα στο φως ... ΑΡΙΜΝΑ ΕΦΗ ΕΛ ... / Α.: Έλειπε. Όλο το πάνω μέρος έλειπε. Γράμματα δεν υπήρχανε καθόλου. M.N.: ΑΡΙΜΝΑ ΕΦΗ ΕΛ ... εκεί, πάνω σ' αυτό το ΕΛ, η πέτρα είχε κοπεί και σπάσει. Το θυμάμαι καλά (Elytis, *Ποίηση*, pp. 361–2).

[219] Elytis, *Collected Poems*, p. 292. ARIMNA approximates the word "Anima"; as the grave stele is broken and difficult to read, the additional "R" assists the poet in turning the anagram into a multireferential riddle (i.e., the word can be decoded as either Marina or anima).

[220] Elytis, *Collected Poems*, p. 292.

It is important to remember that the sentence appears on the grave stele of a "Kore." The Greek word *κόρη* means both "young maiden" and "daughter" (hence the myth of "Demeter and the Kore"). In "The Psychological Aspects of the Kore," Jung describes the figure of the Kore as a common mythological projection of the anima archetype. In connection with Persephone, the anima is presented here as "bipolar"; it can "appear positive one moment and negative the next":

> now young, now old; now a saint, now a whore. Besides this ambivalence, the anima also has "occult" connections with "mysteries," with the world of darkness in general, and for that reason she often has a religious tinge. Whenever she emerges with some degree of clarity, she always has a peculiar relationship to *time*: as a rule she is more or less immortal, because outside time.[221]

It is remarkable to what extent this brief description of the kore as an anima projection applies to the character of Maria Nephele. To begin with, Elytis refers to Maria Nephele as "Kore" a total of three times in the collection (in addition to the "The Presence").[222] In perhaps one of the most astonishing references to the anima archetype, Maria Nephele places herself "always between Lady and Kore," a clear allusion to Demeter and Persephone.[223] Her ambivalent relationship with the poet is also clear: although she is a young girl, in "The Twenty-four-hour Life" she tells us that she "got old about eighteen / you could say in just twenty-four hours."[224] While the Antiphonist constantly describes her as a "Virgin," she tells us that "she has filled love with crosses" and that she tumbles "on the lawn / of anyone when it is night";[225] she further finds solace in the "Electra Bar,"[226] where "Two or three steps below earth's / surface—... all problems [are] solved" (356). Like Persephone, the Kore, Maria Nephele is able to descend to the modern intoxicating underworld—"the Electra Bar"—and ascend to the clouds; her very name, "Maria

---

[221] Jung, *Archetypes*, p. 199.
[222] Elytis, *Collected Poems*, pp. 296, 339, 349.
[223] Elytis, *Collected Poems*, p. 339.
[224] Elytis, *Collected Poems*, p. 352.
[225] Elytis, *Collected Poems*, pp. 314, 326.
[226] Like the mythological character of Electra, Maria Nephele is consumed by her thoughts, and is upset at the world. Consequently, she frequents the "Electra Bar." Unlike Euripides' Electra, however, Maria Nephele is "without more help or some unknown brother" (Elytis, *Collected Poems*, p. 356). She thus "escapes" at the bar: "two or three steps below earth's / surface—and all problems are solved at once!" (The only help she finds is drinking gin fizz until "the mind muddies.") Elytis is, perhaps, making another linguistic association here by associating the name "Ηλέκτρα" (Electra) with "Ηλεκτρονική μουσική" (Electronic Music). In the 1970s, the use of electronic media to produce music (especially the use of the synthesizer) was widespread. In this sense, the "Electra Bar" becomes a symbol of youth's escape from an incomprehensible world by means of drinking and listening to ecstatic—Dionysian—music.

Nephele," exemplifies this duality: Maria is the name of the Virgin, and Nephele literally means "cloud" (and should thus be understood as *ascensional*).[227]

Maria Nephele is undoubtedly one of Elytis's most personal collections. In his interview with Ivask, he explains:

> Maria Nephele means "Maria Cloud." Both names have a mythological connotation. But in my poem Maria is a young woman, a modern radical of our age. My poems are usually rooted in my own experience, yet they do not directly transcribe actual events. *Maria Nephele* constitutes an exception. Having finished *The Axion Esti* (this was sixteen years ago), I met this young woman in real life, and I suddenly wanted to write something very different from *The Axion Esti*. Therefore I made this young woman speak in my poem and express her world view, which is that of the young generation of today. I am not against her, for I try to understand her view point and that of her generation. I attempt to understand her by having us speak in parallel monologues. My conclusion in this poem is that we search basically for the same things but along different routes.[228]

He further concludes: "Maria Nephele is the other half of me; it is as if you would see the reverse of me. Already in my early poem "The Concert of Hyacinths" I wrote, "On the other side I am the same." So here I am showing the other side of myself."[229]

As Jung writes, "archetypes are complexes of experiences that come upon us like fate, and their effects are felt in our more personal life."[230] Thus, the anima is not only projected in mythological motifs, but in a man's "personal misadventure" or his "best venture."[231] Maria Nephele is a "young woman" and a "modern radical of our age." Her radical character fascinates the Antiphonist/Poet, and the creative process—these "conversations with the anima"[232]—leads him to the realization that she is his "other side," that she is, in fact, his anima. "[B]ringing the anima to some degree of consciousness," Walker writes, "is not a task for everyone, especially in the first half of life."[233] "Only as a man grows more mature psychologically does

---

[227] In ancient Greek mythology, Nephele was made by Zeus, from a cloud, in the image of Hera to trap Ixion in his sexual advances. She later married Athamus, who abandoned her for Ino. After being raped by Ixion, Nephele gave birth to the Centaurs. She also had two children with Athamus, Phrixos and Elli, who are central to the myth of the "Golden Fleece."

[228] Elytis, "On his Poetry," p. 640.

[229] Elytis, "On his Poetry," p. 640.

[230] Jung, *Archetypes*, p. 30.

[231] Jung, *Archetypes*, p. 30. Jung further provides the reader with a typical (and quite amusing) anima example in modernity: "when, for instance, a highly esteemed professor in his seventies abandons his family and runs off with a young red-haired headed actress, we know that the gods have claimed another victim" (Jung, *Archetypes*, p. 30).

[232] Walker, *Jung*, p. 50.

[233] Walker, *Jung*, p. 50.

his image of the anima become represented by a single figure."²³⁴ For Elytis, this personal quest came at the age of 67, and was crystallized in the distinct character of Maria Nephele. A descent to the "collective unconscious"—to the world of Maria Nephele—required a break with "all props and crutches,"²³⁵ an abandonment of the poet's elevated language and his Aegean themes. Only through this structured and methodical process could the anima become "the archetype of life itself."²³⁶ Elytis's conclusion in "The Eternal Wager" verifies the existence of the anima as an eternal psychic force, and as a life-affirming experience for the poet. Maria Nephele was right ("so you told me true,"²³⁷ the Antiphonist tells her)—the grave stele of the Kore was representative of that feminine force that the Antiphonist eventually "brings to consciousness." Along with Marina, Ephe, and Eleni, she now becomes part of that stele with a bird in her palm:

> That all the world's unsympathy will turn to stone
> On which you can sit munificently
> With a docile bird in your palm.²³⁸

Modernist Structures: Joyce and Elytis

The study of structure, particularly in the case of modern poetry, is usually approached somewhat skeptically, to say the least, by scholars of modernism. At best, what we see in poetic structure is a kind of radical experimentation exemplified in the visual poems of Apollinaire, Pound's theories on Chinese ideograms or, more recently, the experiments of the Brazilian Concrete Poets of the 1950s. This skepticism around structure is perhaps best expressed by the American poet John Hollander who wrote, in reference to concrete poetry, that "since a true concrete poem cannot be read aloud, it has no full linguistic dimension, no existence in the ear's kingdom. A concrete poem ... remains 'mute poetry' and therefore picture."²³⁹ What Elytis offers in his theory of architectural poetics is a way of overcoming

---

[234] Walker, *Jung*, p. 48.
[235] Jung, *Archetypes*, p. 32.
[236] Jung, *Archetypes*, p. 32.
[237] Elytis, *Collected Poems*, p. 365.
[238] Elytis, *Collected Poems*, p. 365. Ότι όλη του κόσμου η απονιά θα γίνει πέτρα / ηγεμονικά να καθίσεις / μ' ένα πουλί πειθήνιο στην παλάμη σου (Elytis, *Ποίηση*, p. 435). In translating the second line, I use the adverb "munificently" here instead of Carson and Sarris's "as a prince." The word "prince," indicative of a masculine gender in the English translation, does not have a similar connotation in the original Greek, in which the word is a nongendered adverb ("ηγεμονικά"). In fact, it is clear in the original that the "Eternal Wager" is directed to a nameless feminine "you," something that the English translation fails to convey. This nameless feminine "other" might be seen, from a Jungian perspective, as the condensation of the many feminine figures into a single archetypal force.
[239] John Hollander, *Vision and Resonance: Two Senses of Poetic Form* (New Haven: Yale University Press, 1975), p. 266.

the tension between structure and content, as well as between visuality and sound. Structure here remains in the background but it is not at all negligible. It only becomes visible in the process of discovery—a discovery which, for Elytis, must always return to the poem's subject matter.

As I have argued in this chapter, poetic architecture functions as a way of giving shape and significance to poetic content. In the case of *The Axion Esti* and *The Little Seafarer*, such mapping attempts to schematize the imaginary homeland—to render it visible through a concrete architectural schema. In the case of *The Monogram* and *Maria Nephele*, what is structured is more abstract: in the former, loss is given a presence through a reflective structure and in the latter, the poet attempts to give shape to a hidden, or unexpressed, side of himself. The mapping of the homeland as I examined it here, may be compared to Joyce's mapping of Dublin in *Ulysses*. For both Elytis and Joyce, structure works in the background of content and it becomes visible only through a process of uncovering, of solving the riddles that render architecture visible. It is not coincidental, perhaps, that in both cases such structure is linked to an attempt to give a shape to cultural identities that are haunted by the developed West—in the case of Joyce, England (as well as the Catholic church) and in the case of Elytis, Western Europe. Both writers attempted in these works to come to terms, or to place, as it were, history in the configuration of contemporary national identity. And both are remarkable expositions on language: of local dialects, the vernacular, of language's evolution, its mutations and adaptations.

In 1905, Joyce wrote to his brother Stanislaus that "when you remember that Dublin has been a capital for thousands of years, that it is the second city of the British Empire, that it is nearly three times as big as Venice, it seems strange that no artist has given it to the world"[240] Elytis's mapping of the Aegean is based on a similar response. Athens and classical Greece had been mapped time and over again but the islands—a space that captured, as Elytis saw it, a more contemporary sense of Greekness—had not been given neither to the world nor to the Greeks. Yet, such structures should be seen, in my opinion, not as attempts to present what has remained peripheral or repressed; I see their function more as efforts to give shape to what is inevitably a constructed identity. As I have already stressed throughout this book, Elytis is painfully aware that his relationship to the space that he maps is inescapably both personal and metaphysical. In this sense, the architectural poetics of loss as I have discussed them in relation to *The Monogram*, are present in all of Elytis's longer collections—what is mapped, in other words, is a space that is always already lost (even as it is constructed) precisely because it does not belong to the world.

When we consider, alongside the exploration of national identity, the modernist preoccupation with the chaos and disorder of history or the modern crisis of identity, these structures offer ways of shaping the text both subtextually (i.e., imperceptibly) and in opposition to the predominant definitions of nationhood.

---

[240] James Joyce, *Selected Letters* (New York: Viking Press, 1975), p. 78.

Joyce's meticulous schemata and his use of the Homeric subtext in *Ulysses* unflold in the background of a text that is in constant crisis: a crisis of identity, Stephen's anxiety to find a *modern* Irish voice, a marital crisis, a national crisis etc. Similarly, Elytis's structures unfold in the background of history's burden, of what exists only as a personal aesthetic position, of what is lost, or, in short, of what constantly fails to become historical. The crisis of modernism is, in the case of both Elytis and Joyce, a crisis of nationality. Stephen's desperate preoccupation with finding a poetic voice in *Ulysses*—a voice that is Irish without being blindly ethnocentric— is also reflected in Elytis's search for a voice that expresses itself in Greek but that also rejects a narrow designation of Greekness. As I have discussed in the third chapter, his Theory of Analogies was an attempt to describe this Greekness beyond its nationalistic confines. Ultimately, then, Joyce's schemata and Elytis's architectural poetics are manifestations of a modernist crisis that shattered the already porous boundaries of identity (national, individual, or artistic); what they present us with, is an abstract yet schematized space, a certain semblance of order, in which identity can still be explored even as it becomes conscious of its own inevitable foundering.

Appendix:
Odysseus Elytis:
Life and Works

Elytis was born Odysseus Alepoudellis on November 2, 1911, in Heracleion, Crete. He was the sixth and last child of Maria and Panayiotis Alepoudellis, both from the island of Lesbos, who had moved to Crete and established, in 1895, a successful soap factory there. In 1914 the Alepoudellis family business moved to the suburb of Piraeus, in Athens, and young Odysseus, with his brothers, spent his summer vacations on the island of Lesbos, an island often visited by the prominent Greek politician Eleftherios Venizelos, who became a close friend of the family.

In 1916, he enrolled in the Makris Private School, which he attended for seven years. In the years that followed, the Alepoudellis family traveled extensively in Italy, Switzerland, Yugoslavia, and Germany and spent their summer vacations on the island of Spetses. In 1918, the first of two tragedies hit the family. Elytis's eldest sister Myrsini died on December 31 and a shroud of mourning covered the house.[1] In 1925 tragedy struck the family again: while vacationing on Spetses, Panayiotis Alepoudellis, Elytis's father, died of pneumonia. Young Odysseus was deeply affected by these losses and less than two years later, he suffered a nervous breakdown and was forced to spend two months in bed. The aspirations he had of becoming a track athlete were shattered. While recovering in bed, he fervently read Greek and foreign literature. The most profound influence on him was the Alexandrian poet Constantine Cavafy, who ushered him, for the first time, into poetry. "Cavafy was needed for me to be shaken," he would later write in *Open Papers* (1974). "A deep curiosity got hold of me, that was later destined to turn into a deep interest, and later on, a deep admiration."[2]

In 1928, Elytis graduated from high school. That year the poet Kostas Karyotakis (1896–1928), whose pessimistic poetry explored the miserable state of society in the aftermath of industrialization and capitalism, committed suicide, and in subsequent years he became more popular among the youth than any other poet of the time. Deeply influenced by both Cavafy and Karyotakis, Elytis attempted to write his first poems in imitation of them. When, however, he discovered in Kaufmann's bookstore, in Athens, the surrealist poetry of Paul Éluard, he came to the realization that their poetry did not correspond to the way he experienced life as a young man. The discovery of Éluard's poetry is, perhaps, the most significant event in his early poetic orientation.

---

[1] Elytis would later recount the impact of these deep emotional wounds in "The Chronicle of a Decade."

[2] Elytis, *Ανοιχτά Χαρτιά*, p. 334.

In 1930, Elytis entered the Law School of Athens University where he met the young poet Giorgos Sarandaris, who ushered him even more deeply into surrealism. By 1934, he destroyed all the poems he had composed up to that point and wrote a short collection titled "First Poems." These poems would be published in 1939 in the volume *Orientations* (in 310 copies). It is not coincidental that the first lines of the first poem of the collection read: "Eros / The archipelago." The first two words Elytis published would become the most frequently repeated and explored concepts in his poetry. As the poet himself later confided in an interview on National Greek Television, "It is characteristic that the first two verses of my book [*Orientations*] are: 'Eros, the Archipelago.' In a way this foreshadows the entire evolution, in terms of content, of my poetry."[3]

The year 1935 marks the most important one in the early poetic evolution of Elytis. It is the year he met and befriended the poet Andreas Empeirikos, and together they attempted to promote the movement of surrealism in Greece.[4] Along with Empeirikos and the painter Stratis Eleftheriadis-Teriade[5] (1897–1983), Elytis traveled to Lesbos, where he was involved in the discovery and promotion of the art of the recently deceased folk painter Theophilos Hadjimichael (1873–1934). Their efforts eventually culminated in the opening of a "Theophilos Museum" in Lesbos (1964) and the recognition of Theophilos by European artistic circles. Elytis's unique experience in discovering and promoting the art of Theophilos would be recounted in a 1973 long essay titled *The Painter Theophilos*. In the same year (1935), Elytis aligned himself with the literary magazine *Nea Grammata*, which published his first poems, and met the renowned poet George Seferis[6] as well as Giorgos Katsimbalis.[7] In 1936, he also met the poet Nikos Gatsos. In the next few years, this generation of mostly young poets and artists would establish Greece's first literary cafés and produce some of the most profound poetry in modern Greek literature. They would become known as "The Generation of the Thirties."[8]

---

[3] Elytis, *Αυτοπροσωπογραφία*, p. 14.

[4] Empeirikos had recently returned from France and was close to the French surrealist circle.

[5] Teriade was the publisher of the well-known French surrealist periodical *Minotaure*. Elytis's acquaintance with him would prove to be of paramount importance, as Teriade would later introduce him (1949–1951) to the circle of Parisian painters.

[6] Seferis was by that time a well-established and respected poet in Greece. He was a close friend of T.S. Eliot and Ezra Pound.

[7] This is the hero of Henry Miller's novel *Colossus of Marousi*.

[8] The term "Generation of the Thirties" is highly problematic, since these writers had vastly different styles and were concerned with different themes. Although Mario Vitti's description of the generation as the poets who collaborated with the periodical *Nea Grammata* is more specific, the term is often generally used to describe the poets who were concerned with a re-discovery of Greek identity. However, one must keep in mind that, as a poetic symbol, "Greece" assumed different meanings for each writer and, in Elytis's case, its relationship with the historical nation is one of conflict. Nevertheless, Elytis himself uses the term in "The Chronicle of a Decade."

In 1940, Mussolini's army invaded Greece, and Elytis was called to serve as a second lieutenant at the Albanian front.[9] His unit served under fire, and after a long and exhausting campaign, he contracted typhus and was admitted, severely ill, to a hospital in Ioannina. He miraculously recovered and returned to an Athens, which, by that time, was occupied by German forces. During the Nazi occupation of Greece (1941–1944), Elytis worked on two collections of poetry: *Sun the First* and *Song Heroic and Mourning for the Lost Second Lieutenant of the Albanian Campaign*.

Sun the First was first published in 1943 (in 600 copies) and is filled with images of beautiful naked bodies, sunny Greek landscapes, and blooming orchards. It clearly states the refusal of the poet to succumb to the weight of oppression, and his poetic resistance to the violations inflicted by the Nazi occupation. The first poem of the collection—all the poems are numbered and usually bear no titles—expresses precisely this resistance to the "darkness" that is often imposed on people: "I no more know the night death's fearful anonymity / In an inlet of my soul moors a fleet of stars" (I, 1–2).[10] This refusal to compromise and adjust to an oppressive force does not simply refer to the particular historical period of Greece's occupation by the Germans. The suggestions are clearly universal referring to a wider definition of oppression. In some poems, resistance to the historically dark times is suggested in images of natural regeneration:

> It's a long time since the last rain was heard
> Above the ants and lizards
> Now the sky burns boundless
> Fruits paint their mouths
> Earth's pores slowly open
> And by water dripping in syllables
> A huge plant looks the sun in the eye![11]

Sanguine messages of both personal and collective regeneration are scattered throughout the collection: "What I love is born incessantly," "no one will speak our fate," "we come of good stock," "we build and dream and sing."

The second collection that draws from Elytis's wartime experience is *Song Heroic and Mourning for the Lost Second Lieutenant of the Albanian Campaign* (published in 1945 in the periodical *Tetradio*). Elytis described the principal concept behind the collection in an interview with his translator Kimon Friar:

---

[9] Elytis was trained as a Second Lieutenant at the "School of Reserve Officers" in Corfu from January to September 1937. He had joined the army in December 1936 and completed his service in March 1938.

[10] Elytis, *Collected Poems*, p. 75.

[11] Elytis, *Collected Poems*, p. 76. Πάει καιρός που ακούστηκεν η τελευταία βροχή / Πάνω από τα μυρμήγκια και τις σαύρες / Τώρα ο ουρανός καίει απέραντος / Τα φρούτα βάφουνε το στόμα τους / Της γης οι πόροι ανοίγουνται σιγά σιγά / Και πλάι απ' το νερό που στάζει συλλαβίζοντας / Ένα πελώριο φυτό κοιτάει κατάματα τον ήλιο! (Elytis, *Ποίηση*, p. 77).

The virtues I found embodied and living in my comrades formed in synthesis a brave young man of heroic stature, one whom I saw in every period of our history. They had killed him a thousand times, and a thousand times he had sprung up again, breathing and alive. He was no doubt the measure of our civilization, compounded of his love not of death but of life. It was with his love of Freedom he recreated life out of the stuff of death.[12]

As in *Sun the First*, Elytis reconstructs an alternative reality that transubstantiates the enslaving conditions of war and death into a song for freedom. The heroic stature of the second lieutenant is juxtaposed to those forces that violate human freedom: "Those who committed the evil—a black cloud took them / But he who confronted it in the sky's roads / Ascends now alone and resplendent!"[13] The mood of the collection is slowly uplifted with each poem, and, whereas it begins with a mournful lament over the passing of the sun and the coming of darkness, it ends with a hope of regeneration made possible because of the second lieutenant's sacrifice: "Now the dream beats faster in the blood / The world's rightest moment rings out: / Freedom, / Greeks show the way in the darkness: / FREEDOM / For you the sun will weep with joy."[14]

Following the conclusion of World War II and the departure of the German occupying forces from Greece, a civil war broke out between Leftist guerillas and the national government. Elytis was denied a passport, and remained confined in Greece until 1948, when he was finally given permission to travel outside the country. Leaving Greece, he went to Paris, where he met most of the poets he had admired, until then, from a distance: Breton, Reverdy, Jouve, Ungaretti, T.S. Eliot, Éluard,[15] and others. The painter Teriade also put him in contact with Picasso. Still in Paris in 1949, he met the painters Matisse, Léger, and Giacometti. Even though the Greek government refused to renew his passport, Elytis did not return to Greece and in 1950 he met Sartre and Camus.[16] After a three-year-long absence he returned to Athens in 1951.

During the decade of the fifties, Elytis worked on and published two major collections: *The Axion Esti* ["Worthy it is," (in 815 copies)] and *Six and One Remorses for the Sky* (in 550 copies). *The Axion Esti* is, without a doubt, Elytis's most popular collection both inside and outside of Greece. He began working on it around 1954 and sent it to his publisher in 1959. It is a monumental and long work divided into three sections that bear hymnological titles: "Genesis," "Passion," "Gloria." In "Genesis," seven free-verse hymns are presented, each describing stages in the creation of the Greek landscape (by the poet/seer) and the aesthetic principles that accompany it. "In the beginning the light," pronounces the first line

---

[12] Friar, "Introduction," pp. 16–17.
[13] Elytis, *Collected Poems*, p. 115.
[14] Elytis, *Collected Poems*, p. 117.
[15] Elytis had already met Éluard during the latter's visit to Greece in 1946.
[16] His encounters and friendships with these poets, painters, and thinkers are described in the "Chronicle of a Decade."

of the section that brings to mind the Book of Genesis ("Let there be light")[17] as well as the first sentence of John's Gospel ("In the beginning was the Word").[18] The poet continues to "recreate" the Greek landscape (the intense light of the sun, the archipelago, the islands) until his psyche begins to resemble the world he has created: "This then am I / and the world the Small the Great." "The Passion" is the most architecturally complex part. Jeffrey Carson and Nikos Sarris describe the structural division of this section ("sequence") as follows:

> Three forms are represented in this sequence: free verse psalms (P), odes of complex metrical responsion (O), and prose readings (R). There are three sections, identically structured: PPOROPPOROPP. In the first, consciousness confronts tradition (Greeks resist in Albania in World War II); in the second it confronts danger (occupation of Greece in WWII); in the third, it overcomes danger (civil war, post WWII).[19]

"The Gloria" is a celebration of Greek landscape, poetic creation, and the feminine body. It celebrates the triumph of the eternal creative forces over ephemeral human concerns: "Now the Gods' humiliation Now the ashes of Man / Now Now the zero / and Forever the world the small the great!"[20] Though *The Axion Esti* was highly praised in academic and artistic circles, it remained largely unknown to the Greek public until the composer Mikis Theodorakis set it to music in 1964.

Like *The Axion Esti, Six and One Remorses for the Sky* was sent to the publisher in 1959. This collection however, does not present a unified theme (as *Song Heroic and Mourning* and *The Axion Esti* do). but rather it is comprised of seven poems with different themes. In one of the most powerful poems of the collection, "The Autopsy," the body of a young man is dissected but, instead of flesh and blood, what is revealed is emotional or imagistic experiences always connected to Nature: "the olive root's gold" in his heart, "the intense cyan-blue horizon line" beneath his skin, "glaucous traces in the blood," "birds' voices," "the echo of the sky," etc.[21] In what became a recurring technique in Elytis's poetry, landscape is infused with sentiment and becomes a projection and celebration of the human body.

In the1960s, translators abroad began to take notice of Elytis's poetry, and translations of his poems appeared in German, English, Italian, and French.[22] During this period, Elytis traveled extensively. In 1961 he travelled to the United States as a guest of the State Department, where he visited New York, Washington, New Orleans, Santa Fe, Los Angeles, San Francisco, Buffalo, and Boston, and where he met Yves Bonnefoy and Allen Ginsburg. In 1962, invited by the Soviet

---

[17] Genesis 1:3.
[18] John 1:1.
[19] Elytis, *Collected Poems*, p. 136.
[20] Elytis, *Collected Poems*, p. 190.
[21] Elytis, *Collected Poems*, p. 195.
[22] One must note here that George Seferis's 1963 Nobel Prize in Literature, the first given to a Greek poet, also helped to spread interest in modern Greek poetry in general.

government, he visited the Soviet Union along with Giorgos Theotokas and Andreas Empeirikos; the three traveled to Odessa, Moscow, and Leningrad, and met Yevgeny Yevtuchenko. In 1965, invited by the Union of Bulgarian Writers, he visited Bulgaria and toured the country accompanied by the local poet Elisaveta Bagriana (1893–1991). In 1967, just before the military coup, he visited Egypt (Alexandria, Cairo, Luxor, Aswan) and in 1969, unable to work under the fascist regime, he moved to Paris, where he stayed for about a year. In 1971, still in self-exile, he stayed in Cyprus for four months.

In 1961, while aboard the ship bringing him to the United States, Elytis composed the song cycle *Little Cyclades*, which would later be set to music, like *The Axion Esti*, by Mikis Theodorakis. The songs of this collection praise the luminous beauty of the Cycladic landscape, as presented through emotionally charged moments in life. Elytis's interest in lyric poetry and music also led to the composition of a libretto, *The Sovereign Sun*, in 1970 (during his stay in Cyprus), which was put to music by Dimitris Lagios. This collection returns to the symbol of the sun, which reappears in Elytis's poetry, and the metaphysical values it comes to represent in the Greek landscape. As in *Sun the First*, Elytis evokes natural elements of the Greek landscape (sun, winds, mountains, sea) and man-made elements that harmoniously coexist with this landscape (fishing boats, orchards, beautiful young bodies) in order to confront the historical darkness of political oppression and social stagnation. Elytis returns to the composition of songs with his 1972 collection *The Rhos of Eros*, put to music by various Greek composers.

In 1972 the Greek fascist government offered him the Grand Prize for Literature, which he refused. Around the same time, he was awarded a grant by the Ford Foundation, which enabled him to survive the economic hardships of the early seventies. Meanwhile, he continued to compose poetry but refused to publish anything in Athens (due to the dictatorial regime). His two collections of poetry, composed during the Junta rule, were published in Cyprus instead. The *Light-Tree and the Fourteenth Beauty* was written between 1969–1970 and was published in 1971. In these poems Elytis returns, as he explained in a 1979 interview to Andonis Decavalles, to the use of light: "I give Greece again through the analogy of light upon the senses.... I express in them [the poems] my poetic understanding of the quintessence of the Greek realm."[23] Indeed, the 21 poems of the collection are united in their use of light but also, as the critic Mario Vitti notes, in their attitude toward death:

> In the *Light-tree* death is something immanent in humans, a natural, unavoidable, and unknown episode. Fear towards it remains in the boundaries of stoicism. The poet does not attempt a mood of rebellion against it; neither does he try to justify it by turning it into a power tending towards light....[24]

---

[23] Elytis, *Collected Poems*, p. 205.
[24] Vitti, *Οδυσσέας Ελύτης*, p. 311.

The second collection of poetry published by Elytis (in Cyprus) during the junta years was *The Monogram*, which was written and published in 1971. It is one of his most erotic collections, comprised of seven poems, all addressed to an unknown and absent beloved. One of its astounding characteristics is its strict architectural structure. Each poem has a specific number of lines (all multiples of seven) and the lines within each poem are visually symmetric. The first poem (seven lines) has a 3-1-3 line structure; the second poem (21 lines) has a 3-4-7-4-3 line structure; the third poem (35 lines) has a 1-7-5-9-5-7-1 line structure; the fourth and longest poem (49 lines) has a 11-1-7-11-7-1-11 line structure; the fifth poem is symmetrical to the third, the sixth to the second, and the seventh and last poem is symmetrical to the first. This is not the first time Elytis uses symmetry and architecture in his poetry.[25] A prominent characteristic in his structuring of the poems is the use of the number "7." Apart from all the lines of the poems in *The Monogram*, which are multiples of seven, the number appears continually in his poetry: from *Orientations*: "Seven Nocturnal Heptastichs" (seven poems of seven lines each), "Windows toward the Fifth Season" (seven poems), "Orion" (seven poems of seven lines each), "Dionysos" (seven poems), "Clepsydras of the Unknown" (seven poems), "Clear Skies" (21 poems, 3x7), "The Concert of the Hyacinths" (21 poems, 3x7), *Sun the First* (21 poems, 3x7), *Song Heroic and Mourning* (14 poems, 7x2), etc.

In 1974 Elytis published *The Stepchildren* (two units of seven poems each). All the poems of this collection are dated, and are placed in chronological sequence (the first, "Psalm and Mosaic for Spring in Athens," dated 1939, and the last, "Mystic Versicles," dated 1972). Apart from the abundant references to ancient Greek sources, this collection includes Odes or poems referring to particular individuals that Elytis befriended: the painter Pablo Picasso ("Ode to Pablo Picasso"), the poet Giorgos Sarandaris ("Giorgos Sarandaris"), the painter Nikos Hadjikyriakos Ghikas ("Small Analogon"), and the painter Teriade ("Villa Natacha").

After the fall of the Junta, Elytis began working on two poetry collections and various essays. In 1974, he published the *Open Papers*, a volume of essays dating from the mid-thirties to the seventies. This volume includes the lengthy essay "Chronicle of a Decade," one of the most important accounts of the reception of the surrealist movement in Greece and of the first attempts to establish a specifically Hellenic modernist literary tradition in the country. He also worked extensively on a new series of essays that would eventually be published in 1992, under the title *Carte Blanche*. This publication includes the "Report to Andreas Empeirikos"— a moving eulogy of his good friend, who passed away in 1975. Around 1974 he also began working on one of his most powerful collections, which would be published in 1978 under the title *Maria Nephele*.

Maria Nephele is divided into three parts, each representing a "dialogue," or simultaneous monologues, between two voices: Maria Nephele, a young girl of

---

[25] In fact, all his collections are related to the number "7" (usually containing seven poems or multiples of seven). Many of his collections are also symmetrical, as, for example, the poems of *Orientations*—his first collection.

the city, and the Antiphonist, the voice of the poet. Etymologically, "Nephele" in ancient Greek means "cloud," and gives a mood of inapproachable melancholy to the character; apart from its literal meaning as "the other voice," the word "Antiphonist" designates, in the Orthodox tradition, the chanter who sings responsively to, or reciprocates, the main chant. Elytis also returns here to a strict architectural structure and the use of the number "7." Each of the three parts is divided into 14 poems: seven are narrated by the Antiphonist and seven by Maria Nephele. Visually, each poem narrated by the Antiphonist is placed next to a poem narrated by Maria Nephele (or vice versa), forcing an exchange between the two characters. When Maria Nephele is distressed (as in "Bonjour Tristesse"), the Antiphonist transforms sadness into a playful song (as in "Morning Exercises"); Maria Nephele talks about the touristy modern island of Mykonos as the island of her choice, whereas the Antiphonist prefers the more isolated and unpopular island of Patmos; she speaks of her "Twenty-Four-Hour Life," while he speaks of "The Lifelong Moment;" she argues that every age has its Trojan War, and he responds that every age has its Helen.

In 1975 Elytis was offered an honorary doctorate from the Philosophical School of the University of Thessaloniki, and was proclaimed an honorary citizen of Lesbos. In 1979 he was proclaimed an honorary citizen of Heracleion, Crete. In 1975 "Books Abroad" dedicated an entire issue to his poetry; in 1976 *Six and one Remorses for the Sky* was translated into French (*Six plus un remords pour le ciel*); and in 1978 Ingemar Rhedin began translating *The Axion Esti* into Swedish. The greatest surprise for the poet, however, would come in October of 1979, when the secretary of the Swedish Academy announced the awarding of the 1979 Nobel Prize in Literature to Odysseus Elytis "for his poetry, which, against the background of Greek tradition, depicts with sensuous strength and intellectual clear-sightedness modern man's struggle for freedom and creativeness."[26] Other candidates for the 1979 Nobel Prize in Literature included Graham Greene, Jorge Luis Borges, Gabriel García Márquez, and Simone de Beauvoir. This was the second time a Greek poet had received a Nobel Prize—George Seferis was the first in 1963—and the announcement was understandably received with tremendous enthusiasm in Greece. Elytis went to Stockholm in December to receive the prize. In the introduction to his speech, presented in French on December 8, Elytis set the general mood of his poetic ideology:

> May I be permitted, I ask you, to speak in the name of luminosity and transparency? The space I have lived in and where I have been able to fulfill myself is defined by these two states. States that I have also perceived as being identified in me with the need to express myself.[27]

---

[26] The Nobel Foundation, *The Nobel Prize in Literature 1979*, http://nobelprize.org/nobel_prizes/literature/laureates/1979/index.html (accessed November 23, 2007).

[27] Odysseus Elytis, *Nobel Lecture*, December 8, 1979, http://nobelprize.org/nobel_prizes/literature/laureates/1979/elytis-lecture-e.html (accessed August 27, 2006).

The connection between poetical expression and life as well as the association of life with "luminosity and transparency"—inevitably linked with the Greek landscape—are indeed characteristics that describe the conceptualization of his entire poetic creation. To put it simply, ethical values are here linked to physical values. In the *Open Papers* the concept is further elaborated: "In Greece light and history are one and the same thing—meaning that in the final analysis the one reproduces the other, the one interprets and justifies the other, even the void which is blackness; for this country, by offering equality of ethical and physical values [ηθικές και φυσικές αξίες], does not happen to know any other chiaroscuro."[28]

The awarding of the Nobel Prize brought a lot of media attention to the work of Elytis, and for the first time public interest was also drawn to his artwork. Stockholm's Thyelska Galeriet exhibited many of his collages in 1979, and the Zoumboulakis Gallery exhibited them in Athens (1980). Elytis's collages date as far back as 1935. His first artistic attempts were greatly influenced by surrealism and particularly by the paintings of Max Ernst, Yves Tanguy, and Oscar Domínguez.[29] "His first creations" writes Kimon Friar, "were the purely orthodox ones of paradoxical juxtapositions in imitation of the collages of Max Ernst...."[30] Elytis turned to the art of collage more seriously in the 1960s, and after this period, he continued to create collages, inexhaustibly, until his death. His creations are sometimes purely based on color and shape (as in Mondrian, Braque, or Matisse), or they represent images that are often found in his poetry. These collages are published in the following collections: his early collages are included in his song collection *The Rhos of Eros* and in Ilias Petropoulos's *Elytis, Moralis, Tsarouchis*; the collages of the 1980s and 1990s are mainly collected in two publications: the 1985 publication *The Room with the Icons* (collages by Elytis, text by Eugenios Aranitsis) and his 1995 book of prose entitled *The Garden with the Self-Deceptions*.

Elytis lived and continued to create for 17 years after receiving the Nobel Prize in Literature. His post-Nobel popularity kept him very busy. The few years that immediately followed the Nobel presentation were spent almost entirely on award receptions, presentations, and speeches around the globe. In 1980 he was presented with an honorary doctorate from the Sorbonne in France and in 1981 with an honorary doctorate from the University of London.[31] He was also declared an honorary citizen of Larnaca and Paphos (Cyprus) and he was invited by the Spanish Prime minister Soares to visit Spain, where he was declared an honorary citizen of Toledo (in the Fall of 1980). The Royal Philological Association of London further presented him with the Benson award in 1981. Also in 1981, Rutgers University, in the United States, established the Elytis Chair of Modern

---

[28] Elytis, *Collected Poems*, pp. 557–8.
[29] Elytis had seen some of their work in Empeirikos's house.
[30] Kimon Friar, "The Imagery and Collages of Odysseus Elytis," *Books Abroad* 49, no. 4 (1975): 703–11, p. 704.
[31] The medal was presented to him by Princess Anne.

Greek Studies in honor of the Greek poet, and in March of 1982 he was presented, by mayor D. Beis of Athens, with the Gold Metal of Honor of the City of Athens.

The 1980s saw the publication of three collections of poetry by Elytis: *Three Poems Under a Flag of Convenience*, *The Diary of an Invisible April*, and *The Little Seafarer*. He also published three books of translations: *Sappho* (1984), *St. John's Revelation* (1985), and *Krinagoras* (1987). Along with *Second Writing*, published in 1976, these translations are testimony to the wide spectrum of poetic interests and influences in Elytis's work. His translations include, apart from St. John, Sappho, and Krinagoras, the poetry of Rimbaud, Lautréamont, Jouve, Éluard, Mayakovski, Ungaretti, Lorca, and Brecht.

Three Poems under a Flag of Convenience was published in 1982, and it presents three long poems ("The Garden Sees," "The Almond of the World," and "Ad Libitum"), each divided into seven subsections. In "The Garden Sees," the poet reaffirms his conviction that art is a force that creates life: "Whether Plotinus was right / or not will one day become clear / the great eye with its transparency / and a sea behind it like Helen / binding the sun / together with other flowers in her hair / a million signs / omega zeta eta."[32] The Garden *sees*: it is not merely a decorative realm but also a creative force that looks back at the viewer, much like art does. "Life" is also celebrated in "The Almond of the World," where the poet playfully views it as "One more cigarette / which lasts until we expire" yet "with really superb moments."[33] "Ad Libitum" ends with a revealing postscript: "the more I age the less I understand / experience untaught me the world."[34] Old age brings the poet to a wise silence, where "the omega leans to alpha" and "disunites time."

Indeed, Elytis returns to the beginning of his youthful interests with his 1984 collection *Diary of an Invisible April*. It is a dated diary of 49 entries, spanning from Wednesday April 1st to May 7th (1981), and it is reminiscent of his early experiments with surrealism. Although, as he often repeated, he was never an orthodox surrealist, the entries in this collection appear to be more personal; the images are dream-like, often reaching deep into the poet's childhood memories. Elytis's greatest poetic achievement of the 1980s is undoubtedly *The Little Seafarer*, published in 1985. Like *The Axion Esti* and *Maria Nephele*, it is a highly structured collection comprised of four sections in prose, entitled "To Anoint the Repast" (each section is divided into seven short narratives), and three sections in verse, entitled "With both Light and Death" (each section is divided into seven poems). Each prose section is preceded by a separate part, entitled "Spotlight," and each verse section is followed by the section "What one Loves." The entire collection is introduced with an "Entrance" and concluded with an "Exit," shaping its overall structure as follows:

---

[32] A rearrangement of these three letters of the Greek alphabet reveals the word "Zoe" which means Life. Elytis, *Collected Poems*, p. 371.

[33] Elytis, *Collected Poems*, p. 383.

[34] Elytis, *Collected Poems*, p. 394.

Entrance
Spotlight i—To Anoint the Repast—
With Both Light and Death—What one Loves—
Spotlight ii—To Anoint the Repast—
With Both Light and Death—What one Loves—
Spotlight iii—To Anoint the Repast—
With Both Light and Death—What one Loves—
Spotlight iv—To Anoint the Repast—
Exit

The "Entrance" introduces the theme of "journeying" as the underlying theme of the collection. The seven scenes of each "Spotlight" describe dark moments in the history of Greece and specific moments of betrayal from ancient to modern Greece: Miltiades' condemnation and Phidias' imprisonment in the fifth century, BC, Emperor Constantine's arrest of his own son Crispus in the Byzantine years, Kolokotronis's[35] imprisonment in the nineteenth century, etc. "What one Loves" is a compilation of snapshots, or moments, that the poet collects in his travel bag: lines of poetry (from Sappho, Sophocles, Cavafy, Blake, Hölderlin, Novalis, Pound, and others), references to concerts, symphonies, songs, (Vivaldi, Mozart, Beethoven, Theodorakis, Hadjidakis, and others), paintings (Klee, Matisse, Picasso, Braque, Gris, Arp, and others), or simply "words" that the poet finds interesting (Alexandra, anemone, bergamot, bougainvillea, etc.) and geographical places with which he has some emotional connection (Corfu, Lesbos, Aegina, Cyprus, Chios, Cairo, etc.). "Anoint the Repast" (Prose) and "With Both Light and Death" are undoubtedly the most elaborate sections of *The Little Seafarer* where the poet expresses himself in lucid philosophical concepts or emotionally charged images, always traveling within the world he continually constructs en route. The "Exit" ends in a surprisingly pensive tone with the poet speculating whether his personal creations are able to influence the public sphere (and as a consequence provide a sense of justice), or whether they simply remain "small happinesses" relevant only to himself.

Elytis further continues to explore the relationship between the public and the private spheres in two works published in 1990: *The Public and the Private* and *The Private Road*. In the last five years of his life he also wrote two poetic collections, *The Elegies of the Jutting Rock* and *West of Sorrow*. The *Elegies* were published in 1991 and coincided with the celebration of Elytis's eightieth birthday. It is a book of 14 poems that, as Jeffrey Carson suggests, are modeled after the elegies of Hölderlin.[36] Like *The Little Seafarer*, this collection also begins with the announcement of a journey: "Now, I look forward to the boat that, even if you get in it, / Will arrive empty at a long sea Kerameikos / With stone Korai holding flowers."[37] Indeed, the elegies that follow take the reader to a fixed time where the

---

[35] Theodoros Kolokotronis: a celebrated hero of the 1821 Greek revolution against the Ottomans.
[36] Elytis, *Collected Poems*, p. xxxix.
[37] Elytis, *Collected Poems*, p. 511.

actions of poets are "elegized." The poet remembers Hölderlin's mad love for his Susette Gontard (in "Cupid and Psyche"), Novalis's beloved, 12-year-old Sophie von Kühn (in "Elegy of Grüningen"), and one of his favorite nineteenth-century Greek poets, Dionysios Solomos (in "Awe and Whelming of Solomos"). One of the most personal elegies of the collection is "La Pallida Morte," that, as Elytis's translators suggest, was composed after he "spent part of the winter of 1989–1990 in the Evangelismos Hospital in Athens, suffering from anemia."[38] The poem announces this "near-death" experience from its opening line ("Scentless is death yet / The nostrils catch it like / A flower …"),[39] and it gradually moves to declaring Death's inability to kill the poet: "But of these men, death, nobody knows anything to say / Except the poet. Jesus of the sun. Who then rises every Saturday / He. The Is, the Was, and the Coming."[40]

Elytis's final collection published during his lifetime, *West of Sorrow*, was written in the summer of 1995 in Porto Rafti (Greece) where the poet was vacationing with his companion and fellow poet Ioulita Iliopoulou. The seven poems of the collection are "more dense," as Elytis wrote to his translator Jeffrey Carson, "and for this reason more difficult, but closer to my ideal."[41] The title of the collection signals its mood: on one hand, the life of the 83-year-old poet is moving westwards towards its setting but, on the other, it also moves *West of Sorrow*, that is, beyond where sorrow itself sets. The biographical events in the poet's life are insignificant: "what remains," the collection concludes, "is poetry alone."[42]

Elytis died in his apartment in Athens (23 Skoufa Street) of a stroke on March 18, 1996. A posthumous collection titled *From Nearby* was put together by his heir, Ioulita Iliopoulou, and was published in 1998.

---

[38] Elytis, *Collected Poems*, p. 521.
[39] Elytis, *Collected Poems*, p. 521.
[40] Elytis, *Collected Poems*, p. 522.
[41] Elytis, *Collected Poems*, p. xli.
[42] Elytis, *Collected Poems*, p. 554.

Works Cited

Adorno, Theodore. *Prisms (Studies in Contemporary German Social Thought)*. Translated by Shierry Weber Nicholsen. Cambridge, Massachusetts: MIT Press, 1983.
Alcalay, Ammiel. *After Jews and Arabs: Remaking Levantine Culture*. Minneapolis: University of Minnesota Press, 1993.
Aldrich, Robert. *The Seduction of the Mediterranean: Writing, Art and Homosexual Fantasy*. New York: Routledge, 1993.
Amoia, Alba. *Albert Camus*. New York: Continuum, 1989.
Antoniou, David, Than. Kokovinos, and Kostas Petropoulos. *Ερμηνευτικές Αναλύσεις Κειμένων Νεοελληνικής Λογοτεχνίας (Μέρος Β')*. Athens: Pataki, 1982.
Apollinaire, Guillaume. *Selected Writings*. Translated by Roger Shattuck. New York: New Directions, 1971.
Apter, Emily. "Out of Character: Camus's French Algerian Subjects." *MLN* 112, no. 4 (1997): 499–516.
Aranitsis, Evgenios, and Odysseus Elytis. *Το Δωμάτιο με τις Εικόνες*. Athens: Ikaros, 1986.
Bachelard, Gaston. *Air and Dreams: An Essay on the Imagination of Movement*. Translated by Edith Farell and Frederick Farell. Dallas: Dallas Institute for Humanities and Culture, 1988.
———. *The Dialectic of Duration*. Translated by Mary McAllester Jones. Manchester: Clinamen Press, 2000.
———. *Earth and Reveries of Will: An Essay on the Imagination of Matter*. Translated by Kenneth Haltman. Dallas: Dallas Institute of Humanities and Culture, 2002.
———. *New Scientific Spirit*. Translated by Arthur Goldhammer. Boston: Beacon Press, 1984.
———. *On Poetic Imagination and Reverie: Selections from Gaston Bachelard*. Translated by Colette Gaudin. Putnam, Connecticut: Spring Publications, 1988.
———. *The Poetics of Reverie: Childhood, Language and the Cosmos*. Translated by Daniel Russell. Boston: Beacon Press, 1960.
———. *The Poetics of Space*. Translated by Maria Jolas. Boston: Beacon Press, 1994.
———. *The Psychoanalysis of Fire*. Translated by Alan Ross. Boston: Beacon Press, 1964.
———. *Water and Dreams: An Essay on the Imagination of Matter*. Translated by Edith Farell. Dallas: Dallas Institute Publication, 1999.
Bahun-Radunović, Sanja, and Marinos Pourgouris, eds. *The Avant-Garde and the Margin: New Territories of Modernism*. Newcastle: Cambridge Scholar's Press, 2006.

Balakian, Anna. *Literary Origins of Surrealism. A New Mysticism in French Poetry.* New York: New York University Press, 1947.
Barnes, Jonathan. *Early Greek Philosophy.* New York: Penguin, 2001.
Baudelaire, Charles. *Les Fleurs du Mal.* Translated by Richard Howard. Boston: David R. Godine, 2000.
Beaton, Roderick. *An Introduction to Modern Greek Literature.* Oxford: Oxford University Press, 1999.
Belezinis, Andreas. *Ο Οψιμος Ελύτης.* Athens: Ikaros, 1999.
Berman, Jeffrey. *The Talking Cure: Literary Representations of Psychoanalysis.* New York: New York University Press, 1987.
Bradbury, Malcolm. "The Cities of Modernism." In *Modernism: A Guide to European Literature 1890–1930*, edited by Malcolm Bradbury and James McFarlane, 96–104. London: Penguin, 1991.
———. "The Name and Nature of Modernism." In *Modernism: A Guide to European Literature 1890–1930*, edited by Malcolm Bradbury and James McFarlane. London: Penguin, 1991.
———, and James McFarlane. *Modernism: A Guide to European Literature 1890–1930.* London: Penguin, 1991.
Breton, André. *Manifestoes of Surrealism.* Translated by Richard Seaver and Helen R. Lane. Ann Arbor: University of Michigan Press, 1972.
British Broadcasting Corporation. *Clinton: US failed Greek Democracy.* November 20, 1999. http://news.bbc.co.uk/2/hi/world/europe/529932.stm (accessed December 8, 2007).
Brooks, Cleanth. *The Well Wrought Urn: Studies in the Structure of Poetry.* New York: Harcourt, 1947.
Bullock, Allan. "The Double Image." In *Modernism: A Guide to European Literature 1890–1930*, edited by Malcolm Bradbury and James McFarlane, 58–70. London: Penguin, 1991.
Bürger, Peter. *Theory of the Avant-Garde.* Translated by M. Shaw. Minneapolis: University of Minnesota Press, 1984.
Burton, Richard Francis. *One Thousand and One Arabian Nights.* Vol. 10. 16 vols. Forgotten Books, 2008.
Cahm, Eric. "Revolt, Conservatism and Reaction in Paris 1905–25." In *Modernism: A Guide to European Literature 1890–1930*, edited by Malcolm Bradbury and James McFarlane, 162–71. London: Penguin, 1991.
Calinescu, Matei. *Five Faces of Modernity: Modernism, Avant-Garde, Decadence, Kitsch, Postmodernism.* Durham: Duke University Press, 1987.
Calotychos, Vangelis. *Modern Greece: A Cultural Poetics.* Oxford: Berg, 2003.
Camus, Albert. *Lyrical and Critical Essays.* Translated by Ellen Conroy Kennedy. New York: Vintage, 1970.
———. *The Myth of Sisyphus and Other Essays.* Translated by Justin O'Brien. New York: Vintage, 1988.
———. *Notebooks 1935–1951.* Translated by Justin O'Brian. New York: Marlow & Company, 1998.

———. *The Rebel*. Translated by Anthony Brower. New York: Vintage, 1991.
———. *Resistance, Rebellion and Death*. Translated by Justin O'Brien. New York: Vintage, 1988.
———. *The Stranger*. Translated by Stuard Gilbert. New York: Vintage, 1946.
———. *Youthful Writings*. Translated by Ellen Conroy Kennedy. New York: Knopf, 1976.
———, and Jean Grenier. *Correspondences 1932–1960*. Translated by Jan Rigaud. Lincoln: University of Nebraska Press, 2003.
Caroll, David. "Camus's Algeria: Birthrights, Colonial Injustice, and the Fiction of a French-Algerian People." *MLN* 112, no. 4 (1997): 517–49.
Carpenter, Bogdana. "Between DADA and Constructivism: The Polish Avant-Garde Poetic Project." In *The Avant-Garde and the Margin: New Territories of Modernis*, edited by Sanja Bahun-Radunovic and Marinos Pourgouris, 113–28. Newcastle: Cambridge Scholars Press, 2006.
Casanova, Pascale. *The World Republic of Letters*. Translated by M.B. DeBevoise. Cambridge, MA: Harvard University Press, 2007.
Chambers, Iain. *Mediterranean Crossings: The Politics of an Interrupted Modernity*. Durham: Duke University Press, 2008.
Chase, Stuart. "Foreword." In *Language Thought and Reality*, by Benjamin Lee Whorf, v–x. Cambridge, MA: MIT Press, 1978.
Chatterjee, Partha. *The Nation and its Fragments: Colonial and Postcolonial Histories*. Princeton: Princeton University Press, 2007.
Chow, Rey. *The Age of the World Target*. Durham: Duke University Press, 2006.
———. *The Protestant Ethnic and the Spirit of Capitalism*. New York: Columbia University Press, 2002.
Clogg, Richard. *Συνοπτική Ιστορία της Ελλάδας*. Athens: Katoptro, 1995.
Colla, Elliott. *Conflicted Antiquities: Egyptology, Egyptomania, Egyptian Modernity*. Durham: Duke University Press, 2007.
Corbusier, Le. "Θεόφιλος." *Η Λέξη* 172 (Nov–Dec 2002): 968–9.
———. *Κείμενα για την Ελλάδα*. Translated by Leda Pallantiou. Athens: Agra, 1992.
———. *Towards a New Architecture*. Translated by Frederick Etchells. New York: Dover Publications, 1986.
Cromer, Evelyn Baring. *Modern Egypt*. New York: Macmillan, 1916.
Daniels, Stephen. *Fields of Vision: Landscape, Imagery and National Identity in England and the United States*. Princeton: Princeton University Press, 1993.
Daskalopoulos, Dimitris. *Βιβλιογραφία Οδυσσέα Ελύτη, 1971–1992*. Athens: Ypsilon, 1993.
———. "Χρονολόγιο Οδυσσέα Ελύτη (1911–1986)." *Χάρτης* 21–3 (1986): 261–80.
Decavalles, Anthony. *Ο Ελύτης: Από το Χρυσό ως το Ασημένιο Ποίημα*. Athens: Kedros, 1988.
———. "Eros: His Power, Forms and Transformations in the Poetry of Odysseus Elytis." *Books Abroad* 49, no. 4 (1975): 661–74.

Derrida, Jacques. "Faith and Knowledge: the Two Sources of 'Religion' at the Limits of Reason Alone." In *Religion*, edited by Jacques Derrida and Gianni Vattimo, translated by David Webb. Stanford: Stanford University Press, 1998.

———. *Spectres of Marx*. Translated by Peggy Kamuf. New York: Routledge, 1994.

Dimou, Nikos. *Οδυσσέας Ελύτης: Δοκίμια Ι*. Athens: Nefeli, 1992.

Egbert, Donald Drew. *Social Radicalism and the Arts: Western Europe*. New York: Knopf, 1970.

Eleftherotypia. "Αιχμές για τις Χαμένες Πατρίδες από Χριστόδουλο." August 23, 2004.

Eliot, Thomas Stearns. *Poems and Prose*. New York: Knopf, 1998.

———. *Selected Prose of T.S. Eliot*. Edited by Frank Kermode. New York: Harvest, 1975.

Ellis, Havelock. *Sexual Inversion*. Philadelphia: F.A. Davis Company, 1908.

Ellmann, Richard. *James Joyce*. Oxford: Oxford University Press, 1982.

Éluard, Paul. *Capital of Pain*. Translated by Richard Weisman. New York: Grossman Publishers, 1973.

———. *Capitale de la douleur suivi de l'amour la poésie*. Paris: Gallimard, 1966.

Elytis, Odysseus. *2 x 7 ε*. Athens: Ikaros, 1997.

———. *Ανοιχτά Χαρτιά*. Athens: Ikaros, 1995.

———. *Ασμα Ηρωικό και Πένθιμο για τον χαμένο Ανθυπολοχαγό της Αλβανίας*. Athens: Ikaros, 1981.

———. *Αυτοπροσωπογραφία σε Λόγο Προφορικό*. Athens: Ypsilon, 2000.

———. *Δεύτερη Γραφή*. Athens: Ikaros, 1980.

———. *Δυτικά της Λύπης*. Athens: Ikaros, 1995.

———. *Εξη και μία Τύψεις για τον Ουρανό*. Athens: Ikaros, 1979.

———. *Εκ του Πλησίον*. Athens: Ikaros, 1998.

———. *Εν Λευκώ*. Athens: Ikaros, 1992.

———. "Equivalences chez Picasso." Edited by E. Teriade. *Verve: revue artistique et littéraire* VII (1951): 25–6.

———. *Η Αποκάλυψη του Ιωάννη*. Athens: Ypsilon, 1985.

———. *Ηλιος ο Πρώτος*. Athens: Ikaros, 1999.

———. *Ημερολόγιο ενός Αθέατου Απριλίου*. Athens: Ypsilon, 1984.

———. *Κριναγόρας*. Athens: Ypsilon, 1987.

———. *Μαρία Νεφέλη*. Athens: Ikaros, 1999.

———. *Nobel Lecture*. December 8, 1979. http://nobelprize.org/nobel_prizes/literature/laureates/1979/elytis-lecture-e.html (accessed August 27, 2006).

———. *Ο Μικρός Ναυτίλος*. Athens: Ikaros, 1986.

———. "Odysseus Elytis on his Poetry. From an Interview with Ivar Ivask." *Books Abroad* 49, no. 4 (1975): 631–43.

———. "Picasso's Equivalences." *Books Abroad* 49, no. 4 (1975): 649–51.

———. *Ποίηση*. Athens: Ikaros, 2003.

———. *Προσανατολισμοί*. Athens: Ikaros, 2002.

———. *Σαπφώ*. Athens: Ikaros, 1996.

———. *Σηματολόγιον*. Athens: Ypsilon, 2001.

———. *Τα Ελέγεια της Οξώπετρας*. Athens: Ikaros, 1991.
———. *Τα Ετεροθαλή*. Athens: Ikaros, 1996.
———. *The Axion Esti*. Translated by Edmund Keeley and George Savidis. Pittsburgh: University of Pittsburgh Press, 1996.
———. *Τα Ρω του Ερωτα*. Athens: Ypsilon, 1986.
———. *The Collected Poems of Odysseus Elytis*. Translated by Jeffrey Carson and Nikos Sarris. Baltimore: Johns Hopkins, 1997.
———. *The Oxopetra Elegies*. Translated by David Connolly. New York: Harwood, 1997.
———. *The Sovereign Sun: Selected Poems*. Translated by Kimon Friar. Newcastle: Bloodaxe, 1990.
———. *Το Φωτόδεντρο και η Δέκατη Τέταρτη Ομορφιά*. Athens: Ikaros, 1991.
———. *Το Αξιον Εστί*. Athens: Ikaros, 1996.
———. *Το Μονόγραμμα*. Athens: Ikaros, 1996.
———. *Τρια Ποιήματα με σημαία Ευκαιρίας*. Athens: Ikaros, 1982.
Empeirikos, Andreas. *Μια Περίπτωσις Ιδεοψυχαναγκαστικής Νευρώσεως με Πρόωρες Εκσπερματώσεις και Άλλα Ψυχαναλυτικά Κείμενα*. Athens: Agra, 2001.
———. "Un cas de névrose obsessionnelle avec éjaculations précoces." *Revue Française de Psychanalyse* 14, no. 3 (1950): 331–66.
Fleming, K.E. "Orientalism, the Balkans, and Balkan Historiography." *The American Historical Review* (American Historical Association) 105, no. 4 (Oct 2000): 1218–33.
Foucault, Michel. "Nietzsche, Genealogy, History: Selected Essays and Interviews." In *Language, Counter-Memory, Practice*, edited by Donald Bouchard, translated by Donald Bouchard and Sherry Simon, 139–64. Ithaca: Cornell University Press, 1977.
Freud, Sigmund. *Beyond the Pleasure Principle*. Translated by James Strachey. New York: Norton, 1961.
———. *Civilization and its Discontents*. Translated by James Strachey. New York: Norton, 1961.
———. "A Disturbance of Memory on the Acropolis." In *The Standard Edition of the Complete Psychological Works of Sigmund Freud, Volume XXII (1932–1936): New Introductory Lectures on Psychoanalysis and Other Works*, by Sigmund Freud, translated by James Strachey. London: Hogarth Press, 1964.
———. *The Ego and the Id*. Translated by James Strachey. New York: Norton, 1960.
———. *The Interpretation of Dreams*. Translated by James Strachey. New York: Avon, 1998.
———. "Letter from Sigmund Freud to C.G. Jung, July 18, 1908." In *The Freud/ Jung Letters: The Correspondence between Sigmund Freud and C.G. Jung*, edited by William McGuire. Princeton: Princeton University Press, 1974.
———. *Mourning and Melancholia*. Vol. XIV, in *The Standard Edition of the Psychological Works of Sigmund Freud Vol. XIV*, (1914–1916), by Sigmund Freud, translated by James Strachey, 237–58. London: Hogarth Press, 1957.

———. *On Beginning the Treatment (Further Recommendations on the Technique of Psychoanalysis)*. Translated by James Strachey. Vol. XII. London: Hogarth Press, 1958.

———. "The Relation of the Poet to Day Dreaming." In *Character and Culture*, edited by Philip Rieff, translated by Philip Rieff. New York: Collier, 1976.

———. "Remembering, Repeating and Working Through." In *The Standard Edition of the Psychological Works of Sigmund Freud, Vol. XII. (1911–1913)*, by Sigmund Freud, translated by James Strachey, 145–56. London: Hogarth Press, 1958.

Friar, Kimon. "The Imagery and Collages of Odysseus Elytis." *Books Abroad* 49, no. 4 (1975): 703–11.

———. "Introduction." In *The Sovereign Sun: Selected Poems*, by Odysseus Elytis, translated by Kimon Friar, 3–44. Newcastle: Bloodaxe, 1990.

Frye, Northrop. *The Great Code: The Bible and Literature*. London: ARK Paperbacks, 1983.

Gaudin, Colette. "Introduction." In *On Poetic Imagination and Reverie*, by Gaston Bachelard, translated by Colette Gaudin, ix–xxxvii. Putnam: Spring Publications, 1988.

Gourgouris, Stathis. *Dream Nation: Enlightenment, Colonization, and the Institution of Modern Greece*. Stanford: Stanford University Press, 1996.

Green, André. *Time in Psychoanalysis*. Translated by Andrew Weller. New York: Free Association, 2002.

Hawthorne, Nathaniel. *Tales*. New York: Norton, 1987.

Heidegger, Martin. *Being and Time*. Translated by Joan Stambaugh. Albany: State University of New York Press, 1996.

———. *Poetry, Language, Thought*. Translated by Albert Hofstadter. New York: Perennial Classics, 1971.

Herzfeld, Michael. "The Horns of the Mediterraneanist Dilemma." *American Ethnologist* (American Anthropological Association) 11, no. 3 (August 1984): 439–54.

Hochberg, Gil. "'Permanent Immigration': Jacqueline Kahanoff, Ronit Matalon, and the Impetus of Levantinism." *boundary 2* (Duke University Press) 31, no. 2 (2004): 219–43.

———. *In Spite of Partition*. Princeton: Princeton University Press, 2007.

Hölderlin, Friedrich. *Hymns and Fragments*. Translated by Richard Sieburth. Princeton: Princeton University Press, 1984.

Hollander, John. *Vision and Resonance: Two Senses of Poetic Form*. New Haven: Yale University Press, 1975.

Homer. *The Odyssey*. Translated by Robert Fagles. New York: Penguin, 1996.

Horden, Peregrine, and Nicholas Purcell. *The Corrupting Sea: A Study of Mediterranean History*. Malden, MA: Blackwell Publishing, 2000.

Hough, Graham. "The Modernist Lyric." In *Modernism: A Guide to European Literature 1890–1930*, edited by Malcolm Bradbury and James McFarlane, 312–22. London: Penguin, 1991.

Hughes, Edward J., ed. *The Cambridge Companion to Camus*. New York: Cambridge University Press, 2007.
Hyde, George. "The Poetry of the City." In *Modernism: A Guide to European Literature 1890–1930*, edited by Malcolm Bradbury and James McFarlane, 337–48. London: Penguin, 1991.
Iakov, Daniel. *Η Αρχαιογνωσία του Οδυσσέα Ελύτη και άλλες Νεοελληνικές Δοκιμές*. Athens: Zitros, 2000.
Joyce, James. *Selected Letters*. New York: Viking Press, 1975.
———. *Ulysses*. New York: Vintage, 1990.
Jung, Carl Gustav. *The Archetypes of the Collective Unconscious*. 2nd ed. Bollingen Series XX. Translated by R.F.C. Hull. Princeton: Princeton University Press, 1990.
Jusdanis, Gregory. *Belated Modernity and Aesthetic Culture: Inventing National Literature*. Minneapolis: University of Minnesota Press, 1991.
———. *The Necessary Nation*. Princeton: Princeton University Press, 2001.
———. "World Literature: The Unbearable Lightness of Thinking Globally." *Diaspora* 12, no. 1 (2003): 103–30.
Kant, Immanuel. *Critique of Aesthetic Judgement*. Translated by James Creed Meredith. Oxford: Clarendon Press, 1911.
Kazantzakis, Nikos. *Οδύσσεια*. Athens: Eleni Kazantzakis, 1984.
Kearney, Richard. *Poetics of Imagining*. New York: Fordham University Press, 1998.
Kehalioglou, Giorgos. "Ένα ανέκδοτο υπόμνημα του Ελύτη για το Αξιον Εστί." *Ποίηση* 5 (Spring 1995).
Kokkinis, Yiannis. *Ανθολογία της Νεοελληνικής Ποίησης*. Athens: Estia, 1995.
Koutrianou, Elena. *Με Άξονα το Φως. Η Διαμόρφωση και η Κρυστάλλωση της Ποιητικής του Οδυσσέα Ελύτη*. Athens: Idryma Kosta kai Elenis Urani, 2002.
Kuna, Franz. "Vienna and Prague 1890–1928." In *Modernism: A Guide to European Literature 1890–1930*, edited by Malcolm Bradbury and James McFarlane, 120–33.
Lacan, Jacques. *Ecrits*. Translated by Alan Sheridan. New York: W.W. Norton & Company, 1977.
———. *On Feminine Sexuality the Limits of Love and Knowledge*. Edited by Jacques Alain Miller. Translated by Bruce Fink. New York: W.W. Norton & Company, 1999.
———. *The Four Fundamental Concepts of Psychoanalysis* (*The Seminars of Jacques Lacan, Book XI*.) Translated by Alan Sheridan. New York: Norton, 1998.
———. *The Language of the Self: the Function of Language in Psychoanalysis*. Translated by Anthony Wilden. Baltimore: John Hopkins University Press, 1981.
Leakey, F.W. *Baudelaire and Nature*. Manchester: Manchester University Press, 1969.
Levy, Michele Frucht. "A Conversation with Luljeta Lleshanaku." *World Literature Today* 83, no. 1 (Jan–Feb 2009): 16–20.

Loewald, Hans W. "Some Considerations on Repetition and Repetition Compulsion." In *Papers on Psychoanalysis*, by Hans W. Loewald. New Haven: Yale University Press, 1980.
Lorca, Federico García. *In Search of Duende*. Edited by Christopher Maurer. New York: New Directions Publishing, 1998.
———. *Ode to Walt Whitman and Other Poems*. Translated by Carlos Bauer. San Francisco: City Lights, 1988.
———. *Selected Letters*. Translated by David Gershator. New York: New Directions Publishing, 1983.
Marcuse, Herbert. *The Aesthetic Dimension—Toward a Critique of Marxist Aesthetics*. Boston: Beacon Press, 1978.
Mastroianni, Marcello. *8½*. Directed by Federico Fellini. New York: Criterion, 1963.
Miller, Henry. *The Colossus of Maroussi*. New York: New Directions, 1958.
Nadeau, Maurice. *The History of Surrealism*. Translated by Richard Howard. Cambridge, MA: The Belknap Press of Harvard University, 1989.
Nietzsche, Friedrich Wilhelm. *The Gay Science*. Translated by Walter Kaufmann. New York: Vintage, 1974.
———. *On the Advantage and Disadvantage of History for Life*. Translated by Peter Preuss. Indianapolis: Hackett Publishing Company, 1980.
———. *The Portable Nietzsche*. Translated by Walter Kaufmann. New York: Penguin, 1976.
The Nobel Foundation. *The Nobel Prize in Literature 1979*. http://nobelprize.org/nobel_prizes/literature/laureates/1979/index.html (accessed November 23, 2007).
Pamuk, Orhan. *Other Colors: Essays and a Story*. Translated by Maureen Freely. New York: Vintage, 2007.
Pinker, Steven. *The Language Instinct: How the Mind Creates Language*. New York: Perennial Classics, 2000.
Poggioli, Renato. *The Theory of the Avant-Garde*. Translated by Gerald Fitzgerald. Cambridge, MA: Belknap Press of Harvard University, 1968.
Pourgouris, Marinos. "Για μια νέα ποιητική αισθητική: Η έννοια της Ελληνικότητας και η θεωρία των αναλογιών στην ποίηση του Ελύτη" *Εντευκτήριο*, September 2005.
———. "Odysseus Elytis (1911–1996)." *Dictionary of Literary Biography: Nobel Prize Laureates in Literature*. Vol. 329. New York: Thomson Gale, 2008. 422–29.
———. "Topographies of Greek Modernism." *The Avant-Garde and the Margin: New Territories of Modernism*. Edited by Marinos Pourgouris and Sanja Bahun-Radunovic. Newcastle: Cambridge Scholar's Press, 2006.
Psycharis, Yiannis. *Το Ταξίδι μου*. Athens: Ermis, 1971.
Raymond, Marcel. *From Baudelaire to Surrealism*. London: Methuen & Co., 1950.
Reber, Arthur S. *The Penguin Dictionary of Psychology*. New York: Penguin, 1995.
Recio, Virginia López. *Το Φεγγάρι, το Μαχαίρι, τα Νερά: Ο Λόρκα στην Ελλάδα*. Athens: Ekdoseis ton Philon, 2006.
Rimbaud, Arthur. *Complete Works, Selected Letters*. Translated by Wallace Fowlie. Chicago: University of Chicago Press, 1966.

Ritsos, Yiannis. *Ρωμιοσύνη*. Athens: Kedros, 1994.
Robinson, Christopher. "The Greekness of Modern Greek Surrealism." *Byzantine and Modern Greek Studies* 7 (1981): 119–38.
Rosen, David. "T.S. Eliot and the Lost Youth of Modern Poetry." *Modern Language Quarterly: A Journal of Literary History* 64, no. 4 (Dec 2003): 473–94.
Said, Edward. "Narrative, Geography and Interpretation." *New Left Review*, no. 180 (1990): 81–97.
———. "Representing the Colonized: Anthropology's Interlocutors." *Critical Inquiry* 15, no. 2 (Winter 1989): 205–25.
Sandrow, Nahma. *Surrealism: Theatre, Arts, Ideas*. New York: Harper and Row Publishers, 1972.
Sapir, Edward. *Culture, Language and Personality*. Berkeley: University of California Press, 1970.
———. *Selected Writings of Edward Sapir*. Berkeley and Los Angeles: University of California Press, 1951.
Sartre, Jean Paul. *Existentialism is a Humanism: Including, A Commentary on the Stranger*. Translated by Carol Macomber. New Haven: Yale University Press, 2007.
Scott, Clive. "The Prose Poem and Free Verse." In *Modernism: A Guide to European Literature 1890–1930*, edited by Malcolm Bradbury and James McFarlane, 349–68. London: Penguin, 1991.
Seferis, George. *Μέρες Α'*. Athens: Ikaros, 2003.
Shaver, Gilbert J. "Rev. of Poetry, Language, Thought, by Martin Heidegger." *Boundary 2: A Journal of Postmodern Literature* 1 (1973): 742–9.
Shelley, Percy Bysshe. "A Defence of Poetry." In *Criticism: Major Statements*, edited by Charles Kaplan and William Anderson. New York: St. Martin's Press, 1991.
Sheppard, Richard. "The Crisis of Language." In *Modernism: A Guide to European Literature 1890–1930*, by Malcolm Bradbury and James McFarlane, 323–36. London: Penguin, 1991.
Sheridan, Alan. "Translator's Note." In *The Four Fundamental Concepts of Psychoanalysis*, by Jacques Lacan, translated by Alan Sheridan. New York: Norton, 1998.
Stamatakos, Ioannis. *Λεξικόν Αρχαίας Ελληνικής Γλώσσης*. Athens: Vivliopromitheutiki, 1999.
Theotokas, Giorgos. *Το Ελεύθερο Πνεύμα*. Athens: Ermis, 1986.
Todorova, Maria. *Imagining the Balkans*. New York: Oxford University Press, 2009.
Trivizas, Sotiris. *Το Σουρεαλιστικό Σκάνδαλο*. Athens: Kastaniotis, 1996.
Trypanis, Constantine, ed. *The Penguin Book of Greek Verse*. New York: Penguin, 1971.
Tzara, Tristan. *Seven Dada manifestos and Lampisteries*. Translated by Barbara Wright. London: Calder, 1977.
Unwerth, Matthew von. *Freud's Requiem: Mourning, Memory, and the Invisible History of a Summer Walk*. New York: Penguin, 2005.

Valaoritis, Nanos. *Μοντερνισμός, Πρωτοπορία και "ΠΑΛΙ."* Athens: Kastaniotis, 1997.
Varga, Andriana. "Periphery to Center and Back: Exploring Dada and the Absurd in the Context of Romanian Literary Traditions." In *The Avant-Garde and the Margin: New Territories of Modernism*, edited by Sanja Bahun-Radunovic and Marinos Pourgouris, 129–53. Newcastle: Cambridge Scholars Press, 2006.
Vitti, Mario. *Η Γενιά του Τριάντα: Ιδεολογία και Μορφή*. Athens: Ermis, 2000.
———. *Οδυσσέας Ελύτης*. Athens: Ermis, 1991.
———. "Εισαγωγή: Το Εργο του Ελύτη και η Ελληνική Κριτική." In *Εισαγωγή στο Εργο του Ελύτη*, edited by Mario Vitti. Heraklion: Panepistimiakes Ekdoseis Kritis, 2000.
Voutouris, Pantelis. "Odisseas Elitis-Periklìs Ghiannopulos. Dalla linea greca al neoclassicismo surrealista." In *Odisseas Elitis: un europeo per metà*, edited by Paola Maria Minucci and Christos Bintoudis, 253–71. Rome: Donzelli Editore, 2010.
Walcott, Derek. *The Antilles: Fragments of Epic Memory*. December 7, 1992. http://nobelprize.org/nobel_prizes/literature/laureates/1992/walcott-lecture.html (accessed October 10, 2007).
Walker, Steven F. *Jung and the Jungians on Myth*. New York: Routledge, 2002.
Whorf, Benjamin Lee. *Language Thought and Reality*. Cambridge, MA: MIT Press, 1978.
Wilden, Anthony. "Lacan and the Discourse of the Other." In *The Language of the Self: the Function of Language in Psychoanalysis*, by Jacques Lacan, translated by Anthony Wilden, 157–311. Baltimore: John Hopkins University Press, 1981.
Williams, Raymond. *The Country and the City*. New York: Oxford University Press, 1975.
Yea, Michelle. "Contemporary Chinese Poetry Scenes." *Chicago Review* 39, no. 3/4 (1993): 279–83.
Yiannopoulos, Perikles. "Η Ελληνική γραμμή και το Ελληνικό Χρώμα." *Τα Νέα Γράμματα* 4, no. 13 (Jan–March 1938): 117–24, 132–9, 213–14.

Index

Adorno, Theodor 174–5
"Age of Glaucous Memory" (Elytis) 27, 139
alētheia 10, 36, 148, 171
"Alpha Romeo" (Elytis) 124, 125
anagrammatism 100–101, 195
Analogies, theory of 65–109
    analogy as interchangeable with metaphor and correspondence 93–4
    as answer to stereotypical characterizations of Elytis 105, 107
    artists and thinkers with similar theories 69
    Bachelard as influence on 9, 68, 70
    as central metaphysical construct of Elytis 9–10
    concrete examples for clarifying 90
    content as emphasis of 112
    development 86–106
    direct correspondence in 66
    Eros, Death, and Nature in 57
    first thoughts on 87
    Greek identity and 108, 200
    influences on 9, 68–86
    on language and geography 95, 98
    nature and 71
    painting used to explain "analogy" 87–8
    as poetic effort to reconstruct the world 90
    as poetical theory of object relations 65
    principal claims of 65–6
    as revolution of the object 95
    transformation from matter to spirit in 59
    as transposition of intersubjective network through synaesthetic process 67–8, 88–9
"Anniversary" (Elytis) 115, 138, 139
architectural poetics 145–200; *see also* Solar Metaphysics
    absent in early works 27
    in early poems 137–41
    in longer collections only 134, 146
    on poetic structure 10–11, 198–9
    on poetry and mathematics 145
    and Solar Metaphysics as not interchangeable 135
    Solar Metaphysics as theory of 114, 123, 133–5
"Assessment and a New Beginning" (Elytis) 33, 93
automatic writing 29, 31, 78, 82, 143, 171
"Autopsy, The" (Elytis) 56–7, 205
Axion Esti, The (Elytis) 162–75, 204–5
    architectural poetics in 11, 27, 113, 134, 146, 199
    on the body and history 173, 175, 180
    and Foucault's "Nietzsche, Genealogy, History" 11
    "Genesis" 100, 121, 122, 131, 163, 167–8, 204–5
    "Gloria" 141, 167, 168, 174, 175, 184, 204, 205
    on Greek identity 108, 131, 145, 163–5, 172, 175
    interaction of self with natural elements in 59
    as metahistorical 171–5
    mourning in 161
    number seven as structuring principle 141
    "Passion" 167, 168–71, 184, 204
    on Plotinus 121
    prophetic vision in 143
    on repetition in history 177
    set to music 104, 162–3, 205
    structure 165–71
    on sun as source of oppressive beauty 60
    translation 208

Bachelard, Gaston
    Elytis influenced by 7, 69–70
    on four elements 10, 72
    on the hidden real 95
    "Luck-Art-Risk" 69

on material imagination 9, 70, 181n155
on poetic imagination 69–73
theory of Analogies influenced by 7, 9, 68, 69, 70
Baudelaire, Charles
 on correspondences 9, 68n10, 72, 73–7, 83, 93
 Elytis influenced by 7, 10, 75–7
 Elytis on 77
 philosophy of nature 74–5, 91
 on poetry and mathematics 145
 as root of European modernism 74
 on Symbolism 18
 on synaesthetic experience 74, 75
 theory of Analogies influenced by 9, 68, 69
 works
  "La Chevelure" 76–7
  "Correspondences" 72, 74–5, 77
  "Que diras-tu ce soir" 76
"Body of Summer" (Elytis) 55–6
Bradbury, Malcolm 3, 4, 15–16, 18, 19
Breton, André
 on automatic writing 29, 78, 143
 dream poetry 94
 on dream symbolism 84–5
 Elytis meets 204
 Freud misread by 82
 linguistic systems and 95
 Manifesto of Surrealism 32, 84
 on metaphor 95
 misconceptions about surrealism 31
 on nonconformism 32
 theory of Analogies influenced by 68, 69
Brooks, Cleanth 10, 141–2
Burton, Sir Richard Francis 39–40, 61
Byzantium 19, 163–4, 172, 175

Calinescu, Matei 3, 19, 102, 129, 145
Calotychos, Vangelis 6–7, 127, 129
Camus, Albert
 on the absurd 47, 48, 49, 53, 60
 childhood 43n24
 Elytis influenced by 9, 33, 42, 52–3, 59, 204
 Empédocle magazine 42–3, 52, 112, 116
 Le Corbusier and 123
 Mediterranean aesthetics of 8, 9, 37, 42–54, 59, 61, 116

on nationalism 45–6, 61–2
on natural beauty 175
Solar Metaphysics influenced by 116, 123
on sun and sea 47–51, 112
surrealism and Elytis's discovery of 31
works
 L'Eté 43, 46, 47, 48, 50
 "Mediterranean" 52
 The Myth of Sisyphus 48, 161, 170
 "The New Mediterranean Culture" 44
 Noces 43, 46
 "Nuptials at Tipasa" 51, 52
 The Stranger 45, 45n38, 49–50, 51, 60, 62
Carson, Jeffrey 24, 166, 205
Carte Blanche (Elytis) 7, 121, 207
Cavafy, Constantine P. 5, 21, 22, 24, 35, 58, 137, 201
Char, René 42, 43, 52, 112, 116
Chatterjee, Partha 35–6
Chow, Rey 1, 2, 4, 6, 35, 36, 107
"Chronicle of a Decade" (Elytis) 20, 22, 28, 88, 105, 112, 119–20, 126–7, 139, 164, 207
"Climate of Absence" (Elytis) 26
consciousness 168–71
Corti, José 21
cosmopolitanism 4, 9, 35, 36, 55, 62, 142
Crevel, René 21
Cycladic architecture 58n104, 67, 114, 123, 126, 133, 142

dadaism 3, 16–17, 18, 19, 81, 102–3
dialect 106, 129
Diary of an Invisible April (Elytis) 1, 162, 210
"Dionysos" (Elytis) 138, 140
"Divine Light According to Plotinus, The" (Elytis) 121
Dragoumis, Ionas 19, 164–5
"Dream of Giorgos Sarandaris" (Elytis) 85
"Dream of Preciosa, The" (Elytis) 85
dream symbolism
 Elytis on 84–5
 Freud on 9, 78–86
"Dreams, The" (Elytis) 69, 83
Durrell, Lawrence 41, 54–5

Elegies of the Jutting Rock, The (Elytis)
162, 211–12
Eliot, T.S. 5, 20, 35, 54, 128–9, 142, 156, 162, 204
Éluard, Paul
  Elytis influenced by 8, 21, 22–7, 58, 137, 201, 204
  Elytis on poetry of 25, 26
  Elytis translates 210
  Elytis's pen name derived from 23
Elytis, Odysseus
  artwork 209
  characteristics of poetry
    air and water in 72–3
    as comparative poet 35, 142
    continued evolution 13
    death as theme 53n88
    dialect 106
    as Greek poet 1, 35, 45–6, 103–5
    Joyce compared 199–200
    justice and the sun associated 119–20
    linguistic characteristics 99–102
    Mediterranean identity 42, 43n24, 52–60
    as modernist poet 2–3, 13
    nationalism and 1–13, 63
    natural forces as motif 56–7
    number seven as structuring principle 140–41
    as poet of the Aegean 1, 13, 33, 62
    as structured 11, 65, 69, 102n177, 109, 137–41
    sun symbolism 10, 60, 111–12, 115–22
    surrealism and structure combined 137, 138, 140
  critical and theoretical views (*see also* Analogies, theory of; architectural poetics; Solar Metaphysics)
    on Baudelaire 77
    on Cavafy 22
    on deconstruction and reconstruction in poetry 130–31
    dream nation of 11, 131, 133, 163, 175, 179–81
    on dream symbolism 84–5
    on Éluard 25, 26
    familiarity with Lacan 92n125

fragmentary nature of theorizing 11
on gaze of the object 91–3
on Greek myth 54–7
on ideal reader 11–12
on Kalvos 17n10
on Karyotakis 22
on language 95, 97–8
on materialism 182
metaphysical theories used 8
on moments that reveal correspondence of senses and things 83n
as not a theorist 7
on para-semantic relationship 89
on Picasso 86–7
on poetic imagination 71
on poetry and forces of light 115
on poetry as source of revolutionary forces 86
on Solomos 17n10
on three states of reality 89
influences on 7, 9, 68
  Bachelard 7, 69–70
  Baudelaire 7, 10, 75–7
  Camus 9, 33, 42, 52–3, 59, 204
  Cavafy 21, 22, 201
  Éluard 8, 21, 22–7, 58, 137, 201, 204
  Empeirikos 27–8
  Freud 7, 11, 68, 81–6
  Karyotakis 21, 22, 201
  Le Corbusier 123, 126–7, 129, 142
  Picasso 7, 68, 204
  surrealism 8, 20, 21–2, 24, 25, 27–33, 57, 58, 68, 129, 138, 201–2
literary history (*see also Axion Esti, The*; *Light-Tree and the Fourteenth Beauty, The*; *Little Seafarer, The*; *Maria Nephele*; *Monogram, The*; *Orientations*; *Sun the First*; and other works by name)
  complete works published 11
  conservative academicians attacked 103n180
  early poems destroyed 21, 24, 137, 202
  Empédocle magazine article 42, 43, 52, 112, 116
  first published work 24, 202

first serious contact with poetry
20–21
national appropriation of
12–13, 104
pen name 23, 24, 139
publications 7
reluctance to publish 23, 24, 139
translations by 210
personal history and characteristics
asceticism 1, 12
family background 23, 43n24
life and works 201–12
political involvement 85–6
reception of work
misreadings 11–12, 143
stereotypical characterizations
104–5
as understudied 35
as unknown to Western
audiences 5–6
Empédocle (magazine) 42–3, 52, 112, 116
Empeirikos, Andreas 5, 24, 25, 27–8, 29, 81,
85, 92n125, 103, 131, 202, 206, 207
Engonopoulos, Nikos 28, 29
Enneads, The (Plotinus) 121
"Equivalences chez Picasso" (Elytis) 86–7,
87n108
ethnic identity 33–6, 104, 108; *see also*
Greek identity

"First Poems" (Elytis) 24, 25–6, 58,
137–41, 202
"First Things First—Poetry" (Elytis)
105, 192
"For the Optics of Sound" (Elytis) 102
Foucault, Michel 11, 106, 145, 171, 172,
173, 174, 175
Freud, Sigmund
on dream symbolism 9, 78–86
Elytis influenced by 7, 11, 68, 81–6
as Mediterranean 37
on poetry as sublimation 80–81, 86
on ruins 40–41
surrealism rooted in discoveries of 68,
78, 81, 82
as theorist of structure 145
theory of Analogies influenced by 9, 68
theory similar to theory of Analogies 69
on unconscious 8

works
Beyond the Pleasure Principle 154–6
Civilization and Its Discontents 41,
79n76
The Ego and the Id 152, 153
Interpretation of Dreams 70n22,
72, 78–86
"Mourning and Melancholia" 11,
151–4
"The Relation of the Poet to Day-
dreaming" 80–81
"Remembering, Repeating, and
Working Through" 159
Totem and Taboo 79n76, 80
From Nearby (Elytis) 145, 212
futurism 3, 16, 18, 19, 30, 81, 102–3

"Garden Gazes, The" (Elytis) 10, 90–3
Garden of Self-Deceptions, The (Elytis)
88–9, 209
Gatsos, Nikos 129, 202
Generation of the Thirties 202
automatic writing and 29
eastward orientation 128
Elytis included 12
on Greece harmonious with modern
times 126
Greek identity and 1, 3
on modernism and tradition 129–30
myth and 54
Theotokas's *Free Spirit* and 124
"Girl with the Violet Spot, The" (Elytis) 85
"Girls, The" (Elytis) 69, 70n22, 72, 88, 94
globalization 33, 97, 105, 182
Gospels 121, 122, 205
Greek identity (Greekness)
antiquity compared with modern 3
in *Axion Esti* 131, 163–5, 172
Elytis and 1, 3, 103, 104, 143, 200
misperceptions of 5, 175
modernist poets reassess 33–4
Greek myth 54–7, 97
Greek tragedy 46–7, 54

Hadjimichael, Theophilos 131–3, 202
Heidegger, Martin 8, 10, 69, 95, 101, 119,
136, 148, 179
Heraclitus 10, 31, 47, 59, 69, 117–20, 141
Hölderlin, Friedrich 31, 119, 190, 211, 212

Homer 120, 155–6
homosexuality 39–40, 61

Iliopoulou, Ioulita 1, 212
"Image of Boeotia" (Elytis) 27, 139

Jameson, Fredric 10, 107, 108
John, Gospel of 121, 122, 205
Jouve, Pierre Jean 43n24, 58, 69, 137, 204, 210
Joyce, James 41n18, 54, 80, 113, 135, 143, 146, 156, 199–200
Jung, Carl G. 7, 11, 37, 145, 193–8
Jusdanis, Gregory 6, 20, 35, 36, 130, 163–4, 165n84

Kahanoff, Jacqueline 42, 61, 62
Kalvos, Andreas 17, 17n10, 20, 69, 97, 117
Karamanlis, Konstantinos 182
Karyotakis, Kostas 21, 22, 201
katharevousa 103, 106, 163
Katsimbalis, Giorgos 23, 24, 139, 202
Kazantzakis, Nikos 5, 35, 129, 156, 156n47
Kore 196
Koutrianou, Elena 116–17

Lacan, Jacques 8, 10, 41, 88, 91–4
"Laconic" (Elytis) 111–12
language
    Elytis on 95, 97–8
    katharevousa 103, 106, 163
    popular versus academic 106
    radical modernism rejects official 102–3
    Sapir-Whorf hypothesis 8, 10, 88n109, 95–7
    threat to minor languages 105
Lautréamont, Comte de 77, 82, 210
Le Corbusier 123–7
    on Cycladic architecture 58n104, 114, 123, 126, 133, 142
    Elytis influenced by 123, 126–7, 129, 142
    surrealism and Elytis's discovery of 31
    on Theophilos Hadjimichael 132
    theory of Solar Metaphysics influenced by 7, 10, 69, 125
Léger, Fernand 123, 125, 204
Levantinism 41–2, 61, 62
Light-Tree and the Fourteenth Beauty, The (Elytis) 206

acoustic strictness of 99–100
architectural poetics in 135
Mediterranean in 59
number seven as structuring principle 141
sun symbolism 111
written during regime of the Generals 115
Little Cyclades (Elytis) 206
"Little Green Sea, The" (Elytis) 57, 99
Little Seafarer, The (Elytis) 176–85, 210–11
    absence and loss in 143
    architectural poetics in 11, 134, 146, 199
    in defining aesthetics of Greekness 145
    dream nation in 163, 175, 179–81
    on duration 65
    "Entrance" 184, 210–11
    "Exit" 185, 210–11
    on Greek identity 108, 131
    historical and poetic time in 177–80
    linguistic deciphering in 101–2
    polyphony of 181–2
    repetition in 181
    structure 176–7
Lorca, Federico García 37, 156–9, 210

McFarlane, James 3, 4, 19
"Mad Pomegranate Tree, The" (Elytis) 56, 138, 139
Mallarmé, Stéphane 94, 102, 113
Maria Nephele (Elytis) 186–98
    architectural poetics in 11, 134, 146, 199
    "ARIMNA EPHE EL" 195–6
    Bachelard's elements and 73
    consistent language of 189–90
    critical reception 192–3
    epigraphs 102, 192, 194
    "The Eternal Wager" 187, 198
    historical circumstances of composition 191
    Jung's *anima* archetype and 11, 193–8
    as most personal work 145, 197–8
    mourning in 162
    number seven as structuring principle 141, 208
    "The Presence" 186, 187, 194–5, 196, 186, 187, 194–5, 196
    prophetic vision in 143
    "The Song of Maria Nephele" 186, 187

"The Song of the Poet" 186, 187
    structure and conceptual framework of
        186–91, 207–8
    water theme 188
Matisse, Henri 7, 115, 204, 209, 211
Mediterranean 37–63
    being Mediterranean 37–42
    Elytis compares northerners and people
        of 127–8
    in European imaginary 9
    fragmentation of culture 38–9
    modernisms 42–60
    nationalism 43, 61–3
    ruins 40–41
    sexualization of 39–40, 41, 61
"Megali Idea" 17, 19, 22, 29, 163, 164, 172
"Melancholy of the Aegean" (Elytis) 27
Mentzelos, Dimitris 21–2
metaphor
    analogy as interchangeable with 93–4
    Bachelard on nature and 71–2
    Baudelaire on 75
    Breton on 95
    reconstruction of the world through 103
metaphysics 8; *see also* Solar Metaphysics
metonymy 93
modernism 15–36
    aesthetic versus rationalist 19–20
    architectural poetics and crisis of 145
    Baudelaire as root of 74
    destruction and social change as two
        poles of 81
    eastwards movement in 127
    Greek 5, 8, 15, 16, 17, 20, 104, 109,
        128–30, 145, 165
    as inclusive and universal 3–4
    on linear reading of history 181
    maps of 15–16
    materialism and 184
    Mediterranean modernisms 42–60
    metaphor in poetry 94
    national modernisms 33–6
    nationalism versus 19–20, 104, 199
    official language rejected by radical
        102–3
    on poetic form 112–13
    poststructuralism versus 5
    on pure poetry 94

as reconfiguration of national identity
    142–3
on reintegrating art and praxis of
    life 2–3
on representable reality 89
rumination on ruins in 41
science and 68–9
in South-Eastern Europe 4, 15–16
structure in 198–200
tradition and modernity 124–5, 156, 165
Monogram, The (Elytis) 146–62
    absence and mourning in 143, 148
    architectural poetics in 11, 143, 145,
        199, 207
    conceptual structure of 148–51
    Freud's "Mourning and Melancholia"
        as subtext 11, 151–4
    on Greek identity 108
    number seven as structuring principle
        141, 146–8, 207
    reflective pattern in 148, 176

nationalism
    Elytis and 1–13, 63
    Mediterranean 43, 61–3
    modernism versus 19–20, 104, 199
    national modernisms 33–6
    official versus popular definitions of
        nation 106
Nea Grammata (magazine) 23, 24, 69, 139,
    164, 202, 202n8
"Neighborhood of Evrota, The" (Elytis) 85
Nietzsche, Friedrich 4, 42, 145, 172,
    173n118, 177, 178, 181
Nobel Prize 1, 12, 35, 54, 90, 104, 162, 208–9
Novalis 31, 145, 211

"Ode to Santorini" (Elytis) 27
"Of the Aegean" (Elytis) 27, 52, 139
Open Papers (Elytis) 7, 24, 27, 60, 69, 83,
    88, 182, 192, 201, 207, 209
"Orange Girl" (Elytis) 56
Orientations (Elytis)
    "First Poems" 24, 25–6, 58, 137–41, 202
    nature in 27
    number seven as structuring principle
        140, 207
    poetic structure and 113
    reflective pattern in 139, 149

sea as central poetic motif 115
structural component of 138–40
surrealist influence in 57

Palamas, Kostis 18–19, 117
Parnassians 17, 18, 22
Parthenon 66, 67, 114, 124, 125
Picasso, Pablo
   Elytis influenced by 7, 68, 204
   Elytis on 86–7
   Elytis's "Ode to Pablo Picasso" 207
   "La femme fleur" 66–7
   in *The Little Seafarer* 211
   theory of Analogies and 68, 69
Plotinus 10, 117, 121–2, 141
Poggioli, Renato 3, 68–9, 94, 113, 184
"Poor Azakynthos" (Elytis) 85
postcolonialism 6, 35, 142
poststructuralism 1–2, 4, 5, 8, 142
Private Road, The (Elytis) 211
psychoanalysis
   Bachelard and Baudelaire and 10
   Elytis and 69
   Empeirikos and 27, 81n86
   Mediterranean sexuality and 41
   modernist poets refuse analysis 80, 81n85
   on representable reality 89
   as scientific 68
   surrealism rooted in 68, 78, 81, 82
Public and the Private, The (Elytis) 90, 98, 106, 185, 211

Rantos, Nikitas 28, 29
repetition 154–9, 178–9, 181
"Revelation" (Elytis) 122, 141
Rhos of Eros, The (Elytis) 26, 124, 206, 209
Rilke, Rainer Maria 80, 81n85, 112
Rimbaud, Arthur 68, 77, 82, 94, 181, 186, 210
Romanticism 17, 29, 31, 126, 128, 170
Room with the Icons, The (Aranitsis and Elytis) 209

Said, Edward 6, 45, 61
Sapir, Edward 8, 10, 88n109, 95–7, 98n160, 106, 134
Sarandaris, Giorgos 85, 201–2, 207
"Second Nature" (Elytis) 26

Second Writing (Elytis) 25, 210
Seferis, George 5, 15, 35, 54–5, 85, 98, 106, 117, 129, 129n80, 202, 208
"Seven Days for Eternity" (Elytis) 141
"Seven Letters from Royaumont" (Elytis) 112
Sikelianos, Angelos 32, 85, 117
Six and One Remorses for the Sky (Elytis) 111, 141, 204, 205, 208
Solar Metaphysics 111–43
   as applicable only to longer collections 134
   and architectural poetics as not interchangeable 135
   basic premises 114
   as cosmological frame 53–4
   diaphaneity as central notion 111, 135–6
   in Elytis's article for *Empédocle* 43, 112
   Eros, Death, and Nature in 57
   form as emphasis 112, 113–14
   influences on 116–17
   justice as expressible within 120–21
   Le Corbusier's influence on 7, 10, 125
   as search for unity in absence of it 143
   as simultaneously modern and traditional 142
   as "solar" and "metaphysical" 134–5
   sun symbol in 10, 112, 115–22
   as theory of architectural poetics 114, 123, 133–5
Solomos, Dionysios 17, 17n10, 20, 60n115, 97, 185
Song Heroic and Mourning for the Lost Lieutenant of the Albanian Campaign (Elytis) 113, 158–9, 165, 203–4, 207
Sovereign Sun, The (Elytis) 111, 115, 206
"Sporades" (Elytis) 27
"Statement of 1951" (Elytis) 86, 120
Stepchildren, The (Elytis) 123, 207
Sun the First (Elytis) 203
   "Body of Summer" 55–6
   number seven as structuring principle 140, 207
   poetic structure and 113
   sun as central poetic motif 111, 115
   "Variations on a Sunbeam" subcollection 77n66, 100n167
   written during Nazi occupation 115

surrealism
  attempts to combine destruction and social change 81, 85
  automatic writing 29, 31, 78, 82, 143, 171
  Elytis and 8, 20, 21–2, 24, 25, 27–33, 57, 58, 68, 129, 138, 201–2
  Freud's scientific discoveries as foundation of 68, 78, 81, 82
  Greek 20, 29–33, 103
  Heraclitus associated with 117
  on interrelating art and reality 3, 22
  metaphor and 93, 94
  reason attacked 19, 32, 77
  as revolution of the object 95
  and structure combined in Elytis's poetry 137, 138, 140
  theoretical versus revolutionary aspects 29
  theory of Analogies and 68
  in Yugoslavia 15
Symbolism 18–19, 30, 103, 128

Teriade, Stratis Eleftheriades 86, 123, 131, 132, 202, 204, 207

The Painter Theophilos (Elytis) 132–3, 202
Theodorakis, Mikis 104, 162, 205, 206, 211
Theotokas, Giorgos 6n14, 32, 124, 206
Three Poems Under a Flag of Convenience (Elytis) 90, 210
tradition
  Elytis on founding a new 128–33
  modernity and 124–5, 156, 165
  Solar Metaphysics relies on 142
Tsarouchis, Yiannis 77, 102
Tzara, Tristan 16–17, 34

Valéry, Paul 134, 156
Vitti, Mario 11–12, 23, 24, 137, 140, 148, 161n64, 206

Walcott, Derek 115, 174–5
"Well, The" (Elytis) 85
West of Sorrow (Elytis) 162, 211, 212
Whorf, Benjamin 8, 10, 95–7
Williams, Raymond 61, 63

Yiannopoulos, Pericles 19, 164–5

For Product Safety Concerns and Information please contact our EU
representative GPSR@taylorandfrancis.com
Taylor & Francis Verlag GmbH, Kaufingerstraße 24, 80331 München, Germany

www.ingramcontent.com/pod-product-compliance
Lightning Source LLC
Chambersburg PA
CBHW071352290426
44108CB00014B/1518